Christopher Durang
27 Short Plays

Christopher Durang has had plays on and off Broadway including *The Nature and Purpose of the Universe; Titanic; A History of the American Film* (Tony nomination, Best Book of a Musical); *Sister Mary Ignatius Explains It All For You* (Obie Award, off-Broadway run 1981-1983); *Beyond Therapy; Baby with the Bathwater; The Marriage of Bette and Boo* (Obie Award, Dramatists Guild Hall Warriner Award); *Laughing Wild.* Recently an evening of six of his one acts called *Durang, Durang* premiered at Manhattan Theatre Club in 1994.

His plays have been presented extensively in regional theaters in America, and also abroad. He has had the pleasure of working on premiére productions at the Eugene O'Neill Playwrights Conference, the American Repertory Theatre, Arena Stage, Mark Taper Forum, Playwrights Horizons, and the Public Theatre, among others.

Durang has also been active in cabaret, having co-written and performed with Sigourney Weaver in their Brecht-Weill parody *Das Lusitania Songspiel* (both receiving Drama Desk nominations in musical performing); and later having performed his own satiric nightclub act *Chris Durang and Dawne,* first at the Criterion Center in New York, then at Caroline's Comedy Club, and in 1995 at the Bay Street Theatre in Sag Harbor and the Triad in Manhattan. He has been working with Donna McKechnie on her one-woman show, *Inside the Music.* And years ago at the Yale Cabaret, he co-wrote two cabaret pieces with Albert Innaurato, and one with Wendy Wasserstein.

He has also written several screenplays and teleplays: *The Nun Who Shot Liberty Valance* for Warner Brothers; *The House of Husbands* (co-authored with Wendy Wasserstein) for the Ladd Company; *The Adventures of Lola* for Tri-Star and director Herbert Ross; a sitcom, *Disfunction—The TV Show,* again for Warner Brothers.

He is also an actor, sometimes performing in his own plays *(The Marriage of Bette and Boo,* ensemble acting Obie; *Laughing Wild* in New York and L.A.), sometimes in other people's plays (Wallace Shawn's *The Hotel Play,* Charles Schulman's *The Birthday Present* at the Young Playwright's Festival). He performed in the Stephen Sondheim revue *Putting It Together* with Julie Andrews at Manhattan Theatre Club. And he played a conservative Congressman in *Call Me Madam* with Tyne Daly in the City Center Encore Series. He can be heard on the CD's of both shows. And he's had supporting roles in the films *Secret of My Success, Mr. North, Penn and Teller Get Killed, The Butcher's Wife, Housesitter, Life with Mikey, The Cowboy Way.*

He has received a Guggenheim, a Rockefeller, the CBS Playwriting Fellowship, the Lecompte du Nouy Foundation grant, and the Kenyon Festival Theatre Playwriting Prize. In 1995 he won the prestigious three-year Lila Wallace Readers Digest Writers Award; as part of his grant, he is working with the Alcoholism Council Fellowship Center in New York, running a workshop for adult children of alcoholics.

Mr. Durang is a graduate of Harvard College and of Yale School of Drama; a member of the Dramatists Guild Council; and with Marsha Norman is the co-chair of the playwriting program at the Juilliard School Drama Division.

He has written a new play on commission for Lincoln Center Theatre called *Sex and Longing,* and it is scheduled for the fall of 1996.

Christopher Durang
27 Short Plays

Contemporary Playwrights Series

SK
A Smith and Kraus Book

A Smith and Kraus Book
Published by Smith and Kraus, Inc.
Copyright © 1995 by Christopher Durang.
All rights reserved. Manufactured in the United States of America.
Cover and Text Design by Julia Hill. Cover photos ©1995 by Susan Johann.
First Edition: October 1995
20 19 18 17 16 15 14 13 12 11

Library of Congress Cataloging-in-Publication Data
Durang, Christopher, 1949 -
    [Plays]
        Christopher Durang. --1st ed.
        p. cm. --(Contemporary playwrights series, ISSN 1067-9510)
        Contents: v. 1. 32 short plays --
        ISBN 1-57525-023-3 (v. 1. : cloth). -- ISBN 978-1-880399-89-7 (v. 1. : pbk.).
        I. Title. II. Series.
        PS3554.U666A19   1995
        812'.54--dc20   95-38058
                                  CIP

Contents

Introduction

Christopher Durang is relentlessly entertaining. Whether his play is a burlesque of other playwrights or an annihilation of the myth of the happy American family, or a vitriolic challenge to organized religion, homophobia, psychoanalysis, or parenthood, the plays are constantly arousing their audiences with hilarity and mirth. He succeeds because of the extraordinary fertility of his imagination, inventiveness, courage, and audacity. Blessed with twin gifts—originality and an anarchic spirit—he provides an audience with unruly laughter and outlandish amusement. One must guard oneself against the possibility of dying from laughter while watching a Durang play or reading a Durang script.

Coexistent with that power is Durang's tragic vision. Like all GREAT comedy writers, Durang has another significant dimension. From the time of his earliest plays, he has been responsive to the most profound and baffling question, "What is the nature and the purpose of the universe and to the human condition within that universe?". I know that chronology because the first major production of his play, *The Nature And The Purpose Of The Universe*, in 1971 preceded by two months his entering the Yale School of Drama. When he chose to come to Yale, I was the Associate Dean of the Drama School and together with Richard Gilman taught and supervised the training of the student playwrights. That position afforded me the rare good fortune of being in his immediate neighborhood for the three years of his training and his subsequent residence as an ABC Fellow. I had the opportunity to both observe and participate in his development as a playwright. On the day Gilman and I accepted him into the program, I rushed into Dean Robert Brustein's office to announce, "We took in a kid from Harvard who is about twenty-one or twenty-two and who already has a subject: A scream for help in a world he knows provides none, so he keeps on screaming and laughs at it."

Laughter for Durang not only affords a relief but a temporary refuge which might very well be the only remaining source of salvation. The modern playwright closest in spirit and form to him is Ionesco, and the playwright from the history of western dramatic literature most his kin is Aristophanes. A reader of *Sister Mary Ignatius Explains It All For You* will hear echoes of *The Lesson* by Ionesco as will the reader of *Canker Sores and Other Distractions* hear echoes of *The Bald Soprano*. Ionesco's bizarre and fantastic situations which inhabit his illogical universe in a form plotless and replete with non-sequiturs are echoed in Durang's *'dentity Crisis* and *Death Comes To Us All, Mary Agnes*. And just as Aristophanes took Euripedes to task while that playwright was still alive (Thesmophoriazusae), so Durang takes his contemporaries to task in *For Whom The Southern Belle Tolls* and *A Stye of the Eye*. He similarly echoes Aristophanes' habit of taking to task contemporary figures who sat in his audience such as Socrates (*The Clouds*) and Cleon (*The Wasps*) with his plays *Entertaining Mr. Helms* and *Cardinal O'Connor*. Aristophanes' universe was not at all absurd, but his inventions and his fantasy worlds that he created were designed to attack the corruption which was poisoning his beloved Athens.

Durang shouts for reason in an unreasonable universe and in an unreasoning society. He is, in the best sense of the critic, attempting to be corrective while fulfilling his primary purpose of entertaining his audience. He has to be offensive to be effective, just as Aristophanes had to be offensive and Jonathan Smith (Dean of St. Patrick's Cathedral, Dublin) had to be offensive. That offensiveness is in the service of an objective to aid an audience to see not only its follies and vices but also its misplaced values, its lies and deceits, its infirmities, even its cruelty and callousness. Only by having such conditions razed in front of us can we begin the process of building, of correcting. With his uncommon talent, Christopher Durang lights a candle rather than curses a darkness.

Howard Stein, September 1995
Professor Eemeritus, Columbia University
Retired Chairman, Oscar Hammerstein II Center for Theatre Studies,
Columbia University

Preface

The first six plays in this volume were presented together as an evening called, somewhat immodestly, *Durang Durang* at Manhattan Theatre Club in the fall of 1994, directed by Walter Bobbie. This presentation was the first full theatrical evening I had had in New York City since 1987 when *Laughing Wild* premiered at Playwrights Horizons.

The middle section of the book consists of fifteen plays, of which all but one *(Naomi in The Living Room)* have never been published before. Some of these are very short. Some are somewhat short. Some are almost long, but still one act, and thus still shorter than, say, *The Iceman Cometh*. And there is pastoral comedy, pastoral tragedy, absurdist pastoral tragedy, Greek tragic sketch comedy, pastoral Greek absurdist comic tragedy, oh, etc., etc.

The final section consists of six plays, previously published, and ending with two of my best known short plays, *The Actor's Nightmare* and *Sister Mary Ignatius Explains It All For You*.

I have written author's notes for these plays; and after several of the plays, I have included some additional notes, which are geared to actors (and directors). My plays seem to be tricky to perform. I have found that whether a play of mine comes across as funny or funny-touching or loud-and-off-putting or overstated-and-false varies wildly from production to production, depending on the acting tone that is found.

I don't believe there is only one way to perform a play—but really, you don't look at Blanche DuBois in *A Streetcar Named Desire* and say: "I think I'm going to play her like a lascivious loudmouth." And then walk around the stage bellowing and belching while you say "Young, young, young man."

I suppose that seems outlandish as a suggestion, but I have seen the tone and effectiveness of my plays change totally depending on how they're done. And my plays often are written in an exaggerated style that actors and directors sometimes mistakenly think they must match. *Finding the truthful psychological underpinnings to the characters in my plays is very important.*

For instance, a positive example first: Elizabeth Franz, who was the original Sister Mary, was wonderfully complicated, and very real at the same time she was funny. Elizabeth's Sister Mary was a true believer in her faith, she cared about her students, past and present; she was charming to the audience and to little Thomas; but she also flew into full, believable rages when contradicted, and she also had total, unquestioning commitment to all of the opinions I (and the Catholic Church) gave her. Elizabeth never winked at the audience, saying "I know this is funny." She played Sister on her own terms, for real; yet she had the pacing and skill of a comic actress.

Some wonderful actresses followed Elizabeth in the role—Nancy Marchand, Lynn Redgrave, Mary Louise Wilson, Kathleen Chalfant, Claudette Sutherland, Elizabeth Huddle, Merle Louise, Patricia Gage, Valerie Curtin, Peggy Cass, Cloris Leachman—and they all brought their own colors and quirks, but, like Elizabeth, they rooted their acting in true psychology. They played a woman who was complicated and had her own deep faith, no matter how illogical I as the author found most of her thoughts.

However—and now the bad example—I once saw a production where Sister was played one-dimensionally as just mean—as if it were a sketch, and it said "Enter a mean nun." It became boring, and over the top. In the second half when all the exstudents berated Sister, the play in this production came to an emotional stop...we hadn't believed this woman really existed—she seemed like an author's cartoon exaggeration; so we didn't believe that all these people were really upset with her. We couldn't care about this Sister; we didn't even believe anyone would have been that influenced by her; there was no recognizable psychology going on underneath her surface portrayal.

And, alas for me, the audience assumed that this was how I wrote it. The unrelenting and forced meanness that the actress brought to the role was the *fact* they saw before them—they could imagine no other interpretation besides the shrill one before their eyes.

Just as if you saw Blanche DuBois played as a belching, booming-voiced, sloppy drunk, and you had never seen or heard of *Streetcar* before, you might think that that's how Tennessee Williams wrote the character.

So, for those reasons, I write these notes, geared to guiding actors and directors to find the right tone.

And some readers of plays have told me they enjoy the notes. So I hope you do too. And if not, sorry.

Gosh, 27 plays. How odd. What possessed me to write them?

Christopher Durang, June 1995

Christopher Durang
27 Short Plays

Mrs. Sorken

AUTHOR'S NOTE

In attempting to create an evening of theater parodies, I wrote the character of Mrs. Sorken to introduce the pieces and to comment on them.

I don't intend for her to be British, but I must admit many of my inspirations for this kind of humor are British. All those wonderful, scatterbrained ladies in British movie comedies, like Margaret Rutherford or Joyce Grenfell. Very polite, very optimistic, willing to put a chipper spin on whatever they do.

In the late 80s, I had an evening called *Mrs. Sorken Presents* at the American Repertory Theater in Cambridge, Massachusetts, and my original Sister Mary, Elizabeth Franz, played Mrs. Sorken. For that evening, I wrote three appearances for her, before each of three plays she was introducing. And the character's first appearance always went very well, but the subsequent ones kind of did not. It felt as if the audience was unwilling to re-enter Mrs. Sorken's contemplative, verbal world after they had been involved with specific plays (and the plays didn't go that well up at A.R.T.)

So I put the speech away, though I hoped I'd find a future use for the character, since I like her. Then when Manhattan Theater Club expressed interest in doing an evening of one acts by me, I resurrected the character, rewrote some of what she says, and decided to limit her appearance to just at the beginning of the evening.

So here she is, Mrs. Sorken.

ORIGINAL PRODUCTION

Mrs. Sorken was the opening play of the six-play evening, *Durang Durang,* which premiered on November 14, 1995, at Manhattan Theater Club, Stage II, New York City. Lynne Meadow, artistic director. Barry Grove, managing director. Scenery by Derek McLane. Costumes by David C. Woolard. Lighting by Brian Nason. Sound by Tony Meola. Production stage manager was Perry Kline; stage manager was Gregg Fletcher. Directed by Walter Bobbie.

There was one intermission, after the third play. The program included this listing: Act I: Theater. Act II: Everything Else.

The plays had a company of seven actors: Becky Ann Baker, David Aaron Baker, Patricia Elliott, Marcus Giamatti, Lizbeth Mackay, Patricia Randell, Keith Reddin. Understudies were John Augustine, Judith Hawking, Margo Skinner. Mrs. Sorken was played by Patricia Elliott.

CHARACTERS

MRS. SORKEN

MRS. SORKEN

Enter Mrs. Sorken to address the audience. She is a charming woman, well dressed and gracious, though a little scattered. She is happy to be there.

MRS. SORKEN: Dear theatregoers, welcome, and how lovely to see you. I've come here to talk to you about theatre, and why we all leave our homes to come see it, assuming we have. But you have left your homes, and you're here. So, welcome!

Now I have written down some comments about theatre for you, if I can just find them. *(Searches through her purse.)*

Isn't it refreshing to see someone with a purse? *(Looks some more through the purse.)*

Well, I can't find my notes, so I'll have to make my comments from memory.

(From here on, she is genuinely winging it—some of it may be thoughts she's prepared, much of it are thoughts that pop into her head as she is speaking. She is not nervous, though. She loves talking to the audience.)

Drama. Let's begin with etymology, shall we?...etymology, which is the history of the word.

The word "drama" comes from the Greek word "dran," which means to do, and which connects with the English word "drain," meaning to exhaust one totally, and with the modern pharmaceutical sedating tablet, Dramamine, which is the tradename of a drug used to relieve airsickness and seasickness and a general sense of nausea, or "nausée" as Jean Paul Sartre might say, perhaps over a cup of espresso at a Paris bistro. How I love Paris in the spring, or would, if I had ever been there; but Mr. Sorken and I haven't done much traveling. Maybe after he dies I'll go somewhere.

We go to the drama seeking the metaphorical Dramamine that will cure us of our nausea of life.

Of course, sometimes we become nauseated by the drama itself, and then we are sorry we went, especially if it uses the F-word and lasts over four hours. I don't mind a leisurely play, but by 10:30 I want to leave the theatre and go to sleep. Frequently, I prefer Dramamine to drama, and only wish someone would renew my prescription for seconal.

Secondly…we have the word "theatre," which is derived from the Greek word "theasthai," which means to view.

And nowadays we have the word, "reastat," a device by which we can dim the lights in one's house slowly, rather than just snapping them off with a simple switch.

And thirdly, we have the Greek god "Dionysus," the last syllable of which is spelled "s-u-s" in English, but "s-o-s" in Greek, the letters which in Morse code spell *help*— "Dionysos" is the god of wine and revelry, but also the father of modern drama as we know it.

The Greeks went to the theatre in the open air, just like the late and wonderful Joseph Papp used to make us see Shakespeare. Shakespeare's language is terribly difficult to understand for us of the modern age, but how much easier it is when there's a cool breeze and it's for free. If it's hot and I have to pay, well, then I don't much like Shakespeare. I'm sorry, I shouldn't say that. He's a brilliant writer, and I look forward to seeing all 750 of his plays. Although perhaps not in this lifetime.

But back to the Greeks. They went to the open-air theatre expecting the drama they saw to evoke terror and pity.

Nowadays we have enough terror and pity in our own lives, and so rather than going to the theatre looking for terror, we go looking for slight irritation. And rather than looking for the theatre to evoke pity, we look merely for a generalized sense of identification as in "Evita was a woman, I am a woman." Or "Sweeney Todd was a barber, I go to the hairdresser." Or "Fosca in *Passion* should have her moles removed, I know a good dermatologist." That sort of thing.

But did the Greeks really experience terror and pity? And if so, what was it in all that matricide-patricide that so affected them?

I know that seeing Greek drama nowadays, even with Diana Rigg in it, really rather baffles me, it is so very different from my own life. My life with Mr. Sorken is not something that Diana Rigg would wish to star in, even on PBS. My life, I'm sorry to say, is not all that interesting.

Indeed, addressing you at this moment, I'm sorry to say, is the high point of my life to date.

Could I have lived my life differently? Women of my generation were encouraged to marry and to play the piano, and I have done both those things. Is there a piano here? I don't see one. I might have played a sonata for you, or a polonaise.

But back to my theme—Drama, from the Greek word "dran."

When we leave the drama, we return to our homes feeling "drained." And if it's been a good night in the theatre, we leave feeling slightly irritated; and feeling identification with Evita or Fosca or that poor Mormon woman in *Angels in America*.

And so, drained, we get into our nightgowns, we adjust our reastats from light to darkness, we climb into bed next to Mr. Sorken, we fall into a deep REM sleep, dreaming God knows what mysterious messages from our teeming unconscious; and then in the morning we open our eyes to the light of the new day, of the burgeoning possibilities.

Light from the Greek word "leukos," meaning white, and the Latin word "lumen" meaning illumination. In German, *der licht;* in French, *la lumiere.* All art leads to light.

Light. Plants need light to grow. Might people need art to grow? It's possible. Are people less important than plants? Some of them are certainly less interesting.

But there is some connection between theatre and light, and people and plants, that I am striving to articulate. It's about photosynthesis, I think, which is the ingestion of light that plants go through in order to achieve growth.

And you see, it's "light" again— "photo" comes from the Greek word, "phos," which means light and which relates to phosphoresence, or the "light given off." And "synthesis" comes from the Greek prefix, "syn-" meaning together, and the Greek word "tithenai," meaning to place, to put.

Photosynthesis—to put it together with light.

We go to the theatre, *desperate* for help in photosynthesis.

The text of the play is the light, the actors help put it together, and we are the plants in the audience.

Plants, lights, theatre, art. I feel this sense of sudden interconnection with everything that's making me feel dizzy. And Dramamine, of course, is good for dizziness.

Now, to wrap up.

(Warmly.)

Welcome, theatregoers. I hope you enjoy your evening this evening. Act I is theatre parodies. Act II...is not.

The plays are by Christopher Durang, who is one of my favorite writers. He is also my nephew. If David Mamet was my nephew, I'm sure he'd be my favorite writer as well. Although, in truth, I don't think Mr. Mamet would have an aunt like me. I think if he has any aunts, they are probably Chicago gangsters who use the F-word. I'm sorry, was that rude? But anyway, please enjoy this evening. And if you are ever in Connecticut, I hope you'll drop in and say hello to me and Mr. Sorken. He prefers that you call first, but I love to be surprised. So just ring the bell, and we'll have cocktails.

And I hope you have enjoyed my humbly offered comments on the drama. I have definitely enjoyed speaking with you, and have a sneaking suspicion that in the future, it is going to be harder and harder to shut me up.

(Rather grandly raises her arms upward to present the evening that is to follow:)

Let the games begin!

(Lights out. End.)

Mrs. Sorken is happy to talk to the audience, and she has no trouble expressing herself. Thus, stage fright or being upset at misplacing her notes, is not meant to be part of her character.

Although it's logical to play momentary disorientation, I want her to quickly move on. I want her to play that she's immediately resilient, that she has most of what she needs to say in her head, and that she believes other ideas will pop into her head whenever she needs them to. Then I want her to just get on with the task of communicating the words and content of the speech.

Mrs. Sorken is very verbal, her speech is dense. Please do not speak slowly.

Or as director Walter Bobbie would say to all of the actors in *Durang Durang:* Aim for the end of the sentence, don't break it up into little pieces.

Another piece of director advice: Act *on* the lines, not between them.

If you've been acting on the line and not pausing in between, when later you *choose* to take a pause, it can be very powerful because you've "earned" the pause. But you can only earn one from time to time, not every other sentence.

Walter often told the actors to pay attention to the commas and the periods in my writing, especially in long speeches. And to predominantly follow them. Thus the opening sentence is: "Dear theatergoers, welcome, and how lovely to see you." I don't mean for you to abnormally rush it, but the pauses should be very tiny, as a comma suggests; and not a full stop, as a period would suggest. Because if you choose to stop after the word "theatergoers" and then stop after "welcome," you make the first sentence somewhat laborious. You take one thought and make it into three thoughts. If you should do that throughout the speech, the audience will feel bogged down and tired of all Mrs. Sorken's words.

I honestly don't mean to be a controlling ogre. Sure… if you have an acting impulse to stop at a certain place or to stress a certain word, that's fine.

But as a general rule, go for the end of the sentence. Always be communicating the *whole* sentence—it helps the audience understand what you're saying. And with Mrs. Sorken's complicated and formal diction (which is similar in its baroqueness to Sister Mary's diction), it's good to help them hear the whole thought, all at once, not broken up into separate little beats.

If you go too slowly, the audience will get ahead of you.

Plus, with Mrs. Sorken or Amanda in *Belle* or the woman in *Laughing Wild* or Sister Mary—any of the characters I've written who talk in long, convoluted sentences—you must perform them with a high energy. You mustn't dawdle through them. Pace, pace, verbal dexterity. Look at the screwball comedies of the 1930s, and watch how fast everybody talks (*Bringing Up Baby* with

Katharine Hepburn and Cary Grant, *The Lady Eve* with Barbara Stanwyck and Henry Fonda, *His Girl Friday* with Rosalind Russell and Cary Grant). Pray to cinematic heaven and ask it to guide you.

Two additional things about Mrs. Sorken.

Sometimes the humor can lie in saying something matter-of-factly—as when she says, "Maybe after he dies I'll go somewhere," or when she identifies with the "poor Mormon woman in *Angels in America.*"

And also, don't be afraid to figure out what words Mrs. Sorken enjoys saying. Mrs. Sorken's language is ornate, she uses words and phrases like "etymology" and "sedating tablet" and "teeming unconscious." So when your instincts lead you to it, relish the fancy words. It's hard to say "teeming unconscious" without enjoying the word "teeming" a little bit. "Photosynthesis" is probably slightly pleasurable to say.

In most cases, I prefer you not use a British accent, or a "Connecticut" lockjaw one. Just use your own voice and let the character sound how you sound, saying and believing what Mrs. Sorken says.

I don't mean to inhibit your acting impulses, but if you had experienced the difference between say, Patricia Elliott doing the speech in a charming, funny way that took ten minutes and another actress taking many pauses and making the piece be close to 20 minutes—I think you would understand my desire to guide actors through these notes.

Well, that's all.

For Whom the Southern Belle Tolls

AUTHOR'S NOTE

This play is a parody spin-off of Tennessee Williams' *The Glass Menagerie*. Audiences unfamiliar with the play seem able to enjoy it anyway—because parent-child tensions are the core theme of it—but the play is definitely geared to people who know the Williams' play.

I've always had a strong reaction to *The Glass Menagerie*. I think it's quite a wonderful play. I first was captivated by the play in high school when I took home a recording of it from the library which featured the stellar cast of Jessica Tandy as Amanda, Montgomery Clift as Tom, Julie Harris as Laura, and David Wayne as the Gentleman Caller. Tom's feeling trapped, Laura's feeling overwhelmed by the world (and typing class), and Amanda's trying to force them both to be other than who they were—these themes reverberated with me.

In graduate school at Yale School of Drama, however, I discovered that as I got older there was something in me that was starting to find the Amanda-Laura relationship funny—these two souls stuck together, one hopelessly trying to change the other one, who couldn't and wouldn't budge.

I befriended fellow playwright Albert Innaurato and we ended up writing a strange sketch based on *Menagerie* in which he played an overbearing Amanda and I played a shy, withering Laura, but we didn't dress as women, we dressed as priests. Well, it made sense to us at the time.

Our take on *Menagerie* was about seven minutes, and was exceptionally lunatic. (It became part of a cabaret act Albert and I did together called *I Don't Generally Like Poetry But Have You Read "Trees"?*)

I didn't think about *Menagerie* again until I saw yet another production in the mid-80s. I actually quite liked the production, but found that between the various movie and TV versions, a couple of high school productions, and some other stage ones, I felt overexposed to the play. And though I still admired the play quite genuinely, I seemed to have reached that place where I found it hard to respond normally because I knew it too well.

And though I as a child always felt sympathy for Laura, as an adult I started to find Laura's sensitivity frustrating. I mean, how hard was typing class really?

And though in my youth I found Laura's interest in her glass animals to be sweet and otherworldly (with the appropriately perfect symbolism of her loving her glass unicorn best because it was different), now as an adult, I felt restless with her little hobby. Did she actually spend hours and hours staring at them? Couldn't she try to function in the world just a little bit? Why didn't she go out bowling or make prank phone calls or get drunk on a good bottle of bourbon?

Anyway, I started to find Laura annoying and frustrating.

It's out of this irritation with Laura's sensitivity—a feeling greatly at odds with the Williams' original—that I seem to have written this parody, *For Whom the Southern Belle Tolls*. (I say "seem" because I often say "seem" and because I approached writing this parody on impulse, unaware consciously of how my

10 CHRISTOPHER DURANG

feelings toward the play had changed. Writing the parody was a way of playing with, and releasing, some of what I felt after seeing the play for what seemed the 100th time.)

I've been happy that some of the critics have described this parody as "affectionate." I do feel affectionate toward the original play. But there is something about sweet, sensitive Laura that seems to have gotten on my nerves.

ORIGINAL PRODUCTION

For Whom the Southern Belle Tolls was part of *Durang Durang* at Manhattan Theatre Club. The cast was as follows:

Amanda	Lizabeth Mackay
Lawrence	Keith Reddin
Tom	David Aaron Baker
Ginny	Patricia Randell

The spring before this production, the play was presented by Ensemble Studio Theatre as part of its one-act Marathon 94. The cast and the director were the same. And it was partially from this production's good reception that Manhattan Theatre Club approached me and Walter Bobbie about doing a full evening of one-acts, which became *Durang Durang*.

Several years before these two productions, there was a showcase production of an earlier version of *Belle*. It was directed by Scott Allen, and its cast was Laura Waterbury as Amanda, John Money as Lawrence, Timothy Kivel as Tom, and Julie Knight as Ginny.

And subsequent to that showcase, there were two staged readings of *Belle*, one at the Westport Artists Theatre Workshop in Connecticut, and one at a benefit for The Glines Theatre in New York City. Both times E. Katherine Kerr and myself played Amanda and Lawrence; John Augustine and Julie Janney were Tom and Ginny in Westport, and Jeffrey Hayenga and Cristine Rose were Tom and Ginny at the Glines' benefit.

CHARACTERS

AMANDA, the Southern belle mother
LAWRENCE, her sensitive son
TOM, her other son
GINNY, a visitor

FOR WHOM THE
SOUTHERN BELLE TOLLS

Scene: A warm, fussy living room setting. A couch, a chair, homey and warm. Maybe a fringed throw over the couch. Maybe a vase of jonquils. Enter Amanda, the Southern belle mother. Dressed nicely, for company. Feminine clothing, though perhaps an earlier feeling to what she's wearing.

AMANDA: Rise and shine! Rise and shine! *(Calls off.)* Lawrence, honey, come on out here and let me have a look at you!
(Enter Lawrence, who limps across the room. In his 20s [or maybe a young-looking 30], he is very sensitive, and is wearing what are clearly his dress clothes. Amanda fiddles with his bow tie and stands back to admire him.)
AMANDA: Lawrence, honey, you look lovely.
LAWRENCE: No, I don't, mama. I have a pimple on the back of my neck.
AMANDA: Don't say the word "pimple," honey, it's common. *(With hopeful energy.)* Now your brother Tom is bringing home a girl from the warehouse for you to meet, and I want you to make a good impression, honey.
LAWRENCE: It upsets my stomach to meet people, mama.
AMANDA: Oh, Lawrence honey, you're so sensitive it makes me want to hit you.
LAWRENCE: I don't need to meet people, mama. I'm happy just by myself, playing with my collection of glass cocktail stirrers. *(Lawrence smiles wanly and limps over to a table on top of which sits a glass jar filled with glass swizzle sticks.)*

AMANDA: Lawrence, you are a caution. Only retarded people and alcoholics are interested in glass cocktail stirrers.

LAWRENCE: *(With proud wonderment.)* Each one of them has a special
name, mama. *(Picks up one to show her.)* This one is called
Stringbean because it's long and thin. *(Picks up another one.)* And
this one is called Stringbean because it's long and thin. *(Picks up a
blue one.)* And this one is called Blue because it's blue.

AMANDA: All my children have such imagination, why was I so blessed?
Oh, Lawrence honey, how are you going to get on in the world if
you just stay home all day, year after year, playing with your collection of glass cocktail stirrers?

LAWRENCE: I don't like the world, mama. I like it here in this room.

AMANDA: I know you do, Lawrence honey, that's part of your charm.
Some days. But, *honey*, what about making a living?

LAWRENCE: I can't work, mama. I'm crippled. *(He limps over to the couch
and sits.)*

AMANDA: *(Firmly.)* There is nothing wrong with your leg, Lawrence
honey, all the doctors have told you that. This limping thing is an
affectation.

LAWRENCE: *(Perhaps a little steely.)* I only know how I feel, mama.

AMANDA: Oh if only I had connections in the Mafia, I'd have someone
come and break *both* your legs.

LAWRENCE: *(Slightly amused.)* Don't try to make me laugh, mama. You
know I have asthma.

AMANDA: Your asthma, your leg, your eczema. You're just a mess,
Lawrence!

LAWRENCE: I have scabs from the itching, mama.

AMANDA: That's lovely, Lawrence. You must tell us more over dinner.

LAWRENCE: Alright.

AMANDA: That was a *joke*, Lawrence.

LAWRENCE: Don't try to make me laugh, mama. My asthma.

AMANDA: Now, Lawrence, I don't want you talking about your ailments
to the feminine caller your brother Tom is bringing home from the
warehouse, honey. No nice-bred young lady likes to hear a young
man discussing his eczema, Lawrence.

LAWRENCE: What else can I talk about, mama?

AMANDA: Talk about the weather. Or Red China.

LAWRENCE: Or my collection of glass cocktail stirrers?

AMANDA: I suppose so, honey, if the conversation's comes to some godawful standstill. Otherwise, I'd shut up about it. *(Becomes coquettish, happy memories.)* Conversation is an art, Lawrence. Back at Blue Mountain, when I had seventeen gentlemen callers, I was able to converse with charm and vivacity for six hours without stop and never once mention eczema or bone cancer or vivisection. Try to emulate me, Lawrence, honey. Charm and vivacity. And charm. And vivacity. And charm.

LAWRENCE: Well, I'll try, but I doubt it.

AMANDA: Me too, honey. But we'll go through the motions anyway, won't we?

LAWRENCE: I don't know if I want to meet some girl who works in a warehouse, mama.

AMANDA: Your brother Tom says she's a lovely girl with a nice personality. And where else does he meet girls except the few who work at the warehouse? *(Thinking it's odd, but not sure why.)* He only seems to meet men at the movies. Your brother goes to the movies entirely too much. I must speak to him about it.

LAWRENCE: It's unfeminine for a girl to work at a warehouse.

AMANDA: *(Firm, frustrated.)* Now Lawrence—if you can't go out the door without getting an upset stomach or an attack of vertigo, then we have got to find some nice girl who's willing to *support* you. Otherwise, how am I ever going to get you out of this house and off my hands?

LAWRENCE: *(Sensitive, unknowing.)* Why do you want to be rid of me, mama?

AMANDA: I suppose it's unmotherly of me, dear, but you really get on my nerves. Limping around the apartment, pretending to have asthma. If only some nice girl would marry you and I knew you were taken care of, then I'd feel free to start to live again. I'd join Parents Without Partners, I'd go to dinner dances, I'd have a life again. Rather than just watch you mope about this stupid apartment. I'm not bitter, dear, it's just that I hate my life.

LAWRENCE: I understand, mama.

AMANDA: Do you, dear? Oh, you're cute. Oh, listen, I think I hear them.

TOM: *(From offstage.)* Mother, I forgot my key.

LAWRENCE: I'll be in the other room. *(Starts to limp away.)*

AMANDA: I want you to let them in, Lawrence.

LAWRENCE: Oh, I couldn't, mama. She'd see I limp.

AMANDA: Then don't limp, damn it.

TOM: *(From off.)* Mother, are you there?

AMANDA: Just a minute, Tom, honey. Now, Lawrence, you march over to that door or I'm going to break all your swizzle sticks.

LAWRENCE: Mama, I can't!

AMANDA: Lawrence, you are a grown boy. Now you answer that door like any normal person.

LAWRENCE: I can't.

TOM: *(From off.)* Mother, I'm going to break the door down in a minute.

AMANDA: Just be patient, Tom. Now you're causing a scene, Lawrence. I want you to answer that door.

LAWRENCE: My eczema itches.

AMANDA: *(Impatient.)* I'll itch it for you in a second, Lawrence.

TOM: *(From off.)* Alright, I'm breaking it down.

(Sound of door breaking down. Enter Tom and Ginny Bennett, a viva- cious, friendly girl dressed in either factory clothes, or else a simple, not- too-frilly blouse and slacks.)

AMANDA: Oh, Tom, you got in.

TOM: *(Very angry.)* Why must we go through this every night??? You know the stupid fuck won't open the door, so why don't you let him alone about it? *(To Ginny.)* My kid brother has a thing about an- swering doors. He thinks people will notice his limp and his asthma and his eczema.

LAWRENCE: Excuse me. I think I hear someone calling me in the other room. *(Limps off, calls to imaginary person:)* Coming! *(Exits.)*

AMANDA: *(Angry, focused on Tom.)* Now see what you've done. He's prob- ably going to refuse to come to the table due to your insensitivity. Oh, was any woman as cursed as I? With one son who's too sensi- tive and another one who's this big lox. *(Suddenly re-notices Ginny; switches to Southern charm and graciousness.)* I'm sorry, how rude of me. I'm Amanda Wingvalley. You must be Virginia Bennett from the warehouse. Tom has spoken so much about you I feel you're al- most one of the family, preferably a daughter-in-law. Welcome, Virginia.

GINNY: *(Very friendly, and very loud.)* CALL ME GINNY OR GIN! BUT JUST DON'T CALL ME "LATE FOR DINNER"!! *(Roars with laughter.)*

AMANDA: Oh, how amusing. *(Whispers to Tom.)* Why is she shouting? Is she deaf?

GINNY: *(Still talking loudly.)* You're asking why I am speaking loudly. It's so that I can be heard! I am taking a course in public speaking, and so far we've covered organizing your thoughts and speaking good and loud so the people in the back of the room can hear you.

AMANDA: Public speaking. How impressive. You must be interested in improving yourself.

GINNY: *(Truly not having heard.)* What?

AMANDA: *(Loudly.)* YOU MUST BE INTERESTED IN IMPROVING YOURSELF.

GINNY: *(Loudly and happily.)* YES I AM!

TOM: When's dinner? I want to get this over with fast if everyone's going to shout all evening.

GINNY: What?

AMANDA: *(To Ginny.)* Dinner is almost ready.

GINNY: Who's Freddy?

AMANDA: Oh, Lord, No. dear. DINNER IS READY.

GINNY: Oh good. I'm as hungry as a bear! *(Growls enthusiastically.)*

AMANDA: You must be very *popular* at the warehouse, Ginny.

GINNY: No popsicle for me, ma'am, although I will take you up on some gin.

AMANDA: *(Confused.)* What?

GINNY: *(Loudly.)* I WOULD LIKE SOME GIN.

AMANDA: Well, fine. I think I'd like to get drunk too. Tom, why don't you go and make two Southern ladies some nice summer gin and tonics? And see if sister would like a lemonade.

TOM: Sister?

AMANDA: I'm sorry, did I say sister? I meant brother.

TOM: *(Calling as he exits.)* Hey, four eyes, you wanna lemonade?

AMANDA: Tom's so amusing. He calls Lawrence "four eyes" even though he doesn't wear glasses.

GINNY: And does *Lawrence* wear glasses?

AMANDA: *(Confused.)* What?

GINNY: You said Tom called Lawrence "four eyes" even though he doesn't wear glasses, and I wondered if *Lawrence* wore glasses. Because that would, you see, explain it.

AMANDA: *(Looks at her with despair.)* Ah. I don't know. I'll have to ask Lawrence someday. *(Switches to energy, and Southern charm again.)* Speaking of Lawrence, let me go check on the supper and see if I can convince him to come out here and make conversation with you.

GINNY: No, thank you, ma'am, I'll just have the gin.

AMANDA: What?

GINNY: What?

AMANDA: Never mind. I'll be back. Or with luck I won't.

(Amanda exits. Ginny looks around uncomfortably, and sees the table with the collection of glass cocktail stirrers.)

GINNY: *(Looking at stirrers.)* They must drink a lot here.

(Enter Tom with a glass for Ginny.)

TOM: Here's some gin for Ginny. *(Offers drink.)*

GINNY: What?

TOM: Here's your poison.

GINNY: No, thanks, I'll just wait here.

(Ginny now notices the offered drink, and takes it.)

TOM: Have you ever thought that your hearing is being affected by all that loud *machinery* at the warehouse?

GINNY: Scenery? You mean, like trees? Yeah, I like trees.

TOM: I like trees too.

(Tom sort of gives up on conversation, and leafs through his newspaper.)

AMANDA: *(From offstage.)* Now you get out of that bed this minute, Lawrence Wingvalley, or I'm going to give that overbearing girl your *entire* collection of glass gobbledygook—is that clear?

(Amanda pushes in Lawrence, who is wearing a blue night shirt.)

AMANDA: I believe Lawrence would like to visit with you, Ginny.

GINNY: *(Shows her drink.)* Tom brought me my drink already, thank you, Mrs. Wingvalley.

AMANDA: You know, dear, a *hearing aid* isn't really all that expensive, you might look into that.

GINNY: No, if I have the gin, I don't really want any gator ade. Never liked the stuff anyway. But you feel free.

AMANDA: Thank you, dear. I will. *(Takes Tom by the arm, to lead him away; back to charm.)* Come, Tom, come to the kitchen and help me prepare the supper. And we'll let the two young people converse. Remember, Lawrence. Charm and vivacity.

TOM: *(Putting down his newspaper.)* I hope this dinner won't take long, mother. I don't want to get to the movies too late.

AMANDA: *(Irritated.)* Oh shut up about the movies. *(Smiles charmingly at Ginny and Lawrence.)*

(Amanda and Tom exit. Lawrence stands still, uncomfortably. Ginny looks at him pleasantly. Brief pause.)

GINNY: *(Loudly.)* HI.

LAWRENCE: *(Startled.)* Hi. …I'd gone to bed.

GINNY: I never eat bread. It's too fattening. I have to watch my figure if I want to get ahead in the world. *(Suddenly wondering.)* Why are you wearing that nightshirt?

LAWRENCE: I'd gone to bed. I wasn't feeling well. My leg hurts, and I have a headache, and I have palpitations of the heart.

GINNY: I don't know. Hum a few bars, and I'll see.

LAWRENCE: *(Hears her odd statement, can't figure it out; says shyly:)* We've met before, you know.

GINNY: Uh huh.

LAWRENCE: *(Telling a precious memory.)* We were in high school together. You were voted Girl Most Likely to Succeed. We sat next to one another in glee club.

GINNY: I'm sorry, I really can't hear you. You're talking too softly.

LAWRENCE: *(Louder.)* You used to call me BLUE ROSES.

GINNY: Blue Roses? Oh yes, I remember, sort of. Why did I do that?

LAWRENCE: I had been absent from school for several months, and when I came back, you asked me where I'd been, and I said I'd been sick with viral pneumonia, but you thought I said "blue roses."

GINNY: I didn't get much of that, but I remember you now. You used to make a spectacle of yourself every day in glee class, clumping up the aisle with this great big noisy leg brace on your leg. God, you made a racket!

LAWRENCE: *(Sensitive, embarrassed.)* I was always so afraid people were looking at me, and pointing. *(A bit resentful.)* But then eventually mama wouldn't let me wear the leg brace anymore. She gave it to the salvation army.

GINNY: I've never been in the army. How long were you in for?

LAWRENCE: I've never been in the army. I have asthma.

GINNY: You do? May I see it?

LAWRENCE: *(Confused.)* See it?

GINNY: Well, sure, unless you don't want to.

LAWRENCE: Maybe you want to see my collection of glass cocktail stirrers. *(Lawrence limps to the table with his precious collection. Ginny follows behind him.)*

LAWRENCE: *(Holds up a swizzle stick.)* I call this one Stringbean, because it's long and thin.

GINNY: Thank you. *(Cheerfully puts it in her glass and stirs it.)*

LAWRENCE: *(Fairly appalled.)* They're not for *use. (Takes it back from her.)* They're a collection.

GINNY: *(Not having heard, but willing.)* Well I guess I stirred it enough.

LAWRENCE: They're my favorite thing in the world. *(Holds up another one.)* I call this one Q-tip, because I realized it looks like a Q-tip, except it's made out of glass and doesn't have little cotton swabs at the end of it.

(Ginny looks blank.)

LAWRENCE: Q-TIP.

GINNY: Really? *(Takes it and puts it in her ear.)*

LAWRENCE: No!!! Don't put it in your ear. *(Takes it back.)* Now it's disgusting.

GINNY: Well, I didn't think it was a Q-tip, but that's what you said it was.

LAWRENCE: I *call* it that. I think I'm going to throw it out now. *(Puts Q-tip aside somewhere; holds up another one.)* I call this one Pinocchio because if you hold it perpendicular to your nose it makes your nose look long. *(Holds it up to his nose.)*

GINNY: Uh huh.

LAWRENCE: *(Holds up another one.)* And I call this one Henry Kissinger, because he wears glasses and it's made of glass.

GINNY: Uh huh. *(Takes it and stirs her drink again.)*

LAWRENCE: No! They're just for looking, not for stirring. *(Calls.)* Mama, she's making a mess with my collection.

AMANDA: *(From off.)* Oh shut up about your collection, honey, you're probably driving the poor girl bananas.

GINNY: *(Calls off to her.)* No bananas, thank you! My nutritionist says I should avoid potassium. *(To Lawrence.)* You know what I take your trouble to be, Lawrence?

LAWRENCE: Mama says I'm retarded.

GINNY: I know you're tired, I figured that's why you put on the night-shirt, but this won't take long. I judge you to be lacking in self-confidence. Am I right?

LAWRENCE: Well, I am afraid of people and things, and I have a lot of ailments.

GINNY: But that makes you special, Lawrence.

LAWRENCE: What does?

GINNY: I don't know. Whatever you said. And that's why you should present yourself with more confidence. Throw back your shoulders, and say, "HI! HOW YA DOIN'?" Now you try it.

LAWRENCE: *(Unenthusiastically, softly.)* Hello. How are you?

GINNY: *(Looking at watch, in response to his supposed question.)* I don't know, it's about 8:30, but this won't take long and then you can go to bed. Alright now try it. *(Booming.)* "HI! HOW YA DOIN'?"

LAWRENCE: Hi. How ya doin'?

GINNY: Now swagger a bit. *(Kinda butch.)* HI. HOW YA DOIN'?

LAWRENCE: *(Imitates her fairly successfully.)* HI. HOW YA DOIN'?

GINNY: Good, Lawrence. That's much better. Again.
(Lawrence starts to enjoy this game with Ginny. Amanda and Tom enter from behind them and watch this.)

GINNY: HI! HOW YA DOIN'?

LAWRENCE: HI! HOW YA DOIN'?

GINNY: THE BRAVES PLAYED A HELLUVA GAME, DON'TCHA THINK?

LAWRENCE: THE BRAVES PLAYED A HELLUVA GAME, DON'TCHA THINK?

AMANDA: Oh God I feel sorry for their children. Is this the *only* girl who works at the warehouse, Tom?

GINNY: HI, MRS. WINGVALLEY. YOUR SON LAWRENCE AND I ARE GETTING ON JUST FINE, AREN'T WE, LAWRENCE?

AMANDA: Please, no need to shout, I'm not deaf, even if you are.

GINNY: What?

AMANDA: I'm glad you like Lawrence.

GINNY: What?

AMANDA: I'M GLAD YOU LIKE LAWRENCE.

GINNY: What?

AMANDA: WHY DON'T YOU MARRY LAWRENCE.

GINNY: *(Looks shocked; has heard this.)* Oh.

LAWRENCE: Oh, mama.

GINNY: Oh dear, I see. So that's why Shakespeare asked me here.

AMANDA: *(To Tom.)* Shakespeare?

TOM: The first day of work she asked me my name, and I said Tom Wingvalley, and she thought I said Shakespeare.

GINNY: Oh dear. Mrs. Wingvalley, if I had a young brother as nice and as special as Lawrence is, I'd invite girls from the warehouse home to meet him too.

AMANDA: *(Retreating to vague manners.)* I'm sure I don't know what you mean.

GINNY: And you're probably hoping I'll say that I'll call again.

AMANDA: Really, we haven't even had supper yet. Tom, shouldn't you be checkin' on the roast pigs feet?

TOM: I guess so. If anything interesting happens, call me. *(Exits.)*

GINNY: But I'm afraid I won't be calling on Lawrence again.

LAWRENCE: This is so embarrassing. I told you I wanted to stay in my room.

AMANDA: Hush up, Lawrence.

GINNY: But, Lawrence, I don't want you to think that I won't be calling because I don't like you. I do like you.

(Lawrence and Amanda both look hopeful.)

LAWRENCE: You do?

GINNY: Sure. I like everybody. But I got two time clocks to punch, Mrs. Wingvalley. One at the warehouse, and one at night.

AMANDA: At night? You have a second job? That *is* ambitious.

GINNY: Not a second job, ma'am. Betty.

AMANDA: Pardon?

GINNY: Now who's deaf, eh what? Betty. I'm involved with a girl named Betty. We've been going together for about a year. We're saving money so that we can buy a farmhouse and a tractor together. So you can see why I can't visit your son, though I wish I could. *(To Lawrence.)* No hard feelings, Lawrence. You're a good kid.

(Lawrence looks extremely crushed and sad. He limps over to his collection, and takes one of his precious swizzle sticks, and offers it to Ginny.)

LAWRENCE: I want you to keep this. It's my very favorite one. I call it Thermometer because it looks like a thermometer.

GINNY: You want me to have this?

LAWRENCE: Yes, as a souvenir.

GINNY: *(Offended.)* Well, there's not need to call me a queer. Fuck you and your stupid swizzle sticks. *(Throws the offered gift upstage.)*

LAWRENCE: *(Horrified.)* You've broken it!

GINNY: What?

LAWRENCE: You've broken it. YOU'VE BROKEN IT.

GINNY: So I've broken it. Big fuckin' deal. You have twenty more of them here.

AMANDA: Well, I'm so sorry you have to be going.

GINNY: What?

AMANDA: Hadn't you better be going?

GINNY: What?

AMANDA: GO AWAY!

GINNY: *(Hearing the last phrase.)* Well, I guess I can tell when I'm not wanted. I guess I'll go now.

AMANDA: You and Betty must come over some evening. Preferably when we're out.

GINNY: Uh huh. *(Calls off.)* So long, Shakespeare. See you at the warehouse. *(To Lawrence.)* So long, Lawrence. I hope your rash gets better.

LAWRENCE: *(Saddened, holding the broken swizzle stick.)* You broke thermometer.

GINNY: What?

LAWRENCE: YOU BROKE THERMOMETER!

GINNY: Well, what was a thermometer doing in with the swizzle sticks anyway?

LAWRENCE: Its *name* was Thermometer, you nitwit!

AMANDA: Let it go, Lawrence. There'll be other swizzle sticks. Good bye, Virginia.

GINNY: I sure am hungry. Any chance I might be able to take a sandwich with me?

AMANDA: Certainly you can shake hands with me, if that will make you happy.

GINNY: I said I'm *hungry.*

AMANDA: Really, dear? What part of Hungary are you from?

GINNY: Oh never mind. I guess I'll go.

AMANDA: That's right. You have two time clocks. It must be getting near to when you punch in Betty.

GINNY: *(Cheerful, her basic nature.)* Well, so long, everybody! I had a nice time. *(Exits.)*

(Quiet. Amanda walks toward the kitchen and calls off to Tom in a contained voice.)

AMANDA: Tom, come in here please. Lawrence, I don't believe I would play the victrola right now.

LAWRENCE: What victrola?

AMANDA: Any victrola.

(Enter Tom.)

TOM: Yes, mother? Where's Ginny?

AMANDA: The feminine caller made a hasty departure.

TOM: Old four eyes bored her to death, huh?

LAWRENCE: Oh, drop dead.

TOM: We should have you institutionalized.

AMANDA: That's the first helpful thing you've said all evening, but first things first. You played a little joke on us, Tom.

TOM: What are you talking about?

AMANDA: You didn't mention that your friend is already spoken for.

TOM: Really? I didn't even think she liked men.

AMANDA: Yes, well. It seems odd that you know so little about a person you see everyday at the warehouse.

TOM: The warehouse is where I work, not where I know things about people.

AMANDA: The disgrace. The expense of the pigs feet, a new tie for Lawrence. And you—bringing a lesbian into this house. Why, we haven't had a lesbian in this house since your grandmother died. And now you have the audacity to bring in that…that…

LAWRENCE: Dyke.

AMANDA: Thank you, Lawrence. That overbearing, booming-voiced bull dyke. Into a Christian home.

TOM: Oh look, who cares? No one in their right mind would marry four eyes here.

AMANDA: You have no Christian charity, or filial devotion, or fraternal affection.

TOM: I don't want to listen to this. I'm going to the movies.

AMANDA: You go to the movies to excess, Tom. It isn't healthy.

LAWRENCE: While you're out, could you stop at the liquor store and get me some more cocktail stirrers? She broke Thermometer and she put Q-tip in her ear.

AMANDA: Listen to your brother, Tom. He's pathetic. How are we going to support ourselves once you go? And I know you want to leave. I've seen the brochure for the merchant marines in your underwear drawer. And the application to the air force. And your letter of inquiry to the Ballet Trockadero. So I'm not unaware of what you're thinking. But don't leave us until you fulfill your duties here, Tom. Help brother find a wife, or a job, or a doctor. Or consider euthanasia. But don't leave me here all alone, saddled with him.

LAWRENCE: Mama, don't you like me?

AMANDA: Of course, dear. I'm just making jokes.

LAWRENCE: Be careful of my asthma.

AMANDA: I'll try, dear. Now why don't you hold your breath in case you get a case of terminal hiccups?

LAWRENCE: *(Willing; a new possible ailment.)* Alright. *(Holds his breath.)*

TOM: *(Fed up with everything.)* I'm leaving.

AMANDA: Where are you going?

TOM: I'm going to the movies.

AMANDA: I don't believe you go to the movies. What did you see last night?

TOM: *(Somewhat defiant.)* Hyapatia Lee in *Beaver City.*

AMANDA: And the night before that?

TOM: I don't remember. *Humpy Bus Boys* or something.

AMANDA: Humpy what?

TOM: Nothing! Leave me alone!

AMANDA: These are not mainstream movies, Tom. Why can't you see a normal movie like *The Philadelphia Story.* Or *The Bitter Tea of General Yen?*

TOM: Those movies were made in the 1930s.

AMANDA: They're still good today.

TOM: I don't want to have this conversation. I'm going to the movies.

AMANDA: That's right, go to the movies! Don't think about us, a mother alone, an unmarried brother who think he's crippled and has no job. *(See Lawrence, pokes him.)* Oh, stop holding your breath, Lawrence, mama was kidding. *(Back to Tom.)* Don't let anything interfere with your selfish pleasure. Go see your pornographic trash that's worse than anything Mr. D.H. Lawrence ever envisioned. Just go, go, go—to the movies!

TOM: Alright, I will! And the more you shout about my selfishness and my taste in movies the quicker I'll go, and I won't just go to the movies!

AMANDA: Go then! Go to the moon—you selfish dreamer!
(Tom exits.)

AMANDA: Oh, Lawrence, honey, what's to become of us?

LAWRENCE: *(Sees Tom's newspaper on the table.)* Tom forgot his newspaper, mama.

AMANDA: He forgot a lot more than that, Lawrence honey. *(Sits on couch next to Lawrence.)* He forgot his mama and brother.
(Lights dim on Amanda and Lawrence on the couch, perhaps with Lawrence's head on Amanda's shoulder. Lights lower to a dim glow on the two of them, as if they are memory. They are still. Tom enters from

the side of the stage into a bright spotlight, and addresses the audience directly. His tone is mournful and elegiac.)

TOM: I didn't go to the moon, I went to the movies. In Amsterdam. A long, lonely trip working my way on a freighter. They had good movies in Amsterdam. They weren't in English, but I didn't really care. And as for my mother and brother—well they were impossible to live with, so I didn't miss them.

Or so I thought. For something pursued me. It always came upon me unawares, it always caught me by surprise. Sometimes it would be a swizzle stick in someone's vodka glass, or sometimes it would just be a jar of pigs feet. But then all of a sudden my brother touches my shoulder, and my mother puts her hands around my neck, and everywhere I look I am reminded of them. And in all the bars I go to there are those damn swizzle sticks everywhere.

I find myself thinking of my brother Lawrence. And of his collection of glass. And of my mother. I begin to think that their story would maybe make a good novel, or even a play. A mother's hopes, a brother's dreams. Pathos, humor, even tragedy. But then I lose interest, I really haven't the energy.

So I'll leave them both, dimly lit, in my memory. For nowadays the world is lit by lightning; and when we get those colored lights going, it feels like I'm on LSD. Or some other drug. Or maybe it's the trick of memory, or the memory of some trick.

Play with your cocktail stirrers, Lawrence. And so, good-bye.

AMANDA: *(Calling over in Tom's direction.)* Tom, I hear you out on the porch talking. Who are you talking to?

(Lights come back up on Amanda and Lawrence.)

TOM: No one, mother. I'm just on my way to the movies.

AMANDA: Well, try not to be too late, you have to work early at the warehouse tomorrow. And please don't bring home any visitors from the movies, I'm not up to it after that awful girl. Besides, if some sailor misses his boat, that's no reason you have to put him up in your room. You're too big-hearted, son.

TOM: Yes, mother. See you later. *(Exits.)*

LAWRENCE: *(Holding up a swizzle stick.)* Look at the light through the glass, mama. Isn't it amazin'?

AMANDA: Yes, I guess it is, Lawrence. Oh, but both my children are weird. What have I done, O Lord, to deserve them?

LAWRENCE: Just lucky, mama.

AMANDA: Don't make jokes, Lawrence. Your asthma. Your eczema. My life.

LAWRENCE: Don't be sad, mama. We have each other for company and amusement.

AMANDA: That's right. It's always darkest before the dawn. Or right before a typhoon sweeps up and kills everybody.

LAWRENCE: Oh poor mama, let me try to cheer you up with my collection. Is that a good idea?

AMANDA: It's just great, Lawrence. Thank you.

LAWRENCE: *(Holds up yellow swizzle stick.)* I call this one Daffodil, because it's yellow, and daffodils are yellow.

AMANDA: Uh huh.

LAWRENCE: *(Holds up a clear one.)* And I call this one Curtain Rod because it reminds me of a curtain rod.

AMANDA: Uh huh.

LAWRENCE: *(Holds up a blue one.)* And I call this one Ocean, because it's blue, and [the ocean is...]

AMANDA: I THOUGHT YOU CALLED THE BLUE ONE BLUE, YOU IDIOT CHILD! DO I HAVE TO LISTEN TO THIS PATHETIC PRATTLING THE REST OF MY LIFE??? CAN'T YOU AT LEAST BE CONSISTENT???

LAWRENCE: *(Shocked; hurt.)* No, I guess, I can't.

AMANDA: *(Still angry.)* Well, *try*, can't you?
(Silence.)

AMANDA: I'm sorry, Lawrence. I'm a little short-tempered today.

LAWRENCE: *(Still hurt.)* That's alright.
(Silence. Amanda looks at Lawrence, and feels bad for yelling at her pathetic child. She decides to try to make up.)

AMANDA: Do you have any other swizzle sticks with names, Lawrence?

LAWRENCE: Yes, I do. *(Holds one up.)* I call this one "Mama." *(Throws it onto the floor with a sudden sharp motion.)*
(Pause. Amanda has to take this in.)

AMANDA: Well, that's lovely, Lawrence, thank you.

LAWRENCE: I guess *I* can be a little short-tempered too.

AMANDA: Yes, well, whatever. *(Deciding to defuse this argument.)* I think we won't kill each other this evening, alright.

LAWRENCE: Alright.

AMANDA: I'll just distract myself from my rage and despair, and read about other people's rage and despair in the newspaper, shall I?

(Picks up Tom's newspaper.) Your brother has the worst reading and viewing taste of any living creature. This is just a piece of filth. *(Reads.)* Man Has Sex with Chicken, Then Makes Casserole. *(Closes the paper.)* Disgusting. Oh, Lawrence honey, look—it's the *Evening Star. (Holds the paper up above their heads; we see its banner reads* Evening Star.*)* Let's make a wish on it, honey, shall we?

LAWRENCE: Alright, mama.

(Amanda holds up the newspaper, and she and Lawrence close their eyes and make a wish.)

AMANDA: What did you wish for, darlin'?

LAWRENCE: More swizzle sticks.

AMANDA: You're so predictable, Lawrence. It's part of your charm, I guess.

LAWRENCE: *(Sweetly.)* What did you wish for, mama?

AMANDA: The same thing, honey. *(Wistful.)* Maybe just a little happiness, too…but mostly just some more swizzle sticks.

(Sad music. Amanda and Lawrence look up at the Evening Star. *Fade to black. End.)*

TO THE ACTOR

I've seen Amanda played a number of ways, all of which seemed to work.

It was a pleasure to watch Lizbeth Mackay's work on the role at MTC. Lizbeth was a fellow student at Yale School of Drama. As a dramatic actress, she's fluid and effortless and very moving. She brought all this same commitment to the comic exaggeration of my Amanda and it deepened the play. Although the play remained very much a comedy, with Lizbeth doing the part we actually felt for this woman whose life seemed to be over. And because Lizbeth is still young and attractive, she was very believable as someone who would have other possibilities available if only she could unload her impossible son Lawrence.

Lizbeth was wonderfully convincing on the Southern charm. When she'd lecture Lawrence on it, she seemed to have real knowledge to impart.

When the "feminine caller" arrived, her graciousness was an extremely funny starting place for her ongoing realizations of how limited and odd Ginny turned out to be.

The director Walter Bobbie felt that playing the negative was a danger—if Amanda believed that there was *no* chance that this evening would work out for Lawrence, then the actress had nowhere to go and nothing to play. So, in a way,

Walter's Amanda sort of played the same intention as Williams' Amanda in the real play: She's hoping that the "feminine caller" will work out and be a match for Lawrence and will solve her "problem" for her.

I agree with Walter that playing the negative is dangerous; yet because the play is short (30 minutes about), if the actress has the right comedic spin, I think a more despairing attitude can also work.

At the Tennessee Williams Literary Festival in New Orleans, I saw an actress named Ann Meric play Amanda in *Belle* in a very different way that was still very funny. Older than Lizbeth, Ann played Amanda as clearly spent, fed-up, barely able to put up with either son for a moment longer. Because she has a low voice and comic timing and because she said everything with real psychological truth, Ms. Meric made the story a darker one, but still very funny.

But whatever the choices are, the stakes must be high for Amanda. And when she and Tom fight at the end, it must be a full-out, emotional fight, much like the one in the real Williams' play.

Lawrence

To casting directors, I ended up saying things like "We need a male Laura." Just as you would cast Laura in *Menagerie* as sweet and sensitive and appealing but a little odd, so I'd like to see those qualities in an actor playing Lawrence. Thus boyish and slight; preferably not effeminate, just "soft" in soul and aura. And with comic abilities. (Ah, the hard part.)

Lawrence is a hypochondriac, but he does believe in his ailments. He treasures his ailments.

Keith Reddin, who played Daisy for me in my *Baby with the Bathwater* in 1983, played Lawrence at MTC. He has the sweetness to be Lawrence, but he's also a little innately strange and offbeat. And he's boyish still. And he knows how to say odd things in a normal tone of voice, as if there's nothing remarkable about what he's saying. So it was a pleasure hooking up with him again.

Tom

Tom is, frankly, a bit under-written and thus a little hard to play.

What we looked for in casting him was a "regular guy" who had a sexuality to him; we wanted to believe that he was out having a good time with sailors. We also wanted someone who had the anger to play the "I'm going to the movies" argument with Amanda full out and yet also would be believable in hitting the same sensitive sound in his "I didn't go to the moon" speech that an actor would need to play the real Tom. Someone who had the skill to fill in the less written parts—such as his kind of restlessness at home, mostly paying attention to what's going on, but wanting the dinner to be over so he can get to his adventure at the movies.

David Aaron Baker hit all these notes and made an excellent Tom.

Tom's "other life" as a gay man is a minor note in this play and obviously plays off of what we came to know about Tennessee Williams' own active sex life and the fact that Tom in *Menagerie* is acknowledged to be Williams' stand-in. So I just added our knowledge of that sex life to the *Menagerie* story. It's a joke, of course; but that's the basis of the joke.

And *Humpy Bus Boys* is one of my favorite movies.

Ginny

Judging from auditions, Ginny appears to be a hard part sometimes for actors to figure out.

Ginny is a "regular guy" kind of girl and works at the factory with Lawrence's brother. She is hale and hearty and also hard of hearing. She doesn't think she's hard of hearing, however. She thinks she hears fine. Also, she talks rather loudly—both out of enthusiasm and out of her hearing problem.

So for starters, the actress must speak loudly. You can't talk in a normal voice and then leave the actress playing Amanda stuck with the line "Why is she shouting? Is she deaf?" which then makes no sense.

On the other hand, if she speaks so loudly it hurts our ears, then we're in trouble. Or if she just shouts, but forgets to act the content and intention of her lines.

Walter worked with Patricia Randell on choosing when Ginny's speaking would be at its loudest (especially during her opening scene meeting everyone) and when it would be appropriate to have her talk in a more normal tone of voice (especially during her solo scene with Lawrence).

When she's talking in a normal level of loudness, it's not that she suddenly isn't hard of hearing. It's two things: A theatrical convention where we're giving the audience a bit of a break; and it's identifying places in the text where it makes sense psychologically that Ginny is less emphatic, less excited.

Ginny is hard of hearing, but this is *not* a fact she acknowledges. So when she says "What?" to something someone's said, she doesn't in any way play that she thinks it's odd she didn't hear. It's just a fact, the person must have spoken too softly. She's enjoying the conversation immensely, so please tell her again what it is you said so she can keep enjoying the conversation.

Patricia Randell was especially good on her cheerful enjoyment of everything. Her Ginny was a very happy person who tended to think wherever she was, people would like her and she would have fun. When she said "What?" loudly in her opening scene, she always had a happy excited smile on her face. And when people reacted in confusion to the things she said, she never, of course, noticed. Ginny is in her own world and she thinks she's just fine. She has no judgment of herself and no knowledge that she mis-hears things.

(By the way, when she says "What?", keep the "What's" as loud as the rest of what she says. In auditions, actresses sometimes would talk loudly, but then talk softly on the word "What?" It was a choice I didn't understand. If Ginny talks loudly unconsciously, as she does, then she would also be loud on her "What?")

One can choose to cast or play Ginny as fairly "butch," and costume her accordingly in, say, her factory clothes (like a garage mechanic's uniform or something).

Or you can go a less dead-on way, as we did with Patricia Randell. Patricia's Ginny was overly friendly and boisterous but not initially "butch." She was also dressed in a nice pantsuit that one might wear to go to a stranger's house for dinner; a dress would be too feminine for Ginny to wear, but a pantsuit seemed fine. And she wore a colored netting on the back of her hair, kind of 1940s "Rosie the Riveter" style. (The costumes all gently pushed the time back to the time of the real Williams' play.)

At the point when Ginny gets to showing Lawrence how to act "normal" ("The Braves played a helluva game, don'tcha think?"), at that point though, she should be as butch as the actress can be.

And that's almost the limit of what there is for Ginny to play. When the evening's fallen to pieces, she can get quite angry at Lawrence and Amanda, but strangely, her personality is so sunny that she gets over it fast. And on her exit she actually does mean that she had a really good time. She's a happy soul, she fits into the world comfortably—something she shares, in her exaggerated way, with the Gentleman Caller of the Williams' play.

A Stye of the Eye

This is a parody of Sam Shepard's play *Lie Of The Mind*, with bits of some of his other plays thrown in for good measure. (And also with bits of David Mamet and John Pielmeier's *Agnes Of God*.)

Though critically acclaimed in 1985, *Lie Of The Mind* turns out not to be that well known by audiences. So I feared that their not knowing the play would keep my parody from working.

However, the audience at Manhattan Theater Club seemed happy to accept *A Stye Of The Eye* as a parody of a certain kind of macho-poetic symbolic drama, and they seemed quite consistently willing to go with it and have a good time.

Though the parody is not as affectionate as the Williams' one, still the point of doing the parody is to have the audience enjoy themselves and to kind of jointly shake off some irritation from many an evening of pretentious, symbolic drama (and not just Shepard).

I wrote *Stye* a while ago, but added the character of Wesley (who's featured in *Curse Of The Starving Class*) specifically for the Manhattan Theater Club production because I knew that David Aaron Baker was going to be part of the acting company, and Walter Bobbie and I wanted *Stye* to feature all seven actors. So I chose a Shepard character to parody that would suit David's look and abilities. (David is late 20s, handsome, and a most versatile actor. I thought he would play well and comically the spacey, mind-elsewhere mysteriousness of Wesley. And he did.)

Writing the play, I enjoyed myself. Discussing it now, I feel somewhat guilty in that I don't like putting myself in print in a critical role about a fellow dramatist. I know how painful it is to receive criticism in the newspaper, and here I am offering it in print of another author. And I do admire several of Shepard's plays, especially *Curse Of The Starving Class, Buried Child,* and *Fool For Love* (play, not movie).

Lie Of The Mind, though, really irritated me, and the critical kudos it received at the time baffled and discouraged me. (If this was acclaimed, how was I to fit into the New York theater? was the thought that stopped me.)

So, blah blah blah. There you have it, but I hope the parody makes you laugh.

ORIGINAL PRODUCTION

A Stye of the Eye was part of *Durang Durang* at the Manhattan Theatre Club. The cast was as follows:

Jake . . . . Marcus Giamatti
Ma . . . . Becky Ann Baker
Dr. Martina . . . . Patricia Elliott
Agnes/Beth . . . . Keith Reddin
Meg . . . . Lizbeth Mackay
Wesley . . . . David Aaron Baker
Mae . . . . Patricia Randell

CHARACTERS
JAKE
MA, Jake's mother
DR. MARTINA DYSART, a psychiatrist
BETH, Jake's wife
MEG, Beth's mother
WESLEY, Beth's brother
MAE, Jake's sister

(Note: Beth plays "Agnes" in *Agnes Is Odd,* the play-within-a-play section. Beth is written to be played by the same male actor who plays Lawrence. Even if done on a single bill, it is best when played by a sensitive-looking young man rather than by a woman.)

A STYE OF THE EYE

Scene: A desolate prairie. Windswept. Maybe a couple of discarded truck tires piled on one another. Or maybe it's a highway in the midst of a prairie. Anyway, not much scenery. Desolate, isolated, out west somewhere. On part of the stage we see Jake, who is on a pay phone. He is tall, in his 30s, and dressed in dungarees, boots and a T-shirt or work shirt. He is masculine, and has a raging temper.

JAKE: Answer the phone, damn it. Answer the phone. *(Bangs the phone receiver on the side of the phone, or any other surface.)* Come on, come on! *(Into receiver.)* Hello! Hello!
(Lights up on a different part of the stage. Ma is discovered next to a phone, or enters calmly over to the ringing phone. Ma is between 40 and 50, and dressed in a sloppy, comfortable print dress. Her hair is not fussed with, just pulled back out of her face. She is a no-nonsense woman, tough, matter-of-fact, sounds like a Cracker.)
MA: Hello?
JAKE: Hey, Ma?
MA: Who is this?
JAKE: Ma, it's your son.
MA: Who?
JAKE: Your son, ma.
MA: I got two sons. Which one are you?
JAKE: I'm Jake.
MA: Jake?
JAKE: Jake!

MA: You're not the other one? What's his name?

JAKE: Frankie. No, it's not Frankie, Ma. It's Jake.

MA: Jake?

JAKE: Stop saying Jake, or I'm going to come over to your house and punch you in the mouth.

MA: *(Her voice warming, friendly.)* Oh, now it sounds like Jake. How are you, baby?

JAKE: She's real bad, Ma.

MA: Who, Jake?

JAKE: She's all red and blue and purple.

MA: Who you talkin' about, Jake?

JAKE: I had to hit her. She was dressin' real sexy life, and goin' off to rehearsal.

MA: Who is this you're talkin' about, Jake?

JAKE: It's Beth, Ma. My wife.

MA: Are you married, Jake?

JAKE: Ma, you know I am. You wuz at the wedding.

MA: Why didn't you marry your sister, Jake, she always liked you.

JAKE: That would be incest, Ma.

MA: No, it wouldn't. Incest would be if you married me. If you married your sister, it would be...sorority.

JAKE: Shut the fuck up, Ma. I'm tryin' to tell you I killed Beth.

MA: Who's Beth?

(Note: Ma's lapses in memory are complete. When she says something like "Who's Beth," she has no recollection whatsoever that she heard the name Beth a few seconds before. So all her questions are asked innocently, trying her best to get information. There is no "What was that thing you said a moment ago" tone to any of her repeating questions. And thus when Jake seems irritated with her forgetting, she has no idea what is the cause of his frustration.)

JAKE: She's my wife.

MA: I didn't know you were married.

JAKE: You have the attention span of a gnat. Ma, we've been through this. Beth is my wife, you wuz at the wedding, and I just killed her.

MA: *(Suspicious.)* Who is this calling me?

JAKE: It's your son, Ma! I just killed my wife.

MA: Well, I never pay attention to the tramps you start up with. She probably asked for it.

JAKE: She was goin' to rehearsal, Ma. She's into actin', Ma, and she's goes off to fuckin' rehearsal, and every day she dresses more slutty like, and I just know that she's doin' it with some fuckin' actor on her lunch break. And I seen her in a play once. She stank.

MA: *(Upset.)* Whatcha goin' to plays for, baby? I didn't bring you up to spend your time goin' to plays. You're gonna end up like that Sam Shepard boy down the road. Why don't you settle down and marry your sister?

JAKE: Stop talkin' about incest, Ma. I just killed my wife.

MA: Well, did anyone see you?

JAKE: No.

MA: Well, there, you see. Go get a good night's sleep, and in the morning we'll get you another one. Why don't you marry your sis... Oh, that's right, you don't like that idea. You're stubborn like your father. I hate his guts. I wish he wuz dead.

JAKE: He is dead, Ma.

MA: Well, good.

JAKE: I didn't want to kill her, Ma, but she asked for it.

MA: Who you talkin' about, baby?

JAKE: Beth, Beth! How many times do I have to say it!

MA: 33. I'm getting bored with this conversation, Jake. Is your good brother Frankie there?

JAKE: What?

MA: Put Frankie on.

JAKE: He's not here.

MA: Put him on.

JAKE: He's not here.

MA: Frankie, is that you?

JAKE: Wait a minute, Ma.

MA: Did you hear what Jake told me?

JAKE: Hold your horses a minute, Ma. Hey, Frankie! Ma wants to speak to you! Frankie! *(Changes personalities, and switches phone hands; sounds more polite and reasoned though still has a temper.)* Hey, Mom, how are you?

MA: Oh, Frankie, I love it the way you call me "mom" and Jake calls me "Ma." It's so differentiating. Frankie, did you hear that Jake killed his wife?

JAKE: He told me, Mom. He's a crazy, spoiled, mixed-up kid. If only Pa weren't a drunk and a skunk and dead.

MA: Is he dead?

JAKE: You know he's dead. We were all at the funeral, and you spit on his grave.

MA: Was that your pa? Well, he never was no good. But he sure could ride a horse, and shoot a rifle, and wear boots and dungarees.

JAKE: Mom, what are we gonna do about Jake?

MA: Why did I spit on his grave?

JAKE: I don't know. You wuz angry. Everyone in this family has a fierce temper.

MA: *(Proudly.)* We do. We're fierce, us Faberizzi's.

JAKE: Mom, we're not Italian.

MA: Well, what's our last name then?

JAKE: We don't have a last name. Mom, what are we going to do about Jake?

MA: Who?

JAKE: Jake.

MA: Jake's dead. His wife just killed him.

JAKE: You got it backwards, Ma. I mean "Mom."

MA: You know you and Jake sound so much alike that sometimes I think you're both two different aspects of the same personality. That means I gave birth to a symbol, and me with no college edjacation.

JAKE: I'm not a symbol, Ma. I'm a westerner looking for the big open expanses, but they're gettin' smaller and smaller. There's no place to hope, Ma.

MA: You sound like a symbol. But not some prissy Ivy League–type symbol. My children are virile, masculine symbols who carry guns and beat up women. You all got so much testosterone in you, that you got a native kinda poetry in you, even when you spit. Why don't you go kill a woman like your brother?

JAKE: But what woman is like my brother?

MA: That's not what I meant, stupid. The verb was implied in that sentence, as in "Why don't you go kill a woman like your brother *did*," "did" in imaginary bracket signs. And me with no college edjacation. Put Jake back on the line, honey, I'm bored with this conversation. No, never mind, I got an idea. Why don't you go try to find Beth. Maybe she's not dead. Maybe she's only brain damaged, and *you* can marry her. That might have symbolic value of some sort.

JAKE: But what symbolic value would that have, Mom?

MA: I don't know, I'm not a writer. But if we put some jazz music under it, or some good country sounds, it's bound to mean somethin' to somebody. I gotta go now, Frankie, the cactus is whistlin' on the stove. But you keep an eye on your brother, and if you wanna marry your sister, just let me know. *(Hangs up, exits; lights fade on her part of the stage.)*

JAKE: Good bye, Mom. *(Switches to Jake personality; grabs for phone from himself.)* Hey, I ain't done talkin' to her yet! *(Switches back to Frankie, hangs up the phone.)* Well, she's done talkin' to you. Why'd you go and kill her, Jake? *(Switches to Jake.)* Ma? *(Switches to Frankie, annoyed.)* No, not Mom. Beth. *(Switches to Jake.)* I don't know. She just kept goin' to all them rehearsals and…well, it irritated me. *(Switches to Frankie.)* I can understand that. *(Switches to Jake; vehement.)* Especially this one play called *Agnes is Odd* or some such thing, all about this flakey nun who killed her baby.

(Lights change. We see the play Jake is remembering. Jake either exits or stays on the side and watches with the audience. The sound of Stravinsky-like music, or Carmina Burana. Startling, mysterious, other-worldly.)

(Enter Dr. Martina Dysart, in a crisp business suit, smoking three cigarettes, one in her mouth, two in her hands. She takes the one in her mouth out, and addresses the audience. She is intense and concerned, solving a deep mystery.)

DR. MARTINA: The baby was discovered in a waste basket with the umbilical cord knotted around its neck. The mother was unconscious, next to the body. The mother was a young nun called Sister Agnes, Sister Agnes Dei. During the night she had given birth and then seemingly killed her baby. Then she went out to the convent stables and blinded eight horses with a metal crucifix. That much is fact. But she is also a musical genius along the lines of Wolfgang Amadeus Mozart. Furthermore, my life as a psychiatrist is drab and depressing, and even though I think it unappealing that she killed her baby and blinded the horses, still I envy her passion. You wouldn't see *me* getting up in the middle of the night to go down to the stables. And furthermore, I'm a lapsed Catholic who wishes I had her faith, and I wish I had a horse, and I…wish I was a composer. In short, there are many ideas and subtleties to think about here, so stop rattling your programs and let's move on with it. My first meeting with Agnes, I thought she was brain damaged.

(Enter Sister Agnes, the sensitive nun. Dressed perhaps in the strange white nun's outfit Amanda Plummer wore in the Broadway version of

Agnes of God, *which is the same design Sally Field wore in* The Flying Nun *TV series. Or a more conventional nun outfit is okay too. Jake's wife Beth is playing Sister Agnes. Beth is written to be played by a small, sensitive young man.)*

AGNES: Look, stigmata.

(Agnes holds out her palms, which at first glance have gaping red holes in them. A second later one notices that she seems to be holding red rubber things in her palms, with reddish centers to them.)

DR. MARTINA: Nonsense, those are plastic Dr. Spock ears. Look, I'll show you.

(Dr. Martina removes the "plastic stigmata" and puts the Dr. Spock ears on her ears. She leaves them there for the rest of the scene.)

DR. MARTINA: People sell these at Halloween. Do you like Halloween, Agnes?

AGNES: Pooh. Pooh.

DR. MARTINA: Pooh. Winnie the Pooh? Do you like Winnie the Pooh?

AGNES: Pooh. Pooh. Puer. *(Last word is pronounced "Pooh-air".)*

DR. MARTINA: Puer. That's Latin for boy. Do you like boys, Agnes?

AGNES: Pooh-ella.

DR. MARTINA: Yes, puella. Latin for girl. Maybe it's Latin you like. Do you like Latin, Agnes? Hic, haec, hoc, and all that.

AGNES: Puer. Puella. Eck, eck, equus! *(Momentarily mimes blinding horses, then pulls herself together again.)*

DR. MARTINA: Boy, girl, horse. This isn't a very intelligent conversation, Agnes. Don't they make you speak sentences in the convent, Agnes?

AGNES: Agnes Dei.

DR. MARTINI: Yes, that's Latin for Lamb for God. *(With a shock of recognition.)* Oh my God, your name is Agnes Dei, isn't it? Good grief, I wonder if that means you're some sort of sacrificial lamb to God, and that maybe your giving birth was an immaculate conception, and that the father is God Himself!!! Good Lord, what a shocking idea, oh my mind is running, let me try to breath deeply for a moment. *(Puffs on several of her cigarettes.)* Goodness. what dreadful rubbish I was just speaking. Rather like speaking in tongues. Do you like tongues, Agnes?

AGNES: We had tongue sandwiches at that convent, and it made all the Sisters menstruate.

DR. MARTINA: *(Pause.)* I think that's rather an obscene remark you've just made, Agnes. Did you mean to be obscene?

AGNES: Children should be obscene. And not furred.

DR. MARTINA: Furred?

AGNES: Furred like a bird.

DR. MARTINA: What is the matter with you exactly? Are you a saint or are you brain damaged?

AGNES: *(Sings, lasciviously.)*
Erotic, erotic,
Put your hands all over my body!

DR. MARTINA: I see. Well, if you're going to sing, I think I'll go now. By the way, which member of the convent is it who won't let you watch MTV? *(Shudders to herself.)* What a sharp remark of mine. I'm definitely in the right profession.

AGNES: No do with MTV.

DR. MARTINA: Of course, it do. Does. That's the kind of song that's sung on MTV.

AGNES: Noooooooo. Who *sing*, Doctor?

DR. MARTINA: I forget. That slutty woman who changes her look all the time, what's-her-name...oh my God, her name is *Madonna*, which means "Mother of God"!
(Agnes has a screaming fit at this scary coincidence, and falls to the ground rolling around in circles, going "Whoop! Whoop! Whooop!")

AGNES: Whoop! Whoop! Whoop! Whoop! Whoop!
(Lights fade on Agnes and Dr. Martina, and they exit. Lights back up on Jake.)

JAKE: *(As Jake; explaining to Frankie.)* It was after that terrible play that I took Beth out in the parking lot and I beat her to a pulp. "Your play was pretentious!" I said, and then I punched her. "You were unconvincing as a nun, and I didn't know whether you were supposed to be crazy or sane," and then I kicked her in the side. "And I don't like the previous play you wuz in, *The Reluctant Debutante*, either, and then I took her head and I put it under the tire of the Chevrolet, and I dropped it on her. And that's how I killed her. *(Switches to Frankie.)* Oh, Jake. The play couldn't have been that bad. *(Switches to Jake.)* It was. It was. I fuckin' hated it, man. It made me wanna puke. *(Switches to Frankie.)* Yeah, but to kill someone. *(Switches to Jake; big baby, teary.)* Oh, Frankie, I miss her already. I wish she was alive so we could go on a second honeymoon together. *(Switches to Frankie.)* I got some land in Florida I could sell ya. *(Switches to Jake.)* Oh yeah? *(Switches to Frankie.)* It's called Glengarry Glen Ross.

(Switches to Jake.) Oh I don't want to go there. *(Switches to Frankie, who now speaks in a fast, staccato rhythm, with a lot of aggressive salesman energy.)* Why the fuck not? The place is good. Not great maybe, but what I'm sayin' is, it's good. Not great maybe, but good. That's what I'm sayin'. It may be swamp, it may have bugs, but fuck, Jake, what's perfect? You tell me. No, don't tell me, I'll tell you. It's not great, good. Am I right? Do you understand what I'm sayin'? Should I say it again? What I'm sayin' is, fuck shit piss damn, it ain't half bad. Half good, half bad. You gotta settle. It ain't perfect. Settle. Gotta. You gotta settle. A negotiation. Give and take. You know what I'm sayin'? What I'm sayin' is… *(Switches to Jake, frustrated and angered by Frankie's irritating sales pitch.)* Shut up! I know what you're saying, you sound lifelike, granted, but you repeat yourself on and on and on, and you're…insensitive to my upset about my wife. She is dead, you know. I deserve sympathy. *(Switches to Frankie.)* Yeah, but you killed her. *(Switches to Jake.)* Hmmmmm. I wonder if she's not totally dead. *(Switches to Frankie.)* Okay, listen here, Jake, I'm gonna go out across the prairie or the highway or wherever we are, and I'm gonna see if I can find her, and if she's alive or not. *(Switches to Jake.)* Hey, Frankie, one more thing. If it turns out she's alive, I don't wanna hear you been doin' it with her. *(Switches to Frankie.)* Now, Jake, don't start gettin' crazy on me. *(Switches to Jake; violent.)* I don't wanna hear it. *(Switches to Frankie.)* Okay, you don't gotta hear it. *(To himself.)* I'll say it real soft. *(Switches to Jake.)* Whaddit you say? *(Switches to Frankie.)* Nothin', Jake, relax. Nothin'. See ya around. *(Switches to Jake; suspicious, hostile.)* See ya. *(They exit.)*

(Lights change to another part of the stage. It is the home of Meg, who is Beth's mother. At Manhattan Theatre Club, we set this scene outdoors, in front of Meg's house. There was a screen door that led into the house; there were tires on the outside yard, which people could sit on, or fall on. It would be easy, with tiny line adjustments, to set this scene inside Meg's house if you preferred that. But my references here are to the "outside" setting.)

    Meg enters the yard through her screen door, which closes behind her. Meg is 35 to 45, blowsily attractive. She is based on the character Ann Wedgeworth played in Lie of the Mind. *Along these lines, she has red hair, kind of trashy jewelry, tight jeans and boots, and a feminine, off-the-shoulder bright blouse. She is sensual, and has a charming drawl to her speech. She might look like a going-to-seed country western singer.)*

MEG: My, it's hot in that house today. I need some air. Ooo. *(Sound of a sheep from offstage.)* Baylor? Is that you?

(Wesley, a young man in jeans and a T-shirt, comes outside through the screen door. He is the son of Meg, and the brother of Beth. He carries two large paper grocery bags. He is spacey, and mysterious. His speech is often lacking in emotion, and he seems to have his own thoughts going on a lot.)

MEG: Oh, Mike, I thought you wuz your father.

WESLEY: The baby sheep has maggots in it. I brung it in the kitchen.

MEG: That's nice. Where is your father? Is he still out hunting deer?

WESLEY: I guess so. *(Wesley puts his two grocery bags on the ground.)*

MEG: He's been hunting deer a long time. 15 years, is it?

WESLEY: I dunno. I went shoppin'.

MEG: Oh, that's so thoughtful. Your sister Beth should be comin' home from the hospital any minute—Jake didn't kill her after *Agnes is Odd,* he just damaged her brain a bit, I meant to tell ya. And I want to make her a nice home-cooked meal. *(Meg starts to empty the two bags. The entire contents are artichokes.)* Oh, an artichoke, how nice. Oh, another one. Oh, another one. Mike, honey, we gotta teach you how to shop better.

(Meg continues to empty artichokes onto the yard, or inside the tires. Wesley just stares.)

WESLEY: I think I saw Pop in the hunter's cabin. He didn't got no clothes on.

MEG: Lord, how many artichokes are there here? *(Suddenly hearing it.)* What did you say about maggots and the kitchen?

WESLEY: The lamb has maggots. I brung it in the kitchen.

MEG: Mike, honey, you don't bring a critter with maggots into the kitchen.

WESLEY: Why is Pop naked in the hunter's cabin?

MEG: I wonder if your sister Beth even likes artichokes. Oh, I think I hear her now. Beth, honey, is that you?

(Enter Beth, same actor who played Agnes. Beth's head is wrapped in an enormous bandage, and she's in a hospital gown. She also limps, and carries a small suitcase. Due to her brain damage, her speech is peculiar now. She often speaks nonsense syllables, but as if they make sense to her. From time to time, she stares off oddly.)

BETH: Monga raga. Luga mee.

MEG: Oh, Lord, you look awful. Doesn't she look awful, Mike?

WESLEY: My name is Wesley. *(Exits.)*

MEG: Oh Beth honey, the doctors said you had brain damage. Is that right?

BETH: *(Greeting her mother, telling of her recent experiences.)* Mummy. Mommy. Custom. Costume. Capsule. Cupcake. Candle. Campbell. Chunky Beef Soup. Ugga wugga meatball.

MEG: Oh! Well, that made sense. Mike, she's makin' sense to me.
(Enter Jake.)

JAKE: Is Beth still alive?

MEG: Oh my God, he's come to finish her off! Mike, do somethin'.

BETH: *(Excited to see him.)* Jake? Joke? Kill me, joke? Jake?

JAKE: I'm not Jake, Beth. I'm his good brother Frankie.

BETH: *(Disappointed.)* Jake? I want Jake.

MEG: Goodness, he nearly killed her, and she wants him. Isn't the human heart peculiar?

JAKE: *(To Meg.)* I'm sorry about what my brother did to your daughter, ma'am, and I hope you don't mind my comin' here.

MEG: Oh, an apology. Oh my. *(Cries.)*
(Enter Wesley. He's only wearing underpants now, and untied work boots. He has two more bags of groceries, also with artichokes. He puts them down on the ground, and exits.)

MEG: Oh good, more artichokes.

BETH: Jake?

JAKE: No, Beth, I'm Frankie.

BETH: I want Jake.

MEG: No, honey. Jake plays too rough.

BETH: Need. Bleed. I am a Jake Junkie.

MEG: *(Sound of lamb bleating.)* Mike, I hope you're getting that lamb outta the kitchen, honey.

BETH: *(Sudden fear; feeling of significance.)* Lamb? Lamb of God? Agnus Dei?

MEG: What? I guess so, honey.
(Enter Wesley.)

WESLEY: Do we have any mint jelly?

MEG: I don't know, honey. Have you said hello to your sister Beth?

WESLEY: No. *(Exits back into house.)*

BETH: *(To Jake.)* Jelly. Junket. Jacket. Jake.

JAKE: I'm not Jake, Beth. I'm Frankie.

BETH: Frankie? Funky. Fatty. Patty. Head wooooound.

MEG: Oh, it's going to be hard to cast her in plays now. No Restoration comedy for you, young lady!

JAKE: I just wanted to see that you were alright, Beth.

BETH: Wait. Love. Life. The Call of the Wild. Coyote. Aawoooooooooo! I want to marry you.

JAKE: But you already have a husband. You're married to my brother.

BETH: You be my husband. I be your wife. You be, I be, we be.

MEG: She's so much more interesting to listen to since her accident, isn't she? And a wedding, what a good idea. Excuse me, I want to see if there are maggots in the kitchen. Mike! *(Exits.)*

BETH: We become one together, Frankie, and we make a baby out of papier-mâché maybe. Baby maybe.

JAKE: I'm in love with you, Beth, but I feel such guilt at betraying my brother.

(Enter Mae, Jake's sister. She wears a tight, sexy red dress and stands provocatively.)

MAE: And what about betraying your sister?

BETH: Oooh, pretty dress.

MAE: Here, you can try it on.

(Mae takes off her dress, and gives it to Beth, who runs happily into the house with it, very excited. Mae is now dressed in an attractive slip and high heels. Jake and Mae kiss passionately, then rush to opposite sides of the room, banging into the walls, or sides of the stage.)

JAKE: Why'd you come here, Mae?

MAE: I can't get you outta my head, Jake. You run around my brain like a haunting refrain. I love ya.

JAKE: I'm not Jake. I'm Frankie.

MAE: Oh, ain't you realized yet, you're two aspects of the same personality. And you and I are two aspects of the same personality, only we're male and female, and you're male and male, so I wish you'd get yourself into one person so you and I could combine into one person also. But if you remain two people, then when you and I combine, we'll be three people, and that's not what I want.

JAKE: What?

MAE: I can't say that all again. What part didn't you hear?

JAKE: Mae.

(They rush from opposite sides of the yard and embrace. She beats his chest. They roll about on the floor. They are very passionate.)

JAKE: How'd you know where to find me?

MAE: Ma tol' me.

JAKE: Ma. She's a sick lady.

MAE: Do you know how to spell Mae? You spell it just like Ma, but add an "e" to it.

JAKE: What the hell's that supposed to mean?

MAE: I don't know.

(They run from opposite sides again, and embrace passionately. Meg enters.)

MEG: Sorry to interrupt, but I have something to tell you. *(Points to her eye.)* I have a stye in my eye. And it hurts when I close my eye and see nothing, and it hurts when I open my eye and look around. No matter what I do it hurts. This stye in my eye is a symbol. I have a symbol in my eye. *(Smiles.)* I just wanted you to know. *(Exits back into house.)*

MAE: I was in the school orchestra in Texas when I first started to lust after you, Jake, and you know what instrument I played? The cymbals.

JAKE: We come together like two cymbals crashing, don't we, Mae?

MAE: Yes. Let's you run to that side of the yard, and I'll run to the other side, and then we'll run together again.

JAKE: *(Excited.)* Okay.

(They run to opposite sides. Just as they are about to run together, enter Beth, now dressed in Mae's red dress, but with lots of jangly jewelry and a purse, purple stockings, high heels, and a strange, teased wig. It is a demented person's attempt to look attractive. She kind of looks like "Carnaby Street" London fashions of the 60s, which is most incongruous for this prairie setting.)

BETH: I feel like the jewelry counter at Woolworth's.

JAKE: You look like the jewelry counter at Woolworth's.

(Enter Meg, carrying an American flag. She now wears an eye patch over her eye with the stye in it.)

MEG: I found this nice flag in the kitchen. I think it's American. *(Sees Beth.)* Oh, don't you look nice? When's the wedding?

MAE: What wedding?

JAKE: I told Beth I'd marry her. *(Switches to Jake.)* Frankie! What did you say? I thought so! The minute I turn out not to have killed her, the two of you try to betray me! *(Switches to Frankie.)* Now, Jake, stay calm. *(Switches to Jake.)* I can't stay calm. You been doin' it with my wife. *(Switches to Frankie.)* We ain't done it yet, Jake. *(Switches to Jake.)* Yeah, but you were gonna! Yippie-i-o-ki-ay, that makes me mad! I'm gonna have to take out my gun, Frankie! *(Switches to Frankie; in fear for his life.)* Don't take out that gun. Jake! Jake! Don't shoot me! I'm your brother! Jake!

(Sound of a gun shot. Jake falls to the ground, dead.)

MAE: He's dead. Jake shot him.

MEG: *Who* shot him? I didn't follow that visually at all. Maybe it's because of the stye in my eye. Oh dear, I think I'm developing a stye in my other eye.

(The eye patch Meg is wearing on her eye is a double one, and she moves the top one over to cover her remaining eye. She now has eye patches on both of her eyes.)

MEG: Oh, Lord, I can't see anything now.

MAE: Jake, Frankie. Jake, Frankie. We can't be one together. Now I'm just half. Or three-fifths. I need two-fifths.

BETH: *(Chipper.)* Well, I don't care. These clothes make me want to go back on the stage. Good-bye, mother. Good-bye, Jake. I'm going to star with RuPaul and Charles Busch in Edward Albee's *Three Tall Women*. In Act II, I get to be in a coma. Good-bye! *(Beth exits.)*

MEG: She really is brain damaged.

(Enter Ma.)

MA: Hi, everybody. I was just on my way to work at the Roy Rogers chain of restaurants, I'm the French fries girl, when I set my house on fire and decided to come on over here for a nice little set-down and heigh-ho, how are ya?

MEG: Oh, you're just in time to help me fold the American flag.

MA: What American flag?

(Meg and Ma start to try to fold the American flag.)

MEG: I found it in the kitchen. I hope it doesn't have maggots in it.

MA: Maggots in the flag? Oh. That sounds serious.

MAE: Do you have any cymbals in the house? Oh, there they are. *(Mae gets a pair of cymbals easily from somewhere hidden on the stage; at Manhattan Theatre Club they were inside the two tires. To the dead body of Jake.)* Jake, Frankie. Do you remember that song we used to play in high school? *(Sings.)*
Blue moon,

It hangs up high in the sky, *(Bangs the cymbals, sings.)*
Without a dream in my heart,
Without a stye in my eye... *(Bangs the cymbals.)*
I love you, Jake, Frankie. I'm desperate without you.
(Enter Wesley. His underpants are now splattered with some blood. Not too gross, but noticeable.)

WESLEY: The baby lamb is dead.

MEG: Well, please get it out of the kitchen. *(To Ma.)* I'm sorry. Do you know my son Mike?

WESLEY: My name's Wesley.

MA: How ya doin'? I like your bloody underpants. Oooh. Something's wrong with my eyes.

MEG: Are you developing styes?

MA: Don't think so. I think I'm going blind. *(Puts on dark glasses.)*

MEG: Well, we'll just have to fold the flag as best we can.

MA: Alrighty-dighty.
(Meg, with her two eye patches, and Ma, with her dark glasses, try to fold the flag some more. It's not easy for them.)

MAE: You're blind, and you're folding the American flag.

WESLEY: There are maggots in the American flag. Pop is naked in the hunter's cabin. The baby lamb is dead.

MAE: Why does all this information make me want to crash the cymbals again? *(Crashes her cymbals.)*
(Jake stands.)

JAKE: Would you stop that god awful racket? *(Stands, brushes himself off.)* I'm sorry I killed Frankie, but maybe I can be free now that he's dead. Did I kill Beth too?

MAE: Beth has gone back to theatre.

JAKE: That's a kind of death. *(Jake looks out. A lone jazz instrument plays in the background. Moody, yearning. The characters notice the sound of the jazz.)* I'm gonna go out west and look for open spaces. I've been lookin' for love in all the wrong places. I'm sick of women.

MEG: Well, I certainly think Beth was a transvestite anyway. *(Jazz music fades out.)* I always presumed that's why you beat her up. Or maybe I'm the transvestite. Oh, we forget the things we don't want to re-member. That's a theme of the play. Oh the meaning, the meaning. Who am I talkin' to?

JAKE: Me, but I want to talk again. *(Jazz music starts up again.)* I'm sick of women. I'm gonna find me some Mexican whores and some tequila, and I'm gonna drive me down some highway with open spaces on either side of me and I'm gonna sit in the car with my legs spread open real wide so my peter can breath, and I'm gonna live like a real man, away from civilization and from styes in the eye. *(Exits to his new life; jazz music fades out.)*

MAE: He's gone. Love and hate is mixed up in my heart. What'll we do?

MA: We got to stick together. We got to go back to our roots. We got to get our heads examined.

WESLEY: I want to have a speech.

MEG: Honey, we gotta wrap this thing up. Make it short.

WESLEY: Could I have jazz music please? *(Jazz starts again.)* Artichokes. There are three different words in artichoke. There's "art." And there's "choke." And there's "ih."

MAE: What does that mean?

MA: You're the one holding the cymbals, not him.

MAE: I don't think they are cymbals.

MEG: No?

MAE: I think…they represent somethin' else.

MEG: I wonder…if they're connected to… *(Importantly, mysteriously.)* …the styes in my eye.

(Everyone looks out in the distance, and stares importantly. Lights dim. The sound of wind whistling through the prairie. A coyote's howl is heard. End.)

TO THE ACTOR
About Ma

In auditions for Ma at MTC, about 75 percent of the good actresses who auditioned seemed to have trouble finding the part. So for that reason, I offer some clarifications.

Ma is feisty, straight-talkin', a no-nonsense lady who lives somewhere out west. She don't fuss much, she says what's on her mind. She talks loud and bold. She swats mosquitoes on her forehead with the back of her hand, she sits unladylike but comfortable with her legs spread wide. She wears messy, loose, print house dresses with sneakers or boots or something that's comfortable to walk around the farm in.

I've also written, especially in the first scene, that she can't seem to remember anything.

I've already written this into a note in the text itself, but I'll repeat it: The comedy about her not remembering only works if you play Ma as totally forgetting from line to line. The first time her son Jake mentions his wife Beth, Ma asks: "Who's Beth?" Then a moment later Jake mentions Beth again, and Ma says: "Who's Beth?"

If you play it as if she half-remembers and says the second "Who's Beth" with a twinge of "That name sounds familiar, who is it again?", it just isn't funny. While if with feisty authority she keeps asking the same question over and over, with no self-knowledge and no uncertainty—then it is funny. (And it's also much more frustrating for Jake.)

In case it's helpful, the character of Ma reminds me of all the feisty Crackers that Marjorie Main played in the movies of the 1930s and 40s.

Probably only film buffs know Marjorie Main now, but in case you would find it helpful to look up her work on video, she played Ma Kettle in a series of films (starting with *The Egg and I*). Ma Kettle was kind of a hillbilly woman who was blunt with a twang and was a no-nonsense kind of gal; she and Pa had 11 to 15 children, and she'd sort of cook in the kitchen with live chickens wandering about underfoot. She spoke her mind and wasn't afraid of anybody.

Marjorie Main played similar characters in a number of other films, notably in the wonderful 1939 classic *The Women,* where she played unflappable Lucy, the woman who runs the Reno, Nevada ranch for divorced women (and where she doesn't blink an eye when Paulette Goddard and Rosalind Russell scratch and bite and tear one another's hair out; she calmly throws water on them, like they were a pair of dogs); in a film I don't know called *Murder, He Says,* which Pauline Kael mentions favorably as a loony comedy about "homicidal hillbillies." Cracker, hillbilly—these words conjure up Marjorie Main and what I have in mind for Ma.

If that's helpful, you might want to find an old movie on video or on TNT or AMC with Marjorie Main in it.

About Jake

With Jake, it's good if you can find someone who's effortlessly masculine and has a good theatrical temper, the kind that's loud and angry and yet comes out funny.

In Shepard's *Lie Of The Mind* there are two brothers: rabble-rouser problem kid Jake and good, doe-eyed Frankie. I found the dichotomy between "bad" brother and "good" brother a little formulaic and so in my parody I've put him into the same character.

However the actor chooses to switch between being Jake and being Frankie, the switch should be fast. Often just switching looks between the two characters can be enough: Jake talks to Frankie looking left, then switches to looking right as Frankie talks back to Jake. Or you can move your body a bit too, if that feels natural to you.

Frankie as the "good" brother does sound calmer than Jake and more reasoned. Yet in the first scene with Ma on the phone, good Frankie also has reason to get annoyed with Ma. Don't be afraid to let Frankie have an anger too. It doesn't rob them of difference... they both have tempers, the whole family does. It's just Jake is a "rage-aholic" and Frankie only has a temper from time to time and is generally more reasonable.

Jake also has a crybaby side that I thought Marcus Giametti brought out beautifully. One minute he'd be seething about why he had to beat Beth to death, the next minute he'd get all blubbery and weepy about feeling lonely that she was gone. (Just like a wife beater.)

The Mamet speech. Must be staccato and fast, the way Mamet dialogue usually is. Must be. Fast. Must be fast. You know what I mean? Fast? Quick? Are you stupid? Do you know? Am I right? Right! Fuckin' A.

A warning of something we found in rehearsal. Don't get stuck on how "Frankie" would sound doing the speech; just do it the way you would do the speech.

Marcus in rehearsal first did the speech great, then he seemed to get lost and for a while we couldn't figure out what was wrong. Then finally it came out: It had to do with trying to do the Mamet speech in "Frankie's" voice.

As Jake and Frankie, Marcus was using a bit of a western drawl, which sounded good. But this drawl elongated his vowel sounds a bit, and these longer vowels slowed the rhythm in the Mamet speech, and made the speech seem slow and un-Mametlike. So Walter and I gave him permission not to worry about sounding like Frankie during the speech, but just to do it in his own voice in the quick rhythms he initially used instinctively.

It's not that I want the *Glengarry* parody to sound different from Frankie... but if anything is stopping you from being staccato and fast on the Mamet speech, let go of it. (When Marcus changed his interpretation in preview to the faster rhythms, the audience laughter and recognition improved enormously.)

Meg, Mae and Wesley

Meg in *Lie Of The Mind* was played by Ann Wedgeworth and my version of Meg was very much based on her amusing, likable performance. Meg is kind of sexy and very vague; life is in a haze to her. Her look is important; sexy tight jeans (or stretch pants), a kind of trashy, off-the-shoulder blouse or sweater, sexy red hair if possible.

When Mae shows up seductively as Jake-Frankie's sister, she is a parody character from a different Shepard play, *Fool for Love*. And in the Shepard-directed version of that play in New York, the brother-sister lovers were wildly and humorously intense. They would embrace passionately, then separate and pretty much hurl themselves against opposite walls, stare at one another, panting and exhausted, then rush back at one another again. (This was quite funny actually and effective in communicating their weird passion for one another. I liked *Fool For Love* on stage.)

That's why my parody characters of Mae and Jake-Frankie throw themselves around that way.

When Wesley comes in just wearing underpants, that's because in Shepard's *Curse of the Starving Class,* a character named Wesley suddenly wanders about the house totally naked but somewhat inexplicably carrying an ailing sheep. Wesley marches to his own drummer and has slow, deep thoughts that we can only imagine.

Many (most?) in the audience don't get these specific references; but as I said earlier, they seemed to enjoy going for the ride anyway. It's a weird poetic-symbolism play parody.

Finally, Wesley's last speech: "There are three different words in artichoke. There's 'art.' And there's 'choke.' And there's 'ih.'"

That speech should be done with importance and emphasis. But it seems to be important how you say "ih." When David Aaron Baker did it, it seemed to work best when he was his most emphatic and important on the word "ih" and when "ih" had the feeling of the sound you make when you go "ugh" or "bleech" to something you don't like.

Well, I think enough notes. I'm tiring myself out.

Nina in the Morning

This play began as a short story. I really liked it, but didn't know what to do with it.

After the good reviews for *Belle* at E.S.T. happened, Michael Bush, the associate artistic director at Manhattan Theater Club, called me and director Walter Bobbie to see if I had other plays up my sleeve that might make an evening.

Bush and Lynne Meadow had been talking with Walter Bobbie for a couple of years looking for a project to work on with him. Lynne had been the first person to present my work in New York back in 1973 (when she presented me and Albert Innaurato in the aforementioned *I Don't Generally Like Poetry But Have You Read "Trees"?* cabaret evening, and then produced an early one-act of mine, *Better Dead Than Sorry).* I also worked on MTC's multi-authored musical revue *Urban Blight* in 1988.

I had just re-acquainted myself with MTC by singing and doing my best to dance in the Stephen Sondheim revue *Putting It Together.* With Julie Andrews. I said, with Julie Andrews. Isn't that odd that I was in that? It was thrilling; I loved it. And a CD exists of it, so you can check that I'm not making it up. However did I get in a five-person musical with Julie Andrews singing Stephen Sondheim music? Ah, the life of a playwright for me!

So, in any case, MTC had been expressing interest in Walter's work and my work before the nice reviews for *Belle.* So this ended up feeling like good and natural timing.

I knew I had *Mrs. Sorken* and *A Stye Of The Eye* to put on an evening, but I had worries about whether a whole evening of theater parody would wear out its welcome. (A few years earlier, a friend, John Money, had wanted to produce an evening of theater parody by me and to call it *Deranged Theatrics.* I consented, but then got cold feet and withdrew. I became fearful of how the critics would treat such a "light" off-Broadway evening from me. I didn't think I had a "full" evening of theater parody in me. And I was starting to go through a "fear-of-the-*New York Times*-critic" phase.)

It was my belief that Act II should not be theater parody.

I gave Walter a box of unproduced writing and some beginnings of things; we decided to have a reading of various of these scripts at MTC.

From this pile, Walter chose the short story *Nina In The Morning,* which I had indicated I thought I could dramatize.

The style of the story was part of its charm and so I created a Narrator so he could speak in the story's style.

I owe Walter Bobbie a debt of gratitude for his inventive staging of this piece. I had envisioned Nina being quite stationary for most of the piece, but Walter had her moving up and about, especially when she was in memory. This staging helped enliven the piece and let us go in and out of memory with Nina most vividly.

I wrote that Nina's children James and Robert would be played by the same actor. The Narrator also mentions Nina's daughter. I intended to write something to allow for the same actor to play her as well, but before I got to do that, Walter devised a way for the daughter character to enter, using the existing narration. His idea enlivened what I'd already written and took care of the need of my having to add something for the daughter.

I thought his work was especially outstanding in this piece.

The look of the play, Walter and I decided, should be like a Calvin Klein "Obsessions" ad. At first we thought that meant black and white, but the designer, David Woolard, put Nina in a stunning off-the-shoulder bright red evening gown with a comically long train and with her hair slicked fashionably back and off her face. She sort of looked like the Wicked Queen in *Snow White* meets Calvin Klein.

Walter added the presence of a maid to add atmosphere and to help Foote move certain props.

If Calvin Klein's "Obsessions" is one way to think of the play, another is to think of the drawings and stories of Edward Gorey—all those thin creatures with long dresses and capes who stand around staring dispassionately while awful tragedies occur one after another around them.

Nina is not a parody. It is meant to be its own thing. At MTC, because Act I consisted of a monologue about theater and two theater parodies, I was alarmed to learn that many people were racking their brains during *Nina* trying to figure out what it was a parody of. Was it Edward Albee? (The formality of the language and the wealth of the people suggested him a bit.) Was it Noel Coward? Was it the performance art of Robert Wilson? (Some of Walter's staging suggested Wilson a little bit.) What was it?

My mention in the program that Act I was Theater, Act II was Everything Else, was clearly too subtle. Plus lots of people don't read the program.

So, late in the run one afternoon, I talked with the actresses backstage about the problem and said I had thought about giving Mrs. Sorken a line explaining to the audience that Act II was not theater parodies. Patricia Elliott (who played Nina as well as Mrs. Sorken) jumped at this and was extremely game—she was willing to try a new line in the middle of her speech that very afternoon in 10 minutes. So I gave her a couple of possibilities, all fine but a little convoluted. Strangely, when she tried to repeat them back, she came up with her own abridged version that went: "Act I is theater parodies. Act II... is not."

Given her elaborate manner of speaking, the blunt inelegance of this phrasing seemed funny to us in the dressing room. And then to the audience a few moments later. So I wrote it in and it seemed to help. I wish I had thought to put it in earlier in the run.

Note to grammarians: Yes, I know that the proper grammar would be "Act I is theater parody." But I think the audience hears better "Act I is theater parodies;" and so that's how I've left it. And I ended a sentence five paragraphs above with the word "of." "Never end a sentence with a preposition." I could have moved the "of" to earlier in the sentence, but it would have sounded awkward to everyone except grammarians.

Sorry. Why am I talking to grammarians? Time to focus on *Nina*.

ORIGINAL PRODUCTION

Nina In The Morning was part of *Durang Durang* and began Act II. The cast was as follows:

Narrator . . . . David Aaron Baker
The Maid . . . . Patricia Randell
Nina. . . . . Patricia Elliott
James/Robert/La-La . . . . Keith Reddin
Foote . . . . Marcus Giamatti

CHARACTERS

NARRATOR

THE MAID (optional; non-speaking)

NINA

JAMES, ROBERT, LA-LA, THE THREE CHILDREN OF NINA
    (all played by one actor)

FOOTE, the manservant

NINA IN THE MORNING

Scene: A beautiful room in a rather elaborate household—a chateau, a small castle? At Manhattan Theatre Club they had floor-to-ceiling sheer curtains in front of a beautiful azure blue scrim. The sound of the ocean. The curtains gently move to a breeze.

There is a beautiful chaise. And in front of the chaise, a tall, gilt-edged mirror. [The mirror should be only a frame, with nothing where the mirror glass itself would be. Thus an actor can sit or stand behind it, and still be seen by the audience. Seeing a reflection in the mirror is mimed.]

Beautiful, mysterious music is heard. A lovely, haunting soprano aria perhaps.

The Narrator is onstage. He is dressed in a tuxedo and looks elegant.

As the music is finishing, Nina enters.

She is dressed beautifully. [At MTC the designer put her in an off-the-shoulder red gown, with a very, very long train. However she is dressed, it should be elegant and flattering to the actress. And a little extreme.]

Her age is indeterminate—definitely over 40 though—and her face is on the white side, with perhaps too much makeup. She walks toward her chaise with great regalness, as if she's in a procession, on her way to be crowned.

When the Narrator speaks, he is speaking her thoughts, usually. So her facial expressions change with his comments. She does not otherwise look at him or relate to him [with a couple of noted exceptions].

NARRATOR: The mist hangs heavy over the ocean today. Nina woke from an uncertain sleep and walked to the chaise in her dressing room and sat in front of the beautiful, cherished mirror.

(Nina sits on her chaise, and looks out to her mirror and gasps.)

NARRATOR: Her facelift had fallen during the night, and her cheeks were held in place by straight pins.

NINA: *(Looking in the mirror, touching her face delicately.)* Oh, Lord. Oh, Lord. How dreadful.

(Enter James, her child, dressed in short pants and a white shirt. He looks like a well-dressed prep school boy. Played by an actor somewhere in his 20s or young-looking 30s.)

JAMES: Good morning, mother.

NINA: Don't kiss mommy today, her face is precarious.

JAMES: I don't want to kiss you anyway. I hate you.

NINA: Please don't upset me, James. My plastic surgeon is in Aruba.

JAMES: What's this pin for? *(Reaches for her face, pulls out a pin.)*

NINA: James, stop that. Stop it. Foote! Foote! Come quickly, James is at my face again.

NARRATOR: But James kept reaching for Nina's face, over and over.

NINA: Stop it, you unruly child.

(James keeps trying to pull pins out of her face. Nina keeps trying to protect her face. All the pin business is mimed. Foote, the family manservant, enters. Dignified and in a tuxedo.)

FOOTE: You called, Madame?

JAMES: I want to pull your face off, mother!

NARRATOR: Foote, seeing Nina's predicament with her son, pulled James away from her, pushed him to the ground, and sat on him.

(Foote pulls James away, pushes him on the ground and sits on him.)

NINA: Gently, Foote, gently.

JAMES: *(Struggling with Foote.)* I hate you, mother, I hate you.

NARRATOR: Foote took out a hypodermic from his jacket pocket, and gave the misbehaving child a shot.

(Foote does all that.)

JAMES: I hate you. I'm sleepy. *(Passes out.)*

FOOTE: Will that be all, Madame?

NARRATOR: Foote was the family manservant, and often gave the children general anesthesia whenever they became unruly. Foote had once been a dentist.

NINA: Thank you, Foote. James was pulling pins out again. I must have done something wrong raising them. I thought I often smiled. I wonder if they wanted anything else.

FOOTE: Do you wish me to remove any teeth while he's out?

NINA: No, no. Leave his teeth alone, Foote. I just want quiet for a while. Look at how peaceful James is, curled on the floor. I always liked my children best when they were unconscious.

FOOTE: If Madame needs me further, just call.

NINA: Thank you, Foote. You're a jewel.

(Foote exits.)

NARRATOR: Foote withdrew, leaving Nina with her thoughts. She thought about her face. She thought about James. Psychotherapy had been no help for James except perhaps in helping him to express his anger more freely, and how useful had that been.

NINA: *(Sort of to herself.)* Not very.

NARRATOR: Nina's hands shook as she lifted a coffee cup to her face. Her perceptions were off, and she poured hot liquid down the left side of her face. She put cream and sugar on her face, stirred it, and then rang the bell for Foote.

(Nina mimes the actions the Narrator says above while, or shortly after, he says them. She uses a real cup, spoon, cream pitcher, and sugar bowl, but no actual liquids or sugar.

She does all the gestures without emotion. She feels the heat of the coffee and the mess of the liquids after she has done all of them. Then she makes a face of pain, and confusion. Then she rings the bell.)

NINA: Foote, I need you. Bring a wet cloth. I'm sticky.

NARRATOR: Foote brought a basin of warm water and a roll of gauze and sponged her gingerly.

(Foote enters with a Maid as the Narrator speaks. The Maid has a tray with a silver bowl and a wet cloth. Foote starts to pat Nina's face lightly with the cloth.)

NINA: Do you think I'm beautiful, Foote?

FOOTE: You once were very striking, Madame.

NINA: Yes, but now, what do you think of me now?

FOOTE: *(Looks at her.)* You have quite a nasty burn on your face, Madame. Would you care for a shot of Novocaine?

NINA: Go away, Foote. I want to think.

NARRATOR: And again, Foote withdrew, dragging James after him.

(Foote drags James out the door, while the Maid curtsies and follows after them.)

NARRATOR: Nina racked her brain, trying to remember what she wanted to think. The colors of her wall were beige. She had wanted burnt orange, but the designer had run through the house screaming "Beige! Beige!" and they finally had to give him his way.

NINA: *(Out, to imagined designer.)* I wanted burnt orange, but you have given me beige.

NARRATOR: Later the designer turned against her too, like her son James. No, no, Nina wanted pleasant thoughts, nice things. Flowers, butterflies...

NINA: *(Hopefully.)* Little duckies.

NARRATOR: *The Little Prince* by Saint-Exupery. That was a nauseating little book, she had never finished it. Some monk gave it to her when her car had been stopped at a traffic light.
(The Narrator sits stiffly at the bottom of the chaise. He holds his arms as if holding a steering wheel. He stands in for the chauffeur now.)

NINA: Drive on, Lance.

NARRATOR: *(To the audience.)* But Lance, the handsome chauffeur, insisted on the necessity of obeying the red light. *(Speaking as Lance, to Nina:)* "I must obey the red light, Madame."

NINA: Laws are for other people, Lance. Not for me.

NARRATOR: *(Speaking as Lance.)* "I'm sorry, Madame. I don't wish to lose my license."

NINA: I said, drive on, Lance.

NARRATOR: *(To the audience again.)* But the Mercedes just sat there, and the monk had a chance to pass the stupid book through the car window.
(A Monk scurries across the stage, stopping just long enough to drop a copy of The Little Prince *on Nina's chaise-car. He then scurries the rest of the way off.)*

NINA: Kill that monk, Lance.

NARRATOR: *(To the audience.)* But Lance was selective in what commands of hers he followed, and eventually he had to be fired.
(The Narrator stands, no longer playing Lance. He returns to his narration role.)

NARRATOR: A long succession of chauffeurs followed, none satisfactory. Finally she gave up riding in the car. She stayed at home, hoping for visitors.
(Nina rings the bell. Foote appears immediately, and waits for her bidding.)

NINA: Foote, if any Jehovah's Witnesses come today, show them in, will you?

(Foote exits.)

NARRATOR: But no Jehovah's Witnesses came. And Nina found she had to fill the time with thinking, and reminiscing. Nina had once been beautiful.

NINA: I am very beautiful.

NARRATOR: Men would stop on the street to stare at her. She caused traffic accidents. Jealous women would rush up to her in their homeliness and try to kill her.

NINA: Homely women were always trying to shoot me. It was flattering really.

NARRATOR: Everywhere she went, her eyes would anxiously seek out the mirrors. Sometimes she would bring her own mirrors with her.

NINA: Put this up, would you?

NARRATOR: …Nina would say, lugging a large mirror, and few could deny her. Her love affairs were unpredictable and random. Sometimes it would be royalty, other times it would be the men from Con Edison.

(The Narrator turns his back, pretending to look at a power box. He is now the Con Edison man. Nina comes up to him, stands close and seductive.)

NINA: I don't really know where the power box is, I'm afraid. Would you care to lie down?

(The Narrator reverts to his narrator role, and addresses the audience again.)

NARRATOR: Sometimes when she was especially lonely, she would try to seduce her children.

(James enters, dressed as before as a prep school boy. He, though, also carries a lunch box. He sits on the chaise and looks at Nina.)

NINA: Don't you find mommy especially attractive today?

NARRATOR: She would ask James…

(James looks startled.)

NARRATOR: …and Robert.

(The actor playing James puts on black-rimmed glasses, and becomes Robert. His posture changes, and he looks at Nina also surprised, but somehow more adult, more jaded.)

NARRATOR: …and occasionally poor La-La.

(The actor now opens the lunch box, takes out a simple skirt that wraps

around in one gesture, and clips a large yellow bow in his hair. All the while he makes the following sounds:)

LA-LA: *(Happily and monotonously singing to herself.)* La-la-la-la-la, la-la-la-la, la, la, la, la...

(The actor finishes his costume change and sits back down; with a rather foolish and sweetly imbecilic expression, he becomes La-la, staring at Nina.)

NARRATOR: La-La was retarded, and Nina hated her.

NINA: *(Firmly.)* La-La! Pay attention!

(La-La turns away, opens up her lunch box and starts looking through it happily.)

LA-LA: La-la-la-la-la, la-la-la...

NINA: Uhhhh. You're *willfully* retarded.

NARRATOR: Nina would shout this at La-La, and then hit her.

(Nina swats La-La's head. La-La hits her head on the tin lunch box, and sort of stumbles offstage, happy but disoriented.)

NARRATOR: But Nina mustn't think of the past now. The present was what held promise. Her plastic surgeon was due back in several days.

(Nina rings the bell.)

NINA: *(Grandly.)* Foote, I want a cruller!

NARRATOR: She heard what she presumed were Foote's footsteps, but they belonged to her second son Robert, who fired two shots, one of which grazed her shoulder.

(Enter Robert, dressed the same as James but with the addition of the glasses. He shoots a pistol twice at his mother. On the second shot, Nina moves her shoulder as if hit.)

ROBERT: I hate you, mother!

NARRATOR: Then he ran into the garden.

(Robert runs off. Nina holds her shoulder and rings the bell again.)

NINA: Foote, bring the gauze again, please.

NARRATOR: Nina had been presented to the Queen twice.

(Nina forgets her pain, and re-enters memory again. She lets go of her shoulder, and stands proudly to meet the Queen.

Then during the following, Nina moves back to her chaise, and Robert enters and sits close to his mother.)

NARRATOR: It had been shortly after the second presenting that Nina, having been spurned by a member of the Royal Guard on duty, successfully seduced Robert, who was fifteen and seemed to enjoy the activity for a while but then became hysterical.

(Nina and Robert lean in as if to kiss; suddenly Robert starts to scream hysterically. He stands up upset, looks at her, then screams again, running off. Nina looks after him, unconcerned, slightly feeling incomplete.)

NARRATOR: The school psychologists were highly critical of Nina's behavior, but she was uninterested in their judgments. And then when Louis Malle made *Murmur of the Heart* she called them up and said:

NINA: There you see! The critics thought it was charming, so I don't know what all the fuss was about my behavior.

NARRATOR: Nina quite liked the film, which had to do with a mother seducing her son one afternoon, but she felt that the actress Lea Massari was more coarse-grained than she was.

NINA: My features are more delicate, more lovely. I thought Lea Massari was a bit too earthy. I may be sensual, but I am never earthy.

NARRATOR: Neither Robert nor James would agree to see the film, but La-La sort of liked it.

(Enter La-La, happy, in her own world.)

LA-LA: La-la-la-la-la, la-la la-la la-la…

(La-La sits next to Nina and, as if they're watching a movie, stares out with a scrunched up, interested face.)

NINA: *(To audience.)* Yes, La-La loved the movies. *Murmur of the Heart* she liked. And that other Louis Malle film about suicide, *The Fire Within.* And that early Jeanne Moreau film where she makes love in the bathtub, *The Lovers.* Also directed by Louis Malle. La-La really seemed to like the films of Louis Malle…

(La-La leans forward in particular concentration.)

NINA: …which just goes to show she's only retarded when she wants to be. No retarded child is going to like the films of Louis Malle. So I've proved my point, La-La is willfully retarded.

(Nina pushes La-La away; La-La meanders off. Nina's thoughts return to the present, and her wounded shoulder.)

NINA: Where is Foote with that gauze, my shoulder is bleeding. Foote! Foote!

NARRATOR: James' father had been a tax lawyer, but Robert's father had been one of twenty men; La-La's father had been one of fifty-six men that busy summer she had the beach house painted. After a brief burst of self-judgment, she searched the thesaurus for alternatives to the word "promiscuity."

NINA: *(Miming looking in a dictionary.)* Synonyms include "debauchery." "Salacity." And "lubricity." "Lubricity." "Looooo-bricity." "Loooooo-briiiiiiii-ci-teeeeeeeeeee."

NARRATOR: Nina liked the sound of "lubricity" and that summer she would climb up the ladders and whisper the word into the house-painters' ears.

(The Narrator finds himself near Nina. She stands and seductively whispers in his ear, as if he's the house painter.)

NINA: *(Whispering into his ear.)* Lubricity.

(Enter Foote with some more gauze.)

FOOTE: Has Madame been shot?

(Nina's thoughts return to the present, and Robert's recent attack on her.)

NINA: Yes, Foote. Robert said something to me, something mean, and then he shot me. What took you so long?

FOOTE: I'm sorry, Madame. I was giving La-La a hypodermic shot to calm her down. She was complaining about something and acting retarded, and now she's quiet and good as a lamb.

NINA: She is good as a lamb. *(Suddenly remembering; stern.)* Foote. I asked for a cruller. How many times must I ask for a thing before I get it?

FOOTE: We don't have any crullers. Would you like sausages?

NINA: Go away, Foote.

FOOTE: Sorry, Madame. I'll ask Cook to bake some crullers for tomorrow morning.

NINA: Tomorrow morning? Tomorrow, and tomorrow, and tomorrow. Who knows if I'll want a cruller tomorrow, Foote. It doesn't matter. Leave me now, please.

FOOTE: Yes, Madame. *(Foote exits.)*

NINA: Oh my life, my life, my life. What has become of my life? *(Looks in the mirror anew.)* And what has become of my face? Oh my. Pins are for curtains, not for faces.

NARRATOR: Nina stared at herself in the mirror and tried to decide whether or not to kill herself. She stared a long while. She didn't look well. Slowly she took the pins out of her face. *(Nina mimes taking pins out. Then she pulls her cheeks downward, and stares tragically at herself in the mirror.)*

NARRATOR: Her cheeks drooped downward, and her eyes filled with tears. She looked like Simone Signoret. Late Simone Signoret. Of course, when the doctor returned from Aruba, he'd make Nina look substantially better. And she didn't know how to kill herself, unless one of her children shot her. She rang for Foote.

(Nina rings the bell.)

NINA: *(Without force; slipping into despair.)* Foote. Foote.

NARRATOR: In lieu of crullers, Nina decided to have sausages and general anesthesia. And if Robert shot her while she was passed out, so be it; and if she woke from her sleep, she'd have a proper lunch.

NINA: Yes. Death or lunch. Death or lunch. One of the two. *(Nina continues to look in the mirror, touching her face lightly.)*

(Lights dim. End.)

TO THE ACTOR

I already mentioned the sort of "look" of the piece: self-consciously elegant... Edward Gorey... Calvin Klein "Obsessions" ads.

For music I mentioned beautiful and mysterious, perhaps an opera aria. We ended up using a lovely aria for two sopranos from the opera *Lakme* by Delibes. This aria has gotten a bit popular because it was used in an ad for British Airlines and in the vampire movie *The Hunger* (and was included on that movie's soundtrack recording). There are, I'm sure, other ones, too. (Rachmaninoff's "Vocalise" for a soprano voice might be another.)

I think it's important to mime the facelift-pins-in-the-face stuff. I think miming it adds to the stylization and distancing that the piece needs.

When I wrote it, I envisioned Nina sitting still for the whole thing with the Narrator's lines telling us what she's thinking. I think that would still work, though I really enjoyed what Walter Bobbie brought to the staging with Nina walking to different parts of the stage with different memories.

There was an early part in rehearsal where it was all movement and flow and it was hard to follow and enjoy. (Luckily, this was an early rehearsal, not a preview.) One of the things that had gotten lost in this rehearsal was the clarity of events in Nina's mind.

Much of the play takes place on a *particular day:* On that particular day Nina's facelift has fallen; her son James has said he hates her and tried to take pins out of her face; her son Robert has shot her in the shoulder; and she has asked for a cruller which she has not received. It is those events which are current and happening now which bring her to the point at the end of the play where she is legitimately considering whether she wants to continue living or not, whether to have "lunch or death."

All the other things that happen are memories from the past; Nina can and should lose herself in them, but whenever she comes back to a moment in the present day, it's important for the actress to keep in mind that these present-day events are what her major journey is in the play, short though it is. The other things are flashbacks, meant to inform the audience and to comfort and distract Nina, but the present-day events must not be forgotten; they add up for Nina.

Sorry about line readings, but the last line "death or lunch" is important to me. Please don't go for any easy humor of saying "death" portentously and then "lunch" lightly or cutely.

Nina takes herself so seriously that, I think, she would intone both options with equal seriousness, giving both equal weight. It's the giving of equal weight to these ludicrously unequal things that makes the line funny and strange.

Oh, a minor note about the monk. Walter had Keith, who played all three children, play the monk, but the monk wore a large brown robe with an oversized cowl that totally covered his head and face; so the audience never knew it was Keith. I liked not seeing the monk's face and I offer that as a possible way of handling it. (If you did let the monk's face be seen, then choose a different actor, not the actor playing Foote or playing the children.)

Wanda's Visit

This play is based on a teleplay I wrote in 1986 for a PBS half-hour comedy series called *Trying Times,* created by Jon Denny. It was Denny's idea to ask various playwrights to write half-hour teleplays about "difficult times." Denny produced about 12 of them for WCET in Los Angeles. The first ones included Beth Henley on meeting the in-laws; Wendy Wasserstein on learning to drive; Bernard Slade on moving day; George C. Wolfe on having a black maid put a spell on your house; Albert Innaurato on dealing with a tax audit. (The *Trying Times* program shows up from time to time on PBS stations and makes fun watching.)

My episode was number six and my topic was dealing with a visit from someone from your high school days.

The character of Wanda—needy, manipulative, impossible to be rid of—came charging out of my brain and was great fun to write.

The teleplay was filmed in a week, directed by Alan Arkin, and starring Jeff Daniels, Julie Hagerty and Swoosie Kurtz as Wanda.

My professional path had crossed Swoosie's when she played Bette in my play *A History of the American Film* at Arena Stage in 1977 and then repeated her role in 1978 on Broadway, winning a Drama Desk award for her portrayal. In 1977 she also played the pivotal, comic role of Rita in my friend Wendy Wasserstein's play *Uncommon Women and Others,* both onstage and on camera for PBS's *Great Performances.*

Swoosie is a very special comic talent, and it was a thrill to have her play Wanda. Indeed this whole experience of working with Jeff, Julie, Swoosie and Alan was one of the nicest and most artistically successful professional experiences I've had. (And for added fun, I played the role of the Waiter. Nepotism. Authorism?)

I was sorry that more people didn't see it (there's occasionally talk about putting some of the *Trying Times* out on video; I wish they would). So I decided to re-present it onstage as part of *Durang Durang.*

The script is mostly the dialogue from the teleplay. I have made some changes for transition purposes. For instance, on film we could simply fade to later in the evening, with Wanda wrapped in a blanket, talking, talking. On stage, I had to find other ways to make time pass.

As I was adapting it, some new lines also came to me and I often included those as well. (Marsha got some new quirks in the restaurant scene.)

So, *Wanda's Visit.*

ORIGINAL PRODUCTION

Wanda's Visit was part of *Durang Durang* at Manhattan Theater Club. The cast was as follows:

Jim . . . . Marcus Giamatti
Marsha. . . . . Lizbeth Mackay
Wanda . . . . Becky Ann Baker
Waiter. . . . . David Aaron Baker

CHARACTERS
JIM
MARSHA, his wife
WANDA
WAITER
TWO MEN

WANDA'S VISIT

Scene: A comfortable home in Connecticut. Not realistically designed, though—different areas represent different rooms: the living room, the dining room, the bathroom, the kitchen. The dining room table later doubles as a table in a restaurant. The furniture and the colors are taste- fully chosen. A "country" feel.

At Manhattan Theatre Club the setting was very simple: a round table and three chairs. When the chairs were one way, it was the living room. When the chairs were around the table, it was the dining room. For the bedroom, two chairs were put together and the actors sat on them and spread a comforter over themselves. The bathroom was defined by a square of light.

This is the home of Jim and Marsha. They enter and come to speak to the audience.

They are attractive, in their mid-to-late 30s. He's in somewhat preppy relaxed clothes—khaki pants, a button-down shirt. She's in a comfortable skirt and blouse, with warm but pale colors. Her hair may be pulled back.

Their manner in talking to the audience is that of telling a story, but also, perhaps, of explaining themselves to a marriage counselor.

JIM: Our lives had been seeming dull for a while. You know, nothing major, just sometimes being quiet at dinner.
MARSHA: After 13 years, you run out of things to say, I guess. Or else it's a phase.
JIM: I think it's a phase.

MARSHA: Me too. It'll pass.

JIM: We've been married for 13 years.

MARSHA: Our anniversary was in March.

JIM: So in March we went to dinner and tried to get drunk, but we just got sleepy.

MARSHA: We didn't try to get drunk.

JIM: I did.

MARSHA: We had a very nice time, but the wine made us sleepy.

JIM: We were in bed at 10:30. Asleep in bed.

MARSHA: Well, we were tired.

JIM: And then the next week I got this letter from this old classmate of mine.

MARSHA: Wanda. He'd never mentioned her.

JIM: Well, she was just some girlfriend. You know. High school.

MARSHA: Wanda.

JIM: And Wanda wrote me, saying she'd like to visit. And I asked Marsha if she'd mind.

MARSHA: I have trouble saying no, most women do, I think. It's not pleasing or something. Anyway, Jim got this letter...

JIM: ...and Wanda said she was going to be in our neck of the woods...

MARSHA: ...and I hate the phrase "neck of the woods"...

JIM: And I asked you if you'd mind, and you said, it would be fine.

MARSHA: Well, I have trouble saying no. You know that. You should have said "Are you sure" or "Really" or something.

JIM: *(Stymied; out to audience.)* Well, I didn't. I thought it would be fun. You know, to mull over the old high school days—the prom, the high school paper—I was editor...

MARSHA: And really, what a ball for me...

JIM: And Marsha didn't seem to mind. I mean I can't be a mind reader. So I wrote Wanda back, and told her we'd love to have her visit. I mean, really it might have been fun. In high school Wanda had been quite a looker.

MARSHA: And, of course, what an enticement for me. To meet an old high school fantasy. Lucky me.

JIM: So we set a date, and Marsha cleaned the house and baked a chicken.

MARSHA: Jim refuses to cook or clean.

JIM: I mow the lawn, you make the chicken.

MARSHA: We're old-fashioned, I guess.

JIM: And so we waited for her visit.

(Lights change. Sound of a car driving up, stopping, and a door slamming.)

JIM: Oh, I'll go, honey. It must be Wanda.

(Jim goes off to greet Wanda. Marsha straightens up things one last time.

Offstage we hear great whooping and enthusiastic cries of "Jim! Jim!"

Marsha looks startled, curious.

Wanda and Jim come into the room. Wanda is also late 30s, early 40s, but unlike Jim and Marsha, she is not in as good shape. Her clothes are a little gaudy, her hair looks odd or messy, and she carries a sense of emotional disarray with her. But she also looks kind of fun and colorful.)

WANDA: *(With longing.)* Jim!!!

(Wanda throws her arms around Jim with great abandon, and then holds this embrace as if her life depended on it.

Marsha goes closer to them, and waits patiently for the appropriate moment to be introduced.)

WANDA: *(Still embracing him.)* Jim. Jim. Oh, Jim, Jim.

MARSHA: *(Since the embrace doesn't seem to be ending.)* Hello. I'm Marsha, Jim's wife.

WANDA: *(Breaking from the embrace.)* Oh, hello. Nice to see you. I was just so excited at seeing this guy. Hey, guy. Hey. How ya doin'?

JIM: I'm fine. *(A little uncertain he recognizes her.)* Wanda?

WANDA: Are you expecting someone else?

JIM: No, it's just—well, didn't you used to be blond?

WANDA: Yeah, and I didn't used to be fat either—although I'm not really fat, my woman's group doesn't let me say that, I just have a food problem and some of it shows. But really I just lost 20 pounds. You should have seen me last month.

JIM: You seem quite thin.

WANDA: Oh, you're sweet. I may look thin, but I'm really fat. *(To Marsha.)* Do you have anything I can eat?

MARSHA: Well...

WANDA: No, I'm just kidding, it was a joke, it seemed like this set-up, you know, I talk about my weight, and then I say, can I have some food.

MARSHA: But if you're hungry...

WANDA: *I am not hungry. (Glares at Marsha; then becomes friendly again;*

to Jim.) Say, Jim, I love your wife. She reminds me of my mother.
(To Marsha.) No, no, the positive side of my mother. Really. I like
both of you.

MARSHA: *(Innocently.)* Thank you. I like both of you.

WANDA: What?

MARSHA: *(Trying to fix what she said.)* I like you, and I like Jim.

WANDA: You better, you're married to Jim, you lucky dog, you. Oh, give
me another hug, guy.
(Wanda gives Jim another bear hug.)

WANDA: Hrrrrrrrrrrrrr.

JIM: Why don't we go in the living room?
*(Wanda careens into the living room area, looks around her. They fol-
low.)*

WANDA: Oh, I love this room. It's so "country." Did you do it, Marsha?

MARSHA: Well, we bought the furniture. I never thought of it as "doing
it" actually.

WANDA: Oh, it's wonderful. And I should know, because I have terrible
taste.

MARSHA: What?

WANDA: I mean I can evaluate good taste in others because I have such
bad taste in all my own choices. For instance, my house looks like
the interior of a Baskin Robbins. Everything is plastic, and there are
all these bright yellows and dark chocolates. Really the only thing
worse than being married to me is to have me decorate your house.

JIM: Well, I'm sure you underestimate yourself, Wanda.

WANDA: Isn't he a dreamboat? You're a dreamboat, dreamboat. Well, say
thank you!

JIM: *(Embarrassed.)* Thank you.

WANDA: *(To Marsha; with sudden focus.)* Do you have anything to eat?
Pretzels or something?

MARSHA: Well, dinner should be ready soon.

WANDA: Oh, Lord, I don't want dinner yet. Just some pretzels would be
good. Something to munch on.

MARSHA: Would you like some pate?

WANDA: Pate? *(To Jim.)* Where'd you get her, honey, the back of *The New
Yorker? (To Marsha.)* Sure, honey, I can eat pate, as long as you have
crackers with it. And maybe some pretzels.

MARSHA: Fine. I'll be right back. *(Exits to kitchen area.)*

WANDA: Oh, Jimbo, she's a jewel. An absolute jewel. *(Wanda sits next to Jim.)*

JIM: Thank you. We've been married 13 years.

WANDA: Oh. An unlucky number. But she's a jewel. I hope she's not hard like a jewel—just precious.

JIM: Yes, she's very precious.

WANDA: Good.

JIM: You know, I hate to say this, but I don't recognize your face actually.

WANDA: That's very perceptive, Jim. I've had plastic surgery. But it wasn't the fancy-schmancy kind to make your face look better, it was so they couldn't find me.

JIM: Who couldn't find you?

WANDA: I don't want to talk about it. Not on the first night, at least.

JIM: Now you've piqued my interest.

WANDA: Oh, you men are always so impatient.

(Wanda squeezes his knee. Marsha comes in with the pate, and notices the knee-squeezing. Marsha sits down with the pate. Wanda is seated between Jim and Marsha.)

MARSHA: Here is the pate.

WANDA: Thanks, honey, I'll just have the crackers. *(Munches enthusiastically on a cracker.)* Stoned wheat thins, I love this. *(To Jim.)* She's a jewel, Jim.

JIM: *(Rather miserably.)* I know. You're a jewel, Marsha.

MARSHA: Thank you. *(To Wanda.)* Would you like a drink?

(Wanda pauses for a moment, and then begins to sob, very genuinely.)

MARSHA: *(At a loss what to say.)* Don't feel you have to have a drink.

JIM: Wanda, what's the matter?

WANDA: *(Through sobs.)* Oh, I don't want to burden you. Or your wife.

MARSHA: That's all right, I'm sure we'd love to be burdened. I mean, if it would help you.

JIM: Yes. Tell us what's the matter.

WANDA: I don't know where to begin. I'm just so unhappy!

JIM: Gosh, Wanda. What is it?

(Wanda pulls herself together, and tries to explain why she felt so upset.)

WANDA: Well it all started the summer after high school graduation. *(To Marsha.)* Jim and I had gone to the prom together, and though of course nothing had been said, everyone just kind of presumed he and I would get married.

JIM: Really? Who presumed this?

WANDA: Well, everyone. My mother, my father, me, everyone.

JIM: Gosh. I mean, I knew we dated.

WANDA: Dated, Jimbo, we were inseparable. From about February of senior year to June senior year, we spent every spare moment together. You gave me your class ring. Look, I have it right here. *(Looks through her purse.)* No, I can't find it. *(Keeps looking.)*

MARSHA: Jim, gave me the nicest engagement ring.

WANDA: Uh, huh. Now, where is it? *(Wanda dumps out the messy contents of her purse; looks through the mess.)* No. No. Here's the prescription for seconal I always carry with me in case I feel suicidal.

MARSHA: I don't think any of the pharmacies are open this late.

(Wanda stares at Marsha for a moment, like a child who's crying and has suddenly been distracted. Before she can go any further comprehending whatever Marsha said, Jim speaks up.)

JIM: Forget about the ring, Wanda. Tell us why you cried a few minutes ago.

WANDA: Isn't it obvious?

JIM: Isn't what obvious?

WANDA: Seeing the path not taken. I could have had a happy life if I married you. Excuse me for talking this way, Marsha, I just want you to know how lucky you are.

MARSHA: Oh, that's fine. Whatever.

WANDA: No, not whatever. Jimbo. *(Kisses him; looks at Marsha, speaks to Jim.)* You see, I do that in front of Marsha so she knows how lucky she is.

MARSHA: Thank you. I feel lucky.

WANDA: Well, don't you forget it. Are you listening to me?

MARSHA: No one else is speaking.

WANDA: *(Genuinely laughs.)* Oh I love her sense of humor. So anyway, after the prom, Jimbo went away for the whole summer, and he didn't write me...

JIM: I didn't know you wanted me to...

WANDA: And then you and I went to different colleges, and *then* when you didn't write me, I was heartbroken...

JIM: Really? I'm terribly sorry... I thought we were kind of casual. I mean, we were 17.

WANDA: I was 18. They held me back in 3rd grade.

JIM: Wanda, if you felt this way, why didn't you tell me at the time? You haven't said anything in 20 years.

WANDA: Well, I've been very busy, and it's hard to be open about emotions, especially painful ones. *(Chomps on a cracker.)* So then I went to Ann Arbor, and oh, Jim and Marsha, I'm so ashamed to tell you this—I was promiscuous.

MARSHA: Really?

WANDA: Yes. *(Emphatic, cranky.)* Gosh, these crackers are sure making me thirsty. When you offered me something to drink, I didn't think it was going to be my one chance.

MARSHA: *(Startled, disoriented.)* I'm sorry. Would you like something to drink?

WANDA: *(Sweetly.)* Yes, thank you, Marsha. Anything at all. Preferably with vodka.

(Marsha exits off to kitchen.)

WANDA: She really is a jewel. She really is. Now where was I?

JIM: You were saying you had been promiscuous.

WANDA: It was awful. I became a campus joke. But it was because I was drowning my sorrow, you see—in flesh.

JIM: In flesh. Ah. Well, that's too bad.

WANDA: There was this one night a whole bunch of guys from the football team stood outside my window and they chanted my name.

JIM: Oh. Well, at least you made an impression.

WANDA: Yeah, but it was because I was missing a certain somebody. And also I liked sex.

(Marsha comes in, just in time to hear this last remark.)

JIM: *(Startled.)* Oh, Marsha's here. Hello, Marsha. We missed you.

MARSHA: *(A bit of an edge.)* Here's your drink. I hope you like Kool-Aid.

WANDA: Oh, I love it! *(Gulps her entire drink.)* Mmmm, delicious.

(Marsha looks disappointed.)

WANDA: So anyway, the campus minister once had to give a whole sermon against me, which made me feel just awful. *(To Jim.)* And all because I was pining for you.

MARSHA: I wonder if I should check on the chicken.

JIM: Please don't go just now. *(Jim gets up, to stand by Marsha.)*

WANDA: And, of course, I was raised Catholic, so I knew what I was doing was very, very wrong, but I was so unhappy... *(Weeps copiously.)* *(Jim and Marsha stare at her for a little while.)*

JIM: *(Without too much enthusiasm.)* There, there, Wanda.

MARSHA: Yes. There, there.

WANDA: And then my second husband gave me herpes, and every time the first one would call to threaten my life, it would trigger an outbreak...

(Marsha sits back down in a chair, Jim sits on the arm.)

WANDA: ...herpes is often set off by emotional turmoil, you know.

JIM: *(Forcing interest.)* Oh, yes, I've read that.

WANDA: And then I thought to hell with men, maybe I should become a lesbian. And I tried that, but the problem was I just wasn't attracted to women, so the whole experiment was a dismal failure.

MARSHA: Doesn't anyone want dinner yet?

WANDA: *(Suddenly switching moods.)* Marsha sounds hungry. Sure, honey, let's go eat.

(Wanda bounds up and moves to the dining room table. Jim and Marsha follow.

The dinner is not realistically done. It may be mimed with plates and silverware already set on the table.)

WANDA: Oh the dinner looks beautiful. Marsha, you're so talented as a homemaker. Now where was I?

JIM: Something about you were promiscuous.

WANDA: Well, I don't like to use that word. I slept around uncontrollably, that's what I prefer to say. Did you ever do that, Marsha?

MARSHA: No, I didn't. I was a late bloomer.

WANDA: Uh huh. So then, there was that guy from prison. And then there was his father, Fred. Did I tell you about Fred? Well, Fred said to me, I married you because I thought you would be my anchor in the port of life, but now I think you're stark raving mad...

MARSHA: Could I have the salt please?

(Jim passes Marsha the salt.)

WANDA: ...and I said, you think I'm crazy, who's the one who has hallucinations, and thinks that shoes go on the hands instead of the feet? Not me, buddy boy.

JIM: *(To Wanda.)* Did he take drugs or something?

MARSHA: Please don't ask her questions.

WANDA: What?

MARSHA: *(To Wanda.)* Well, I mean I want you to tell the story your own way.

WANDA: Thank you, Marsha. You know, Jim. I really feel close to Marsha.

JIM: I'm glad. *(To Marsha.)* Could I have the salt please?

WANDA: *(Responding to him.)* Sure, honey. *(Passes him the salt; to Marsha.)*

Don't you just love him? *(Continues on with story.)* So one day the washing machine blew up, and Fred said to me, you did that, every- thing about you is chaos, I'm leaving and I'm taking Tranquility with me.

JIM: He actually said "tranquility"?

MARSHA: *(Muttered.)* Don't ask her questions.

WANDA: *(Explaining.)* Tranquility was our dog. And I said, I'm the one who fed Tranquility, and walked her and took care of her worms, and she used to throw up on the rug, and, of course, you can't just leave it there...

MARSHA: Excuse me, I'll be right back.

JIM: Marsha, are you all right?

MARSHA: I'm fine.

WANDA: I hope my talking about vomit didn't make you feel sick.

MARSHA: *(Nearly out of the room.)* No, it's fine.

(Marsha has left the dining area and gotten to the bathroom area. She holds her head in pain, or leans on a wall for a support. She just could- n't stand to be at the table for a minute longer.)

WANDA: She's a little hard to talk to.

JIM: I think she had a hard day.

WANDA: Really? What did she do? Spend it making up the guest room for me?

JIM: Oh.

WANDA: Really, I can sleep anywhere. I think I'm being evicted tomor- row anyway, so I'd prefer not to be there.

JIM: That's too bad.

WANDA: I roll with the punches. I enjoy the little things in life. I enjoy colors. I like textures, I like silk and cotton, I don't like corduroy, I don't like ridges...

JIM: *(On his way to find Marsha.)* Uh huh. Hold onto the thought. I'll be right back.

(Jim exits and goes to the bathroom area where he finds Marsha still crouched or leaning.)

JIM: Why are you hiding in the bathroom?

MARSHA: I needed aspirin. Then I just couldn't go downstairs again. When is she leaving?

JIM: I think she's staying overnight.

MARSHA: What?

JIM: I think she's staying ov...

MARSHA: Did she say that, or did you say that?

(Wanda, bored alone, bounds into the bathroom area with them. The area is small, and they're all crowded together.)

WANDA: What are you two talking about?

JIM: Oh, nothing. Marsha was just brushing her teeth.

WANDA: It's so intimate brushing your teeth, isn't it? When you live with someone, you don't have any secrets. I remember David said to me, why didn't you tell me you had herpes, and I said, I forgot, okay? People forget things, all right? And he said, not all right, I'm going to have this for life, and I said, so what, you have your nose for life, is that *my* fault?

MARSHA: *(Tired, but sort of annoyed by the logic.)* Yes, but his nose wasn't your fault, while…

WANDA: What?

MARSHA: Nothing. I see your point.

WANDA: So then I thought I'd stay out of relationships for a while, and I went to work for this lawyer, only he wasn't a regular lawyer, he was a king pin.

JIM: King pin?

WANDA: Of crime. He was a king pin of crime, only I didn't realize it. Eventually, of course, I had to get my face re-done so they couldn't find me. But, I better not say anything more about this right now.

MARSHA: *(Trying to tell her no.)* Jim says you were expecting to stay over night…

WANDA: Thank you, I'd love to! I feel I'm just starting to scratch the surface with old Jim-bo here. Jim-bo, do you remember that girl with the teeth who won Homecoming Queen, what was her name?

JIM: I don't remember. She had teeth?

WANDA: Big teeth.

MARSHA: I would like to leave the bathroom now.

WANDA: What?

MARSHA: Well, we need to make your room up for you. I didn't know you were… well, we need to make it up…

WANDA: *(A little girl.)* I hope there's a quilt. I love quilts.

MARSHA: I'll look for one.

(Wanda stares at her, happy, but doesn't get out of the way.)

MARSHA: You have to move or I can't get out of the bathroom.

WANDA: *(Serious.)* I'm holding you hostage.

MARSHA: What?

WANDA: *(Shifting, cheerful.)* Isn't it awful the way they take hostages now? *(Cheerfully leaves the bathroom, talking away.)* It reminds me of my life with Augie. He was really violent, but he was really little, so I was able to push him down the stairs.

(Jim and Marsha look at one another, a little alarmed by the "hostage" exchange.

Lights change. The prominent sound of a clock ticking. Time is passing.

Wanda, Jim and Marsha standing, in a "hallway" area, about to make their goodnights.)

WANDA: *(Happy.)* Oh, you guys, it's been a great evening. I can't believe we played games for 4 hours!

MARSHA: I'm really sorry I shouted at you during Monopoly.

WANDA: That's okay. I know somebody who got killed playing Monopoly.

JIM: But you were really good at charades.

WANDA: Thanks, but I'm sorry I broke the lamp.

MARSHA: It's perfectly all right. Now the guest room is right down this hall.

WANDA: Well, good night, you two. See you in the morning.

MARSHA: Good night.

(Wanda exits off to the guestroom.

Jim and Marsha go to their bedroom, or rearrange the set to stand in for a bedroom—move two chairs together into a "bed," put a comforter over themselves.

They're too tired to talk. They kiss one another briefly, and close their eyes to sleep.

Wanda enters, wrapped up in a quilt.)

WANDA: Oh, is this your bedroom? Oh, it's so pretty.

(Jim and Marsha open their eyes, very startled.)

MARSHA: Is something wrong with your room?

WANDA: No, it's lovely. Although not as nice as here. But then this is the master bedroom, isn't it?

MARSHA: Can I get you a pill?

WANDA: No, thanks. Marsha, I love this bedroom. I feel very "enveloped" here. It makes me never want to leave. *(Wanda pulls up a chair right next to their bed. Keeps wrapped in her quilt.)* I just love New England. I worked in Hartford for three weeks once as a receptionist in a sperm bank.

MARSHA: Wanda, I'm sorry. I really think I need to sleep.

WANDA: You can sleep, I won't be offended. So I got fired from the sperm bank, and then I went to Santa Fe, cause I heard the furniture was nice there.

(Clock ticks. Time passes. Jim and Marsha change positions in bed.)

WANDA: And then Arthur's ex-wife kept making threatening phone calls to me.

(Clock ticks. Jim and Marsha change positions, now look more uncomfortable.)

WANDA: *(Coquettish.)* And I said, "Billy, why didn't you tell me you were 16?"

(Clock ticks.)

WANDA: *(Chatty voice, just telling the facts.)* And then the policeman said, let me see your pussy, and I thought, hey, maybe this way I won't get a ticket.

(Clock ticks.)

WANDA: *(Teary voice, telling a tragic turning point.)* And Leonard said, Wanda, you are a worthless piece of trash. And I said, don't you think I know that? Do you think this is news?

(Clock ticks.)

WANDA: *(Energized, telling a fascinating story.)* And Howard said he wanted me to kill his mother, and I said, "Are you crazy? I've never even *met* your mother." And he said, "All right, I'll introduce you." *(Jim and Marsha have closed their eyes, either asleep or pretending to be. Wanda looks over at them, suspicious.)*

WANDA: Are you asleep? Jim? Marsha?

(Wanda looks to see if they're asleep. She shakes their shoulders a bit, to see if she can wake them.)

WANDA: Jim? Marsha? You're not pretending to be asleep, are you? Jim? Marsha?

(Wanda opens Marsha's eyelid with her finger.)

MARSHA: Yes?

WANDA: I was just checking if you were asleep.

MARSHA: Yes I am. Goodnight. Sleep well.

WANDA: Goodnight.

(Wanda takes her comforter and curls up at the bottom of their bed. Then she pulls their blanket off them, and on to her. Jim doesn't notice, he's asleep for real. Marsha is startled. But gives up, what to do. Lights dim.

Clock ticks.

Lights up for the morning. Wanda sound asleep. Jim and Marsha wake up, and abruptly leave the bedroom for the dining room area.)

MARSHA: You know, she doesn't snore. I'm really surprised.

JIM: Want some coffee?

MARSHA: I think I'd like some heroin.

JIM: Maybe Wanda has some connections.

MARSHA: I'm sure she does. Oh God, why did she sleep on our bed? She seemed like some insane nightmare Golden Retriever.

JIM: Now I feel sorry for her.

MARSHA: Well good for you. Was she always this way?

JIM: Well she was always vivacious.

MARSHA: I see. High school prom queen. Girl Most Likely to Get Herpes.

JIM: Lots of people get herpes.

MARSHA: Yes, but they don't talk about it for 3 hours.

JIM: Why are you so hostile to her? *(Not meaning to say this.)* Is it because she's attracted to me?

MARSHA: *(Not expecting to hear that.)* Yes. *(Marsha goes off to the kitchen.)*

JIM: Are you getting coffee?

(Marsha re-enters with two coffee mugs, one of which she kind of shoves at Jim.)

MARSHA: And are you attracted to her?

JIM: Now come on, Marsha, she's an emotional mess.

MARSHA: You're putting up with it very patiently. Why is that?

JIM: Well that's because... I feel sympathy for her. She's someone I knew once who had a life, and look what's happened to her.

MARSHA: She's attracted to you.

JIM: Now don't make a big thing out of it. It's just slightly interesting for me, that's all.

MARSHA: Well, fine. I understand. I think I'll make a trip to the nearest loony bin, and find some mental patient who finds *me* attractive. Then I'll bring him home and make you suffer through a 48-hour visit while he drools on the carpet.

JIM: Oh, come on, stop making such a big deal about all this. It's no big deal...it's just...well, haven't you ever found it kind of exciting if someone finds you attractive?

MARSHA: I've forgotten. *(Starts to leave.)* I'm going to the A & P. I have to get out of here. *(Marsha grabs a purse and exits.)*

JIM: Don't be mad.

(Jim sighs. With his coffee he walks after her, but Wanda, stirring on the bed, hears him.)

WANDA: Is that life out there?

JIM: You awake? *(Jim comes back into the bedroom area, holding his coffee mug.)*

WANDA: Do I smell coffee? Oh, thanks, Jimbo. *(Wanda takes Jim's coffee, thinking it's for her.)* Uh, I love this. You're like a little house slave. I knew I should've married you. Where's Marsha? Did she wake up dead or anything?

JIM: No, she went to the A & P.

WANDA: That's terrible of me to say. I don't want her dead. I'm just teasing cause I'm jealous of what she has.

JIM: Oh, I'm not so special.

WANDA: Oh, Jimbo, you are. *(Wanda starts to get up; then shows a grimace of pain. A bit flirtatious.)* Uh. I've slept wrong on my back, I think. You know, a tense muscle or something.

JIM: *(Thinking to himself, is this code?)* Oh. Your back is sore? Um, I'm not a professional masseur, but do you want me to rub it?

WANDA: Oh, would you?

(Wanda pretty much flops over in delight. Jim starts to massage her back, sort of in the center.)

WANDA: It's the lower back, Jimbo.

JIM: Oh. Okay. *(He starts to massage her lower back.)*

WANDA: Uh. Yes. Oh yes. Oh, yes. Ohhhhhhh. Uhhhhhhhh.

(Marsha comes back in the house, holding the purse and car keys. She stops and hears Wanda's moaning. She marches into the bedroom, finds Jim and Wanda in the midst of their orgasmic backrub.)

MARSHA: I'm back, if anybody cares.

JIM: *(Really jumps.)* Oh, Marsha. I didn't hear the car.

MARSHA: I don't blame you. It was very noisy here.

JIM: I'm...giving Wanda...that is, her back hurts.

WANDA: He gives the most wonderful back-rub.

MARSHA: I'm so pleased to hear it. Do you need the number of a back specialist, perhaps? I could call my doctor. If you can't walk, we can arrange for an ambulance to take you there.

JIM: Now, Marsha, please, it's really quite innocent.

WANDA: Hey, Marsha, really—I know he's your guy. *(To Jim.)* You're her guy, Jimbo. *(To Marsha.)* It's just my back hurt.

MARSHA: Yes, I follow what you say. Probably tension in the lower back. I have a tension headache in the back of my head today, it feels like it might split open. I think I'll go lie down. In the guest room that you never got to. *(Starts to leave.)* Jimbo, when you finish with her back, the car has a flat tire on the corner of Pleasantview and Maple. I thought you might do something about that.

JIM: Oh. I'll go now.

MARSHA: No, finish the back rub. You've convinced me it's innocent, so finish it.

(Marsha walks out. Jim and Wanda look at one another uncomfortably.)

WANDA: Well, she said to finish it.

JIM: I don't feel comfortable with her in the house.

WANDA: Look, she said it was fine, let's take her at her word.

(Jim looks dubious and touches her back lightly. At the merest touch, Wanda starts to moan loudly again.)

JIM: *(Stopping the back rub.)* Can't you be more quiet?

WANDA: It feels so good.

JIM: Look, that's enough. I'm gonna go deal with the flat tire.

WANDA: Can I come?

JIM: Why don't you...soak in the bathtub for your back?

WANDA: All right. Thank you for the back rub, Jimbo. *(Gets up; calls after where Marsha went.)* Marsha? Do you have any bubble bath?

(Marsha comes back.)

MARSHA: What?

WANDA: Do you have any bubble bath? Jim won't continue with the back rub, and I need to relax.

MARSHA: The back rub...I...what was the question?

JIM: Bubble bath. Do we have some?

MARSHA: Yes, I'm sure we do. Maybe Jim would like to pour it on you in the bathtub.

JIM: Marsha. Please.

WANDA: Oooh, kinky. *(Loudly.)* Hey! I have an idea! Why don't I cook dinner for you guys tonight? Do you like octopus?

MARSHA: Thank you, Wanda, no. I thought we'd go to a restaurant tonight. The walls in this house are starting to vibrate.

WANDA: They are?

MARSHA: Yes. So we'll go to a nice, soothing restaurant where they will take care of us. All right?

WANDA: Sure! Fine by me.

(Lights change. Maybe lovely classical music to change the mood. Jim, Marsha, Wanda sit at the table.

The Waiter comes out and puts a tasteful flower arrangement on the table, turning it into the restaurant.)

WANDA: This is such a pretty restaurant. The music is so classical.

WAITER: Enjoy your meal.

JIM: Thank you.

(Waiter exits. Wanda and Jim mime eating from their plates.)

WANDA: Ohhh, I think I know someone. *(Waves, calls out to imaginary table.)* Hi, there! Oh, no, I don't know them. *(Calls out again.)* Never mind! I thought you were my gynecologist.

MARSHA: You thought he'd be up here?

WANDA: Well, he travels a lot. He also sells encyclopedias.

(Waiter re-enters with a tray of wine glasses. He gives each person a wine glass, Wanda last.)

WAITER: And here is your wine.

WANDA: They didn't have Kool-aid?

WAITER: White Zinfandel was the closest we could get, Madam.

WANDA: Well, all right. *(To Marsha and Jim.)* Here's mud in your eye.

(Everyone drinks. All of them finish their drinks in several quick gulps. The Waiter starts to leave.)

JIM: Waiter! *(Makes signal to Waiter of "another round.")*

(The Waiter nods and exits.)

WANDA: I can't believe they didn't have octopus. It's a delicacy.

JIM: *(Referring to their plates.)* Well, the trout's pretty good.

WANDA: Yeah, but they put nuts on it or something.

JIM: Well, eat around them maybe.

WANDA: You know, Jim, tomorrow we should get out the old yearbook. You know, Marsha, you wouldn't believe how dashing he was back then. *(To Jim.)* Not that you're not now, of course.

JIM: You're sure a shot for my ego.

MARSHA: I'd like to shoot your ego.

JIM: What?

MARSHA: Nothing. Go back to talking about high school. I'll try to achieve a Zen state. *(Closes her eyes, puts her arms loose by her side, tries to relax her body.)*

JIM: I... I wonder where the waiter is with the drinks.

MARSHA: *(With eyes closed; chant-like.)* I am sitting by a tree, and there's a lovely breeze.

WANDA: This restaurant is so adorable. This whole town. You know what I'm thinking? I'm thinking of maybe moving up here to the country with you all, finding a little house to rent. Nothing's happening in my life right now, this might be just the change I might need.
(The Waiter arrives with three more glasses of wine, which he passes out to them. Marsha's eyes are open again; Wanda's comments above pretty much blew her attempt at a Zen state.)

WANDA: I'm almost through with my facial surgery. I've had everything done on my face except my nose. I kept that the same.

JIM: You're right. I recognize your nose now. Yes.

WAITER: Will there be anything else?

WANDA: What? Done to my face?

WAITER: Anything else I can do for you at the restaurant?

JIM: We wanted three more glasses of wine.

WAITER: I just brought them.

JIM: Oh. So you did. Well, thank you.
(The Waiter leaves. Wanda starts to eat her fish.)

MARSHA: So you're going to move up here, are you? Going to sweep up and stick your feet in the ground and root yourself in our "little neck of the woods," are you?

JIM: Marsha, we don't own this area.

MARSHA: I feel differently. *(To Wanda.)* I don't want you moving here, is that clear? I don't want you invading my life with your endless ravings anymore, is that clear?
(The Waiter returns. Wanda keeps eating, seemingly just listening to what's being said, finding it interesting rather than upsetting.)

WAITER: Is everything all right?

MARSHA: No, everything is not all right, this woman is trying to invade my life, and this man is too stupid to see it, and hide from her. *(To Jim.)* Don't you realize she's insane?

JIM: Marsha, could we just finish dinner please?

MARSHA: No, I'd like the check.

WAITER: Are you unhappy with your fish?

MARSHA: I'm very unhappy with it. It has too many bones in it.
(Almost on cue, Wanda starts choking on a bone. She gasps and chokes. Jim, Marsha and the Waiter look at her shocked for a moment.)

JIM: Shouldn't one of us do the Heimlich maneuver?

MARSHA: I don't want to do it, I don't like her.

(Wanda looks startled, even in the midst of her choking. She keeps choking and pointing to her throat.)

JIM: Marsha! *(To Waiter.)* Can you do it?

WAITER: I don't know how to do it yet. It's my first day. Can't you do it?

JIM: Oh, very well.

(Jim gets up and gets the choking Wanda to stand. He stands behind her and then, not sure what to do, puts his arms under her arms, and locks his hands behind her neck: That is, he puts her in a half nelson, and keeps jerking her head forward with his hands, hopefully, as if this should fix her choking.)

MARSHA: *(After a second.)* Oh, for God's sake.

(Marsha gets up, pushes Jim away. She stands behind Wanda, puts her arms around Wanda's lower stomach and then rather violently and suddenly pulls her arms into Wanda's lower stomach. This does the trick, and Wanda spits out the bit of fish and bone, and starts to breathe again.

Wanda sits back down, exhausted.)

WANDA: Oh, thank God, I thought I was a goner.

(Suddenly into the restaurant burst Two Men with handkerchiefs tied around their mouths, and carrying guns. They aim their guns at everyone, but make straight for Wanda.)

MAN: There she is!

WANDA: Oh my God, they've found me!

(The Men grab her and, pointing the guns at everyone else, drag Wanda out of the restaurant.)

WANDA: *(Being dragged or carried out.)* Oh, God, it's the kingpin. Help me! Jim! Jim!

(All this happens very fast and very suddenly. And now Wanda is gone. Jim, Marsha and the Waiter seem stunned for a moment.

A "talking-to-the-audience" light comes up, and the Waiter crosses down into it and addresses the audience:)

WAITER: The next day at the restaurant was considerably less intense, and eventually as time went on, I was made head waiter. For a while I liked the added responsibility and the additional money, but after a while, I realized I wasn't doing what I wanted to do with my life. I wanted to be an actor. But then the story isn't really about me.

(Humbly, the Waiter exits.

Jim and Marsha look confused by the Waiter's behavior, and now address the audience themselves again.

They also straighten the set a bit, while they talk, so that it resembles their house as it was at the beginning of the play.)

JIM: *(To audience.)* Well, all that happened a few weeks ago. Wanda hasn't been found yet, but she's probably fine.

MARSHA: I feel guilty about what happened. I wasn't a good hostess.

JIM: Now, honey, she's probably fine. Wanda's sort of like a bacteria—wherever she is, she seems to grow and go on and on just fine, so you shouldn't feel bad.

MARSHA: Yes, but right before Wanda started to choke on the fish bone, I had this momentary, stray thought of wishing she would choke on a fish bone. And then suddenly she did. I know it's not logical, but on some level, I feel I tried to kill her. And then thugs came and carried her away. I mean, in a way, it's just what I wanted.

JIM: Now, Marsha, you're not responsible for what happened.

MARSHA: I chose the restaurant.

JIM: Now, Marsha. You're not omnipotent. Besides, awful things are always happening to Wanda. She's like a magnet for trouble.

MARSHA: *(To the audience.)* Well, it was just the most awful two days. Three days, counting meeting with the police.

JIM: But some good came out of it.

MARSHA: Yes. We had a big argument, and that was good.

JIM: It cleared the air.

MARSHA: I said what I was feeling, and it was mostly negative, but it was good to say it.

JIM: It cleared the air.

MARSHA: And one of the things I said was that we don't feel joy enough. Or hardly at all.

JIM: Right. We don't feel joy much. So we joined an aerobics class…

MARSHA: To get the blood moving… When you move around, you tend to feel better…

JIM: And we're going to a marriage counselor who specializes in breaking down fear of intimacy in people who've known one another for over 10 years…

MARSHA: And, of course, we fit that. And all told, I guess Wanda's visit helped to stir us up in a good way, all told.

JIM: Right.

MARSHA: Blessings come in unexpected ways.

JIM: Right.

MARSHA: Now if only we were happy.

JIM: Right.

(They look at one another. Then they look out at the audience. Some friendly, possibly optimistic music plays. Lights dim on Jim and Marsha. End.)

TO THE ACTOR

This play is a real relationship piece and I'm proud of it. Sometimes it was a little hard for the audience to shift gears to get into it because it's in a very different style than the first four plays in *Durang Durang*, but once they did shift I felt they all identified with the familiar feelings about marriage and about long-term relationships. On the best nights I felt they were highly amused, and alarmed, by Wanda, and very much rooted for Marsha, the realist, who wanted this nut out of there.

"Nut" is a dangerous word, though. I think Wanda should be fun and have her charm—that's part of what Jim responds to (though primarily he's responding to her flirting with him; he's hungry for someone to think he's special at this point in his life).

But Wanda's very selfish and has literally no ability to wonder how anyone else is feeling. She finds her own story fascinating and assumes everyone else will too.

Wanda mentions her weight early on and there are references to food as well. In the TV version, Swoosie Kurtz, who is very thin, did all the same lines about feeling she looked heavy. They worked in that version as the diet-obsessed chatter of a thin woman. We all know some of those thin women who think they have a weight problem when they don't.

When we auditioned for stage, however, Walter and I decided that as long as we were doing a new version, we wanted to see what it was like with heavier actresses in the role. We ended up liking what happened when a somewhat overweight actress read for the part... somehow Wanda is so needy, that it sort of fit that she "feed" her anxiety with food.

In terms of casting, it's important though that it be believable that Wanda likes sex and has had a lot of it. Sometimes being overweight is a way of keeping oneself protected from sex (sorry to be an amateur psychologist) and sometimes it isn't, but it's important in terms of casting that Wanda be convincing in her flirtations and in her desires.

Because of the three-quarter thrust stage, it was kind of impossible to lug furniture on to change from scene to scene; so Walter and the designer Derek McLane chose to be really simple—three somewhat fancy dining room chairs and one round table. They arranged the chairs to stand in for everything: chairs in the living room and, most stylized, the bed in the bedroom (by bringing two chairs together, having the actors sit down and then throw a comforter over themselves).

I thought this was a good solution and the few set pieces also made for a "light" feeling, where the setting was secondary to the characters and their interactions.

If you had a wider stage and could have different playing areas with furniture already set up; or if you had ways of getting furniture on and off quickly—I think other solutions would be fine too. The one we had worked for MTC.

For the two henchman at the end (who work for the "kingpin"), we ended up using Keith and Patricia, but with both playing men. With pants, raincoats, fedoras and large machine guns, you never had a sense that it wasn't two men.

The henchmen should happen fast.

I think it's obvious from the script, but Jim and Marsha are both nice, intelligent people. Jim is feeling bored and restless, Marsha's feeling sort of ignored and left out. During their speeches at the beginning and the end, I think we should want things to work out for the two of them; they seem well suited, actually, and to care for one another. But I was pleased, in both the TV version and the stage version, that Marsha's and Jim's last two lines seemed very right and a little sad.

I praised the actors in the teleplay version, so I would like to salute the MTC cast as well: Lizbeth Mackay, Marcus Giamatti, and Becky Ann Baker as Wanda.

Business Lunch at the
Russian Tea Room

I wrote this playlet directly for *Durang Durang*. It's about a playwright, named Chris, having a meeting with a film development person for a possible screenwriting job.

It's not a deep piece and many writers have had their go at how Hollywood treats writers and thoughts and ideas—for instance, David Mamet's *Speed-The-Plow*, John Patrick Shanley's *Four Dogs And a Bone*, Arthur Kopit's *Road To Nirvana* (which started as a parody of the Mamet play and once had the loonier title of *Bone-The-Fish*). Christopher Guest's movie *The Big Picture* with Kevin Bacon as a young filmmaker getting jerked around on his first film was quite funny.

Writers have a history of hating to work with Hollywood. My favorite example is J.D. Salinger. He sold his short story "Uncle Wiggily in Connecticut" to the movies and they turned it into a soggy love story called *My Foolish Heart* (1949). He was so horrified that he vowed never to sell another thing to Hollywood, ever. And he never has. (He lives in seclusion in New Hampshire. And he only speaks three sentences a day, two of them to his dog. No, I made up that last sentence.)

I'm more willing for things to work out with Hollywood and me, but so far it's been disappointing. I wrote a screenplay with Wendy Wasserstein that wasn't made. I wrote many versions of *Sister Mary Ignatius Explains It All For You* for an independent producer, but funding could never be completed. I wrote a screenplay for Warner Bros. I'm very proud of, a Monty Python-esque comedy called *The Nun Who Shot Liberty Valance,* which I keep wishing someone would make. And the only script of mine that was filmed was a disaster: an unfunny, forced version of my play *Beyond Therapy,* which the director Robert Altman radically rewrote. I wish I had taken my name off of it, but I didn't. If ever you see it, I apologize.

My only happy writing experience, so far, in films was being hired to rewrite some of the scenes in the Michael J. Fox movie *Secret Of My Success.* I had a supporting role in that film and I was asked to rewrite certain scenes a day or so before they were scheduled to shoot. It sounded intimidating, but it ended up being fun. I like the scenes I wrote and think it's a good commercial movie directed by Herbert Ross, whom I enjoyed working with.

So I keep hoping I'll hook up with the right director, and the right project, and so on.

Many of my experiences (and those of my writer friends) have been writing for "development" people.

In this play, the character of Melissa Stearn is a "development person"— that is, her job is to "develop" projects and ideas into movies or TV movies or TV series.

I hope to work in movies and TV again (especially in New York, the non-earthquake capital of the world), so I want to admit and stress that I do not regard all development people with disdain.

But there have been some. "Ideas" for movies are so debatable. Many development people seem to have no background in writing, directing or acting...they seem to have studied Opinion in college and then they proclaim their opinions about "what works" and "what can't work" in a screenplay with total self-confidence.

They want everything in outline form. I'm afraid I don't think (or create) in outline form. Do you?

I see many a movie where I can recognize the outline, but it's not abetted by any good dialogue, any interesting character development, indeed any actual writing talent anywhere, just this damn outline that sounded good at the meeting.

From so many of these "outline" movies something vital is missing: The actual human desire to communicate is not there. What's replaced it is the desire to make money, and then, rather pathetically, to judge success by how expensive your car is, or your watch, or what restaurant you eat in. The Catholic schoolboy in me (and the writer) disapproves of this materialism. I like to earn money, but it's pretty far from my *sole* interest in life.

So maybe I should move to New Hampshire and talk to a dog. Salinger, by the way, was right about *My Foolish Heart,* it isn't very good. Most of it is a flashback to what might have happened *before* the short story begins. However, the first 10 minutes are rather close to the story, and Susan Hayward is quite good for that brief section in capturing the story's bitter, edgy take on an unhappy, alcoholic woman. And the theme song is quite pretty.

Maybe Melissa Stearn can convince Salinger to finally let *Catcher in the Rye* become a movie. In a few years Macauley Culken will be old enough. And I'd like to play Madame Arcati.

ORIGINAL PRODUCTION
Business Lunch At The Russian Tea Room was part of *Durang Durang* at Manhattan Theater Club. The cast was as follows:

Chris . . . . Keith Reddin
Margaret . . . . Patricia Elliott
Waiter . . . . Marcus Giamatti
Melissa Stearn . . . . Patricia Randell
Priest . . . . David Aaron Baker
Rabbi . . . . Lizbeth Mackay

(Note: At MTC we didn't list the Priest and Rabbi as characters; we didn't want the audience to expect to see them. So in production, I'd prefer you didn't list them as well. Also, at MTC, we cast an actress as the Rabbi because all three actors already had parts in the play. Since Keith Reddin had been playing children and women for much of the evening up until now, it seemed only fitting, and kind of fun, to have Lizbeth Mackay play the male rabbi. However, if you are using a larger company and want to cast a male as the rabbi, that is fine also.)

CHARACTERS
    CHRIS, a playwright
    MARGARET, his agent
    WAITER
    MELISSA STEARN, a Hollywood development person

BUSINESS LUNCH AT THE RUSSIAN TEA ROOM

Scene: Chris, a playwright, is going through a large basket of laundry, mostly white sweat socks. He is laboriously matching the socks, checking the tops of the socks to see if the stripes are blue or red or black, thin or thick, etc. The phone rings. On another part of the stage is Margaret, Chris' agent. She is holding a phone, calling him. She is any age over 45, worldly, smart, quick, a little inexact in her listening. Chris answers the phone, which is near his laundry. (It can be a cordless battery phone.)

CHRIS: Hello?

MARGARET: Hello, Chris, it's me. Are you awake yet?

CHRIS: Is this public television again? I *have* renewed my membership, and I don't care about the umbrella, so please stop calling.

MARGARET: Chris, this is your agent.

CHRIS: Oh, Margaret. Hi.

MARGARET: Are you writing on your play?

CHRIS: No. No, I'm doing laundry. I'm matching socks actually. Making sure I don't put a blue stripe with a black stripe, or a thin double red stripe with a thick single red stripe.

MARGARET: Well, that won't earn me my 10%, will it?

CHRIS: No. But I need socks in order to wear shoes.

MARGARET: Yes, yes, details. Um . . . I'm reminding you that you have a meeting at the Russian Tea Room with Melissa Stearn.

CHRIS: Oh, right, yes, I'd almost forgotten. Who is she again?

MARGARET: She's a new script development person at Zovarax.

CHRIS: Zovarax? Isn't that a medication for cold sores?

MARGARET: Oh, is it? Well, maybe it's Zylaphone. You know, one of those film production companies. She's apparently very hot in Hollywood right now. And she likes writers from the theatre. Apparently Lanford Wilson wrote something for her.

CHRIS: Oh well, that's good. Do you have any checks coming in for me?

MARGARET: Well, the royalty for your one act is coming in.

CHRIS: How much is it again?

MARGARET: $250.

CHRIS: Oh yes. That's not very much.

MARGARET: Now, darling, the play was only 10 minutes.

CHRIS: It was half an hour.

MARGARET: Well, it just flew by. Chrissy, dear, we know theatre pays less, that's why you should go meet with Melba Stringer, and make one of those development deals. Write a movie, write a TV show.

CHRIS: Melba Stringer?

MARGARET: Who's Melba Stringer?

CHRIS: You mean, Melissa Stearn.

MARGARET: Yes, Melissa Stearn. Call me later. *(Hangs up and exits.)*

(The sound of chatter and clinking silverware. The stage transforms itself into the Russian Tea Room. The Russian Tea Room has a lot of red in it. A booth appears; the booth is in the form of a half-circle, and the seating and back are made of red leather or naugahyde. A round table with a pink tablecloth on top of it fits into the booth. This may be achieved with stage hands dressed as waiters. But however it's done, it should be fast and a little overwhelming. Chris does not exit, but lets this activity swirl around him. He is still holding his laundry basket. He sits in the booth that's been brought out, and puts his laundry basket on the seat next to him. A Waiter, in a red tunic with a Russian feel to it, brings him a bowl of something.)

WAITER: Here's your borscht, sir.

CHRIS: I didn't order borscht. This isn't mine.

WAITER: *(A bit surly.)* You don't want it?

CHRIS: I didn't order it. I just got here.

WAITER: *(As if Chris had changed his mind.)* I'll take it back then. *(Exits.)*

(Enter Melissa Stearn. She's in her late 20s, early 30s. Very high energy,

very forceful. Dressed in a "power" dress. 100% sure of her opinions, and loves the movie business.)

MELISSA: Christopher! Melissa Stearn. I'm sorry, I'm late, I just flew in from L.A. and the limousine got stuck in traffic, but luckily I ran into Kim Basinger in the airport, and she rode in the car with me, so I had a movie star to talk to the whole way. I'm so pleased to meet you. I love your work. *Prelude to a Kiss* was my favorite play, it was my life story exactly.

CHRIS: It was your life story? You mean, on your wedding day your spirit left your body and entered the body of an old man?

MELISSA: Well, not literally, of course, but I just loved the play. It was my life story exactly. Although I've never been married, I like to have affairs with black men, and then just move on from one to another. Eventually I'll have a baby though, I think that's part of the point of being a woman, you should do every thing once.

CHRIS: Uh huh. You mean, ice hockey. Mass murder. Working in a library.

MELISSA: Exactly. Waiter!

(She's so certain of herself that the Waiter comes immediately.)

MELISSA: I'll have blinis and beluga, and tall ice tea, stirred with a stick not a spoon. And what will you have?

CHRIS: I'll have scrambled eggs.

MELISSA: You should have borscht. It's delicious here.

WAITER: He doesn't like borscht.

CHRIS: Thank you for remembering.

MELISSA: Bring it to him anyway.

(Waiter starts to exit.)

CHRIS: I'll have scrambled eggs please.

(Waiter exits; we don't know if he heard Chris or not.)

MELISSA: Christopher, all of us at Zerofax feel that we want to return to the old-fashioned kind of movie where the characters have dialogue and thoughts and emotions—you know like *Four Weddings and a Funeral,* we think that was great, you know, Hugh Grant and romance and people buying tickets. That's what it's about, and that's what makes Zerofax a different kind of movie company. We're interested in quality.

CHRIS: You know. I have to tell you, I didn't actually write *Prelude to a Kiss.* That was Craig Lucas.

MELISSA: Oh, that's right. Well, he wasn't available, so then we called you. My assistant Jane loves your work, she said, why don't you call Christopher, he's a very funny writer. And I thought that was a brilliant idea.

CHRIS: Thank you.

MELISSA: I love theatre writers. I produced "Sleaze-O-Rama" for television last year. Did you see it? It got great numbers. It was about a serial killer who became president but who found his humanity after he got AIDS and died. Everyone loved it. Lanford Wilson wrote the first script, which was beautiful, but we had to throw it out because none of the network people liked it, so we had Babaloo Feldman rewrite every single word. But Lanford understood. He thought we wanted something sensitive, but we didn't. I hope he brings the caviar soon, I have a meeting with Nora Ephron in 15 minutes. Nora Ephron is the kind of quality writer we want to work with. That's why I'm meeting with you as well.

CHRIS: Thank you.

MELISSA: We want Nora to write a movie for Meg Ryan where Meg is a widow who misses her husband dreadfully, they had this really special relationship, and then some man hears her talking on the radio, and he's really moved by what she says and he wants to contact her, but the switch is it's her husband who hears her on the radio, she's not a widow at all, he disappeared at sea just like Julia Roberts did in the movie watcha-ma-call-it, and then he shows up and he kills her. It's sort of like *Sleepless in Seattle* meets "Psycho." What was that Julia Roberts' movie called?

CHRIS: *Sleeping with the Enemy?*

MELISSA: Yes. *Sleeping with the Enemy in Seattle.* Something like that. Waiter! I need my food *now* please.

(Waiter has just started to enter with food.)

WAITER: Alright, alright, here's your fucking caviar. *(Gives her caviar, gives Chris borscht.)*

MELISSA: Oh, terrific. I love caviar. Not the taste exactly, but the sense of status it gives me. It's sort of like going to the bank and eating your money. Mmmmmm, delicious. Yummy.

CHRIS: *(To Waiter.)* I didn't order borscht. I don't like borscht. I want scrambled eggs. Truthfully I'd like a BLT, but I'm sure the Russian Tea Room doesn't have BLT's.

WAITER: Enjoy your meal. Fuck you. *(Exits.)*

CHRIS: Why is he being so rude?

MELISSA: Rudeness doesn't bother me. Stupidity does, but not rudeness. I love to stand in a long line, and then just walk to the front and cut in, and if someone doesn't like it, I just say: Fuck you! Oh, you ordered the borscht. Good for you. I thought you didn't like it. So do we have a deal? Do you want to write the movie?

CHRIS: What movie?

MELISSA: Oh I haven't told you the idea. I told you the Nora Ephron. *(Suddenly serious.)* Now that's meant for her. Don't steal it, we'll sue you. I'm involved in six lawsuits right now, one of them against my mother. I'm gonna make her beg. *(Back to energy, friendliness.)* Now here's the idea for you. Shall I tell you?

CHRIS: I guess so. I'm here.

MELISSA: Okay. Here goes. *(Carefully, so the excellence can be savored)* It's about a Catholic Priest and a Rabbi, who fall in love and then, O. Henry–style, each has a sex change without telling the other one.

CHRIS: Ah.

MELISSA: So do you want to do it?

CHRIS: Um…

MELISSA: You see, you're the perfect person because Janet tells me you know all about the Catholic Church, you wrote a play about it once, you went to Catholic school apparently for 100 years or something.

CHRIS: Yes, well, twelve years.

MELISSA: That's amazing. You must have incredible stories.

CHRIS: *(His energy seeping away.)* Uh huh.

MELISSA: And so this story is perfect for you.

CHRIS: *(Has trouble saying no.)* Well, I'm glad you thought of me, but…you know…

MELISSA: What? Don't you think it's brilliant?

CHRIS: Yes, but…I don't really know anything about Rabbis.

MELISSA: Well, we'll call up a Jew and get them to tell you. I had dinner once with Philip Roth, I'll call him at home. *(Takes out her mobile phone.)*

CHRIS: No, please, don't call him yet. I'm not sure if this idea is right for me.

MELISSA: It's a great idea. Conceptual, but with lots of feeling. I wonder if you can do feeling. Well, we'll get Bo Goldman to come in and put in some feeling. But we really think you'll understand the religious angle.

CHRIS: Uh huh.

MELISSA: Do you like the idea?

CHRIS: Uh, well, I can see why you want to do it.

MELISSA: This idea really pushes the envelope.

CHRIS: Yes it does.

MELISSA: So when can you start?

CHRIS: I'm not sure that I'm available actually. I'm trying to write a play, and I have some letters to answer. And I haven't finished sorting my laundry.

MELISSA: I think it's great you brought your laundry to the Russian Tea Room. Very individual. Janet said you were a real person. And I like that, because I'm a real person.

CHRIS: Funny. You don't seem like one.

MELISSA: That's just my LA cover. Underneath I'm a real person, with throbbing, shrieking needs and neuroses. If we work together, you'll get to see that side of me. My mother knows that side. She's gonna go bankrupt and then if she apologizes in public, maybe we'll keep her from going to jail.

CHRIS: Really. Now that sounds like an interesting story.

MELISSA: No, no, just mother-daughter stuff, you know, competition for the father, the mother's a bitch. It's been done. *Terms of Endearment, Postcards from the Edge.* It's not new, it's not fresh. Now this priest-Rabbi-sex-change-but-it's-touching, that's new.

CHRIS: Gee, I'm very flattered, but I don't think I actually want to do it. I can't explain why. Sometimes I make decisions intuitively.

MELISSA: I'm not sensitive. You don't like this idea? I have 22 more of them. Wanna hear?

CHRIS: Shouldn't you be getting to Nora Ephron?

MELISSA: I have a helicopter waiting to take me to the Upper West Side, so I have a couple more minutes still. Let me tell you my other ideas.

CHRIS: Alright.

MELISSA: Did you see the movie *Cruising?*

CHRIS: Yes.

MELISSA: S & M Murders. Al Pacino as a undercover cop posing as a homosexual in leather.

CHRIS: Yes, I remember it.

MELISSA: Re-do the whole movie, but with children.

CHRIS: What? You mean 10-year-olds in leather?

MELISSA: Exactly. Did you see *Bugsy Malone?* It would be like that, only sick. We could get Gus Van Sant.

CHRIS: Yes, I might write that one. Wouldn't we all go to prison?

MELISSA: Clinton likes Hollywood. We'd get Janet Reno to give us a special dispensation.

CHRIS: Uh huh. Well, I can't believe we'd be allowed to make that movie.

MELISSA: Push the envelope. Back in 1939 they couldn't say "Frankly my dear, I don't give a damn." Now we can say fuck and show decapitations. So life moves forward.

CHRIS: *(Calls.)* Check please.

MELISSA: No, no, I'll pick up the check, every word I say is tax deductible, 80%. Mmmm, this caviar is delicious. I don't want to gain weight though. Excuse me while I make myself throw up in the ladies room, and then I'll hop in that helicopter and go see Nora Ephron. I'll call your agent, you tell me which idea you want to write, the Priest-Rabbi thing or the kiddie *Cruising.* Either one is fine, we just want quality but accessibility, something everyone in the world can identify with. It's going to be great. Zerofax is really excited about working with you. It was great meeting you.

(Melissa puts out her hand; before Chris takes it, she puts her fingers down her throat and starts to gag.)

MELISSA: Which way is the ladies room, do you know? *(Puts fingers down throat some more; exits.)*

(At Melissa's exit, the restaurant transforms itself away again. Chris gets out of the booth and grabs back his laundry basket, as the booth disappears away. We are now back in Chris' apartment, where he had been folding laundry before. Phone rings again. It's Margaret.)

CHRIS: Hello?

MARGARET: Hello, Chrissy. This is Margaret. How did your meeting with Melissa Stearn go?

CHRIS: It went very well.

MARGARET: Do you want to write it?

CHRIS: I think I need to finish matching my socks, and then maybe take a bath. Then I need to take my brain out and let it soak overnight in Clorox or something, and then...maybe I should consider moving to Europe.

MARGARET: Oh you didn't like her. Well, just take a nap. She's not the only person in Hollywood.

CHRIS: Yes, but sometimes it feels like she is.

MARGARET: Now, now. Don't overreact. Sleep on it. Remove her personality from the equation, and maybe her idea is actually good. Trust me, open your mind, don't be so judgmental. Mull over the idea for the evening. Alright?

CHRIS: Alright.

(Margaret and Chris both hang up. Margaret exits. Chris stares and tries to think through Melissa's idea.)

CHRIS: A Priest. A Rabbi. They fall in love. It's funny, it's touching. Different cultures, they clash, they contrast. Easter versus Passover. Baptism versus briss. They meet cute, in an S&M bar with Al Pacino. No, that's the other idea. They meet at a communion breakfast. *(Church bells are heard. On a different part of the stage, enter a handsome young Priest.)*

PRIEST: *(Out, to imaginary person.)* Good morning, Mrs. McGillicutty. Thank you. I'm glad you liked the sermon.

CHRIS: He's young, he's handsome, he's celibate. Rabbi Teitelbaum comes into the church, looking confused.

(Enter the Rabbi, played by an actress. She is dressed as an orthodox rabbi, and has a beard and a black hat.)

RABBI: Oi, oi, vhere am I?

PRIEST: May I help you?

CHRIS: Their eyes meet. They consider dating. They go to discos. *(Suddenly disco music, flashing lights. The Priest and Rabbi start dancing together. From another part of the stage, Melissa appears...a voice in Chris' head.)*

MELISSA: No, no, no, not vulgar. We want sensitivity. Zerofax is big on sensitivity.

CHRIS: They don't go to a disco. They go for long walks in the autumn. They discover one another's humanity.

(Sweet music. The Priest and Rabbi hold hands, mime walking.)

RABBI: Vhat beautiful trees. I see God's face in the autumn leaves.

PRIEST: Yes, Rabbi, me, too.

RABBI: Oi, oi, but I feel so guilty.

PRIEST: Don't feel guilty. Oh, Moishe. Even though we have different beliefs, I see more and more that your immortal soul looks just like mine.

MELISSA: Yeah, but sexy. Sensitive, but sexy.

(The Priest and Rabbi stop walking, look at one another intently.)

PRIEST: You make me hot.

RABBI: You make me hot too.

PRIEST: I don't think I'm gay, and yet I long to touch your penis.

RABBI: Oi, oi, please, I'm a Rabbi.

PRIEST: It's a sin. But can love be a sin?

RABBI: I think it can.

MELISSA: Good. Good tension. Sex versus religious belief. Excellent. They're gay, they're not gay. Makes it easier to cast the actors. *Philadelphia* made money, but they didn't kiss enough. Have them kiss.

PRIEST: I feel so drawn to you, Moishe.

RABBI: Oh, Patrick, Patty boy, even though it's against the Torah, inside my heart I know I vant to schtupp you.

PRIEST: Oh, Moise. Oh yes, oh yes.

(The Priest and Rabbi keep looking intently at one another.)

MELISSA: We don't need them to say "schtupping", that's bad writing. Just have them kiss, and we'll cut to a close-up of their tongues.

(The Priest and Rabbi embrace and kiss intensely.)

CHRIS: Then, there's an earthquake, and God strikes them dead. It's a re-play of Sodom and Gomorrah, and He kills the Priest and the Rabbi... *(Aimed at Melissa.)* ...and everyone in the movie business in Los Angeles.

MELISSA: Good idea, but save it for the end. They haven't had their sex changes yet.

CHRIS: I don't want to write this.

(The Priest and Rabbi have been continuing to kiss, but at the above line, they stop and look at Chris.)

MELISSA: Keep kissing.

(The Priest and Rabbi go back to kissing.)

MELISSA: No, keep writing, you're doing well.

CHRIS: No, I won't write this. It's idiotic. You should write it yourself, you like the idea so much.

(The Priest and Rabbi stop kissing again when Chris says "I won't write this." They stare at Chris and Melissa.)

MELISSA: Good idea! I'll write it myself. I'll get help from Nora and Bo and Babaloo. I'll pay myself $300,000. It'll be great! *(She exits, happy.)*

CHRIS: *(To himself.)* So I don't make the money. So what. I'm going to focus on what's simple and true. I'm going to fold my laundry.

(With dignity and importance, he starts to match his socks. The Priest and the Rabbi come over to Chris.)

PRIEST: May we help?

CHRIS: Please.

(The Priest and Rabbi help match the socks, and perhaps fold T-shirts.)

CHRIS: Red stripe with red stripe. Double blue stripe with double blue stripe. Light blue stripe with light blue stripe. Green sock with green sock.

(Chris, Rabbi and Priest keep trying to match the socks. For some reason it is very hard to make a match. The Rabbi in particular keeps holding up one sock with another, and discovering that it is not a match. They are not upset or frustrated doing this. It's just the task they've committed to do. Happy, contented music plays. Lights fade on Chris, the Rabbi and the Priest, matching the socks in the laundry basket. End.)

TO THE ACTOR

Chris should be polite and also have trouble saying no. He finds it embarrassing to say something is a bad idea, so he says things like "ah" and "I can see why you want to do it."

Margaret's part is small, but she's crisp, lively, she knows her client well and cares about him; she's just a trifle scattered and gets names wrong.

Melissa is very sure of herself, she loves her job, she loves her opinions, she's very much "in the business" and loves throwing around the names of Meg Ryan and Nora Ephron.

When she has her long speeches, usually telling a movie idea, she is always energetic, she enjoys telling the idea, she thinks they're always great. On a line like "He disappeared just like Julia Roberts did in that movie watchamacallit," don't slow down and get lost in thought, trying to think what it was, or feeling momentarily uncertain. She's a happy, fast-talking executive, and she breezes by "watchamacallit," it doesn't stop her. She assumes you know the one she means and titles are only details anyway, she doesn't get bogged down in mere details.

When Chris says to Melissa, "Funny, but you don't sound like a real person," Walter Bobbie directed Patricia Randell to just accept the comment without taking any offense; somehow she is beyond being insulted. I thought that was very right.

The Priest and Rabbi; The Ending

In the earliest draft of this there was no final scene with the Rabbi and the Priest showing up; Chris just folded socks on his own and he didn't have a fantasy about what he'd write. We were going to originally end with *Wanda's Visit,* but that ending seemed too thoughtful a tone to send the audience home on. So then we decided that *Business Lunch* in its lightness and punchiness seemed the proper way to conclude the evening. But I needed to end it more satisfactorily than I had. So then I came up with the Rabbi-Priest variation on the ending.

When the Priest and the Rabbi break into disco dancing, I was in seventh heaven; most of the audience was too. It was truly loony.

A couple of things about this section. Please don't make the priest talk in an Irish accent. That is a cliché that is way past being funny. I know I have him talking to "Mrs. McGillicutty;" that's because most of the Catholics I grew up around in my youth in the late 50s were Irish; *none* of them, though, spoke in an Irish accent.

To me the real joke of the priest is how "Hollywood" he is: He's handsome, he's well-spoken, he's charming, he's all a leading man character should be. Then when the Rabbi comes out, dressed so otherworldly and never ever presented in a sexual way, it's partially that juxtaposition that's funny; he's not in any way a Hollywood fantasy.

I initially planned to have the Rabbi be played by a man; it is, after all a gay affair between the priest and the rabbi that Melissa wants written.

However, we only had three actors at our disposal and all three had parts already. We could have brought Marcus back, who had played the Waiter, but somehow it seemed wrong in the world of this play to have any actors double in parts. You didn't want the audience to have a moment of looking at the Rabbi and going: Oh, right, he was the waiter a minute ago.

So we cast Lizbeth Mackay in the part, who was the Southern mother in *Belle*, poor white trash Meg in *Stye*, and straitlaced Marsha in *Wanda's Visit*. And now the Rabbi. Talk about stretching yourself in an evening!

There was something fun about including the role of the rabbi in the transgender casting that had happened throughout the evening, especially in *Stye* where Beth is meant to be played by a young man. So if you want to also cast a woman as a rabbi, that's fine. Just be sure to give her a beard and a big black hat.

Casting a woman, though, did lower the emotional "shock" about the gay romance. So if you do the evening with more than three men and want to consider a man as the Rabbi, that's how I originally envisioned it.

The ending, about folding the laundry: I don't want it to be a "down" ending. It's a strangely happy ending. In Chris' world he may have lost a good-paying job—that he felt mixed about anyway—but now he doesn't have to listen to Melissa's opinions anymore; he's going to do, as he says, "What's simple and true. I'm going to fold my laundry."

At this moment in time folding the laundry represents something good, valuable, and worth doing in his universe. When the two characters break the convention of being in his head and offer to help, he's pleased to get their help.

I thought the ending was going to just be the somewhat sweet image of the three of them matching the socks together. But in tech rehearsal it became clear that for whatever reason actually making a match with a sock was hard. So the ending shifted to the rather funny sight of these three people—Chris, Priest, and Rabbi—dutifully going through socks, holding them up together, not finding a match, and then going on to look for the next pair.

So I recommend playing that they're having trouble making a match (and thus there have to be lots of socks to make this believable). Don't then "color" this difficulty of matching with too much upset or frustration. Just a little… they continue on with their resolve to do this "simple and true" thing. It's just that we see that their task is a little harder than we at first thought.

Finally, I think the music you choose to fade out on at the end is important.

Walter came up with Irving Berlin's "It's a Lovely Day Today," which was perfect. It was upbeat but not frenetic, the lyric was quickly and easily understood; it also left the audience in a good mood (as did the last few beats of the play itself).

Other choices are possible, but whatever you choose, the ending should be pleasantly upbeat, contented.

(Note: There are additional production notes on the six plays in *Durang Durang* in the Dramatists Play Services acting edition of those plays, including some comments on sets, scene changes between the plays, and some cut suggestions. If you're going to produce these plays, I hope you'll consider looking at the expanded notes in that edition.)

The Book of Leviticus Show

AUTHOR'S NOTE

Public access TV shows came about in the mid 70s, I think; I find them fascinating, these homemade shows, where average (or non-average) citizens can rent their own time on TV and put forth whatever they want. In New York City they tend to be quite strange, but they exist around the country as well. I tend to check them out with real regularity.

And the Book of Leviticus is a part of the Old Testament in the Bible. I'd never read it or barely heard of it until Anita Bryant quoted it in her antihomosexual rights campaign in Florida in the late 70s. Then I took it out and read it.

So this play is about these two things: public access TV and this particular book of the Bible.

I created a character named Lettie Lu, who starts her own public access TV show and who finds comfort in the Bible. I've had two actresses play her—my classmate friend from Yale, Kate McGregor-Stewart, who did it years ago on film for a prospective TV project, and Becky Ann Baker, who performed it recently on video to be used as part of *Durang Durang*. The TV project never happened; with regret, we cut the Leviticus video because *Durang Durang* was too long. But both Kate and Becky were brilliant in their acting of Lettie Lu, and I hope something further with this piece happens.

I wrote it originally for camera, and meant for it to be filmed in that homemade public access kind of way, with weird zooms and no cuts, and so on. For *Durang Durang* I rewrote it so it could be done on stage, though the director decided to shoot it for camera anyway, feeling it would be an interesting addition to a theatre evening. Either way I think it works.

And so now, Lettie Lu.

The Book Of Leviticus was filmed for *Durang Durang* and had the following cast:

Lettie Lu	Becky Ann Baker
Tommy	Marcus Giamatti (off-camera)
Grandma	Patricia Elliott
Maggie Wilkinson	Lizbeth Mackay
Maggie's daughter	Keith Reddin
Two Guests	David Aaron Baker
	Patricia Randell

(Note: Lettie Lu mentions motel owner Maggie Wilkinson and her daughter in her dialogue and Walter Bobbie added the silent presences of motel owner Maggie Wilkinson and her daughter, standing in the doorway, watching Lettie Lu film her public access TV show.

Because the camera controls what you see when, the viewer only saw Maggie and her daughter briefly twice, once when Lettie first mentioned them and once at the end when the camera was moving around. It was a fun addition to a filmed version, but should not be done onstage where their ongoing presence would likely be distracting.)

CHARACTERS
LETTIE LU
TOMMY, her husband and camera man
GRANDMA, Lettie Lu's mother
TWO GUESTS ON HER SHOW, a man and a woman

THE BOOK OF LEVITICUS SHOW

VOICE: You are watching the Wheeling, West Virginia Community Public Access Station, Channel 61. The West Virginia Community Public Access Station is in no way responsible for the content of any program on this channel. The views expressed belong to the public access individual producers. By law we must broadcast whatever people want to say. If we could shut down this entire public access station, we would be glad to. But by law we can't. So stay turned for our next public access program, on Channel 61. We think it is a premiere episode.

(A somewhat rundown motel room in West Virginia. A bed with an elderly Grandma asleep on it. An empty bird cage. Suitcases around, opened, not quite unpacked. A standing screen, with clothes flung up over the top. A chair. Near the chair is Lettie Lu, about 35, in a print dress, wandering around. She has a fair amount of energy. Her husband Tommy has a video camera, which he has trained on her.)

LETTIE LU: Are we on the air?

(Lettie Lu realizes that she is on the air, and talks out toward Tommy's camera. Sometimes she sits in her chair, sometimes she bounds up out of it, down to the edge of the stage, to be closer to the camera.)

LETTIE LU: Hello there. Can you hear me? If you can't hear me, call 556-7421, and ask for Lettie Lu in Room 12, and then I'll talk up. This here is our first show, and so I don't know if I need to shout.

TOMMY: *(From behind the camera.)* You don't have to shout, Lettie.

LETTIE LU: That's my husband, Tommy. He's the cameraman. And this is Momma. Show Momma, Tommy. Momma is eighty-three years old and she brought me up all her life in West Virginia and she's a good woman. Bring the camera back to me, Tommy, people must be tired of looking at Momma. *(Smiles at camera.)* Hi again. I'm Lettie Lu and this is the first *Book of Leviticus Show* installment. *(Lettie Lu holds up a cardboard sign with the hand-printed words, "Book of Leviticus Show.")*

Now I was minding my business back in Tommy's and my house in West Virginia. The children had growed up, one of them is a country Western star, one of them is a teller in a bank. Jimmy, he hasn't found himself yet, he don't do nothing. But we were havin' our quiet life when God set our house on fire. Well it wasn't God really, it was Momma; leastwise, we think it was Momma, she denies it, but who else was up cookin' at two in the morning, not me or Tommy, we wuz asleep.

But our house burned to the ground, all of it; and we wuz real bitter. We slept in the truck for a couple of nights, but then I said to Tommy, "What are we complainin' about, we got our lives. God gave us our lives, and we have got to be grateful."

And then we took the Bible out of the glove compartment, and I said, "Tommy, this is God's word, and it will comfort us." *(She picks up the Bible and shows us.)* You know, you can open up the Bible to any old page and it will have a message for you. *(Chooses a section at random.)* Like here, in the Book of Numbers: *(She reads:)* "And the names of the men are these: of the tribes of Judah, Caleb the son of Jephunneh. And of the tribe of the children of Simeon, Shemeul, the son of Annihud. And the prince of the tribe of the children of Dan, Buddi the son of Jogli." Well, this here don't mean a thing to us, but then we read that lovely passage about the Lord is thy shepherd and the green pastures, didn't we, Tommy?

TOMMY: Yes, we sure did, Lettie.

LETTIE LU: And we had some money in the bank, so we thought we'd just come on over to this motel, where the owner is a good Christian woman and her daughter with the harelip, but really it doesn't look bad if you don't look at it. And then Tommy said, "Lettie, read another passage from the Bible."

And then I turned to the Book of Leviticus.

(Reads with great importance:) "And the man that committeth adultery with another man's wife, even he that committeth adultery with his neighbor's wife, the adulterer and the adulteress shall surely be put to death." *(Bounces out of her chair to explain this.)* Well, that made a lot of sense to us because in all our years of marriage, and I

married Tommy when I was fourteen or something just like Loretta Lynn did 'ceptin' I don't sing none; well, in all that time, Tommy and I has never been unfaithful to one another because we believe in God and religion and marriage. And I got to thinkin' about how people say they believe in the Bible but they don't follow through and do nothin' about it.

TOMMY: Sit back down and read them the other part, Lettie.

(Lettie Lu sits back down.)

LETTIE LU: Oh yeah. This is from the same page as the thing about adultery. *(Reads from the Bible again:)* "And if a man also lie with mankind, as he lieth with a woman, both of them have committed an abomination, they shall surely be put to death." *(Slams the Bible shut, bounces up again.)* Well, we checked with the minister about the wordin' just to make sure we understood, but what we thought was true *was* true: This is about homos! And notice that God says *surely* someone will put them to death. I mean, God thinks it's so much what the right thing to do, that he just *presumes* somebody's gonna do it for him!

But we've gotten mighty far from followin' God's commands.

TOMMY: Sit back down and get to the point, Lettie.

LETTIE LU: You're right, Tommy. So what we done is, we went to Sally Bowden's house, and she's got herself two strappin' big sons, Big Jake and Big Harry, and we went into town and Big Jake and Big Harry went out and they captured an adulteress and a homo for us, and they tied 'em up and brung 'em here. I mean, they're here right now.

(Lettie Lu goes and moves the screen. Behind it, tied up on the floor and with gags in their mouths, are a Woman and a Man. They struggle slightly; they've probably been there a while.)

LETTIE LU: See? I kept 'em behind the screen to add to the suspense. I hope you like our show. It's our first episode.

TOMMY: Get back to the point, Lettie.

LETTIE LU: Oh right. And so now we're going to follow the teachings of God in the Book of Leviticus. Wake up, Momma.

(Lettie Lu goes over to Grandma, tries to wake her, but she seems to be sleeping deeply.)

LETTIE LU: *(To Grandma.)* We're gonna do the first ones. Momma. God, I hope she's not dead. Oh, there she goes. You havin' a dream, Momma?

GRANDMA: Where's my teeth?

LETTIE LU: Well, did you go to sleep with them in your mouth, or did you take them out first?

GRANDMA: I don't know where they are.

LETTIE LU: We know that, Momma. That wasn't the question. Now we are on television, and nobody out there wants to hear about your teeth.

GRANDMA: I had a dream about pancakes.

LETTIE LU: Pancakes? Oh dry up, Momma, you're irritatin' everybody. *(Gets a gun from somewhere easy.)* Old age is a terrible thing. Okay, you ready, Tommy?

(Lettie Lu gets in a position, aims at the two people on the floor. Aims well, but maybe looks the other way; she's not bloodthirsty, just doing her best to follow the Bible.)

LETTIE LU: Pay attention now, Momma, we're gonna kill 'em. In the name of God's will, you shall *surely* be put to death.

(Lettie Lu fires the gun twice. One or both of the bodies twitch violently; because they're tied together, it's hard to tell if one or both has been hit.)

LETTIE LU: Did I get 'em, Tommy?

TOMMY: Looks like it. Wrap it up now, Lettie, we're outta time.

GRANDMA: Do we know these people?

LETTIE LU: *(Annoyed to explain it again.)* We met 'em in town, Momma, Jake and Harry tied 'em up, and I read in the Bible that God wanted somebody to kill 'em.

GRANDMA: *(Understanding.)* Oh.

LETTIE LU: Well, I'm gonna sign off now. Read your bible, follow everything it says. And next week, we're gonna do the part from the Book of Leviticus about how to sacrifice turtle doves to please God.

GRANDMA: Where we gonna get a turtle dove?

LETTIE LU: You're really awake now, aren't you, Momma? I don't know. Maybe Woolworths'll have one of those 98 cents parakeets and then I'll kill that.

GRANDMA: Kill the parakeet?

LETTIE LU: That's what it says in the Bible. God, you can't follow anything, it's amazing I grew up to be as smart as I am. Good-bye, all! God bless you! Tune in next week for more readings from the Book of Leviticus Show!

(Lettie Lu waves at the camera. So does Grandma, though she looks back at the dead bodies a bit too. Music. Lights down. End.)

Naomi in the Living Room

AUTHOR'S NOTE

In 1988 I saw a funny play by Charles Mee at the Home for Contemporary Theater on Walker Street in Soho; and at intermission the artistic directors of the theater asked me to write a short play for their ongoing "home" series. For each evening in this series, they chose a room in the "home," and then asked authors to write plays taking place in that room. And so far they'd already had an evening of plays set in the bedroom, and in the kitchen, and now they were up to the living room. I said yes.

When I thought about what to write, my mind went to actress Sherry Anderson, whom I had just seen in a play reading where she acted Phyllis Diller in a nightmare. She didn't do an imitation; because it was a nightmare scene, she played the part as this really odd character with a pink wig and turquoise blue dress, who had a crazy glint in her eye and some sort of inner logic that you could tell she followed, even if you didn't.

I felt the character Sherry came up with had nothing really to do with Phyllis Diller, but was a creation of her own. And I felt this desire to write something for her to play this irrational character.

And since this was to be part of the "living room" series, in my mind I heard this clunky first line of "And this is the living room." And then the character going on to explain each additional room of the house.

I knew Sherry through my good friend, actor-writer John Augustine—they grew up in Canton, Ohio together—and so I wrote a part for John, and for our friend Elizabeth Alley as well.

And the atmosphere at *Home* was so pleasingly loose that they didn't want to have casting approval or anything, they just wanted me to show up the day before tech with a rehearsed cast, ready to use the single set all the "living room" shows did.

We were the final play of the evening, after plays by Eve Ensler, John PiRoman and Barry Kaplan. And the play went over great with this downtown audience; all three actors were terrific, and Sherry in particular was outstanding as this really odd woman.

In describing her take on the character, I think of the Monty Python actors playing women—it had that kind of exaggeration, yet she also had this believable look in her eye that truly crazy people do—everything she said and thought made perfect sense to her. And she was a force of nature. When she offered a seat, but then suddenly screamed that no, she wanted to sit there and charged at them like a suddenly furious rhino—I found her hilarious.

The play was a "hit" at *Home;* and when they had an evening of the best of the *Home* series, we redid the play again. (Also on this "best of..." bill was a play by John Augustine, *Scab Writes A Song,* where Sherry played yet another crazy mother—though this time in another room of the house, the dining room. Crazy mothers may be found anywhere.)

It was great fun doing this play at *Home.* Later we did it again at Ensemble Studio Theater where it worked some of the time, getting good laughs, but then other times sat there like a big mess, with a mostly silent, baffled audience. It was very disorienting. Different theater, different aura, different order (we were first, and maybe the play is too weird to be first; it's better as a nutty dessert).

So we prefer to remember the two times we did the play at *Home.*

ORIGINAL PRODUCTION

Naomi in the Living Room was first presented by Home for Contemporary Theater in New York City in December 1988, on a bill of plays set in the living room by Eve Ensler, John PiRoman and Barry Kaplan. It was directed by the author. The productions all shared the same set, designed by Geoff MacStutis. Artistic directors, Randy Rollison and Denise Lancot. The cast was as follows:

Naomi . . . . Sherry Anderson
John . . . . John Augustine
Johnna. . . . . Elizabeth Alley

It was subsequently performed again at Home in 1989; then again at Ensemble Studio Theater as part of their one-act marathon 1990. The cast was always the same, though Ms. Alley was unable to play her part at E.S.T., so Ilene Kristen played Johnna in that production.

CHARACTERS
NAOMI
JOHN
JOHNNA

NAOMI IN THE LIVING ROOM

Scene: A living room. Enter Naomi, followed by John and Johnna, an attractive young couple. John has a mustache and is dressed in a suit and tie. Johnna is wearing a dress with a string of pearls. Naomi, though, looks odd. Naomi plants herself somewhere definitive—by the mantelpiece, for instance—and gestures out toward the room.

NAOMI: And this is the living room. And you've seen the dining room, and the bedroom, and the bathroom.

JOHN: Yes, I know. I used to live here.

NAOMI: The dining room is where we dine. The bedroom is where we go to bed. The bathroom is where we take a bath. The kitchen is where we…cook. That doesn't sound right. The kitchen is where we…collect kitsch. Hummel figurines, Statute of Liberty salt and pepper shakers, underpants that say Home of the Whopper, and so on. Kitsch. The kitchen is where we look at kitsch. The laundry room is where we do laundry. And the living room is where Hubert and I do all of our living. Our major living. So that's the living room.

JOHNNA: What do you use the cellar for?

NAOMI: *(Suspicious.)* What?

JOHNNA: What do you use the cellar for?

NAOMI: We use the cellar to…we go to the cellar to…replenish our cells. We got to the attic to…practice our tics, our facial tics. *(Her face contorts variously.)* And we go to the car port, to port the car. Whew! Please don't ask me any more questions, I'm afraid I may not have the strength to find the answers. *(Laughs uproariously.)* Please, sit down, don't let my manner make you uncomfortable. Sit on one of the sitting devices, we use them for sitting in the living room.

(There is a couch and one chair to choose from. John and Johnna go to sit on the couch.)

NAOMI: *(Screams at them:)* DON'T SIT THERE, I WANT TO SIT THERE!!

(John and Johnna look frightened. Naomi charges over to the couch, and John and Johnna almost have to run to avoid being sat on by her.)

NAOMI: Shits! Ingrates! It's my house, it's my living room. I didn't ask you, I can ask you to leave.

(John and Johnna start to maybe edge out of the room.)

NAOMI: No, no, sit down. Please, make yourselves at home, this is the living room, it's where Rupert and I do all our living.

(There's only one chair, so with some hesitation Johnna sits in the chair, and John stands behind her.)

NAOMI: *(Stretching her arms out on the couch.)* Wow. Boy oh boy. I need a big couch to sit on because I'M A BIG PERSONALITY!!!! *(Laughs uproariously.)* Tell me, are you two ever going to speak, or do I just have to go on and on by myself, or *WHAT!!!!!!*

(Naomi stares at John and Johnna intensely. They hesitate but then speak.)

JOHNNA: This is a very comfortable chair. I love it.

JOHN: Yes, thank you.

NAOMI: Go on.

JOHNNA: Ummmm, this morning I washed my hair, and then I dried it. And we had coffee in the kitchen, didn't we, John?

JOHN: Yes, Johnna, we did.

JOHNNA: *(Pause, doesn't know what else to say.)* And I love sitting in this chair.

NAOMI: I think I want to sit in it, get up, get up.

(Naomi charges over, and John and Johnna move away from it, standing uncomfortably. Naomi sits and moves around in the chair, luxuriating in it.)

NAOMI: Hmmmm, yes. Chair, chair. Chair in the living room. Hmmm, yes. *(Looks at John and Johnna, shouts at them:)* Well, go sit down on the fucking couch, you morons!

(John and Johnna look startled, and sit on the couch.)

NAOMI: *(Screams offstage.)* Leonard! Oh, Leonard! Come on in here in the living room and have some conversation with us. You don't want me to soak up everything our son says all by myself, do you?

(Naomi stands and walks over to John and Johnna on the couch. She smiles at Johnna.)

NAOMI: You probably didn't know John was Herbert's and my son, did you?

JOHNNA: Yes, he told me. I've met you before, you know.

NAOMI: Shut up! *(Calls out.)* Hubert! Rupert! Leonard! *(To them.)* I hope he's not dead. I wouldn't know what room to put him in. We don't have a dead room. *(Smiles; screams.)* AAAAAAAAAAAAAAAAAAA-HHHHHHHHH! *(Looks at them.)* Goodness, my moods switch quickly. *(Naomi sees a tiny stuffed pig in a Santa Claus suit perched on the mantelpiece. With momentary interest, she picks it up and looks at it, then puts it down again.)*

NAOMI: *(Focusing on John and Johnna again; a good hostess.)* Tell me all about yourselves, do you have children? *(Sits, listens attentively.)*

JOHNNA: We had five children but they all died in a car accident. The babysitter was taking them for a ride, and she was drunk. We were very upset.

NAOMI: Uh huh. Do you like sitting on the couch?

JOHN: Mother, Johnna was telling you something sad.

NAOMI: Was she? I'm sorry, Johnna, tell it to me again.

JOHNNA: We had five children...

NAOMI: *(Tries to concentrate, but something impinges on her consciousness.)* Wait a minute, something's bothering me!!!! *(She rushes over to the little stuffed Santa pig, snatches it up and throws it against the wall in a fury.)* This belongs in the kitchen, *not* the living room. The living room is for living, it is not meant for sincerely designed but ludi-crously corny artifacts! Kitsch! *(She sits down again.)* Do you like Hummel figurines?

JOHN: Very much. Now that the children are dead, Johnna and I have begun to collect Hummel figurines, especially little boy shepherds and little girl shepherdesses.

NAOMI: Uh, huh, isn't that interesting? Excuse me if I fall asleep. I'm not tired yet, but I just want to apologize in advance in case your bor-ing talk puts me to sleep. I don't want to offend you. *(Screams.)* AAAAAAAAAAAAAAAAAHHHHHHHHH! I'm just so bored I could scream. Did you ever hear that expression? AAAAAAAAAAA-AAAAAHHHHHHHHH!

JOHN: Excuse me, I want to change my clothes. I'm tired of my color scheme. Do you have a clothes changing room?

NAOMI: No, I don't have a clothes changing room, you certainly are an idiot. Use the bedroom or the bathroom. Really, children these days have no sense. In my day we killed them.

JOHN: *(To Johnna.)* Excuse me, I'll be right back.

JOHNNA: Must you go?

JOHN: Darling, I don't feel comfortable in these colors. They're hurting my eyes.

JOHNNA: Well, bring it back.

JOHN: What?

JOHNNA: *(Sincere, confused.)* I'm sorry, I don't know what I mean.
(John exits.)

JOHNNA: He's constantly talking about his color scheme. It's my cross to bear, I guess. That and the death of the children.

NAOMI: So who the fuck are you, anyway?

JOHNNA: I'm Johnna. I'm married to your son. All our children recently were killed.

NAOMI: Stop talking about your children, I heard you the first time. God, some people can't get over their own little personal tragedies, what a great big crashing bore. Lots of people have it worse, girlie, so eat shit! *(Calls offstage.)* Hey, John, where did you get this turd of a wife, at the Salvation Army? I'd bring her back! *(Laughs uproariously.)* Ahahahahahahahaha!

JOHNNA: I think I want to go.

NAOMI: Boy, you can't take criticism, can you? Sit down, let's have a conversation. This is the conversation pit. You can't leave the pit until you converse on at least five subjects with me. Starting now, go: *(Waits expectantly.)*

JOHNNA: I was reading about Dan Quayle's grandmother the other day.

NAOMI: That's one. Go on.

JOHNNA: She said there should be prayer in the schools...

NAOMI: That's two. *(Naomi starts to remove her boots, or high heeled shoes, in order to massage her feet.)*

JOHNNA: And that we should have a strong defense...

NAOMI: That's three.

JOHNNA: And that the Supreme Court should repeal the Wade vs. Roe ruling that legalized abortions.

NAOMI: That's four.

JOHNNA: And that even in the case of pregnancy resulting from incest, she felt that the woman should be forced to carry the child through to term.

NAOMI: That's four-A.

JOHNNA: And then she said she hoped the mother would be forced to suffer and slave over a horrible job and take home a tiny teeny paycheck to pay for some hovel somewhere, and live in squalor with the teeny tiny baby, and that then she hoped she'd be sorry she ever had sexual intercourse.

NAOMI: That's still four-A.

JOHNNA: Don't you think she's lacking in Christian charity?

NAOMI: That's five, kind of. Yes, I do. But then so few people are true Christians anymore. I know I'm not. I'm a psychotic. (*She throws her boot in Johnna's direction.*) Get up off the couch, I want to sit there. (*Naomi rushes over, Johnna has to vacate fast. Then Naomi starts to luxuriate in sitting in the couch, moving sensuously. She luxuriates all over it.*)

NAOMI: Oh, couch, couch, big couch in the living room. I have room to spread. Couch, couch, you are my manifest destiny. Mmmmm, yes, yes. (*Calls out.*) Edward, hurry out here, I'm about to have an orgasm, you don't want to miss it. (*Back to herself.*) Mmmmmm, yes, couch, couch pillows, me sitting on the couch in the living room, mmmmm, yes, mmmm... (*Calls.*) Forget it! It's not happening. (*To Johnna.*) Tell me, can you switch moods like I can? Let me see you. (*Johnna stares for a moment.*)

NAOMI: No, go ahead, try.

JOHNNA: Very well. (*Happy.*) I'm so happy, I'm so happy. (*Screams.*) AAAAAAAH! Do you have chocolates for me? (*Desperate.*) I'm so sad, I'm so sad. Drop dead! (*Laughs hysterically.*) Ahahahahahahahaha! That's a good one! (*Looks at Naomi for feedback.*)

NAOMI: Very phony, I didn't believe you for a moment. (*Calls offstage.*) Herbert! Are you there? (*To Johnna.*) Tell me, do you think Shubert is dead?

JOHNNA: You mean the composer?

NAOMI: Is he a composer? (*Calls out.*) Lanford, are you a composer? (*Listens.*) He never answers. That's why I sometimes worry he might be dead and, as I said, I don't have a room for a dead person. We might build one on, and that would encourage the economy and prove the Republicans right, but I don't understand politics, do you?

JOHNNA: Politics?

NAOMI: Politics, politics! What, are you deaf? Are you stupid? Are you dead? Are you sitting in the chair?

(Enter John. He is dressed just like Johnna—the same dress, pearls, stockings, shoes. He has shaved off his mustache, and he wears a wig that resembles her hair, and has a bow in it like the one she has in her hair. They look very similar.)

JOHN: Hello again.

NAOMI: You took off your mustache.

JOHN: I just feel so much better this way.

NAOMI: Uh huh.

JOHNNA: *(Deeply embarrassed.)* John and I are in couples therapy because of this. Dr. Cucharacha says his cross-dressing is an intense kind of co-dependence.

NAOMI: If this Dr. Cucharacha cross-dresses, I wouldn't see him. That's what John here is doing. Too many men in women's clothing, nothing gets done!

JOHNNA: *(To John.)* Why do you humiliate me so this way?

JOHN: I want to be just like you. Say something so I can copy you.

JOHNNA: Oh, John. *(Does a feminine gesture and looks away.)*

JOHN: Oh, John. *(Imitates her gesture.)* That doesn't give me much. Say something else.

JOHNNA: Maybe it's in your genes.

JOHN: Maybe it's in your genes.

(Johnna, in her discomfort, keeps touching her hair, her pearls, shaking her head, etc. John imitates everything she does, glowing with glee. His imitations drive her crazy, and is undoubtedly part of what has them in couples therapy.)

NAOMI: This is a disgusting sight. *(Calls.)* Sherbert, our son is prancing out here with his wife, you should really see this. *(To them.)* I find this uncomfortable. This makes me want to vomit.

JOHNNA: Maybe we should go.

JOHN: Maybe we should go.

NAOMI: *(Upset.)* How come you don't dress like me? How come you dress like her?

JOHN: I want to be noticed, but I don't want to be considered insane.

JOHNNA: John, please, just stay quiet and pose if you must, but no more talking.

NAOMI: Insane? Is he referring to someone in this room as insane?

(Calls.) Sally! Gretchen! Marsha! Felicity! *(To them.)* I'm calling my army in here, and then we'll have some dead bodies.

JOHNNA: Maybe we should go.

JOHN: Maybe we should go. *(Keeps imitating Johnna's movements.)*

JOHNNA: Will you stop that?

(Naomi, very upset and discombobulated, stands on the couch and begins to pace up and down on it.)

NAOMI: Insane, I'll give you insane! What's the capital of Madagascar? You don't know, do you? Now who's insane? What's the square root of 347? You don't know, do you? Well, get out of here, if you think I'm so crazy. If you want to dress like her and not like me, I don't want you here.

(Naomi lies down on the couch in a snit to continue her upset. John begins to walk back and forth around the room, pretending he's on a fashion runway. Johnna slumps back in her chair and covers her eyes.)

NAOMI: I can have Christmas by myself, I can burn the Yule log by myself, I can wait for Santa by myself. I can pot geraniums. I can bob for apples. I can buy a gun in a store and shoot you. By myself! Do you get it? *(Stands and focuses back on them.)* You're dead meat with me, both of you. You're ready for the crock pot. You're a crock of shit. Leave here. I don't need you, and you're dead!

(Pause.)

JOHNNA: Well, I guess we should be going.

JOHN: Well, I guess we should be going.

(Johnna and John, looking the same and walking the same, leave the house. Naomi chases after them to the door.)

NAOMI: Fuck you and the horse you came in on!

(John and Johnna exit. Naomi comes back into the room and is overcome with grief. She sits back on the couch and lets out enormous, heartfelt sobs. They go on for quite a bit, but when they subside she's like an infant with a new thought, and she seems to be fairly contented.)

NAOMI: Well, that was a nice visit.

(End.)

TO THE ACTOR

Naomi is a "large" character. She needs to be able to shout and run around the room and be very inconsistent. She must find an inner logic where all this makes sense… she's rather like an infant who changes her focus with total concentration from moment to moment, but with little sense of continuity. One minute she's fine, the next minute she's angry at something and screaming, the next minute she's over it. When the people around her are still upset by her outbursts, she has no understanding of that; she has an infant's sense of time and appropriateness.

John and Johnna are important parts; they both are the normative figures. The play needs their normal presence to set off Naomi's craziness. As John Augustine and Elizabeth Alley played the parts, John was initially doing his best not to react in irritation to his mother, but had a certain just-holding-the-lid-on impatience listening to her. Johnna, less familiar with the mother and more drawn to people-pleasing, was more willing to make nice and overlook really odd things.

When John disappears and comes back in drag (John Augustine played these sections in sheer delight), he was pleased as punch to be in this other reality where he got to imitate his wife's way of dressing, her way of moving, and so on. At that point he seemed as crazy as his mother, though not hostile.

Johnna's continuing attempt to act normal and make the best of things is very important to the last part of the play. She's the only "normal" one left at that point and the other two characters need her discomforted reactions to bounce off of.

As for Naomi in the last third of the play, Sherry seemed to play a disassociated irritation at John's drag—she didn't exactly mind (or even quite notice) that he's now in a dress, instead she seemed grouchy and dissatisfied about something larger that was nagging at her—probably the fact that now that he's in a dress and striding all over the room, she senses that he's getting more attention than before, and this doesn't make her happy. And she strikes out at them unreasonably, her sense of well-being all discombobulated.

Well, it's a silly play. Good luck. Make of it what you can.

Woman Stand-up

AUTHOR'S NOTE

This is a strange piece, and I quite like it. My idea was to make use of all the jokey self-deprecations that are in a lot of women stand-up acts (like Joan Rivers, always talking about what a "dog" she is or women talking about their weight), and to make those attempts at jokey self-deprecation come out of the mouth of a truly vulnerable, wounded young woman who has obviously been damaged by all the awful things her mother (and others) have said to her. Thus we are meant to believe what this young woman says. She has a *truly* damaged self-image. The conceit of the piece is that she's trying to turn the pain and emotional abuse of her life into comedy, but she isn't succeeding. Thus it "sounds" like comic stand-up, but it's not working... her vulnerability is too clear.

I wrote the sketch for a multi-authored musical revue about city life called *Urban Blight,* which was produced by the Manhattan Theatre Club in 1988.

Since this is a monologue, I was very anxious during the casting to find out who would do the piece. Director John Tillinger told me they found this talented woman who made the piece work in auditions and her name was Faith Prince. And when I saw her, she was wonderful—she played the part as inwardly wounded, she was clearly telling the truth about what her mother said to her, she had the proper sound of someone trying to imitate the rhythms of stand-up comedy she had heard, but she kept looking uncertain, panicked. She was the walking wounded, though played by an actress with a comic gift, so it didn't just get serious.

Faith was a stand-out in other people's material in the whole evening as well, and it's been fun to follow her upward rise since then: a Tony nomination for *Jerome Robbins' Broadway,* stopping the show in a supporting part in *Nick and Nora,* and then winning all the awards (including the Tony) for her Miss Adelaide in the hit revival of *Guys and Dolls.* But the first time I saw her was doing this piece, *Woman Stand-Up.*

ORIGINAL PRODUCTION

Woman Stand-Up was part of *Urban Blight,* which premiered May 18, 1988, at the Manhattan Theatre Club, Lynne Meadow, artistic director, Barry Grove, managing director. Based on an idea by John Tillinger, the evening was directed by Mr. Tillinger and Richard Maltby, Jr.; with music by David Shire, lyrics by Mr. Maltby, Jr., with an additional song by Edward Kleban. The twenty authors who had sketches in the evening were John Augustine, John Bishop, Christopher Durang, Jules Feiffer, Charles Fuller, Janusz Glowacki, A.R. Gurney, Jr., Tina Howe, E. Katherine Kerr, David Mamet, Terrence McNally, Arthur Miller, Reinaldo Rovod, Jonathan Reynolds, Shel Silverstein, Ted Tally, Wendy Wasserstein, Richard Wesley, August Wilson, and George C. Wolfe. The sets were by Heidi Landesman; *Blight* was performed by a company of seven actors: Larry Fishburne, Nancy Giles, E. Katherine Kerr, Oliver Platt, Faith Prince, Rex Robbins, and John Rubinstein.

Woman . . . . Faith Prince

CHARACTERS

WOMAN, trying to be a stand-up

128 CHRISTOPHER DURANG

WOMAN STAND-UP

A comedy club. A Young Woman crosses to a microphone and speaks. She looks sweet and a bit frightened.

WOMAN: Hi, and welcome to the Comedy Club, New York's premiere comedy spot. My name is Cindy, and I am a stand-up comedienne.

Let me tell you about myself. I am fat, I am unmarried, I have roaches in my kitchen, I use feminine hygiene spray on my hair, and I have such a low self-esteem that when my mother told me to get a nose job, I bought a Pit Bull and had it bite my nose off.
(There is the sound of recorded laughter over the sound system. The Woman smiles.)

That's my laugh track.

Don't you just love Joan Rivers? Don't you just love her on Hollywood Squares? Don't you just love the tragedy behind Hollywood Squares? Joan Rivers' husband kills himself, Paul Lynde was a closeted homosexual and had a heart attack while doing poppers—I can't prove that, that's just hearsay, so please don't sue me—and John Davidson uses feminine hygiene spray on his dimples. But I sure do like that show. *(Laughs.)*

Don't you love New York? Don't you love the rats in the sewers? Don't you love the beggars on the street while you go looking to buy a co-op? It's so much contrast everywhere, it makes my head spin. My head is on a washer-dryer cycle, every morning I hook my brain up to the sink and I wash it out for 15 minutes. This is my form of meditation. My brain is very clean, and it's very damaged.

I think I'd like the sound of a laugh track again please. *(Laugh track.)*

Thank you. Tell me, do you find me funny or do you find me disturbing?

My mother said to me, Cindy, don't give away your pussy to any man unless you marry him, you're worthless so don't give away your one claim to fame. And then on my first date with Teddy, I learned he was allergic to cats, so I got rid of my pussy. But now we had nothing to do on our honeymoon, so we played pictionary and he went out with prostitutes. Could I have the laugh track again please? *(Laugh track.)*

Thank you. I'm a stand-up comedienne, but I'm too insecure to go anywhere without my laugh track. My mother says I'm not only worthless, but I'm not funny. I wish my mother would die. Then I'd have everybody over for brunch and serve Bloody Mary's made with her blood.

I'm sorry, that's really not funny, is it? It's New York, you see, I'm not well, all the suffering and the tension and the years of abuse, mental as well as physical, that I received at the hands of my parents, has made me not fit to be a comedienne, but what else can I do with my life?

I went to a party the other day, and all the men in the room were homosexual. My mother says I am the cause of homosexuality in New York. So I said to her, okay, then I'm responsible for a lot of art and good musical comedies, and she said to me, no, you're just responsible for homosexuality. And for the dropping off in the birthrate because no man in his right mind could possibly like you. *(Cries briefly.)* Do you understand why I have low self-esteem, or do you think I should tell more jokes like Joan Rivers? Laugh track, please. *(Laugh track.)*

Don't you just love living in New York? I was in the subway the other day and everybody was covered with blood and was screaming. It was on the E train, and that's usually one of the nicer trains. Then they took us all to the emergency room at B. Dalton, and Joan Collins was autographing one of her books. The clerks covered the dying people with gauze, and then Joan Collins took the gauze off the dying people and put it on the camera lens so she could look younger. I think she looks fine if you like a 50-year-old whore with a face life.

I'm sorry, I don't mean to be catty to other women, it's just that I have low self-esteem and I'm afraid to criticize men. *(Laugh track.)*

I didn't ask for the laugh track, but thank you.

Well, I think it's time for me to go now. *(Laugh track again; she looks confused.)*

Living in New York is really like living in hell, but in hell at least you know there's a heaven somewhere, but when you live in New York, there's only Newark and Trenton to think about. New Brunswick probably isn't bad. Maybe I could marry some professor from Rutgers…but no, I forgot, I'm hideous and worthless. Well, I apologize for taking up your time. You've been a great audience, well, not great, but not totally worthless like me. There must be a better way to live, but I don't know what it is! *(Laughs uncomfortably.)* But if you see me in the gutter and I'm starving, I hope you give me a nickel! Goodnight! *(Waves good-bye. End.)*

TO THE ACTOR

I have seen this piece done so that it doesn't work at all, so I am going to offer some notes.

The key to making it work seems to be to cast an actress who is innately vulnerable. She then must play that the awful things that her mother has said to her—which she tells in the form of conventional, stand-up comedy rhythms—are nonetheless the truth, her mother actually has said them. And so, even though she's trying to fit into the world of stand-up comedy, she's still too upset by believing the dreadful put-downs she's grown up with. So it's a strange piece… it is funny, but it's uncomfortable.

When an actress only plays the rhythm and sounds of stand-up, the piece literally doesn't work.

If the portrayal is only about capturing a stand-up comedy style (copying the delivery rhythms of, say, Joan Rivers or Elayne Boosler or Rosie O'Donnell)—but with no undercurrent of vulnerability and pain—then the piece appears to be about a brash young woman having a failed comedy act. The audience thinks the point is that they're supposed to find it funny that her jokes fail.

When this happens, this is painful for me, because the piece isn't written to function that way. Yes, her act fails, but it's not the failure of a brash, loud, *confident* young woman who just doesn't have good material; it's meant to be the failure of an insecure, extremely non-confident woman, and her material, good or bad, has grown directly out of her psyche, it's not just that she came across some bad joke writing.

Her vulnerability and pain have collided with the sounds of self-deprecating humor that is in some stand-up, and it combines to create a very strange mixture. (If Elayne Boosler or Joan Rivers put themselves down, I never for a minute actually worry about them; we should worry about this woman.)

Aside from Faith Prince (who you may not know if you haven't seen her on Broadway), think of the sensitive souls of actresses like Julie Hagerty or Dianne Wiest (especially in *Parenthood*) or young Judy Holliday (especially in *Adam's Rib*), imagine them doing the piece, and then you'll have an idea of how to approach it.

I also saw the piece done in showcase by a young woman named Margaret Innouye, who seemed like a young Marilyn Monroe in terms of prettiness and spaciness. Her pain was not as clear as Faith's, but it was replaced, effectively, by a cloudiness that Marilyn used to have, as if she was almost medicated. This also worked—it wasn't that she was druggy, it was as if she lived under a psychological cloud that protected her from knowing what she was really feeling. When she would smile seductively, in a generalized way, after what she thought was a punch line, you thought: This woman is out to lunch; something's happened to her; what was it? So that was another interpretation that I thought worked.

But not brash, not confident. Vulnerable, trying to sound like a stand-up comic, but not succeeding too well. (After all, she's brought her own laugh track out of insecurity.)

DMV Tyrant

This is a simple sketch about a man trying to renew his license at the Division of Motor Vehicles.

It was included in early previews of *Urban Blight,* but then was dropped. It went well, it just didn't stand out that much in comparison to *Woman Stand-up*, so I understood leaving it out as well.

But I think we all live in fear of places like the Division of Motor Vehicles, which is why I wrote the piece. So I include it here.

ORIGINAL PRODUCTION

DMV Tyrant was part of *Urban Blight* at the Manhattan Theater Club. Its cast was as follows:

Customer. . . . . John Rubinstein
DMV Lady . . . . E. Katherine Kerr

CHARACTERS
CUSTOMER
DMV LADY

DMV TYRANT

Scene: A window at the Division of Motor Vehicles. Sign on desk reads "Division of Motor Vehicles." A Woman at a window (DMV Lady), approached by a Customer.

CUSTOMER: Is this window 7?

DMV LADY: Yes?

CUSTOMER: I'm afraid something rather complicated has happened with my driver's license.

DMV LADY: I'm sorry to hear that. What happened? *(With great disinterest she begins to read a book.)*

CUSTOMER: Well, you see, I moved here from another state, and I let my driver's license lapse...and...*(Waits.)*

DMV LADY: *(Looks up.)* Yes?

CUSTOMER: Should I wait until you finish?

DMV LADY: I don't think so. It's a very long book.

CUSTOMER: But...are you listening to my problem.

DMV LADY: I can read and listen at the same time. Go on. *(Goes back to reading.)*

CUSTOMER: Oh. Well. Uh, anyway, I took the driving test again, and I passed it and got this temporary license, which has now expired, and I've never gotten my permanent one, and when I called about it, they said they had lost me in the computer, and they had no record of my taking the test, and so they couldn't send me my license even though I did take and pass the test. *(Pause.)* Your turn to say something.

DMV LADY: Wait a minute. *(Reads some more. Looks up.)* I wanted to finish the paragraph. Now what seems to be the matter?

CUSTOMER: Well...

DMV LADY: In one sentence.

CUSTOMER: I haven't received my driver's license.

DMV LADY: Let me see if you're on the computer.

CUSTOMER: I'm not on the computer.

DMV LADY: What is your name?

CUSTOMER: I'm not there.

DMV LADY: How do you spell that?

CUSTOMER: I'm not on the computer. I went to Window 3 and they told me there was no record of me on the computer.

DMV LADY: I am not Window 3, I am Window 7, and I need to know your name.

CUSTOMER: James Agnes.

DMV LADY: Is that A as in aardvark, g as in gesundheit, n as in nincompoop, e as in excruciating, s as in seltzer water, pause pause, j as in Jupiter, a as in Agnes, m as in Mary, e as in excruciating, and s as in slow, lingering death?

CUSTOMER: Yes.

DMV LADY: *(Types into computer; looks.)* Well, you're not on the computer.

CUSTOMER: I told you I wasn't.

DMV LADY: Fine. I will give you an award at the end of the day. How else may I help you.?

CUSTOMER: I...I would like to get my permanent license.

DMV LADY: I'm sorry. There is no record of you on the computer.

CUSTOMER: Yes, but I have my temporary license. *(Hands it to her.)*

DMV LADY: This temporary license has expired.

CUSTOMER: Yes, I know it's expired.

DMV LADY: It is no longer a valid license.

CUSTOMER: I know that. That's why I want my permanent one. I hadn't noticed it hadn't come in the mail until this one had already expired. I had presumed everything was alright.

DMV LADY: What a funny thing to do. *(Suspicious.)* If you do not have a valid driver's license, how did you get here to the Division of Motor Vehicles?

CUSTOMER: I took a taxi.

DMV LADY: Can you prove that to me?

CUSTOMER: What?

DMV LADY: Did you keep a receipt from the taxi?

CUSTOMER: No, I didn't.

DMV LADY: I trust you did not drive here yourself, did you, Mr. James Agnes?

CUSTOMER: No, no, I realize my license is not valid.

DMV LADY: That is correct. You have an invalid license. Good morning.

CUSTOMER: But you're not helping me.

DMV LADY: *(Pleasantly.)* How may I help you?

CUSTOMER: I want my driver's license.

DMV LADY: You must take the driving test.

CUSTOMER: But I took the driving test.

DMV LADY: I have no record of that.

CUSTOMER: I know you have no record of it, some *schmuck* lost it in the computer...

DMV LADY: Kindly do not speak Yiddish to me. If you wish to make an appointment to take the driving test, go to Window 4. *(Goes back to reading.)*

CUSTOMER: I DON'T WANT TO TAKE THE TEST AGAIN!

DMV LADY: *(Irritated.)* Well, when did you take the test before?

CUSTOMER: It's the same date as that on my temporary license.

DMV LADY: February 3, 1894. The Division of Motor Vehicles did not exist in 1894.

CUSTOMER: Let me see that. *(Looks.)* Alright, it's a typo. It's clearly meant to be 1994.

DMV LADY: I am willing to agree with you that it is more likely a typo. You see, I don't stick to the rules on everything, I am human. What is your name again?

CUSTOMER: James Agnes.

DMV LADY: Is that a as in aardvark, g as in gesundheit...

CUSTOMER: James Agnes!

DMV LADY: Let me see if we have a record of you in the computer. *(Types into computer.)*

CUSTOMER: You don't, you don't, I told you you don't!

DMV LADY: Why are you shouting at me? When I am shouted at, I do not feel like cooperating.

CUSTOMER: But you haven't *been* cooperating.

DMV LADY: I have been cooperating. If I had not been cooperating, you would have been shouting at me much earlier than this.

CUSTOMER: I want my license.

DMV LADY: Well, you can't have it. You're not on the computer.

CUSTOMER: But that's not my fault.

DMV LADY: And it's not my fault. We are both blameless. Isn't it a nice feeling?

CUSTOMER: You are not helping me.

DMV LADY: I am doing everything in my power.

CUSTOMER: But don't you have more power than you're using? Can't you, for instance, type me into the computer, and then send me my license?

DMV LADY: No. Only the secretary at the driving test site can do that.

CUSTOMER: But when she forgets to do that at the time of the driving test, can't someone else do it then?

DMV LADY: If the secretary at the driving test site is willing to write a note admitting that she had forgotten to type in your name, then I can enter your name into the computer. And then we will fire her. Do you want her to lose her job?

CUSTOMER: No, I don't. I want you to lose *your* job.

DMV LADY: I don't see how you can expect me to help you if you're going to be hostile.

CUSTOMER: Isn't there anything you can suggest to solve my problem?

DMV LADY: *(Thinks.)* If you could re-live the initial driving test, when it was finished, you could ask to watch the secretary type in your name and your test result into the computer.

CUSTOMER: Your suggestion is that I *re-live* the initial driving test?

DMV LADY: It is a hypothetical suggestion, I admit, but it is the limit of what I can think of to assist you.

CUSTOMER: Could I see your supervisor please?

DMV LADY: My supervisor if shredding documents in the other room, and cannot be disturbed.

CUSTOMER: *(Angry.)* Look into my eyes. I want you to tell me what I should do that will solve my problem, and I want you to tell me *right now!*

DMV LADY: Move out of New York.

CUSTOMER: *(Taken aback, but it might be worth it.)* That's a good suggestion. Thank you. *(He storms out.)*

DMV LADY: *(Calling after him.)* Ohio's nice. *(She goes back to reading.)* *(End.)*

Funeral Parlor

This is a sketch that was part of a Carol Burnett TV special, *Carol, Carl, Whoopi and Robin,* that aired on ABC in 1987. The two main parts in the sketch are a widow played by Carol and a crazy mourner at the funeral parlor played by Robin Williams.

I'm a fan of Carol Burnett and so was excited when I was asked to submit a sketch for this special. My original sketch was between two women; I envisioned the crazy mourner as a nutty part for Carol.

From the sketch, I was asked to come work for four weeks in L.A. as a staff writer for the special under the head writers, Dick Clair and Jenna McMahon. Dick and Jenna had written many of Carol's funniest sketches for years, including all the ones about Eunice and her mother fighting on and on and on.

Once I was on staff, I learned that Carol didn't actually want to play the crazy part, she was more interested in playing the "normative" role, the reactor role. And on learning that Robin Williams was to be a guest star, changing the mourner to a man seemed a natural.

The special was filmed three times—the rehearsal and two run-throughs, all in front of audience.

The first two times Robin did the sketch more or less as written and rehearsed, but he made it clear that he wanted to try a wilder version where he could ad-lib further crazy comments. So Carol announced to the audience on the last run-through that Robin was going to pull stuff out of his hat, "I have no idea what he's going to do, and so I figure... let 'im." Then she added "Pray for me."

Robin's ad-lib version was quite funny, though the "story" of the sketch no longer really registered. (And Carol had wanted the sketch to have a "point," she wanted the crazy man to actually have a positive effect on the woman in the long run.)

When I saw the first edit a couple of months later, I was distressed by what had happened. They had edited the three takes together so that sometimes Robin seemed to be playing a part, and Carol was reacting to what he was doing as that character; and sometimes he'd be riffing, and Carol would actually be playing reactions to Robin himself and his free-associating, not to the character he was playing. (And Robin sometimes seemed a character and sometimes seemed himself.)

Sense of my own authorial propriety aside, I found the sketch schizoid and confusing when edited that way. I preferred that they either keep to the versions where he played the material as written or go to the other extreme and just show all of his ad-libbing one.

But wonder of wonders, fate sort of gave me the best solution. There was another sketch in the evening that was just not working as they edited it together (which was a shame; it was funny when they worked on it). And so suddenly they had a whole 10-minute section to fill in the special.

The solution they came up with was to first show the full version of my sketch with Robin staying in character; then to follow it with his own ad-libbed version in its entirety—and his ad-libbed version was much funnier when you knew what he was riffing on top of.

I was delighted with this result, and Robin won an Emmy actually.

So, here is my version of the sketch. (To see Robin's riff version of it, watch for the repeat of the special. It seems to show up on the Disney channel with some regularity.)

ORIGINAL PRODUCTION

Funeral Parlor was included in the TV special *Carol, Carl, Whoopi and Robin,* which originally aired February 10, 1987. Marcy Carsey and Tom Werner, executive producers. Stephanie Sills, Dick Clair and Jenna McMahon, producers. Writing supervised by Dick Clair and Jenna McMahon. Directed by Harvey Korman and Roger Beatty. Written by Chris Durang, Jim Evering, Ken Welch, Mitzi Welch, Dick Clair and Jenna McMahon. Musical material by Ken Welch and Mitzi Welch. The cast was as follows:

Susan . . . . Carol Burnett
Marcus. . . . . Robin Williams

CHARACTERS
SUSAN
MARCUS

FUNERAL PARLOR

Interior: A Funeral Parlor. Quiet, grave (sorry) setting. Perhaps a bit of casket shows. Certainly lots of flowers. Hushed atmosphere. Susan, the mourning widow, is dressed in black, with pearls. She is sedate, proper, formal. A few people are in line, offering their condolences, shaking her hand. She acknowledges them with a little nod and little smile, and a whispered "Thank you." As we begin, at the end of the line to see Susan is a man named Marcus. Marcus is dressed in a nice suit, but it's kind of a light color and his tie and shirt are kind of flowery, not really right for a funeral, but maybe he had to come straight from work (or Hawaii). Otherwise he looks appropriate enough. The person before Marcus makes quiet sounds of condolences, and leaves. Marcus reaches Susan. He is sincere and genuine, it's just that he's, well, odd.

MARCUS: Susan, I'm so sorry. My deepest condolences.
SUSAN: Yes, thank you…(??) *(She doesn't know who Marcus is.)*
MARCUS: Marcus.
SUSAN: *(Still doesn't know him, but is gracious.)* Yes, Marcus. Thank you for coming.
MARCUS: We'll all miss him terribly.
SUSAN: Yes. It's a great loss.
MARCUS: We'll all miss him.
SUSAN: Yes.
MARCUS: You must feel terrible.
SUSAN: Well…I don't feel good. It was a terrible shock.
MARCUS: Death is always a shock. You're sitting home doing nothing,

and then suddenly death goes "Boo!", and somebody falls down dead.

SUSAN: Yes. *(Looks around, hopes someone else will come over.)*

MARCUS: What were his last words? Were they "Boo"?

SUSAN: What? "Boo"? No. He didn't really have any last words.

MARCUS: Did he make any last noises?

SUSAN: Noises? What?

MARCUS: Guttural sorts of noises? Or high-pitched-shrieking ones? *(Makes high-pitched sounds.)* Eeeeeeek! Eeeeeeeeek! Awooooga! Awooooooga!

SUSAN: Just noises, I don't know. They were lower than that. Don't do that anymore.

MARCUS: *(Sympathetically.)* Oh, Susan, you poor, poor thing. *(Turns to someone who's gotten in line behind him.)* I wouldn't wait if I were you, I'm going to be a while.

(The person in line looks surprised but goes away; Susan looks alarmed.)

MARCUS: All alone in the house now. Alone in the kitchen. Alone in the dining room. Alone in the living room—living room, that's a mocking phrase now, isn't it? Alone, alone, alone. All alone. Alone, alone, alone.

SUSAN: Please don't go on.

MARCUS: Yes, but you have to mourn, Susan, to *mourn*. I always thought the Irish were right to do all that keening. Do you want to keen, Susan?

SUSAN: Not really. Thank you anyway.

MARCUS: How about singing a Negro spiritual?

SUSAN: I don't think so. *(Looks about madly for people.)*

MARCUS: *(Sings.)*
Swing low, sweet chariot,
Comin' for to carry me home…

SUSAN: Thank you for coming.

MARCUS: Don't you want to sing?

SUSAN: I don't want to keen or sing. I'm an Episcopalian. I'll cry quietly in my room later this evening. Now I must attend to the other mourners.

MARCUS: Susan, you're avoiding the sadness, I can't let you do that.

SUSAN: Please, please let me do that. It's been a terrible day. I have to bury my husband.

MARCUS: Is he in the casket? It's a closed casket, he's not actually in some other room, propped up in some stuffed chair or other, waiting there to startle someone, is he?

SUSAN: Certainly not. Thank you so much for coming.

MARCUS: That would give someone quite a fright. They'd be standing by this chair making conversation and then realize they were talking to him, only he was stark, stone dead! Ahahahahaha, that would be a good one!

SUSAN: Yes, very good. *(Calls.)* Oh, David! *(No luck.)*

MARCUS: I'm going to miss him too, you know.

SUSAN: Ah, how nice. Or rather, how sad. Well, time heals everything.

MARCUS: You're not the only one with sorrow written on your forehead.

SUSAN: What?

MARCUS: I should say not. *(Shows his forehead, previously covered with bangs; it has "sorrow" written on it.)* Magic marker. Doesn't wash off. We're going to miss him on the commuter train. We used to exchange morning pleasantries. "Nice morning," or "Cold enough for you?" or "The train seems to be on time today for a change."

SUSAN: I see. Excuse me. I think the mortician is signaling me.

MARCUS: You know, your husband was the only person on that whole damn train who was even willing to speak to me.

SUSAN: *(Very much at a loss.)* How interesting.

MARCUS: The other people would get panic in their eyes if I even started to walk in their direction, and they'd move away, or pretend to be sleeping. But they didn't fool me, I'm no dope, *You can't sleep standing up!*

SUSAN: *(Trying to make small talk.)* Well, if you're tired enough maybe you can.

MARCUS: Your husband, though, was always very friendly to me. Not like my father. Nowadays my father won't even return my phone calls, I went to a seance and everything.

SUSAN: What?

MARCUS: Well he's dead, but I have this medium friend who gave me this special 800 number that lets you call the dead. Maybe you'd like the number to try to reach your husband on the other side.

SUSAN: I don't think so. Well, que sera, sera. Ah me. La dee dah. Well, thank you so much for coming.

MARCUS: *(Warmly.)* Well, you're welcome. I just feel so terrible about your husband being gone, and I don't know what I'm going to do on the train in the morning.

SUSAN: Yes. Well—why don't you read a book?

144 CHRISTOPHER DURANG

MARCUS: That's an idea. Do you have any suggestions?

SUSAN: Oh my, I don't know. *The Thorn Birds, Great Expectations.* Any book, I don't care.

MARCUS: My favorite book is *Babar the Elephant.*

SUSAN: Yes, that is excellent.

MARCUS: Have you read it?

SUSAN: No, but I hear wonderful things. Ah me. My, my. Well, thank you for coming. Good-bye.

MARCUS: *(Surprised.)* Are you leaving?

SUSAN: *(Losing her temper.)* No, I'm not leaving. I want *you* to leave. You're making me hysterical. Can't you take a hint. When I say "Thank you for coming," that's code for "Go away now." Don't you understand that?

MARCUS: *(Terribly abashed, a bit hurt.)* Oh. I'm sorry. I thought it just meant "Thank you for coming." I'm sorry. I didn't realize. I…Is there anything else you've said in code I haven't understood?

SUSAN: No. Nothing. I don't think so.

MARCUS: *(Still a little thrown.)* Oh good. *(He looks very abashed and embarrassed.)*

SUSAN: It's…just…well… *(Feeling badly for him.)* Oh dear, now I feel terribly guilty about having expressed my emotions.

MARCUS: *(Friendly again, thinking of her.)* Oh don't feel guilty about expressing emotions. That's a *good* thing to do. You've had a terrible loss.

SUSAN: *(Somewhat seriously, realizing.)* Yes, I have.

MARCUS: Are you sure you don't want to keen yet? I'm not Irish, but I think it's a very appropriate thing to do at a wake.

SUSAN: Oh I don't know. Maybe another time.

MARCUS: This would be the most likely time.

SUSAN: Well, I don't know. *(A little interested.)* What does keening sound like exactly?

MARCUS: Oh, it's real interesting. It's sort of like this.

(Marcus makes an enormously strange, low, sustained moan-whine that goes up and down the scale. The rest of the people present come to a dead halt and stare.)

SUSAN: *(To crowd; slightly annoyed.)* Please stop staring. Go back to your conversational buzz.

(The crowd goes back to its hum.)

MARCUS: Did I do something wrong again?

SUSAN: Well, it was a very startling sound

MARCUS: It's just like crying, but more dramatic. I love to cry. You loved your husband, didn't you?

SUSAN: *(Genuine.)* Yes.

MARCUS: Well, then, don't you want to keen just a little?

SUSAN: Well, I see your point a little but...I don't know that I really could.

MARCUS: You could do it softer than I did.

SUSAN: I don't think so.

MARCUS: Oh please, I'm sure it would make you feel better.

SUSAN: *(Wanting to feel better.)* Would it? *(Starts to, but freezes.)* This is difficult to do in public. Couldn't I call you later this evening, and do it on the phone?

MARCUS: No, it's much more healing to keen at the funeral. You shouldn't do it on the phone.

SUSAN: Oh, I don't know.

MARCUS: Come on. It'll help.

SUSAN: *(Hesitates, but then.)* Oooooooo. *(It's very soft. Sounds like a ghost sound, or a person imitating the wind.)*

MARCUS: That's good.

SUSAN: Oooooooo.

MARCUS: That's good.

SUSAN: Oooooooo.

MARCUS: That's good. AAAAAAOOOOWWWWWOOOOOOOO!!!!
(Susan looks aghast for a moment. The crowd stops and stares again. Momentary silence. After a beat, Susan gives in to some odd combination of grief and having fun, and makes extremely loud keening sounds simultaneously with Marcus.)

BOTH: AAAAAAAAAAOOOOOOOOOOOOOOOOOWWWWWW-OOOOOOOOOOOOOOOOO!!!!!!!
(From out of these very satisfying, if shocking noises, Susan starts to cry loudly and uninhibitedly. Marcus pats her on the back in a comforting manner, looking out at the crowd a bit proudly as if to say "See what I did?" Susan's crying subsides, and her breathing returns more to normal.)

MARCUS: There, that's better.

SUSAN: *(Drying her eyes.)* Thank you so much for coming. *(Just as Marcus begins to wonder.)* No, no, not code. Thank you. I feel much better.

MARCUS: Oh good. Well, you're welcome.
(Marcus and Susan shake hands warmly. Marcus smiles at her, moves aside, as other mourners come over to speak to Susan. Quick fade. End.)

Canker Sores
and Other Distractions

This is another sketch I wrote with Carol Burnett in mind. I thought she could be the difficult waitress Midge.

However, it's never been done. I found it in my trunk (or rather on my computer, which sometimes is like a trunk).

CHARACTERS
    MARTIN
    PRUNELLA, his ex-wife
    MIDGE, a waitress

CANKER SORES AND
OTHER DISTRACTIONS

Scene: A restaurant. Martin and Prunella, a well-dressed couple.

MARTIN: Prunella, it's so good to see you.

PRUNELLA: You too, Martin.

MARTIN: Prunella, how I've missed saying your name. Prunella, Prunella, Prunella. Like prunes with vanilla.

PRUNELLA: Martin, Martin. I…can't think of anything equivalent to say.

MARTIN: How long has it been?

PRUNELLA: It's been a long time.

MARTIN: It's been a long time, hasn't it. Prunella. Prunella, Prunella.

PRUNELLA: Ten years. Ever since our divorce.

MARTIN: That dreadful day. We had a particularly contentious divorce too, didn't we? Swearing, crying, hurling accusations. I said so many awful things. You said so many awful things. Then you got all our possessions and the house and the kids and the car.

PRUNELLA: I know. We really hated one another back then. As a matter of fact, we've continued hating one another until…just yesterday, that chance meeting on the street.

MARTIN: It's true, Prunella. When I saw you yesterday, the sunlight shimmering on your wig, all of a sudden all the hate and anger fell into perspective, and I thought, I love this woman, I always have loved this woman. I mean, who cares who got what in the settlement—those are only "things."

PRUNELLA: Yes. *My* things.

MARTIN: Right, but the point is, Prunella, after 10 years of hating you, suddenly that hate has lifted and in its place is…well, it's corny to say it, but in its place is love.

PRUNELLA: I feel the same way, Martin. The kids are grown, the car is broken, the house needs repair. But our love for one another is real.

MARTIN: Prunella, I know this is crazy, and the last thing either of us thought would ever happen, but I think we should get back together. I want us to remarry.

(A rather unwilling waitress named Midge approaches their table. She's not hostile, it's just there are about twenty other places she would rather be.)

MIDGE: Hello, my name is Midge, and I will be your waitress for the evening. Let me tell you about our specials, and then take a cocktail order.

MARTIN: Could you come back in a minute?

MIDGE: What?

MARTIN: I'm sorry. Would you come back in a minute. I was in the middle of a thought.

(Midge thinks and mutters to herself, and sort of sluffs away.)

MARTIN: Now where was I?

PRUNELLA: Oh, Martin, it's amazing you feel this way because I feel absolutely the same.

MARTIN: You do?

PRUNELLA: Yes. I haven't felt anything like…

MIDGE: *(Trying again.)* We got duck and chicken and fish, all almondine.

MARTIN: I'm not ready now.

MIDGE: *(By rote; as if repetition will make this work out.)* My name is Midge, and I'm your waitress.

MARTIN: My name is Martin, and I'm not ready yet.

MIDGE: Well, when you're ready you let me know. Okay?

MARTIN: Yes, Midge.

MIDGE: I'll be waiting. *(Walks away.)*

MARTIN: Now what were you saying?

PRUNELLA: I forget.

MARTIN: Oh I hate it when this happens. Well, let me tell you more about my feelings then. Stop me if you've heard it before. I feel so thoroughly renewed, young, in love…I… *(Suddenly realizing.)* I think I'm developing a canker sore.

PRUNELLA: What?

MARTIN: Yes, right on my inner cheek. *(Puts his tongue there.)* Ow, it hurts when I put my tongue on it.

PRUNELLA: Don't put your tongue on it then.

MARTIN: I have to. It hurts.

PRUNELLA: When did you get it, darling?

MARTIN: *(Cranky.)* I don't know, I don't know, it just happened.

PRUNELLA: Darling, I'm sorry.

MIDGE: *(Holding a tray of five drinks.)* Did you all order drinks?

MARTIN: No we didn't.

MIDGE: Well somebody did. I wonder who it was. *(She puts the drinks down on their table, and looks through her notes.)* No…no…no…

PRUNELLA: *(To Martin.)* Go on, dear, I'm listening.

MARTIN: *(In pain, grouchy.)* I was saying I feel so alive, so renewed… damn it, Prunella, this canker sore is just hurting, it's sitting in my mouth and it's hurting me.

PRUNELLA: Maybe you could drink something. *(To Midge.)* Is there any drink you could recommend that makes a canker sore feel better?

MIDGE: Grapefruit juice.

MARTIN: Better, not worse!

MIDGE: I'm not sure if we have grapefruit juice. We have Mimosas, but somebody said the orange juice tasted like grapefruit juice. I'll go check. *(Leaves her pad on the table and exits.)*

PRUNELLA: Don't forget your pad.

MARTIN: I don't want grapefruit juice, Midge.

MIDGE: I'll check. *(Is gone.)*

MARTIN: I'm becoming very sorry we've come to this restaurant.

PRUNELLA: Now, Martin, don't let it ruin this evening for us.

MARTIN: Are you telling me what to do already?

PRUNELLA: It's just a suggestion, don't be angry.

MARTIN: *(Angry.)* I'm not angry. I'm just coping with a canker sore.

PRUNELLA: More like a "cranker" sore.

MARTIN: What?

PRUNELLA: Canker and cranky sound alike. I was just noticing.

MARTIN: Canker and cranky. They don't sound particularly alike.

PRUNELLA: "Anker" and "anky." Well, they're more alike than, say, "canker" and… "geranium."

MARTIN: This is becoming a stupid conversation.

PRUNELLA: Well, I'm sorry I brought it up.

(Silence for a moment.)

MARTIN: *(Puts tongue in his cheek again.)* This really hurts.

PRUNELLA: Don't keep feeling it then.

MARTIN: It's hard not to.

PRUNELLA: Well, suit yourself. *(Pause.)* So you think we should get married again.

MARTIN: What? *(Distracted.)* Oh yes. I do.

(Midge comes back.)

MIDGE: Did I leave my pad here? *(Picks it up.)* I don't know how you expect me to remember anything if I lose my pad.

MARTIN: We don't expect anything from you. Except service.

MIDGE: Well, that's expecting something. *(Takes her pad and leaves.)*

PRUNELLA: Martin, we're getting distracted, and letting petty things interrupt our wonderful reconciliation. Let's not do that. Oh, oh, oh.

(Blinks her eye madly, throws her head back.)

MARTIN: What is it?

PRUNELLA: Something in my eye. Oh dear. Oh my, it stings dreadfully. *(Prunella dabs her napkin in her glass of water and dabs her eye madly.)* Oh my. Ow. Ow.

MARTIN: I don't understand. Something just flew into your eye?

PRUNELLA: Well, I'm not making it up. Ow ow ow. Oh dear. Ow.

MARTIN: Must you say ow? It sounds peculiar.

PRUNELLA: Well it hurts. Ow.

MARTIN: I believe it hurts. It just seems peculiar to have to be vocal about it.

PRUNELLA: Ow.

MARTIN: Seems unnecessary.

PRUNELLA: Don't try to control my pain. It's my pain.

(Midge comes back.)

MIDGE: Here's your grapefruit juice.

PRUNELLA: Ow, ow.

MARTIN: I didn't order grapefruit juice.

MIDGE: Well, I wrote it down. *(Shows him her pad.)*

MARTIN: I don't care what you wrote down, I don't want it.

MIDGE: Do you want a mimosa?

PRUNELLA: Ow, ow. Do you have an eye cup?

MIDGE: What?

PRUNELLA: To rinse my eye.

MIDGE: I can get a shot glass.

PRUNELLA: Yes. Please. Ow ow.

(Midge goes off to the bar.)

MARTIN: Well, my canker sore hurts too. *(To her, sort of.)* Ow. Especially when I touch it. Ow ow ow.

PRUNELLA: It's not a contest, Martin.

MARTIN: You always get this way when there are difficulties.

PRUNELLA: It's called appropriate response, Martin. My eye hurts.

(Midge comes back with the shot glass.)

MIDGE: Here's the shot glass.

MARTIN: I don't want to get married again. It was stupid idea. Life is nothing but pain and misery, it's stupid to have even thought about trying to look for something to work out.

PRUNELLA: Martin, you're overreacting. Eventually I'll get the thing out of my eye, and eventually your canker sore will leave.

MARTIN: It doesn't matter, something else awful will happen.

PRUNELLA: *(Still holding a napkin to her eye.)* Well, fine. I'm remembering what being married to you was like.

MIDGE: Oh, he's right. You get your hopes up and something awful happens. I got a call last week from representatives of Ed McMahon and they said I won a million dollars. And then I thought, I'm going to quit my job as a waitress. But I misheard them. They said I might win a million dollars, if I agreed to subscribe to some magazine. So I ordered TV Guide for thirty-six weeks. And then last night my apartment got robbed, and I don't have a TV anymore. But I'm going to get TV Guide for thirty-six weeks.

MARTIN: Well that's too bad. I wonder if you could not talk to us so much this evening.

MIDGE: What?

PRUNELLA: Martin...

MARTIN: Well, I didn't realize when I came in here that this was one of those talky-chatty restaurants.

MIDGE: What?

MARTIN: I would like to have conversation with my ex-wife, but with you I would like to say hello and good-bye, and here's my order please.

MIDGE: Oh, you'd like to order now. *(To Prunella.)* He's difficult to understand.

MARTIN: I am not difficult to understand. I would like some politeness and decorum with the people whose work it is to serve me.

PRUNELLA: Just the check, please.

MIDGE: What?

PRUNELLA: Martin, I remembered why I divorced you. You're really horrible. You should be in therapy.

MIDGE: I'd love to be in therapy, but I can't afford it.

MARTIN: Where's the manager? I want this woman fired.

PRUNELLA: Just bring him the check. I'm going to go to a fast-food restaurant. *(Leaves, holding her eye.)*

MARTIN: Where's the manager, please?

MIDGE: I don't know if we have a manager. You want to see the cook?

MARTIN: Oh, forget it, forget it. Life is hopeless. You've ruined my remarriage. *(Stalks off.)*

MIDGE: Yeah, yeah. Big deal.

(End.)

The Hardy Boys and the Mystery of Where Babies Come From

AUTHOR'S NOTE

Back when I wrote this sketch, *The Hardy Boys* was a series on television, featuring cute Shaun Cassidy and cute Parker Stevenson looking preppy and wearing sweaters.

The title was actually given to me by my friend Stephen Paul Davis. Thank you, Stephen.

I rather fear the title is funnier than the sketch. But then, nothing's perfect.

CHARACTERS

FRANK HARDY, a cute young man

JOE HARDY, another cute young man

NURSE RATCHED, a terrifying nurse

MR. HARDY, Frank and Joe's father

(Note: I wrote this piece for camera, but think it could be done on stage with minor adjustments.)

THE HARDY BOYS AND
THE MYSTERY OF WHERE
BABIES COME FROM

The title above shows on the screen.
Interior: The Hardy Boys' Bedroom.
*Bunk beds. Posters on the wall. "Episode One" is superimposed on
the screen. Frank Hardy sits at his desk. He's around age 20, nice looking, preppy, wearing a collegiate sweater. Joe Hardy, his brother, comes
in. He's around age 20, nice looking, preppy, wearing a collegiate
sweater.*

JOE: Hi, Frank.
FRANK: Hi, Joe.
JOE: Neat sweater, Frank.
FRANK: Yours too, Joe.
JOE: Dad gave me mine.
FRANK: He gave me mine too.
JOE: Dad's great.
FRANK: Yeah, he is. Great.
JOE: You wanna play Monopoly?
FRANK: Not now.
JOE: Chess?
FRANK: No, you have to think too hard.
JOE: Clue?

FRANK: No, but you're getting closer. Why don't we do some sleuthing?

JOE: Oooh, I love the word "sleuthing," Frank. It makes me feel excited right in the pit of my stomach.

FRANK: Me too. It's a great word.

JOE: Is there some mystery to solve, Frank, that we can use our sleuthing powers on?

FRANK: Yes, Joe, there is. But let's change sweaters first.

(Music and fade to: The same, a few minutes later. The Boys are wearing different sweaters.)

JOE: Nice sweater, Frank.

FRANK: Yours too, Joe.

JOE: Now what's the mystery?

FRANK: Well, I heard someone at school say that Nancy Drew may have to get married because "She has a bun in the oven."

(They both look baffled.)

JOE: Gosh, Frank, that doesn't make any sense at all. Our housekeeper Mrs. Danvers has had whole cakes in the oven, and she's never had to get married.

FRANK: That's just it. Something's fishy here.

JOE: I love the word "fishy." It makes me feel excited right in the pit of my stomach.

FRANK: Me too, Joe. And you're right—this whole thing *doesn't* make sense. Let me think. *(Thinks.)* No, it hurts.

JOE: Well, how shall we solve this mystery. I know—let me interrogate you! Frank, who told you this crazy thing about "buns in the oven"?

FRANK: I don't remember.

JOE: Well, that finishes that investigation.

FRANK: No—wait. The school nurse said it!

JOE: Nurse Ratched!

(Ominous music.)

JOE: Gosh, that music sure is ominous. I wish Mrs. Danvers would leave our stereo system alone. Maybe we can get Dad to fire her. Then it would be just guys living in the house. I'd prefer that.

FRANK: Me too. At least she doesn't sleep here.

JOE: And she's so crazy. Always trying to get me to jump out the window.

FRANK: That's just her sense of humor.

JOE: Well, I don't find it funny. Women are terrifying, aren't they?

FRANK: That's what Dad always said.

JOE: Say, speaking of terrifying women, maybe we should go see Nurse

Ratched and ask her what she meant about all this bun in the oven stuff.

FRANK: We *could* ask her, but that seems too simple.

JOE: Why don't we do some sleuthing then? *(Shudders with delight.)* Oooooh, my stomach again. It's just like late at night when I...well, never mind. Why don't we go see Nurse Ratched, but we won't actually ask her anything, we'll pretend we're sick, and we'll kinda talk around things listening for clues, and that way it'll still be sleuthing! Ooooooooh!

FRANK: That's a good idea, Joe. But let's change sweaters first.

JOE: OK.

(They start to take off their sweaters as we fade. "End of Episode One" is superimposed.)

(Interior: The School Nurse's Office. Nurse Ratched is there, looking through a Sears Roebuck catalog. "Episode Two" is superimposed. Frank and Joe come in, in new sweaters.)

FRANK: Hello, Nurse Ratched.

NURSE RATCHED: Well, hello, boys. Nice sweaters. What can I do you for?

JOE: We wanted to ask you a que...

(Frank jabs him in the ribs.)

FRANK: One of us is sick. We think it might be strep throat.

NURSE RATCHED: Strep throat, huh? Which one of you has it?

JOE: We're not sure. We thought you better examine both of us.

NURSE RATCHED: Sure, I'll examine you. Oh, you boys are so cute, I could eat you up!

FRANK: Eat us up...like "buns in the oven"?

NURSE RATCHED: No, not like buns in the oven. Like hot dogs! *(Laughs hysterically.)*

JOE: Gee, another terrifying woman whose sense of humor I don't understand.

NURSE RATCHED: Now which of you is Frank, and which of you is Joe, I get confused.

FRANK: I'm Frank.

JOE: I'm Joe.

NURSE RATCHED: And I'm ready for action. *(Laughs hysterically.)* Oh I'm going to be fired if I don't watch it. I just love young men. That's why I took this job. Alright, boys, take your shirts and pants off, I want to look at your throats.

JOE: OK, but you gotta promise that you'll talk some more about buns in the oven.

NURSE RATCHED: Sure. Hot cross buns, French pastries, French movies, X-rated x-rays. Anything you want, Joe.

JOE: Frank.

NURSE RATCHED: I thought you said you were Joe.

JOE: Oh, I'm sorry, I am Joe. I just got confused.

FRANK: You bozo.

NURSE RATCHED: OK, boys, now take off your clothes.

(Ominous music. Boys start to remove their sweaters. Camera pans to a clock that reads three o'clock. Fade to the same clock, now reading seven fifteen. It is now darker. Frank and Joe are in T-shirts and boxer shorts, tied up back-to-back on the examining table. They are alone.)

FRANK: I didn't know they had to tie you up to check for strep throat.

JOE: Neither did I.

FRANK: Okay, let's add up the facts we know so far about the mystery.

JOE: Well, Nurse Ratched says we don't have hernias because she gave us that coughing test for two hours.

FRANK: Alright, that's fact number one. What else?

JOE: Well, she thinks we're cute.

FRANK: I think we're cute too, but we need more clues than that to solve this mystery. Nancy may be in trouble!

JOE: I find it hard to think all bundled up this way. I wonder when Nurse Ratched is coming back with the bicycle pump?

(Mr. Hardy, Frank and Joe's father, comes into the office, wearing a suit and looking annoyed.)

MR. HARDY: Frank, Joe! What are you two boys doing here all tied up?

FRANK: We're sleuthing, Dad.

JOE: Ooooooh.

MR. HARDY: You two boys really are retarded. I should have my sperm analyzed. Don't you know the Nurse Ratched is a sex maniac?

JOE: Gosh, Dad, no! Is she?

FRANK: Wow. And what's sperm?

JOE: And what's sex, and what's maniac, and what's retarded?

FRANK: And why should Nancy have to get married because of some breakfast food she has in her oven?

MR. HARDY: What? Breakfast food?

FRANK: There must be some reason she has to get married.

MR. HARDY: She's pregnant.

(Joe and Frank look at one another, astonished.)

FRANK: Pregnant!

JOE: Gosh!

FRANK: What's pregnant?

MR. HARDY: Well, I guess you boys are old enough to be told the facts now. I kinda wanted to wait until you were thirty-five or so, but maybe now that you already know this much, I better tell you the rest. OK, fellas, listen up. I'm about to explain where babies come from.

JOE: Babies! What do babies have to do with buns in the oven?

MR. HARDY: Well, it's complicated, and a little bit disgusting.

FRANK: Go ahead, Dad, we can take it.

MR. HARDY: We'll start with the flower and the bee. The bee pollinates the flowers, by taking pollen from the stamen, and delivering it to the pistil, which in the human species is like fertilizing the egg, which is…

(Nurse Ratched appears behind Mr. Hardy and puts a cloth soaked in chloroform over his mouth.)

NURSE RATCHED: That's about all the filth I think the boys should learn today, Mr. Hardy.

(Mr. Hardy falls to the floor.)

JOE: Gosh, Dad, you've been chloroformed. *(To Nurse Ratched.)* Why did you do that? Are you crazy?

NURSE RATCHED: Is the Pope Catholic?

JOE: I don't know. He's Polish. Is he Catholic too?

FRANK: Wait, Joe, we got some clues from Dad right before he lost consciousness. He said something about eggs, and you make eggs on *top* of the oven, while you make buns *inside* of the oven. Maybe there's some clue about being on top, and being inside.

JOE: It doesn't ring any bells with me, Frank. I think we have a lot more sleuthing to do, oooooh.

NURSE RATCHED: Something make you shiver, honey?

FRANK: The bee, the flower. Inside, on top.

NURSE RATCHED: That's very nice. That's almost a haiku.

JOE: Hi coo? Gosh, I just don't understand women.

NURSE RATCHED: That's cause we have different hormones.

JOE: I heard about that in health class. We had to do a paper on what makes a hormone.

NURSE RATCHED: And what makes a hormone?

JOE: I don't know. I got an F. Is that a good grade?

NURSE RATCHED: Oh, I like a good F.

FRANK: Can you go away for a minute? I need to think.

NURSE RATCHED: Well, I'll be right back, and then we'll take some pictures. *(She leaves.)*

FRANK: I'm so confused. I feel we're on the brink of learning a really big mystery, but I'm finding it hard to concentrate because we're all tied up in our underwear, and that crazy woman keeps coming in here acting all funny.

JOE: But she said she wasn't crazy. She said she was a Polish Catholic.

FRANK: I don't know. *(Sees something, tense.)* Joe, look!

(The camera pans over to the floor, where their sweaters are lying in a heap.)

FRANK: Joe. She didn't even fold our sweaters!

JOE: Gosh.

FRANK: Joe—I think maybe she *is* crazy.

(Ominous music. "End of Episode Two" is superimposed on the screen. Then: "Next week Frank and Joe join a health club and get a fungus in a strange place." End.)

1-900-Desperate

AUTHOR'S NOTE
I found a version of this sketch, written for camera, on my computer. I decided to rewrite it for stage and to include it here. No big deal, but here it is.

CHARACTERS
GRETCHEN, home alone
RECORDED VOICE
SALLY, over-anxious
ZELDA, mysterious
LITTLE BOY, age 5 or so
SCUZZY, sexy, stupid 20-year-old guy

1-900-DESPERATE

Scene: Gretchen, a woman in her mid-30s, is on the phone. Elsewhere on the stage are other people seated in chairs, who eventually will be on the phone also. But for now, lights only on Gretchen.)

GRETCHEN: No, mother, I don't have a date tonight. I know it's Saturday night. Yes, I know my sister Rebecca is married and has children. I've met the children. Yes, they're lovely... *(Listens.)* Well, I'm sorry my life makes you unhappy, mother. I'm very happy here alone in my apartment on Saturday. Oh I don't know. Maybe I'll rent a video tonight. Or eat an entire cake. No, I'm kidding. You know I don't keep food in the house. I have water and baking soda, so if I get acid indigestion from not eating anything, I'm well prepared. *(Listens some more; holds her head.)* Mother, please don't say that about me, you make me feel worthless and desperate. No, I don't want you to lie to me. No, I take that back—I *do* want you to lie to me. Tell me it's fine that I'm alone on Saturday night, and I'm fine. Say that, mother. *Say it. (Listens; it's brief.)* Uh huh. That's very good. Now the other part. Uh huh. Good. Thank you, mother, it's very sweet of you to feel that way. Now I have to go put my frozen dinner in the microwave, so let me hang up... I don't feel like cooking, mother... Well, I get radiation at the dentist too... Let's drop it, let me get off the phone now. Goodnight. *(Grouchy.)* Yes, I love you too. *(Hangs up.)* Oh, thank God, I'm off the phone. *(Looks around; disoriented.)* But what should I do now? Oh, I feel desperate.

VOICE: Feeling desperate? Then call 1-900-DESPERATE. That special someone may just be waiting for you.

GRETCHEN: Oh, Lord, now I'm hearing voices. Oh that's right, the TV is on. I guess that was on the TV. Oh good, I'm not crazy. I'm not crazy. I'm just desperate. *(Starts to dial.)* 1-900-Desperate.

(As soon as Gretchen finishes dialing, we hear the sound of ringing. Then a click, and a recorded voice.)

RECORDED VOICE: Hello there, swinging singles. You have reached 1-900-Desperate, where you can meet the man or woman of your dreams. The call costs $1.99 a half minute, $3.98 for a full minute. And there is a $25 minimum for 6 minutes and 28 seconds. If you don't want to be charged, hang up now. Too late.

(Gretchen is taken aback. She might have hung up, but it happened too fast.)

RECORDED VOICE: You didn't hang up immediately, you might as well listen in on the line, we're going to charge you whatever you do. Enjoy yourself!

(There is another click, and lights come up on some of the other people who are talking or listening on this 1-900 party line. We see Sally, who is extremely overanxious to make a connection with someone. She is either not too attractive, or doesn't think she is. Maybe has a bottle of something, but she is not drunk. Her desperation keeps her sober. And we also see Zelda, who looks highly intelligent and sardonic. She seems to be on the line for purposes other than of meeting people.)

SALLY: *(Having heard the click of Gretchen coming on the line.)* Hello?

GRETCHEN: *(Tentative.)* Hello?

SALLY: Are there any men on this line?

GRETCHEN: Is this 1-900-Desperate?

SALLY: It sure is. Are you a man with a high voice?

GRETCHEN: No, I'm a woman.

SALLY: Damn it. Any men out there?

ZELDA: We've got to stop looking to men to give us meaning.

SALLY: Who the fuck is that?

GRETCHEN: I think she's right. I have meaning even though I'm home alone on Saturday, thinking of renting a video and using the microwave.

ZELDA: You mean to kill yourself.

GRETCHEN: No. To cook.

SALLY: Hello? Any men there?

(Lights up on a little boy.)

LITTLE BOY: Hello?

SALLY: Are you a man?

LITTLE BOY: I'm five years old.

SALLY: Oh, great.

LITTLE BOY: My name is Billy.

SALLY: I don't care what your name is, shut up.

GRETCHEN: Please, don't be abusive to a child.

SALLY: Oh, God, why are there no men on the line?

LITTLE BOY: *(Calls.)* I'm not doing anything, mommy. *(To the phone.)* Bye!

(Little Boy hangs up, lights go off him.)

GRETCHEN: I guess I'd hang up too, but...

SALLY: But what?

GRETCHEN: Well, I guess I've paid for it.

SALLY: Uh huh. Any men out there? Please God.

ZELDA: Women were once warriors. We hunted like Diana, we carved the turkeys at dinner. We must return to those times.

SALLY: Will you shut up?

ZELDA: You need a woman's support group.

SALLY: I need a man. I don't need women yapping at me.

(Lights come up on Scuzzy, a kind of sexy 20 year old with slicked-back hair and a leather jacket.)

SCUZZY: Hey, ladies, how's it hangin'?

SALLY: Oh my God, a man! Hello! Hello!

SCUZZY: You ladies feelin' desperate tonight?

ZELDA: Not really. I'm reading the diaries of Anais Nin. She was very spiritual.

SCUZZY: Hey, ladies, I'm eighteen. How old are you?

SALLY: I'm twenty. *(She's much older.)*

ZELDA: I'm one hundred and five.

SCUZZY: Anyone else out there?

GRETCHEN: Yes. Although I can't stay long. I dialed by mistake.

SCUZZY: Ooooo. A happy mistake for me. What's your name, baby?

GRETCHEN: My name is ...Gretchen.

SALLY: My name is Sally.

SCUZZY: What you look like, Gretchen?

GRETCHEN: Oh...I don't know.

SALLY: I look like a model. I have large breasts and a tiny waist and...do you like big or small hips?

SCUZZY: Who is this? I'm talkin' to Gretchen.

SALLY: Well, I can't lie. I have small hips. And blond hair and bright red lips and I've studied the Kama-Sutra.

SCUZZY: Hey, Gretchen, talk to Scuzzy again.

GRETCHEN: Hello.

SCUZZY: Hey, baby, you sound hot.

GRETCHEN: What kind of name is Scuzzy?

SCUZZY: It's my nickname. You got a nickname?

GRETCHEN: Gretchen. Well, it's not a nickname...it's a name.

SCUZZY: So, what you want, baby?

GRETCHEN: Oh, I don't know.

SALLY: Sometimes I have an orgasm just walking down the street. That's the kind of passionate person I am.

SCUZZY: Butt out, butt head. I'm talkin' to Gretchen. Gretchen, you still there?

GRETCHEN: Yes. Hello. How are you? Where's the woman reading Anais Nin?

ZELDA: Women don't need men.

SCUZZY: Oh yeah? How ya gonna fertilize your eggs then?

GRETCHEN: Excuse me. I think I'm going to get off now.

SCUZZY: You want me to call you?

GRETCHEN: Call me??

SCUZZY: You know. On your number. We can have a "better talk" that way.

GRETCHEN: Oh, I don't know, I don't feel I know you properly yet.

SCUZZY: What do you want to know?

GRETCHEN: Oh, gosh. What books do you read?

SCUZZY: Books. I read the TV Guide.

GRETCHEN: Yes, that's a good publication.

(Lights back up on the Little Boy.)

LITTLE BOY: I have a little red wagon.

SCUZZY: Who the hell is that?

SALLY: Oh, I give up. I hate you all!

(Sally hangs up. Lights go down on her.)

SCUZZY: Gretchen, I wanna call you, baby. Give me your number.

GRETCHEN: Well, I don't know.

SCUZZY: What do you look like, Gretchen?

GRETCHEN: Oh, I don't now.

SCUZZY: You don't know.

GRETCHEN: Well, let's see. I'm 5'9", I have brown eyes.

SCUZZY: What are your measurements? Heh, heh, heh.

GRETCHEN: Um…my measurements are 36-46-77. I look like a large teepee. And I invite men up to my lair and poison them at dinner and serve their bodies to the raccoons outside my house.

SCUZZY: Oooooh, this lady's intriguing!

ZELDA: Good for you, Gretchen. Feed him to the raccoons.

SCUZZY: We got a nut case on the line. Shut up, nut case! Hey, Gretchen, baby, gimme your number.

GRETCHEN: I'm sorry. I don't think we're right for one another. I'm sorry, Scuzzy. I'm sure you're very nice, for someone.

SCUZZY: Damn right I am.

(There is a pause.)

LITTLE BOY: I have a little doggie, and a big doggie.

SCUZZY: Any hot chicks on the line?

ZELDA: *(With a glint, does a feminine, girlish voice.)* I'm here. Who's this?

SCUZZY: My name is Scuzzy.

ZELDA: Oh, I think I'm gonna like you, Scuzzy. Can I give you a good time?

SCUZZY: What's your number?

ZELDA: Let me call you.

SCUZZY: Okay. My number's 666-0666.

ZELDA: Ooooh, that's a sexy number.

SCUZZY: I'm a sexy guy.

ZELDA: I'll call you right up.

SCUZZY: Okay, baby.

(Scuzzy hangs up. Lights go off of him.)

ZELDA: *(Regular voice.)* Good night, Gretchen. I'm gonna make him suffer. And all for you, baby. And for women everywhere.

(Zelda hangs up. Lights off of her. Now only Gretchen and the Little Boy are lit.)

GRETCHEN: Well, calling this line has been a terrific success.

LITTLE BOY: I have a little red wagon.

GRETCHEN: Do you? That's nice.

LITTLE BOY: My mommy and daddy are asleep in front of the television.

GRETCHEN: I wish I could sleep.

LITTLE BOY: I'm five.

GRETCHEN: I'm thirty-five. I guess I could consider waiting for you. In fifteen years, you'll be twenty.

LITTLE BOY: I have a boo-boo on my knee.

GRETCHEN: I don't think this relationship is going to work out.

LITTLE BOY: I can tie my shoelaces.

GRETCHEN: On the other hand, that's better than a lot of the men I know, I'm starting to get interested again.

LITTLE BOY: I have two doggies.

GRETCHEN: Uh huh.

LITTLE BOY: And one's small, and one's big.

GRETCHEN: Really?

LITTLE BOY: And I have a teddy bear named Fred.

GRETCHEN: Uh huh…

LITTLE BOY: And I can count to ten, and some higher numbers too.

GRETCHEN: Uh huh.

LITTLE BOY: One, two…

GRETCHEN: Uh huh.

LITTLE BOY: Three, four, five.

GRETCHEN: Really. How interesting.

LITTLE BOY: Five. And six. And seven.

GRETCHEN: Uh huh…

(Lights dim on the Little Boy counting and Gretchen going "uh huh"… End.)

Women in a Playground

I graduated from Yale School of Drama in spring 1974. A play I co-authored with Albert Innaurato, *The Idiots Karamazov,* was chosen by Robert Brustein for production that fall at the Yale Repertory Theater. Brustein, having seen me perform and sing at the Yale Cabaret, chose to cast me as the monk Aloysha Karamazov who, in Albert's and my version, becomes a rock singer under the tutelage of Anais Nin. I also got cast in a small but interesting role in a serious production of Dostoevesky's, *The Possessed,* directed by Polish filmmaker Andrej Wajda.

Once these two acting jobs were over, I found myself suddenly facing the real world and having no money. I then went through a six-month period of supporting myself (still in New Haven) with three part-time jobs: I taught acting at Southern Connecticut State College; I helped a doctor at the Yale Medical School index his book on schizophrenia; and through the Katy Cook Temporary Employment Service, I got a typing job at the Yale Medical School, writing to people who had donated their bodies to science after death to tell them that Yale had a glut of bodies and they should make other plans. Did you perhaps receive a letter from me?

Why am I telling you all this? No real reason, except it was during this period and for one of those jobs that I wrote the following two pieces.

Teaching acting twice a week, I mostly used Viola Spolin's book of theater games as my guide. But after a while, I started to want to experiment with the students on acting intentions and how much they could change a text. We especially used ambiguous scenes from Harold Pinter, which in their ambiguity were especially able to shift radically depending on what intentions you played. (We did one scene two ways: First the actor played that he intended to kill his wife, though nowhere does the text suggest such a thing; then the next time doing the same scene, he played that he was deeply depressed and intended to kill himself. Same scene, same words, but obviously wildly different meanings and effect.)

As I got more comfortable with the class, I started to write short scenes of my own that I'd bring in for them to work on. These two are the only ones I can still find. (The others are in a box somewhere.)

CHARACTERS
    ETHEL, fairly happy
    ALICE, not too happy

WOMEN IN A PLAYGROUND

Ethel, Alice

ETHEL: Which one is yours?

ALICE: What? Oh, the little boy in the blue jacket.

ETHEL: Oh. That's a nice jacket.

ALICE: Yes. *(Silence.)* Which is yours?

ETHEL: That's Mary playing with your son.

ALICE: Oh yes.

ETHEL: She's five.

ALICE: Oh. She's a pretty child.

ETHEL: She's very well behaved and never gives me a moment of worry.

ALICE: That must be nice for you.

   (Silence.)

ETHEL: How old is your son?

ALICE: He's five also.

ETHEL: What's his name?

ALICE: James.

ETHEL: James. Do you call him Jimmy?

ALICE: No. Not yet.

ETHEL: But you might?

ALICE: No, I don't think we will. James.

   (Silence.)

ETHEL: Does he give you any trouble?

ALICE: Not yet.

ETHEL: That's nice he hasn't given you any trouble.

ALICE: Well, you never know when he'll start though.

ETHEL: That's sort of a pessimistic attitude to take.

ALICE: Oh, I am pessimistic.

ETHEL: I'm an optimist, and me and my husband are very happy.

ALICE: Are you?

ETHEL: Yes we are.

ALICE: Well, that may change.

ETHEL: I hope not.

ALICE: We all hope not, but that doesn't stop things changing.

ETHEL: I don't think I could stand to have your attitude. I wouldn't want to get up in the mornings.

ALICE: And you do now?

ETHEL: Of course I do.

ALICE: Why?

ETHEL: Well, to make breakfast for my husband. Bill. And for my little girl Mary. And to take Mary to the playground. And to see what the day has in store.

ALICE: To see what's in store, eh?

ETHEL: Yes.

ALICE: I don't see why anyone would be anxious for that. Lots of terrible things can be in store.

ETHEL: Well, of course, I know that. I may be an optimist, but I'm no Pollyanna. But you have to proceed as *if* things will be all right, you have to proceed that way, or you'll never get things done.

ALICE: You've gotten that philosophy from some saying or other. You sound like the back of a match pack.

ETHEL: Well, I hope you don't give your philosophy to your little boy. You'll have a suicide case on your hands before he's eight.

ALICE: Six. Look, they're climbing up the slide. Do you think either one will fall off?

(End.)

Phyllis and Xenobia

AUTHOR'S NOTE
Here's the other one. It's about two sisters.

CHARACTERS
PHYLLIS, controlling, rather cheerful.
XENOBIA, her sister; unhappy, resistant.

PHYLLIS AND XENOBIA

Scene: The kitchen of Phyllis and Xenobia. Pretty, feminine, fussy curtains and kitchen table cloth, and so on. Phyllis and Xenobia are sisters. They can be as young as 35, or as old as 65. Both wear print dresses with busy tiny flower patterns on them. They're sitting at the kitchen table, chatting and maybe having tea, like every day of their lives.

PHYLLIS: I like pudding. I like vanilla pudding and chocolate pudding and tapioca pudding and butterscotch pudding.

XENOBIA: I don't like pudding.

PHYLLIS: I do. I like pudding.

XENOBIA: I know. I don't though.

PHYLLIS: Yes, you do. Oh, the puddings our mother used to make. And the cookies. She used to bake dozens and dozens of cookies a day. And you know where she put 'em?

XENOBIA: I don't like cookies. I never have. I never will. They're not good for you.

PHYLLIS: Well, what is, these days? *(Fondly remembering.)* She used to put them all over the room. In the cookie jars, of course. But under the sofa, and behind the sofa pillows, and behind the china cabinet, under the carpets, behind the curtains, embedded in the floor boards, in little holes in the walls, up above the door frames—just everywhere you looked, there were cookies. That woman was obsessed with cookies.

XENOBIA: She was a bad housekeeper, mother was. She never should have done that. We got bugs everywhere.

PHYLLIS: You're right, we did. It started, of course, with the rugs, that's where the bugs started. But they didn't stop there. I didn't mind them though. Did you?

XENOBIA: Yes, I did mind the bugs. I couldn't stand them.

PHYLLIS: Well, you learn to stand everything after awhile, don't you? *(Suddenly reaches over and hits Xenobia hard on the side of her head. Xenobia is shocked and angry.)*

XENOBIA: What did you do that for?

PHYLLIS: You had a bug in your hair.

XENOBIA: I didn't!

PHYLLIS: You did.

XENOBIA: I did *not* have a bug there. I did *not.*

PHYLLIS: Either you had a bug in your hair, or you're wearing a bobby pin that crawls on little legs. And for your sake I hope it's bugs. *(Hits her in the head again.)* There's another one! *(Xenobia looks shocked and upset. Stares at Phyllis. They're silent for a moment.)*

XENOBIA: I hated mother. I'm glad I killed her.

PHYLLIS: Xenobia, you've got to stop thinking you did it. Stephen did it. We saw him do it, and then we watched him be put away, don't you remember?

XENOBIA: I'd like a cookie now.

PHYLLIS: You can't have one. You don't want one. *(Xenobia thinks for a second.)*

XENOBIA: I killed mother. I remember. Because she was in the kitchen and she was making French toast and she was dipping the bread into the egg batter, and she was spreading little chocolate nuggets on the floor with her feet for the baby to eat, and I remember thinking, *This woman is crazy!* So I picked up a mop...

PHYLLIS: No, no, no, no, it wasn't that way at all. It was much more pleasant for one thing. And it was egg meringues, not French toast. Light and fluffy and filled with egg-y goodness. It was like eating an angel's head.

XENOBIA: Well, it doesn't really matter whether it was egg meringues or French toast, the point is that mother's dead, and now we can keep the house clean again. Only you won't let us. You're always hiding Tasty Cakes underneath the sofa, and behind the curtains, and in the cabinets. You're no better than mother. You're just like mother.

My doctor says I shouldn't live with you anymore. He says I should...

PHYLLIS: Should? Should what?

XENOBIA: *(Thinks; evasive.)* Should not live with you anymore.
    (Pause.)

PHYLLIS: You do like pudding.

XENOBIA: I don't.

PHYLLIS: You do.

XENOBIA: I don't.

PHYLLIS: You do.

XENOBIA: I don't.
    (Phyllis hits Xenobia in the arm.)

PHYLLIS: Another bug.
    (End.)

Desire, Desire, Desire

This is a parody of several Tennessee Williams' plays. I wrote it as a companion piece to the early version of *For Whom The Southern Belle Tolls,* but then realized that they were not a good pairing, it was too much. Plus, *Southern Belle* has a kind of precision to its writing and *Desire* is all over the place.

In the early 80s Robert Brustein, who had been so encouraging to me when he was the head of Yale School of Drama and Yale Repertory Theater, moved his theater to Harvard and created the American Repertory Theater. In 1983 ART presented the premiere of my play *Baby With The Bathwater* (in a very good production directed by Mark Linn Baker, with Cherry Jones and Tony Shalhoub, among others).

In spring 1987, Brustein offered me a slot for some short plays. I came up with a hodgepodge called *Mrs. Sorken Presents.* This was an earlier version of the *Mrs. Sorken* which starts this book and Elizabeth Franz played Mrs. Sorken. I wrote three separate appearances for Mrs. Sorken and I liked all of them (and what Elizabeth did with them); but the evening as a whole did not work.

One of the pieces was *Desire, Desire, Desire.* During rehearsals I thought it was good, but in front of the audience it seemed not to work. Either there's something wrong with the piece or the actress playing Blanche spoke way too slowly. Or both. .

I offer the play here anyway. There are parts of it that are funny and maybe it can work in production; I don't actually know.

(Note: The same Mamet speech that appears in *Stye Of The Eye* also appears in this play. Indeed it originated in this play and I took it out and put it into the *Stye* play.)

CHARACTERS
    BLANCHE, sensitive and on the brink
    STANLEY, a sexy lout
    YOUNG MAN, an 18-year-old census taker
    MAGGIE, desperate and in her slip
    CORA, a good-time gal
    BIG DADDY, very fat and angry about mendacity
    MAGGIE 2, also desperate and also in her slip
    STELLA, Blanche's sister

(Note: Maggie and Cora may be double-cast, as may Maggie 2 and Stella, if you can do the costume change fast enough.)

DESIRE, DESIRE, DESIRE

Scene: A shabby New Orleans apartment. Stanley in a ripped T-shirt sits at the table, guzzling beer. Blanche, dressed in frilly feminine clothes that contrast with Stanley's slobbiness, is sipping a cocktail and trying to look elegant. Stanley finishes his beer, crushes it on his head and throws it on the ground. Blanche winces slightly. Stanley opens another beer and downs half of it, pouring the rest of it over his T-shirt.)

STANLEY: *(Sighing in satisfaction.)* Ahhhhhh!

BLANCHE: Yes, it is rather hot, isn't it? Humid weather always makes me feel nervous, the least little sound makes me jump.
(Silence. Suddenly Stanley lets out with an enormous yell. Blanche just about jumps out of her skin.)

STANLEY: Stella!!!!!!!

BLANCHE: Good Lord, Stanley, you startled me half to death. Oh if I only I knew a doctor who could give me a sedative.

STANLEY: What's a sedative?

BLANCHE: Oh, you'll never need one, you great big lout.

STANLEY: I am not a Polack! I am an American!

BLANCHE: I didn't say you were a Polack, Stanley, I said you were a lout.

STANLEY: Oh, that's different. *(Suddenly bellowing again.)* STELLA!!!!

BLANCHE: Stanley, please, you must stop doing that. My nerves. Besides, Stella isn't coming back. She went out that door to get me a lemon coke about six years ago, and the fact she hasn't returned leads me to believe she doesn't intend to.

STANLEY: Where'd my baby go? I miss her. STELLA!!!!

BLANCHE: Oh Lord. There's no hope.

(Doorbell.)

BLANCHE: Oh good, the doorbell.

(Stanley burps. Blanche goes to the door, lets in a Young Man.)

YOUNG MAN: Good evening, ma'am. I'm the census taker.

BLANCHE: I see. How interesting. Won't you come in?

YOUNG MAN: Thank you, Ma'am.

BLANCHE: Look, Stanley, how nicely he's dressed. And his carriage shows off his figure. Yes, a woman can notice a young man's figure sometimes, when she's feeling desperate and wanting to escape from her dreadful life by indulging for a few moments, or a few hours, of...desire.

STANLEY: What?

BLANCHE: Nothing, Stanley. Just talking to myself.

YOUNG MAN: How many people live here?

BLANCHE: Five. Stanley, myself, the milkman, the paper boy, and the French pastry chef.

STANLEY: French pastries are sissy.

BLANCHE: You're just not a *gourmet*, Stanley. We have to work on expanding your taste buds.

YOUNG MAN: And what are the professions of the people who live here?

BLANCHE: Well, the milkman is a milkman, the paper boy delivers paper, the pastry chef cooks pastry, Mr. Kowalski here drinks beer and bowls on Monday, and I create an atmosphere of elegance and refinement, and just a little bit of magic. Would you like to come in the other room and lie down with me?

YOUNG MAN: What?

BLANCHE: Oh, nothing, it's just you remind me of someone else, someone young and tender who touched my heart when I was a young girl at Belle Reeve. Oh, desire, desire, desire. Stanley, I'm hot. Cool me off.

(Stanley throws a can of beer in her face.)

BLANCHE: Oh, thank you. Refreshing. Some people wash their hair in beer, did you know that? Stanley doesn't wash his hair though, do you, Stanley?

STANLEY: Lay off.

BLANCHE: And he doesn't use a deodorant. I really can't stand being here with him, if it weren't for the milkman, and the paper boy and the pastry chef, why, I do declare, I'd just go mad.

STANLEY: I bought you a bus ticket. Why don't you never use it?

BLANCHE: I'm waiting for Stella to come back, Stanley.

STANLEY: Stella!!!!

BLANCHE: Waiting, waiting. If only we knew.

YOUNG MAN: Are you registered democrats or republicans?

BLANCHE: Oh I'm sorry. I forgot you were here. Did any one ever tell you you look like a Prince out of the Arabian nights?—cause you do, honey lamb.

STANLEY: What poetry.

BLANCHE: Mr. Kowalski doesn't like poetry. He rejects the elevated visions of Wordsworth, Sheets and Kelly. *(Correcting herself.)* Kates and Shelley. Keets and Shelley. And Gerard Manley Hophead. Hopscotch. Oh, I'm all confused.

YOUNG MAN: Are you registered democrats or republicans?

BLANCHE: I'm a registered southern belle. I belong to the party of the heart, but I have been foolish, I have cast my pearls to swine. Do you want to come in the other room and lie down for a while?

YOUNG MAN: What, Ma'am?

BLANCHE: Oh, nothing. Desire, desire, desire. Hit me again, Stanley.
(Stanley throws another beer in her face.)

BLANCHE: Oh, thank you. Very refreshing. Mr. Kowalski does come in handy sometimes.

YOUNG MAN: When will the milkman and the paper boy and the pastry chef be back so I could ask them questions?

BLANCHE: You pose such difficult queries. How can I say when they will be back, or even if they're coming back? I'm such a needy person, I scare them all away. Oh, desire, desire, desire.

YOUNG MAN: I see.

BLANCHE: *(Looking into his eyes deeply.)* Do you? Do you, honey?

YOUNG MAN: Well, I didn't mean anything too profound. I'm just here for the census.

BLANCHE: Census. The five senses. Sensual. Sensuous. Sensuosendilipidity. Are you sure you don't want to lie down in the other room for a while?

YOUNG MAN: Thank you kindly, Ma'am, but I'm on the job.
(Enter Maggie, in a white slip. She goes up to Stanley.)

MAGGIE: *(To Stanley.)* Brick, Brick. Big Daddy is dying of cancer and he wants us to have a child, Brick. And you can't want Gooper and

Mae and the no-neck monsters to inherit all the money, do you, Brick?

BLANCHE: Do you have the right apartment?

MAGGIE: *(Looks around, sees she's in the wrong place.)* Oh, I'm sorry. *(To Stanley, friendly.)* Good-bye. *(Exits.)*

BLANCHE: Young, young, young man.

YOUNG MAN: Yes?

BLANCHE: Wait, I've forgotten what I was going to say. *(Thinks.)* Oh yes. Don't you just love these long rainy afternoons in New Orleans when an hour isn't just an hour—but a little drop of eternity dropped into your hands?

YOUNG MAN: Not really.

BLANCHE: Well, fuck you.

STANLEY: That's tellin' him.

BLANCHE: *(Deeply apologetic.)* Oh, I'm sorry. How rude of me. I'm just half-mad with desire. I feel like a cat on a hot tin roof.
(Re-enter Maggie.)

MAGGIE: Brick, Brick, I know about you and Skipper. You disgust me.

BLANCHE: You have the wrong apartment, go away!

MAGGIE: *(Looks at them; realizes again.)* Oh, I *beg* your pardon. I have dyslexia and I must be reading the number on your door backwards. I have to remember to reverse everything I see, and I get all confused. You should see me dial a phone. It's hilarious. *(Pause.)* Good-bye! *(Exits.)*

STANLEY: I used to have a cousin who could open a beer bottle with his teeth. And then when snap-top cans become popular, he became all ashamed and useless. He became a geek in a carnival and now he bites the heads off of chickens they sell in the supermarket before they wrap them in cellophane and put them in the meat counter.

BLANCHE: Thank you for sharing that, Stanley. It was fascinating. *(To Young Man)* He talks so rarely, I think it's important to encourage him when he does.

YOUNG MAN: Are you in favor of tuition tax credits for citizens who send their children to private school?

BLANCHE: Oh I don't know. Ask me something about art, or poetry.

YOUNG MAN: Do you think "Ode on a Grecian Urn" is John Keats' best poem?

STANLEY: What's a Grecian urn?

BLANCHE: Oh, about $3.50 an hour. *(Laughs hysterically.)* Oh, my God, I've made a joke, I'm so sorry.

(Enter Cora, dressed in a bright polka-dot, trampy-dress. She has a corny New York accent, saying "Poil" for "Pearl" and "goil" for "girl." and so on.)

CORA: Hiya, everybody. Bejees, me and Pearl was just at Harry Hope's saloon talkin' about pipe dreams, and Hickey came in for his usual bender, and he told his iceman story that he tells every year, and then he said we all had too many pipe dreams, and when Chuck and me talked about our pipe dream of saving' up enough money to get married and live on a farm if only Chuck could stay on the wagon for a coupla weeks, Hickey looked at us with this kinda mean smile on his ugly map, and he said, beejees, *pipe dreams*, you kids run your life wid *pipe dreams*, but I just killed my wife and now I don't got no *pipe dreams*, and, Pearl, you'd be better off without *pipe dreams* too, and so Chuck and me realize, we did have a *pipe dream* our lives would get better, but now we see that ain't gonna happen, I'm a whore and he's a drunk. But at least we ain't got no pipe dreams anymore!

BLANCHE: *(Irritated.)* Please, please! You've said the word "pipe dream" fifty times! Can't you say the word "illusion"? "Illusion," "illusion." Try it.

CORA: So we've given up our... *(Says it slowly.)* ...il-lu-sions...and we want everyone else to too. *(Energetically to Blanche.)* Face it, you're old and ugly, you're never going to find happiness, and you're going to end up in a mental institution. There! Don't that make you feel better?

BLANCHE: I don't...think so. Let me just go throw up in the other room, and then I'll tell you. *(Runs out.)*

CORA: Did I upset her? Bejees, I didn't mean to upset her. Chuck and me, we wuz cheered up when we let go of our pipe dreams...il-lu-sions.

STANLEY: Oh, Blanche is so sensitive it makes you wanna barf. *(Goes to bathroom.)* Hey, canary bird, get outta the bathroom, I gotta pee! *(Re-enter Blanche.)*

BLANCHE: No need to shout, Stanley. Young man, you are going to have to change the information on your census sheet. There will be only four people living here in a few minutes.

STANLEY: You're finally going to use the bus ticket. Hot damn.

BLANCHE: No, Stanley. I am making an exit, but it's going to be a final one, Stanley. Because it's So Long, Sam; it's good-bye, Charlie; it's night, mother. *(Takes out long sheet of paper.)* Now I've made a list of where everything is so you won't be confused. The paper lanterns are in the top shelf in the bedroom closet, along with broken dreams and extra filters for the vacuum cleaner. The little white tie-things that go with the plastic garbage bags are up above the refrigerator in an empty Nestles Quik box. Extra ice trays are under the bed along with the papers about Belle Reeve and old love letters, yellowin' with antiquity. But you're not to read the love letters, I want to be buried with them.

STANLEY: Yeah, yeah, yeah.

BLANCHE: There are sour balls and Hostess Twinkies in the second cabinet next to the refrigerator, and there are Hershey bars and peanut brittle in the third draw in the kitchen next to the fire extinguisher and the Aunt Jemima cookie jar. The Eiffel Tower place settings are in the fourth drawyer along with the orange juice squeezer and the paper napkins, and scattered pieces of my heart. Linen napkins are in the hall closet with the towels and licorice strings, but I don't want you usin' the linen towels, Stanley Kowalski, I want to be buried with them too.

STANLEY: *(Not able to remember.)* Where's the peanut brittle?

BLANCHE: In the third drawyer in the kitchen, next to the fire extinguisher.

STANLEY: I might get some later.

CORA: Me too.

BLANCHE: Isn't anyone going to try to talk me out of suicide?

CORA: *(Friendly but a bit off-hand.)* Oh, sure, honey. Don't go kill yourself.

BLANCHE: No, I must.

CORA: How come you wanna kill yourself?

BLANCHE: Young woman, say you've been on a streetcar a long time. It's hot and it's bumpy and noisy, and you want to get off, but your stop isn't for fifty more blocks when it reaches Elysian Fields. But then you realize maybe the streetcar may not ever get to Elysian Fields, so you figure, why not get off the streetcar now?

CORA: Take a taxi to Elysian Fields.

BLANCHE: I don't have the money.

CORA: Or use the bus ticket Stanley gave you.

BLANCHE: It's a ticket to somewhere called Glengarry Glen Ross, and I don't want to go there.

STANLEY: *(Suddenly very energetic, staccato, aggressive.)* Why the fuck not? The place is good. It's not great maybe, but what I'm sayin' is, it's good. Not great, good. That's what I'm sayin'. It may be swamp, it may have bugs, but fuck, Blanche, what's perfect? You tell me. No, don't tell me, I'll tell you. It's not great, good. Am I right? Do you understand what I'm sayin'? Should I say it again? What I'm sayin' is, fuck shit piss damn, it ain't half bad. Half good, half bad. You gotta settle. It ain't perfect. Settle. Gotta. You gotta settle. A negotiation. Give and take. You know what I'm sayin'? What I'm saying' is...

BLANCHE: Shut up. I know what you're saying. She says pipe dream 300 times, you repeat yourself endlessly. It's lifelike, granted, one *could* hear it on a bus, if you were listening to a stupid person talking on and on, but I'm on a streetcar, not a bus, and I want poetry and art and music, and if I can't have them, I'd rather be dead.

STANLEY: What I'm sayin' is you gotta be fuckin' realistic.

BLANCHE: I don't want realism, I want magic!

YOUNG MAN: Well, I've been silent for a very long time.

BLANCHE: Yes, and I've appreciated it. Thank you.

YOUNG MAN: But now I want to talk about cable TV.

BLANCHE: What?

YOUNG MAN: There's constant need for new product. This is my last week as a census taker. Next week I'm starting my new job as vice president in charge of script development for Home Box Office. We're always on the look-out for new ideas. Comedies about attractive people who have terminal cancer. Dramas about handicapped people who learn to run in the Olympics with a wooden leg. Musicals about high school students with Bubonic plague who raise money to send homeless people to dancing school. Laughter, tears, exploitation. So if any of you have any ideas, here's my card.

BLANCHE: Thank you, honey lamb.

CORA: Excuse me, I'm going to go get some peanut brittle. *(Exits.)*

BLANCHE: Young man, why don't you make a program about me? A women with illusions shattered, livin' in a place where death is as close as you are, and where the opposite of death is desire. Desire, desire, desire.

YOUNG MAN: I don't mean to be rude, but I don't think you're commercial enough.

(*Enter Big Daddy, looking enormously fat and round, with fat padding that makes him look like Tweedledee and Tweedledum. He has a big cigar in his mouth.*)

BIG DADDY: Brick, Brick. Big Mama is drivin' me crazy, Mae and Gooper are drivin' me crazy, why can't you and Maggie the Cat have a child together? What's the matter between you and Maggie, Brick?

(*Enter Maggie, but played by a different actress then who played her before. She is Maggie 2, and is wearing the same slip as the first one. She crosses to Stanley.*)

MAGGIE 2: Brick, you left your crutches in the other room, Brick. It's my time of month to conceive now, Brick. Do you want to go in the other room and lie down?

BLANCHE: That sounds like me. (*To Young Man.*) You don't want to go lie down, do you, desire desire? (*Young Man politely shakes his head "no."*)

MAGGIE 2: Brick, what's the matter between us?

(*The first Maggie comes in from the kitchen, from where Cora had exited. She is the first Maggie, and she is chomping on a piece of peanut brittle.*)

MAGGIE: Brick, honey, you want some peanut brittle? It's good, baby.

(*Maggie 1 and Maggie 2 look at one another, both feeling threatened.*)

BIG DADDY: I'd like some peanut brittle. (*Exits to the kitchen.*)

MAGGIE 2: Brick, I want to have your baby.

MAGGIE: *I* want to have his baby.

STANLEY: Stella!!!!!

BLANCHE: Please, there seems to be some misunderstanding. Can't the two of you go away and sort it out? I feel as if I'm not at the center of attention when you're both here, and it distresses me.

MAGGIE 2: (*To Stanley.*) Is it because of Skipper that you won't go to bed with me? (*She goes over to the Young Man, addresses him as Skipper.*) Skipper, is that the reason?

BIG DADDY: (*Entering from kitchen, eating peanut brittle.*) Mendacity, mendacity! (*Exits back to kitchen.*)

MAGGIE 2: Brick, Brick, I'll tell you where I'm hiding the alcohol if you'll go to bed with me.

MAGGIE 1: Will you leave him alone?

MAGGIE 2: I feel like a cat on a hot tin roof.

MAGGIE 1: *I* feel like a cat on a hot tin roof.

BLANCHE: I feel left out. Please, everyone leave, this is my apartment, and my story, and my sensitivity, and my desire, so I want you all outta here. Except for Stanley.

STANLEY: SKIPPER!!!!! *(Puts his arm around the Young Man's shoulder.)* Maggie the cat, you make everything dirty. What's between me and Skipper is good and holy and there ain't nothing dirty about it. Oh, sometimes when we wuz on the road together, we'd reach across the bed and shake hands, like men would. Oh, and sometimes, if it was hot, we might take showers together. And sometimes, if we had nothin' better to do, we might dress up like lumberjacks and French kiss for an hour, but it was nothin' dirty. Was it, Skipper?

YOUNG MAN: I don't quite know what to say.

STANLEY: Skipper!!!!

YOUNG MAN: *(Agreeably, conversationally.)* Brick.

MAGGIE 2: *(Desperate.)* Brick!

MAGGIE 1: *(Desperate.)* Brick!

BIG DADDY: *(Entering from the kitchen.)* Big Mama! Big Mama! Oooooohhh! *(Exits.)*

STANLEY: *(To Young Man.)* Come on, Skipper, you and me is gonna go back to high school together, and play on the football team again. And go find a motel room. Don't that sound great?

YOUNG MAN: I'm sorry. What?

(Stanley and Young Man exit.)

MAGGIE 2: Brick!

MAGGIE 1: Brick!

(The two Maggie's exit. Big Daddy comes in from the kitchen, carrying lots of bags of candy and various things mentioned in Blanche's suicide speech.)

BIG DADDY: Thank you for your kind hospitality, Ma'am. *(Exits.)*

(Blanche is still for a moment or two.)

BLANCHE: *(Suddenly.)* Oh my God, I'm alone! *(Runs to door.)* Help! Help! I'm all alone! Help! Help! *(Runs to where the kitchen is.)* Help! Help! I'm alone! *(Goes to telephone.)* Operator, operator, get me Western Union, I want to send a telegram! "Help, help, caught in a trap, can't stand solitude, am afraid I'll go mad. Signed Blanche DuBois." What? Beckett? Samuel Beckett? No, I don't know him. Uh huh. Uh huh. I see. Alright. *(Hangs up; sits, stares out; lights dim to a spotlight on her.)* Nothing to be done. We'll just keep waiting. Waiting for Stella to come back with the lemon coke. Year after year, staring ahead with our lips tightly compressed. Waiting, waiting.

(Lights start to dim, as if play is over. But then they come back up to pretty full, somewhat to Blanche's surprise as well. Stella then enters. She carries a large paper cup of coca-cola.)

STELLA: Blanche, honey, I'm back with your lemon coke.

(Blanche looks pretty surprised to see her.)

STELLA: I'm sorry I was gone so many years. The store on the corner was closed. Where's Stanley?

BLANCHE: He went off to a motel with a young man, rather like my first husband did. We have trouble choosing men, Stella.

STELLA: Oh, Stanley, he's such a card. Well, are you happy to see your baby sister, Blanche?

BLANCHE: Stella, Stella for star. At last my lemon coke. My nerves have needed a lemon coke. *(Goes to sip the coca-cola.)* Stella for Star. This is not a lemon coke. This is a cherry coke. *(Hands the coca-cola back.)*

STELLA: Oh, I'm sorry.

BLANCHE: Would you mind bringin' it back and gettin' the proper one for me? My nerves need a lemon coke, honey.

STELLA: Sure, Blanche. I'll be back as soon as I can. *(Exits with the coke.)*

BLANCHE: *(Said fairly quickly; not fast exactly, but each thought should "feed" into the next.)* She's gone. I'm all alone. For six years at least. Alone, alone. All alone. Oh desire, desire, desire. Desire under the elms; desire under the arms. Farewell to arms. For whom the bell tolls. For whom the *southern* belle tolls. Waiting, waiting. Nothing to be done. We stare out, our lips compressed. Christ on the cross. One of the thieves was saved. One of the thieves had roast beef. One of the thieves went wee wee wee, all the way home. You can never go home again, Blanche. I, I, I took the blows in my face and my body. Body, body. Is anybody there? Stanley? Stella? Young, young, young man? One of the Maggies? Oh please, God, let someone come to the door.

(She runs to the door, opens it. It is a man in a very large rabbit suit.)

RABBIT: *Flores. Flores para los muertos.*

BLANCHE: Are you, Harvey? From the Pulitzer Prize-winning play by Mary Chase? That was a lean year.

(Rabbit shakes head "no".)

BLANCHE: You're not Harvey. Well, whoever you are, I have always depended on the kindness of strangers.

(The Rabbit takes off its head, revealing Stanley.)

BLANCHE: Stanley. You're back. What about Skipper?

STANLEY: It was a phase. It's over now.

BLANCHE: Why are you wearing the rabbit suit, Stanley?

STANLEY: I wore this rabbit suit on my wedding night, and I'm gonna wear it again when Stella has a baby, and then I'm gonna rip it off and wave it like a flag.

BLANCHE: Is Stella pregnant, Stanley?

STANLEY: I don't know. I ain't seen her in six years.

BLANCHE: *(Remembering.)* Oh, she was back briefly while you were out with Skipper and all those Maggies. But she went off again.

STANLEY: She was here? And she left? When's my baby comin' back, Blanche? When's she comin' back?

BLANCHE: I don't know, Stanley. I don't know. Well, Stanley, it's you and me again.

STANLEY: We've had this date from the beginning.

BLANCHE: Yes, we have. Sweet of you to say so.

STANLEY: Stella!!!!

BLANCHE: Oh, you're back on that again.

STANLEY: Stella!!!!

BLANCHE: Oh God, there's no hope. *(Sits.)*

STANLEY: Stella!!!!!

BLANCHE: Oh desire, desire, desire.

STANLEY: Stella!!!!!

(Mournful saxophone music—as in the soundtrack of the Streetcar *movie. Blanche sadly puts the rabbit head on her own head. She sits there, tragically, sadly. Lights dim. End.)*

TO THE ACTOR

I don't have much advice to give because I haven't really worked on a production of this one. I remind actors about keeping the pace fast. Though Blanche should have a sultry Southern accent, something must be done to keep her pace fast nonetheless. Comic lines don't "land" if all the vowels are long and drawn out.

Most people who know theatre well will get the allusions I'm making in this play, but in case there are some who don't, I'm going to risk being obvious and just out and out tell you who's from what.

Blanche, Stanley, Stella and the Young Man are from Williams' *A Streetcar Named Desire.*

Big Daddy and Maggie are from Williams' *Cat On A Hot Tin Roof.*

Cora is a character from O'Neill's *The Iceman Cometh.*

When Blanche gives a long, mundane list of "where everything is" for Stanley to know after she's dead, this is a reference to and parody of Marsha Norman's play *Night, Mother* (which originated at American Repertory Theater).

The man in the rabbit suit, as is mentioned in the play, is a reference to Mary Chase's popular comedy from the 1950s, *Harvey,* where James Stewart played a chatty man who drove his sister crazy by talking to his invisible friend, Harvey the rabbit. (I recently saw the movie and discovered I can't stand it. Sorry to be lacking a sense of humor, but Stewart's hallucination is clearly written to come out of his being an alcoholic. Chase's take on this is very poetic and false... she thinks it's adorable that he sees the rabbit and that he talks in hazy circles all the time. Maybe you have to have grown up around alcoholics to find this movie so irritating.)

Medea

co-written with Wendy Wasserstein

AUTHOR'S NOTE

I co-wrote this sketch with Wendy Wasserstein for a celebration of the Juilliard School's 25th anniversary of the Drama Division in spring of 1994.

Wendy and I went to Yale School of Drama together. (So why were they asking us to write a benefit for Juilliard? Well, Juilliard until two years ago didn't have a playwriting program, so why not ask us, I guess.)

My third year at Yale was Wendy's first year. Wendy and I became laughing pals together. We crammed for Theatre History exams the night before by using insane mnemonic devices. We drove to the New Haven airport together for milkshakes. We spent a New Year's together drinking champagne and eating an entire mocha cake. (We both like sugar. And cake. And icing.) We liked and encouraged each other's writing.

When she finished at Yale, I put all of her plants (about 15 of them) in the back of my car and planned to drive her to New York... though we both discussed how odd it would be if instead of driving to New York, we drove into the ocean together. We weren't feeling suicidal actually; we were just thinking, wouldn't it be odd. "They put all her plants in the car, and then they just drove into the ocean," they'd say.

Are Wendy and Chris OK? Yes, fine. Thank you for asking.

Wendy and I have written together twice—a cabaret show at Yale (*When Dinah Shore Ruled The Earth*) and a screenplay (*House of Husbands*) out in the real world. We have also written two benefits together, including this recent one for Juilliard.

Our assignment for Juilliard was to write something about classical theatre. At first we were going to do something about *The Trojan Women*. But Diana Rigg in *Medea* was playing on Broadway, so Wendy and I went to that. Then we wrote this.

ORIGINAL PRODUCTION

Medea was co-written by Chris Durang and Wendy Wasserstein for the Juilliard School's Drama Division's 25th anniversary, April 25, 1994 at the Juilliard Theater, New York City. The evening was directed by Gerald Gutierrez, produced by Margot Harley, choreographed by Christopher Chadman, musical direction by Tom Fay. The cast for the evening consisted of many Juilliard graduates. For this particular sketch the cast was as follows:

Medea .... Harriet Harris
The Chorus .... Laura Linney
Diane Venora
Denise Woods
Jason .... Kevin Spacey
Messenger .... Randle Mell
Angel Ex Machina .... David Schramm

CHARACTERS
MEDEA, an angry woman
THE CHORUS
JASON, Medea's husband
MESSENGER
ANGEL

MEDEA

The actress who is to play Medea comes out and makes the following introduction.

ACTRESS: Hello. I am she who will be Medea. That is, I shall play the heroine from that famous Greek tragedy by Euripides for you.

I attended a first rate School of Dramatic Arts. At this wonderful school, I had classical training, which means we start at the very beginning, a very good place to start. Greek tragedy. How many of you in the audience have ever acted in Greek tragedy? How many of your lives are Greek tragedy? Is Olympia Dukakis here this evening?

As an actress who studied the classics, one of the first things you learn in drama school is that there are more roles for men than for women. This is a wonderful thing to learn because it is true of the real world as well. Except for *Thelma and Louise.* At drama school, in order to compensate for this problem, the women every year got to act in either *The Trojan Women* or *The House of Bernardo Alba.* This prepared us for bit parts on *Designing Women* and *Little House on the Prairie.* Although these shows are canceled now, and we have nothing to do.

Tonight, we would like to present to you a selection from one of the most famous Greek tragedies ever written, *The Trojan Women.* Our scene is directed by Michael Cacoyannis and choreographed by June Taylor. And now, translated from the Greek by George Stephanoulous, here is a scene from this terrifying tragedy. *(Names the cast members. Then says dramatically:)* And I, will play Medea. *(The actress playing Medea exits with purpose and panache. Enter the three actresses who play The Chorus. They are dressed in togas. Most of the time they speak in unison. Sometimes they speak solo lines. In the style of the piece, they are overdramatic and overwrought. But most of the time they should act their lines as if they are the words from genuine Greek tragedy, full of intonation and emotional feeling. Don't send them up, or wink at the audience. Let the juxtaposition of Greek tragedy acting style and the sometimes silly lines be what creates the humor.)*

CHORUS: *(In unison.)*

So pitiful, so pitiful

your shame and lamentation.

No more shall I move the shifting pace

of the shuttle at the looms of Ida

CHORUS MEMBER #3: *(Echoes.)* Looms of Ida.

CHORUS: Can you not, Queen Hecuba, stop this Bacchanal before her light feet whirl her away into the Argive camp?

CHORUS MEMBER #3: *(Echoes.)* Argive camp.

CHORUS: *(In unison.)*

O woe, o woe, o woe,

We are so upset we speak in unison,

So pitiful, so wretched, so doomed,

Women who run with wolves

Women who love too much,

Whitewater rapids, how did she turn $1000 into $100,000?

Oh woe, oh woe, o woe.

Here she comes now.

Wooga, wooga, wooga.

(Enter Medea in a dramatic, blood red toga. She is in high, excessive grief and fury.)

MEDEA: Come, flame of the sky,

Pierce through my head!

What do I, Medea, gain from living any longer?

Oh I hate living! I want

to end my life, leave it behind, and die.

CHORUS: *(In unison; chanted seriously.)* But tell us how you're really feeling.

MEDEA: My husband Jason—the Argonaut—has left me for another woman. Debbie.

CHORUS: *(In unison.)*

Dreaded Debbie, dreaded Debbie.

Debutante from hell.

MEDEA: She is the daughter of King Creon, who owns a diner on 55th

Street and Jamaica Avenue. Fie on her! And the House of Creon! And the four brothers of the Acropolis. I am banished from my husband's bed, and from the country. A bad predicament all around. But I am skilled in poison. Today three of my enemies I will strike down dead: Debbie and Debbie's father and my husband.

CHORUS: *(In unison.)* Speaking of your husband, here he comes.

(Enter Jason, dressed in a toga, but also with an armored breastplate and wearing a soldier's helmet with a nice little red adornment on top. Sort of like a costume from either Ben Hur *or* Cleopatra. *He perhaps is not in the grand style, but sounds more normal and conversational.)*

JASON: Hello, Medea.

MEDEA: Hello, Jason.

JASON: I hear you've been banished to China.

MEDEA: *(Suddenly Noel Coward brittle.)* Very large, China.

JASON: And Japan?

MEDEA: Very small, Japan. And Debbie?

JASON: She's very striking.

MEDEA: Some women should be struck regularly like gongs.

JASON: Medea, even though thou art banished by Creon to foreign shores, the two innocent children of our loins, Lyle and Erik, should remain with me. I will enroll them at the Dalton School. And there they will flourish as citizens of Corinth under the watchful eye of Zeus and his lovely and talented wife Hera.

MEDEA: Fine, walk on me some more! I was born unlucky and a woman.

CHORUS: *(In unison.)*

Men are from Mars,

Women are from Venus.

JASON: Well, whatever. I call the gods to witness that I have done my best to help you and the children.

MEDEA: Go! You have spent too long out here. You are consumed with craving for your newly won bride, Debbie. Go, enjoy Debbie!

(Jason shrugs, exits.)

MEDEA: O woe, o woe. I am in pain for I know what I must do. Debbie, kill for sure.

CHORUS: *(In unison.)*

Debbie's done, ding dong, Debbie's done.

Done deal, Debbie dead,

Dopey Debbie, Debbie dead.

MEDEA: But also my sons. Never shall their father see them again. I shall kill my children. *(Ferociously, to the Chorus.)* How do you like that????

CHORUS: *(In unison.)* Aaaaaaagghghghghghghgghhhhh!

O smart women, foolish choices. Stop the insanity! Stop the insanity! You can eat one slice of cheese, or sixteen baked potatoes! Make up your mind.

MEDEA: Why is there so little *Trojan Women* in this, and so much of me?

CHORUS: *(In unison.)* We don't know *The Trojan Women* as well as we know *Medea.*

(Spoken, not sung.)

Medea, we just met a girl named Medea.

And suddenly that name

Will never be the same.

MEDEA: Bring my children hither.

CHORUS: *(In unison.)*

O miserable mother, to destroy your own increase, murder the babes of your body. The number you have reached is not in service at this time. Call 777-FILM.

MEDEA: *(In a boiling fury.)* I want to kill my children. I want to sleep with my brother. I want to pluck out the eyes of my father. I want to blow up the Parthenon. I need a creative outlet for all this anger.

(Enter the Messenger, carrying a head. He kneels before Medea.)

MESSENGER: I am a messenger. Caesar is dead.

CHORUS: *(In unison.)*

Caesar is dead. How interesting. Who is Caesar?

MESSENGER: I am sorry. Wrong message. *(Reads from piece of paper.)* Lady Teazle wishes you to know that Lady Windermere and Lady Bracknell are inviting you and Lady The-Scottish-Play to tea with her cousin Ernest, if he's not visiting Mr. Bunberry.

MEDEA: Mr. Bunberry? I do not need a messenger. I need a *deus ex machina.* *(Elaborate music. Enter an Angel with great big wings. Descending from the ceiling, or revealed on a balcony. Or dragging a step ladder that he stands on. Very dramatic whatever he does.)*

ANGEL: Oh Medea, O Medea.

I am a deus ex machina.

In a bigger production, I would come down from the sky in an angel's outfit, but just use your imagination. Theatre is greatly about imagination, is it not.

I am an angel.

I I I I I I I, yi yi yi.

I I I I am the Bird of Greek Tragedy.

Do not kill your children. Do not sleep with your brother. Rein in your rage, and thank Zeus. I come with glad tidings. Debbie is no more a threat. She's been cast in a series. She has a running part on *Home Improvements*.

CHORUS: *(In unison.)*
Home improvements.

ANGEL: Jason will return to you. He sees the error of his ways. He has been lobotomized.

CHORUS: *(In unison.)*
O fortunate woman, to whom Zeus has awarded a docile husband.

MEDEA: O, *deus ex machina*, o, Angel
O, Hecuba, oh, looms of Ida.

CHORUS: *(In unison.)*
Ida Ida Ida Ida.

MEDEA: I am eternally grateful to you.

CHORUS: The things we thought would happen, do not happen.
The unexpected, God makes possible.
(Spoken, not sung.)
The camptown races sing a song,
Do da, do da.

CHORUS AND MEDEA: ˙ (Singing.)
Medea's happy the whole day long,
Oh the do da day!

Things will be just fine,
No need to kill her children,
Medea's feeling happy now,
Oh the do da...

(Big musical coda:)
Oh the do da,
Zeus and Buddha,
They're as nice as
Dionysus,
Oh the do da
Work it through da,
Oh the do da, do da, do da day!
(End.)

One Minute Play

AUTHOR'S NOTE
I wrote this for a "one minute play festival" to benefit the American Repertory Theater in Cambridge, Massachusetts.

The previous time I wrote them a "one minute" play it was seven minutes—*Entertaining Mr. Helms*. This time I wanted to really let it be only one minute.

ORIGINAL PRODUCTION

One Minute Play was written for a benefit for the American Repertory Theater in Cambridge, Massachusetts, some time in the spring of 1992. The cast of this brief play was as follows:

Polly. . . . . Anne Pitoniak
Dave . . . . Michael Malone Starr

CHARACTERS
POLLY
DAVE

ONE MINUTE PLAY

POLLY: Hello, Dave, how are you today?

DAVE: Well, I don't have a sense of myself today. I feel rather worthless. Do you think of me as worthless?

POLLY: Oh, I don't know. I was just trying to make a pleasantry.

DAVE: You know my wife left me. She married my father. He's eighty, but she prefers him.

POLLY: Gee, I'm sorry to hear that. Are there any restaurants you can recommend? My Aunt Helen is coming to town.

DAVE: I'm thinking to going out to find a copy of "Final Exit." Is that the correct title? Do you have a copy?

POLLY: Gosh, no, I never read books. I don't have the time.

DAVE: I have a lot of time now that I've been fired.

POLLY: Gee, I didn't know you'd been fired. What happened?

DAVE: Well, I was incompetent. I don't know why they hired me.

POLLY: What was your profession exactly?

DAVE: Well, it's hard to say really.

POLLY: Well, forget it then, I don't want to know. And you can't recommend a restaurant, I guess?

DAVE: I've lost my appetite. I'm not sleeping. I'm losing weight, and my hair is falling out.

POLLY: *(Stares at him.)* Well, you know, I hope this isn't some call for psychological help that I'm not picking up, but basically I think you're just having a really bad day, and I'm sure you'll feel a lot better tomorrow. And you know, your wife—well, she was rubbish, good riddance. Your father, so he's sexy for an 80-year-old. Your job, you didn't like it anyway. And you needed to lose some weight, so all this sleep loss and body loss is really quite attractive. So tomorrow you'll see it all differently. Well, good-bye. *(Exits.)*

DAVE: *(Calling after her.)* Tomorrow I'll see things differently. Tomorrow I'll be dead! Oh you there! I haven't finished talking to you. *(Pause.)* I've thought of a good restaurant! *(Pause.)* But you'll never get the name of it from me. So long. Good riddance. *(Pause; to himself with some comfort.)* Well, death tomorrow.

(End.)

John and Mary Doe

The first couple of pages of this piece have been sitting in my computer for a year and a half. I think the entire country seems to be riveted by a desire to live back in the 1950s, when life seemed simpler (at least in retrospect). Though I think it's foolish to try to return to the past—it's not a do-able thing, and there are lots of stupid things about the 1950s that we're forgetting in our haze—still it's equally foolish to pretend that our present times aren't upsetting. These two thoughts are the theme of these pages. And I keep thinking this beginning could grow into a full play.

But maybe it won't. I sort of liked the weirdness of what I'd written so far, so I wrote a few more pages to kind of wrap it up, in a short version at least; and I include it now.

CHARACTERS

JOHN DOE, an upstanding husband in his late 30s
MARY DOE, an upstanding wife in her 30s
JOHN, JR., their son
JOHN THE SECOND, their other son
JOHNNA, their daughter

JOHN AND MARY DOE

JOHN DOE: Hello, my name is John Doe. That is my name, I do not mean that I am a representative everyman. That is my family-given name. My middle name is Ferdinand, if it helps you distinguish me. My name is John Ferdinand Doe. John Doe for short.

My wife's name is Mary Doe. Her maiden name was Smith. We met in elementary school. She was always very sweet, and I knew I wanted to marry her the moment I met her when we were nine. I never went through that period of hating girls. No, I was firmly heterosexual even at age nine.

My wife's middle name, to help distinguish her in your mind, is Mother of God. Her name is Mary Mother of God Doe, nee Mary Mother of God Smith.

We have three children. John Jr., John the Second, and our daughter Johnna, Daughter of Mother of God Doe.

We have three pets. We have a dog named Sputnik. And we have a cat named John F. Kennedy, Jr. And we have a goldfish we call Jason Robards, Jr. My son sometimes dresses up in drag and pretends to be Lauren Bacall.

My wife and I have never molested our children. Or if we have, we've forgotten it entirely. And we hope they have. We are not attracted to children anyway. We are attracted to one another, and sometimes to other couples, and sometimes we have drunken orgies, but I don't think we've really done that, I'm just kidding. Absence makes the heart grow fonder.

Why did I say that I wonder. Oh yes. My wife Mary Mother of God Doe nee Smith was murdered last year by our next door neighbor, Tommy Psycho Babbit. We miss my wife very much, Tommy and I do. Tommy is in a mental institution. We all agree he's crazy. We all forgive him for killing my wife, and we all hope he gets better and that he's learning skills that he can use in the outside world, skills like getting mail from the mailbox without axing someone to death and hiding parts of their bodies around the yard like some sort of demented Easter egg hunt. Do you remember Easter egg hunts? Weren't they fun? How I miss my childhood, all the good times. I wish I could be four-years-old again.

We still haven't found my wife's knees. I sometimes get afraid opening certain drawers in the house, afraid we'll find them. Tommy Psycho Babbit swears he never put any of her body parts in the house, but then we did find that Adam's apple in the refrigerator. Of course, my wife didn't have an Adam's apple, so it didn't belong to her. We don't know who it belonged to.

I'm sorry. Is this becoming gruesome? Do you wish this were going to be nicer? Let me start over.

Everything I've said has been a lie. Nothing bad has happened in our family, I just told you all this awful stuff because I wanted to get you to like me. And also to upset you. And also to give you nightmares. But I know where to draw the line. I think the line should be drawn right now. No more awful things from me. Only nice things.

My daughter Johnna drew a picture of a snowman today. My wife Mary and I put it up on the refrigerator. And then we gave Johnna a warm, parental, nonsexual hug, and we told her we love her. Then my wife played Chopin on the piano, with Johnna tied to the piano leg and filled up with enema water, which she was not allowed to expel. *Sybil* was one of my wife's favorite movies, and try and try as we do, her therapist and I cannot get her to stop torturing little Johnna with enemas.

Who invented the enema? Was it a caveman who had indigestion? He had just invented the wheel, and so then he invented the hose, and water pressure, and he thought: I know! I think I'll stick this hose up my ass, that should be fun.

Let me start over. I've gotten disturbing again.

Lovely little duckies frolicking in the water. Beautiful delicate butterflies landing on pretty yellow flowers and daintily sipping nectar. Fuzzy big bumble bees who make a nice sound but don't want to sting people, floating about in the summer sun. Endangered species frolicking in a waterfall and being forcefed Prozac by Dr. Kevorkian.

I think if you want to die you should have every goddamn right to do it. I think if you want to have Dr. Kevorkian or some other doctor you know come over and give you a delicious cocktail that'll kill you, or hook you up to some sort of gas-inhaler or something…well, I say, bully for you, and so long!

And now the first scene.

(John and his wife Mary.)

JOHN: Mary. I love you.

MARY: And John. I love you.

JOHN: Mary, I love you.

MARY: And I love you, John.

JOHN: Mary, I love you.

MARY: Yes, thank you. I cherish your love, John.

JOHN: And I cherish your love, Mary.

JOHN: And now the second scene.

MARY: John, I'm concerned about our country.

JOHN: You are? What about it?

MARY: Well, I feel there is a lack of morality now. The children seem to carry guns in school now. We never did that when I was younger. Why are they carrying guns?

JOHN: Let's ask them. John, Jr., John the Second. Why are you carrying guns to school now?

JOHN JR.: It's cool. Also, we have to protect ourselves from Tommy Psycho Babbit who lives next door.

MARY: Oh, that's right. I think I'm dead. I think I'm dismembered. What a terrible tragedy. *(She lies down on the ground, and scatters her body parts about the room.)*

JOHN: Oh, Lord, how will we ever stage this in a real production? We must hold auditions for an actress to play my wife, and see who can break up into different pieces and scatter themselves around the room. John Jr.! John the Second! Johnna! Come clean up your rooms, and gather your mother's body parts together. This is no way to live, with a tragedy strewn about the kitchen or living room this way like so many snap peas.

JOHNNA: *(Calling from the living room.)* I can't help, Daddy! I'm still tied to the grand piano leg, and I'm holding my enema water. May I please be untied and allowed to expel my water and then go live with my grandparents or something?

JOHN: You kids! You're just impossible. Here, let me beat you.

(John beats all three children to within an inch of their lives.)

Stop crying, I'll give you something to cry about. *(Hits one of them.)* There! That's something to cry about! *(Punches another one.)* And *that's* something to cry about! Why aren't you crying? Did I knock the breath out of you? Well, good! I am a very angry man, and I am learning to express my anger. *(Punches and kicks them to the death.)* Oh, Lord, now they're all dead. Oh, dear. Oh, my. Oh, well. *(To audience.)* Sorry, I feel I've gotten dark again. Let me start over. My wife is not dead. I have not killed the children. We have not mentioned enemas or the movie *Sybil* or a murderous next-door neighbor named Tommy Psycho Babbit. *(To the pieces of Mary on the ground.)* Come on, Mary, pull yourself together now. Stand up. None of this being in the dumps, spread around the room.

(The actress playing Mary re-constructs herself and becomes a whole, living person again.)

JOHN: We certainly were right to cast you, that was excellent! Mary, I love you.

MARY: ...nd...ee...uhb...oooo,...ohn.

JOHN: No, dear, the mouth's half hanging off your face, can you fix it? Ah, that's better. And I love you, Mary.

MARY: And I love you, John.

JOHN: Thank goodness we live in the fifties. We're safe here. The atom bomb may destroy the world in big blasts, following then with long, lingering radiation sickness. And there may be foreign communists in our midst, who are disguising themselves as Margaret Chase Smith and Adlai Stevenson, and who may take over our country and enslave us at any minute. But if those two things *don't* happen, then we will live very very happy lives together.

MARY: I'm very happy, John. I love you. Look at the ducky on the yard.

JOHN: Yes, a lovely ducky. I love you, Mary.

MARY: I'm happy.

JOHN: I'm happy, Mary.

(Mary's eye falls out.)

JOHN: Pick it up, would you, Mary?

MARY: Sorry, John. *(Picks up eye, puts it back in socket.)*

JOHN: Well, let's go to bed. Before anything else falls apart. We'll try to

bring the children back to life tomorrow. But I don't want anything
else to go wrong tonight. So, hurry, let's go to sleep.

MARY: I made you a casserole, Mary.

JOHN: You're Mary.

MARY: I'm Mary. I love you, John.

JOHN: Fine. And I love you, Mary. And thanks for the casserole. We can
microwave it in the morning, if it won't cause cancer or make the
whole goddamn house be riddled with radiation. Let's nap. Dr.
Kevorkian is due shortly after 8:00 P.M. He's going to sell us some
life insurance, and then make himself the beneficiary. And then
we'll finally have rest.

MARY: Oh, I need to rest, I'm exhausted. I love you, John.

JOHN: I love you, Mary.

*(They go to bed, exhausted. The house waits for the visit of Dr.
Kevorkian. End.)*

Diversions

AUTHOR'S NOTE

This is a very old play of mine. I hesitate to tell you how old. I hesitate to tell you. Shall I tell you? Maybe later. Well…I wrote it in 1967, when I was eighteen. My freshman year at Harvard College I put on a production of it in the Loeb Experimental Theater. After that, I went into a two-and-a-half-year depression, and did nothing else until 1971.

One reason I felt an impulse to include this play is that it was the first thing I wrote that started to be in "my style."

For some reason I had written plays for most of my youth. I wrote my first one—a brief version of *I Love Lucy*—when I was eight. After that, with parental cooing and encouragement (for which I'm grateful), I wrote short plays every year. Once I wrote a play called *Dinner at 8* based on the title alone. At that point I hadn't seen the Kauffman-Hart play.

With Kevin Farrell, a school friend who composed music, I started to write musical comedies. The very first one, written when he and I were thirteen, was called *Banned In Boston*. It was extremely innocent and precocious, and ended like a Shakespearean comedy with four marriages. (Its subplot had to do with two conservative aunts trying to shut down a local show they found "offensive;" odd foreshadowing, given the protests my play *Sister Mary Ignatius Explains It All For You* eventually received, including in Boston.)

Banned In Boston was performed at Kevin's and my all boys Catholic high school. The administration "borrowed" girls from a local girls' Catholic school. The priests at my school thought the show was fun, but the nuns at the girls' school were offended by a number where one of their girls dropped a shoulder strap seductively. (Clearly, they didn't relish an *hommage* to *Gypsy* as I did.) That girls' school vowed not to loan out girls for plays at my school again.

Our second musical, when we were fifteen, was getting a bit more cynical and was called *Businessman's Holiday.* (We borrowed girls from another school and had no trouble.) It ended with the heroine realizing the hero was a jerk, turning down his marriage proposal, but otherwise seemed very much like an imitation of a "commercial" musical from the 50s.

Diversions, for what it's worth, seemed to come from a different place in me. It has a young person's existentialism, I guess; it also is drawn to absurdism, which I seemed to know from Edward Albee's *The American Dream* and maybe from some Fellini movies.

So, hoping it's worth reading, here's *Diversions.*

ORIGINAL PRODUCTION

Diversions was presented at the Loeb Experimental Theater at Harvard College in Cambridge, Massachusetts, in the fall of 1967. It was directed by the author. The cast was as follows:

Man . . . . Chris Durang
Nun . . . . Pat Pilz
Aloysious Kain . . . . Mike Stone
Policeman 1 . . . . Ernst Louis
Hysteria . . . . Bonnie Raitt
Policeman 2 . . . . Lynn Stephens
Judge . . . . Burton Craig
Clerk . . . . Richard Bock
Deborah Kain . . . . Jane Stein
Prosecuting Attorney . . . . Dean Sheppard

(Note: Bonnie Raitt is indeed the same person who went on to become the much-enjoyed singer-composer. She was quite good as an actress too.)

CHARACTERS

MAN, who's feeling depressed
NUN, who's not depressed, and is very sure of herself
ALOYSIOUS KAIN, a bit of a milquetoast
POLICEMAN
HYSTERIA, who screams a lot
POLICEMAN 2
JUDGE, who's a bit irritated
CLERK, who's trying to do his best
DEBORAH KAIN, Aloysius' sultry wife
PROSECUTING ATTORNEY, who's virile, knows his place
    in the world

DIVERSIONS

Scene: A Man is standing at the edge of a small platform, preparing to jump. A Nun enters right. She sees him and screams. The Man almost loses his balance because of her scream.

NUN: Don't jump!
(*The Man looks at her, then prepares to jump again. The Nun repeats her scream; then rushes up to him and pulls on his arm.*)
NUN: Don't jump!
MAN: (*Tired.*) Why not?
NUN: It's against the fifth commandment.
(*The Man struggles to free himself from her grasp and to attempt jumping again.*)
NUN: (*Yanking at his arm harder now.*) Don't jump!
(*The Man looks at her.*)
NUN: Think of your wife.
MAN: My wife left me five years ago.
NUN: Think of your children.
MAN: I did. (*Vaguely sarcastic.*) And I appreciate your concern, but please leave me alone. (*He prepares to jump again.*)
NUN: (*In a booming voice.*) If you do that, you're going to go straight to hell.
(*The Man glares at her, starts again.*)
NUN: DON'T JUMP!
MAN: (*Exasperated, getting angry.*) My good woman...
NUN: I'm not a woman, I'm a nun.

MAN: My good woman, would you kindly go away and let me be in *peace!*

(He throws off her clutching hand. She seethes.)

NUN: Who do you think you are? Who do you think you are, to speak to me that way? How very typical of our modern secular world you are. Someone tries to help you, to reach out, and you turn on them, tell them to leave you in peace. Well, I'm finished helping you. I'm finished with you completely. As a matter of fact, I'll help you jump. I'll push you.

(She rushes toward him; they struggle. From left enters Aloysius Kain, a New York Times *under his arm. Seeing the trouble, he raises his newspaper and charges over.)*

ALOYSIUS: Hey! Stop that. Stop that at once.

(He starts to pull the Nun away from the Man.)

NUN: Help! Let go!

ALOYSIUS: Stop this! Stop this!

(A policeman enters, sees the three people struggling. He blows his whistle.)

MAN: *(Amidst the struggling.)* If you'd all just leave me alone.

(The policeman struggles to pull Aloysius off the Nun; Aloysius tries to pull the Nun off the Man; and the Man tries to keep his balance. Suddenly through a quick motion, the policeman loses his balance and falls off the platform, lying in a lump on the floor. [The policeman, not the platform.] A scream offstage. Aloysius, the Nun, and the Man stare aghast at the body at their feet.)

MAN: He fell.

ALOYSIUS: My God.

NUN: Do you think we're...murderers?

ALOYSIUS: Don't say that.

(Enter an Hysterical Woman with another policeman.)

HYSTERIA: I saw it! I saw it! They pushed the policeman over. I saw it!

(She gives an ear-splitting scream.)

ALOYSIUS: *(Nervous.)* For God's sake, woman, not so loud.

NUN: *(Frightened.)* She's a liar! We didn't push that man over. *(She points to Aloysius.)* He did.

ALOYSIUS: I did! How can you say that? You saw me. I didn't do anything. I was trying to...

(The Hysterical Woman screams again.)

(As the above commotion has been going on, a Clerk has entered, carrying a desk, followed regally by the Judge. The Clerk drags the dead

body of the first policeman offstage. The Judge sits behind the desk. The second policeman ushers the group [Aloysius, the Nun, the Man, and the Hysterical Woman] over to the Judge. Much noise and commotion.)

JUDGE: *(Rather tired.)* What is it? Be quiet, please. I can't think.

COP: Your Honor, these three people have been accused of murdering a policeman?

JUDGE: *(Looks at the people in front of him.)* Which three people?

COP: *(Pointing to Aloysius, the Nun, and the Man.)* That woman and the two men.

JUDGE: *(To the three.)* How do you plead?

ALOYSIUS: Not guilty.

MAN: Not guilty.

NUN: Clergy. And I demand to be tried in an ecclesiastical court.
(The Judge frowns.)

JUDGE: *(To the Cop.)* Who is the other one?

COP: She is the witness.
(The Hysterical Woman screams very loudly, followed by a series of sobs. The Clerk rushes in with a pair of pants.)

CLERK: Here are your pants, Your Honor.

JUDGE: *(Distracted.)* What?

CLERK: Here are your pants.

JUDGE: *(Checking.)* But I have my pants.

CLERK: I don't know. The dry cleaners just sent them, that's all.
(Clerk exits. The Judge puts pants on desk.)

JUDGE: *(To Hysteria.)* And what did you see, my good woman?
(Hysteria, terrified, breaks down into further sobbings.)

HYSTERIA: *(In between sobs.)* I demand to call my lawyer.

JUDGE: *(Truly exasperated.)* I can't understand her.

MAN: She said she wants to call her lawyer.

JUDGE: Very well. Clerk! Bring in a telephone. *(Enter the Clerk with telephone and another pair of pants.)*

CLERK: Here are your pants, Your Honor.

JUDGE: I have my pants. *(The Clerk looks sternly at him.)* Oh, very well. I won't argue.
(He takes pants, gives telephone to Hysteria. Exit Clerk. Hysteria, calmer, picks up telephone. Silence. She starts to cry again.)

JUDGE: Now what's the matter?

HYSTERIA: I don't have a lawyer. Everyone else has a lawyer but me. *(Her sobbing is making her talk unintelligible again.)* I'm only a simple working woman...etc.

ALOYSIUS: I don't see why she needs a lawyer. We're the ones who need a lawyer.

HYSTERIA: *(At climax.)* But he's trying to intimidate me!!

JUDGE: My good woman...

(Hysteria gives a horrifying scream.)

COP: Your Honor...

JUDGE: I'm sick of this case. I want nothing more to do with it. It's disgusting.

COP: But Your Honor...

JUDGE: Clerk! Clerk! *(Enter the Clerk.)* My pills, quickly.

CLERK: Which ones?

JUDGE: Ulcer, liver and kidney. *(Motioning toward the Hysterical Woman.)* And please take this woman out. I'm going to rest. Court recesses for my pills. *(To Clerk.)* Tell the Prosecuting Attorney I want to see him when he comes. *(Exit Judge L.)*

CLERK: *(To the Nun.)* I tried to contact your Mother Superior but she was praying.

NUN: You needn't have done that. I have God. I could levitate right up to the ceiling if I wanted.

CLERK: *(To the Man.)* I wasn't given any number to call for you. Do you want to call anyone?

MAN: No.

ALOYSIUS: Did you call my wife?

CLERK: Yes. She's coming down here any moment. Alright. All of you wait in the other room until court begins again. Come on. *(Clerk leads everyone offstage right. Moment's pause. Enter Deborah Kain, Aloysius' wife. She stands alone on stage, takes out her compact. She arranges her hair and powder. Enter the Prosecuting Attorney. They stare at one another, somewhat startled. The Prosecuting Attorney then exits right. Enter the Clerk.)*

CLERK: You are the wife of Aloysius Kain?

DEBORAH: Yes.

CLERK: I'll send him in to you.

(Exit Clerk. Enter Aloysius. Silence.)

ALOYSIUS: Nice of you to come.

DEBORAH: *(Rather loudly.)* I got a phone call which said you were being held for murder. Are you, Henry?

ALOYSIUS: Why did you call me 'Henry'? You know my name is Aloysius. Have you been seeing Henry again?

DEBORAH: I've asked you not to pry into my personal life.

ALOYSIUS: Have you?

DEBORAH: Now, Aloysius. Don't badger me.

(Silence. Aloysius looks away uncomfortably. Deborah takes out a cigarette, waits for him to light it.)

ALOYSIUS: I'm sorry. I don't have my lighter with me.

(She puts away the cigarette, disgusted.) Are you going to stay for the trial or go to your bridge club?

DEBORAH: Bridge club was called off today.

ALOYSIUS: Oh. Well, I guess I'll wait in the other room.

(Deborah stares vacantly into nowhere. Aloysius exits. Enter The Prosecuting Attorney.)

ATTORNEY: You're one of the defendants' wives, aren't you?

DEBORAH: Yes.

ATTORNEY: *(Close to her.)* I'm the Prosecuting Attorney. *(They kiss.)*

DEBORAH: Henry...darling. *(Breaks away.)* We must be careful not to be seen like this. Aloysius doesn't approve.

HENRY: I like the new shade your hair's dyed.

(He lights her cigarette. She begins to pace.)

DEBORAH: Henry, just think. Now that Aloysius has been arrested, we can get married. And if he gets the electric chair, I won't have to leave the Church.

(Silence.)

HENRY: You didn't tell me you were Catholic.

DEBORAH: I didn't think it really mattered.

HENRY: It does.

DEBORAH: But why? Henry. You're not...prejudiced, are you?

HENRY: Well I wouldn't want my daughter to marry a Negro.

DEBORAH: Who would? But, are you prejudiced against...Catholics?

(Henry turns away.)

DEBORAH: Henry, what a horrid thing to come between us. Henry, please. Believe me. I haven't been to Church for years, except for Christmas. And I'd even give that up for you.

HENRY: It wouldn't matter. It would be a blot on our past.

DEBORAH: Henry, does this mean we're through.

(He refuses to turn towards her. She begins to sing softly.)

DEBORAH: "We kiss in a shadow, we hide from the moon, our meetings are few..."

(He turns and they embrace. They kiss.)

DEBORAH: I didn't know you had a daughter.

HENRY: I don't. I was speaking figuratively.

DEBORAH: Oh.

(They kiss again. Enter the Nun, the Man, Hysteria, the Clerk, and Aloysius. Upon seeing the kissing couple, Hysteria gasps. Henry and Deborah break away, startled. The Nun goes to the couple, pulls them apart.)

NUN: Are you married?

DEBORAH: Take your hands off me.

NUN: God have mercy on your souls.

(Enter the Judge. Hysteria screams.)

JUDGE: Is she still screaming?

ALOYSIUS: *(Humiliated, angry.)* Deborah, this is the end of us.

DEBORAH: Aloysius, don't be dramatic.

ALOYSIUS: But I'll never divorce you. Just to spite you.

JUDGE: What is everyone talking about? Court come to order, please.

(Clerk provides chairs. Hysteria, Man, Nun, Henry sit. Clerk exits. Aloysius and Deborah continue talking.)

DEBORAH: You spiteful thing! But I love Henry so.

ALOYSIUS: You are incapable of love.

DEBORAH: Then why did you kill that policeman if you didn't think he was my lover?

(She sits down triumphantly. Hysteria stands up and applauds. The Clerk enters and admonishes her, slapping her palms. He gives the Judge a pair of pants. Exits.)

ALOYSIUS: I didn't kill the policeman!

JUDGE: Order in the court. Who is the Prosecuting Attorney?

HENRY: I am.

JUDGE: Oh yes. I spoke to you a moment ago. And the Defense Attorney?

ALOYSIUS: Your Honor, this thing is so simple, I will defend myself. It can all be over in a minute. Now you see, I saw this nun *(He points.)* trying to push this man off the roof, and I came to stop her. Then a policeman came along, and apparently thinking I was trying to push the nun or both of them off, came and joined the struggle. By mistake, one of us pushed him off. *(Silence.)*

JUDGE: That is the most preposterous story I have ever heard in my life.

DEBORAH: Aloysius! Tell the truth. *(To the Judge.)* He thought the policeman was my lover, while the Prosecuting Attorney here really is.

ALOYSIUS: That's a lie!

HENRY: No, it's not. I am your wife's lover.

ALOYSIUS: I know that. I mean it's a lie that I thought the policeman was my wife's lover.

JUDGE: Oh, so you admit that the policeman was not her lover. Then what possible reason could you have for killing him?

(Pause. Everyone stares at the Hysterical Woman.)

JUDGE: That's funny, I could've sworn you were going to scream.

(Hysteria smiles at him. Henry suddenly stands.)

HENRY: I call to the stand the prosecution's first witness, the eye witness.

(Hysteria comes to the stand, terrified. Silence. Henry begins to shout.)

HENRY: And did you not see that man, Aloysius Kain, willfully push that policeman off the roof, while that horrified couple over there watched aghast? I put it before you. did you not!!!???

HYSTERIA: *(Screaming.)* I did!!! I did!!!

HENRY: And did you not see that innocent couple try to stop Mr. Kain from this horrible murder?

HYSTERIA: *(Screaming.)* YES!!

HENRY: *(Abruptly stopping shouting.)* Your witness, Mr. Kain.

JUDGE: *(Not hearing; out of it.)* What did you say?

HENRY: I said to Mr. Kain that if he should like to cross examine the witness, he might do so.

(Judge nods.)

ALOYSIUS: *(Standing.)* My good woman…

HENRY: *(Shouting.)* Objection! Your Honor, he is browbeating the witness! *(To Hysteria.)* Isn't he???!

HYSTERIA: *(Anguished.)* YES!!!

HENRY: She can no longer stand it. Can you?

HYSTERIA: NO! *(She breaks down wildly.)*

JUDGE: Clerk! Clerk!

(Enter the Clerk. He takes Hysteria out.)

HENRY: Your Honor, I submit that we rid those two people over there, the nun and the man, of any charges. It is obvious that they had nothing to do with the policeman's murder.

JUDGE: Quite obvious.

ALOYSIUS: But Your Honor…

DEBORAH: Aloysius! Don't involve two innocent people! Don't!

JUDGE: *(To Nun and Man.)* You may go.

NUN: Thank you, Your Honor. *(To Aloysius.)* I shall pray for your soul. *(Exits.)*

MAN: *(Starting to leave, but turning back.)* Your Honor, this man didn't...

JUDGE: Shush. My head. Wait—do you play bridge?

MAN: Yes. Sometimes.

JUDGE: Good. And you, Mrs. Kain?

DEBORAH: I am one of the best players in my bridge club. I'd be at my bridge club today if one of the members hadn't killed herself.

JUDGE: What an inconvenience for you. And you, Mr. Prosecuting Attorney?

HENRY: Indeed, I do, Your Honor.

JUDGE: Good.

ALOYSIUS: *(In a small voice.)* I play bridge.

JUDGE: The defendant is never allowed.

ALOYSIUS: Oh.

JUDGE: Clerk!

(Enter the Clerk.)

CLERK: Yes, Your Honor?

JUDGE: What? No pants?

CLERK: I forgot them in the other room.

JUDGE: Well, never mind. Bring me a pack of cards instead.

(The Clerk produces them from his pocket.)

JUDGE: I presume Mr. Kain will not mind if we play bridge to make the trial go faster.

ALOYSIUS: I don't think it's fair, Your Honor.

JUDGE: That was meant as a statement, not a question.

(The Clerk exits.)

JUDGE: *(To the other players.)* I'll deal.

DEBORAH: *I'll* deal.

(She takes the cards and deals at the Judge's desk. They are seated thusly: r to l, the Man, the Judge, Deborah, and Henry. Aloysius isolated right. The Man looks at Aloysius, then away. Deborah is finished dealing—sloppily. They arrange cards.)

HENRY: Your Honor, I suggest that since we have heard all the evidence, we send the jury out for a verdict.

JUDGE: My God! I knew there was something I'd forgotten. There is no jury.

DEBORAH: Well then, make the decision yourself.

JUDGE: Oh. Alright. Who bids first?

HENRY: I do. One club.

MAN: I pass.

JUDGE: You're supposed to say two clubs.

MAN: I pass.

JUDGE: You're supposed to say two clubs.

(Deborah kicks the Man under the table.)

MAN: I pass, I said.

(The Judge twists the Man's wrist. Deborah kicks the Man under the table.)

JUDGE: Say two clubs.

(The Judge, Henry and Deborah begin to chant together.)

CHANT: Two clubs, two clubs, two, clubs…

MAN: TWO CLUBS!

(The three laugh, go back to their places.)

DEBORAH: Good. Start over.

HENRY: One club.

MAN: Two clubs.

JUDGE: Three clubs.

DEBORAH: Four clubs!

(Judge, Deborah and Henry laugh, clap their hands in glee.)

ALOYSIUS: Your Honor…

HENRY: Objection!

JUDGE: Contempt of court.

DEBORAH: Judge, the verdict.

JUDGE: *(Looking up from his cards.)* Oh, yes. *(Shouts at Aloysius.)* The Court has come to the decision that you are guilty. Sentence: death! Clerk!

(Enter the Clerk, with a pair of pajamas.)

CLERK: Your pajamas, Your Honor.

JUDGE: So I see. Clerk. Execute Mr. Kain, please.

(Aloysius does not move. The Clerk takes a gun from the Judge and shoots Aloysius. No one looks or moves except the Man. The Clerk then drags the dead body off.)

MAN: I think I'll quit.

JUDGE: No you don't.

DEBORAH: Henry, darling. Now that Aloysius is dead, we can get married. Your Honor, can you marry us?

JUDGE: I can do anything. Do you, Henry, take this wo…

HENRY: I do.

JUDGE: Do you, Mrs. Kain…

DEBORAH: I have already, but I will again.

JUDGE: I pronounce you man and wife. You may kiss the bride.

(Henry and Deborah kiss very coldly.)

JUDGE: May I kiss the bride?

DEBORAH: Certainly.

(Deborah and the Judge kiss passionately.)

DEBORAH: Let's play bridge.

JUDGE: Alright.

DEBORAH: *(Looking at her cards.)* Let's start over. I don't like my hand.

HENRY: Deborah, what about a honeymoon?

DEBORAH: *(Shouting.)* If you're going to nag me, I won't let you play with us. Judge, I want a new fourth.

JUDGE: Very well. Clerk!

(Enter the Clerk.)

JUDGE: Do you play bridge?

CLERK: Very well indeed.

JUDGE: Then come play it with us.

(Clerk sits down where Henry was.)

HENRY: But Deborah, what about me?

DEBORAH: What about you, Aloysius?

(Silence. Henry is shaken.)

HENRY: *(Correcting her.)* Henry.

DEBORAH: Henry. Sorry. *(Looking at her cards.)* Four spades.

CLERK: Pass.

MAN: Pass.

JUDGE: Pass.

DEBORAH: *(To Man.)* You're dummy.

MAN: I know.

HENRY: *(Shouting.)* DEBORAH! WHAT ABOUT ME?

(Deborah does not hear him; no one does, except the Man; and he turns away.)

HENRY: Deborah, answer me!

DEBORAH: *(To Man, who keeps looking back at Henry.)* You're not concentrating.

MAN: Bridge makes me sick. *(He turns his back to all of them.)*

HENRY: DEBORAH!

(Deborah hands him a revolver from her purse. Henry shoots himself.)

JUDGE: How many hearts are out?

DEBORAH: *(Gaily.)* All of them. *(Putting down her cards.)* I'm tired of bridge. What other games can we play?

(They all put down their cards.)

JUDGE: I don't know.

CLERK: *(Discreetly.)* There's always double solitaire.

JUDGE: But there are three of us. Only two people can play that.

DEBORAH: Clerk, why don't you play it with me?

CLERK: Alright.

DEBORAH: We can play it in your room so we won't be bothered.

(The Clerk, carrying the Judge's pajamas, starts to exit with Deborah and the cards.)

JUDGE: But Deborah, wait! Wait! What about me? What about me?

(Deborah and the Clerk, dragging the dead Henry out after them, are followed by the Judge, who keeps calling after them. They exit.

The Man is now alone on stage. He gets up from his chair, looks about him. He arranges the chair next to the desk, and then climbs up onto the desk. He looks down to the floor. He prepares to jump. Enter the Nun.)

NUN: *(Sternly.)* Don't jump.

(The Man looks at her very seriously. She remains stern, uncompromising. He sits down on the desk.)

MAN: *(Barely audible.)* Why not? *(To the floor, more or less.)* Why not, why not, why not...* (His voice trails off. He just stares at the floor. End.)*

The Nature and Purpose
of the Universe

This has been a lucky play for me.

It marked the end of a writing block that had been with me for most of my college years. I had been accepted at Harvard at least partially because of my having written plays that were produced in high school (and locally in the summers), and now here I was not writing or feeling I could write.

Midpoint my freshman year, after an initial energetic four months at school, I slipped further and further into depression. Life seemed hopeless; being asked to write an essay on the poetry of George Herbert seemed a preposterous waste of time, plus I felt I had nothing to say about poetry, George Herbert, or being alive.

My sophomore year was the worst...I started skipping all my classes, without acknowledging that that's what I was doing; I withdrew from the friends I had (whom I found too chipper and happy anyway); I slept all morning, sometimes through lunch, getting up just in time to do my term time work-study job of cleaning fellow students' bathrooms two hours a day. Then at night I'd go to the movies.

My taste in movies was good, but on the grim side—lots of Ingmar Bergman, Antonioni, Fellini. So a typical day I might sleep all morning, talk to no one, scrub bathtubs and sinks for two hours, eat alone, then go out to see Death stride around Sweden in *The Seventh Seal.*

I really wasn't very well, was I? In any case, both sophomore and junior years I kept pulling myself back together just in time, in order to pass my classes, getting professors to let me hand in papers two and three and four months late. I flunked one class junior year—on the 18th century, which I just couldn't bear at that point for some reason; Alexander Pope in particular made my head throb with boredom. But then that summer I organized myself to make up the class in summer school so that I could still graduate on time.

I have lots of opinions about what caused my depression, but that's for another time. But I lucked out with a helpful therapist through Harvard's health services.

Indeed Harvard's offering mental health counseling for free was a very significant thing for me. My parents came from that World War II generation that believed that you solved your problems "yourself," you didn't talk to anyone about anything, and it was a sign of weakness and self-indulgence if you couldn't pull yourself together. Psychiatrists were for people like Olivia De Havilland in *The Snake Pit,* they weren't for "regular" people. (This was a corollary to the notion that Alcoholics Anonymous was only for people who were literally falling down on the ground, drunk, preferably on the Bowery.)

So for my parents' generation (and their parents), psychological problems of a complex sort were really ignored, denied, and pushed under—though it was typical for some of the women from time to time to have mental "breakdowns" and have to go away for a while, perhaps for shock treatments. Then they'd come back, and little would be said about it.

But Harvard's offering psychological counseling was like an imprimatur to me; this important university was acknowledging that its students might need help, and that help was a valuable thing to seek.

So I'm very glad to have been part of that next generation for whom psychological help was a good thing, needed by many intelligent people, not some sign of failure or disgrace. (My play *Beyond Therapy* makes fun of some of the excesses possible in therapy, but to me, it's a friendly play, I'm not actually angry about the topic. I think therapy is very valuable.)

My senior year the depression lifted…it was an enormous relief, and I still don't know exactly why things got better. (Though my committing to making up the failed course was a help—I made a decision I wanted to graduate, and I followed through on it. My follow-through cheered me up.)

I also decided I *had* to get a less depressing term-time job, and I sought out and got a tutoring job, helping high school students with their math and English homework.

One afternoon no students came by, and I took out a notebook and started to write *The Nature and Purpose of The Universe*. It sort of came flying out of me, with this enormous energy and glee…it was like the flip side of my depression, it included a lot of my hopeless feelings about life and love and relationships and people's inability to find happiness or to get on with one another—but where those feelings had previously overwhelmed me, as I wrote this I found the excess of the suffering funny.

Years later, when I've attended Al-Anon meetings, I've sometimes felt something similar: A person will be sharing some awful event in their life, and how hopeless it all looks, and the way they describe what's going on suddenly sounds funny—to everyone in the room. And then we all laugh, including the speaker, at this thing that isn't actually funny, but we've all had this sudden surge of "perspective" and distance where we've seen the overview of the person's patterns. It's a healthy feeling actually…though for those people who remain stuck in the specifics of the pain, it can seem callous. But it isn't callous, it's this strange place where perspective meets pain. It is the beginnings of something healthy.

Well, this may be a bit serious to introduce this play. But it gives you a sense of my psychological state when I wrote it.

A few other things about it.

The title came from a misunderstanding. During my college years (1967–1971), there were many protests against the Vietnam war, and many times students took over buildings and vented a lot of anger at college administrators, sometimes about the college's ties to the war, sometimes in what seemed like an obvious misplaced anger at their parents. I passed an entire course due to the invasion of Cambodia...isn't that a pathetic and puny offshoot of wartime tragedy?

In any case, Harvard, like many universities, wanted to somehow cope with all these building takeovers and accusations of complicity, and so on. And so one morning, each Harvard student received a pamphlet under his door entitled "The Nature and Purpose of the University." I misread it and thought it said "The Nature and Purpose of the *Universe*," and was momentarily thrilled and amazed to think that Harvard had taken upon itself the explaining of this extremely important issue. But, alas, it was about other matters.

But my misreading gave me this title. And I wanted to tell the story of someone whose life was really, really, really terrible; and how God sat up in heaven and consciously participated in making that life worse. (It's the Book of Job, though I didn't think of that when I was writing it.)

By the way, I got into Yale School of Drama with this play. (I hope you find that interesting, and not irritating.)

ORIGINAL PRODUCTION

The Nature and Purpose of the Universe was presented in the spring of 1975 for a few performances at the Direct Theatre in New York City, directed by Yannis Simonides. To allow for using fewer actors, it was done as a "radio version," in front of microphones. (Further information on the "radio version" may be found in the *To the Actor* notes that follow the script.) I can no longer find the full cast list, but three cast members were fellow graduates from Yale School of Drama: Diana Belshaw as Elaine, Nicholas Hormann as Ronald, and Sigourney Weaver as Eleanor.

In September 1975, this "radio play" version was re-presented at the Direct Theatre, this time co-directed by Allen R. Belknap and Yannis Simonides. The "radio version" allows more doubling among the men. The cast of this version was as follows:

Ronald . . . . Justin Rashid
Elaine . . . . Lynnie Godfrey
Eleanor Mann . . . . Anne De Salvo

```
Steve Mann . . . . . . . . . . . . . . . . . . . . . . . . . . . James Nisbet Clark
Andy, Coach Fr. Hemmer . . . . . . . . . . . . . . . . . . David Wilborn
Donald, Ralph . . . . . . . . . . . . . . . . . . . . . . . . . Nick Mariano
Gary, The Pope . . . . . . . . . . . . . . . . . . . . . . . . . Lars Kampmann
```

The Nature and Purpose of the Universe was presented again by the Direct Theatre at the Wonder Horse Theatre in New York on February 21, 1979. The production was directed by Allen R. Belknap, setting by Jonathan Arkin, lighting by Richard Winkler, costumes by Giva Taylor. (This was not the "radio" version, but was staged full-out). The cast was as follows:

```
Ronald . . . . . . . . . . . . . . . . . . . . . . . . . . . . . . . . . Jeff Brooks
Elaine. . . . . . . . . . . . . . . . . . . . . . . . . . . . . . . . . Caroline Kava
Eleanor Mann. . . . . . . . . . . . . . . . . . . . . . . . . . . Ellen Greene
Steve Mann. . . . . . . . . . . . . . . . . . . . . . . . . . . . . . Tom Bade
Donald Mann . . . . . . . . . . . . . . . . . . . . . . . . . . . Ethan Phillips
Andy Mann . . . . . . . . . . . . . . . . . . . . . . . . . . . . . Eric Weitz
Gary Mann. . . . . . . . . . . . . . . . . . . . . . . . . . . . . . Chris Ceraso
Coach Griffin . . . . . . . . . . . . . . . . . . . . . . . . . Robert Blumenfeld
Ralph . . . . . . . . . . . . . . . . . . . . . . . . . . . . . . . . . . T.A. Taylor
Fr. Hemmer. . . . . . . . . . . . . . . . . . . . . . . . . . . . . T.A. Taylor
The Pope. . . . . . . . . . . . . . . . . . . . . . . . . . . . . . Robert Blumenfeld
```

CHARACTERS
   RONALD, an agent of God
   ELAINE, an agent of God
   ELEANOR MANN, a housewife
   STEVE MANN, her husband
   DONALD MANN, her oldest son
   ANDY MANN, her youngest son
   GARY MANN, her middle son
   COACH GRIFFIN
   RALPH, a friend of Gary's
   FR. HEMMER
   THE POPE

THE NATURE AND PURPOSE
OF THE UNIVERSE

Scene: A kitchen–living room setting, not too elaborate and flexible enough to accommodate easy changes. A few chairs, a kitchen table set for breakfast. Cereal boxes and the like. Enter Ronald, an agent of God. He is dressed neatly in a suit and tie, or perhaps in a tuxedo.

RONALD: The Nature and Purpose of the Universe. Chapter One. It was an ordinary Tuesday morning, much like any other Tuesday morning. The frost was on the pumpkin and a nip was in the air. It was an ordinary Tuesday morning, much like any other Tuesday morning. Steve and Eleanor Mann were just getting up. Eleanor was still crying softly into her bathrobe because her oldest son was a dope pusher, and her middle son was a homosexual and wore purple scarves, and her youngest son had recently lost his penis in a strange McReilly's reaper accident.

(Ronald exits. Enter Eleanor and Steve Mann. Eleanor looks bedraggled, and carries a frying pan and spatula; she stands by the kitchen table and scrambles eggs; she cries softly into a dish towel. Stove, eggs not necessary. Steve, in a suit, sits at the table, reading a newspaper and drinking coffee. For a while there's just the scrambling, the reading, the quiet crying.)

STEVE: Eleanor! Why are you crying? You just got up.

ELEANOR: Oh, Steve. I don't understand it. Not any of it. Our house is worth forty-five thousand dollars. Where did it all start to go wrong?

(Enter Donald, about 25, seedy and vicious.)

DONALD: Hey, Mom, where's my spare hypodermic?

ELEANOR: Oh, Steven. Speak to your son.

STEVE: I saw it in the hall closet.

DONALD: God damn it.

(He exits. Enter Andy, about fourteen, wearing short pants with a large white bandage covering the crotch of the pants.)

ANDY: Good morning, Mom. Good morning, Dad.

(Eleanor looks at him and, overcome with grief, cries into a dish towel.)

STEVE: Good morning, son. How's the boy?

ANDY: Okay.

(Enter Donald.)

DONALD: God damn it! The needle's not there! Now where is it? One of you must have taken it. Who was it?

ELEANOR: *(Sobbing.)* Oh, Donald, why must we live like this?

DONALD: *(Hurls her to the ground.)* Shut up, you stupid drudge! Did you throw my hypodermic out? Did you, you slut? Slattern! Trollop! Tramp!

ELEANOR: Steven! Don't let him treat me this way!

STEVE: Donald, have a little patience with your mother please.

DONALD: You threw the needle out, didn't you, bitch? *(He kicks her.)*

ELEANOR: *(Screams.)* You shouldn't take drugs! You shouldn't sell drugs! We'll all be arrested!

ANDY: We need more sugar, mom, for the cereal.

DONALD: What do you know? You're going to pay me for that needle and I'm going to kill you if you take any of my things ever again!

(He kicks her. She screams.)

ELEANOR: Steven!

STEVE: Don't despair, Ellie. Have faith. God provides.

ELEANOR: I know, but look what He's provided!

STEVE: *(Furious.)* Don't you dare to talk against God, you whore of Babylon. *(He kicks her.)* Do you want the children not to believe in God?

ELEANOR: Oh, Steve, please! Let me finish making the eggs.

STEVE: What sort of example is that?

ANDY: We don't believe in God, Dad. Ever since that earthquake in Peru.

STEVE: You see what you've done, Pig?

ELEANOR: I didn't cause the earthquake! Oh, Steve. Let me finish the eggs.

DONALD: Hurry up, I'm hungry.

(The sons and father go calmly back to eating, Eleanor gets up from the floor, cries into the dish towel and starts scrambling the eggs again. There is silence except for the eggs and her whimpering.)

STEVE: *(After awhile.)* Eleanor, don't snivel. It's depressing.

ELEANOR: I'm sorry, Steven.

(Enter Gary, the middle son, dressed entirely in purple.)

GARY: Good morning, Dad. Good morning, Donald. Good morning, Andy. *(He kisses his father and brothers on the cheek.)*

ELEANOR: Don't you say hello to your mother?

GARY: *(Chilly, doesn't like her.)* How are you, Eleanor?

ELEANOR: Oh, Gary. Gary, Gary.

(Gary starts to nuzzle Andy's shoulder, and then kiss behind his ears. Eleanor after a bit:)

ELEANOR: Gary, stop it! Your brother has no genitals! Leave him alone.

(Donald kicks over the table.)

DONALD: Can we have no peace in the morning? Is there no civilization left anywhere in this stupid house? What kind of town is this? What kind of people are these? *(He hurls his mother to the ground.)*

ELEANOR: Steven, help me! Help!

(Enter Ronald. Action freezes. Then actors exit, except for Ronald.)

RONALD: The Nature and Purpose of the Universe. Chapter 2. It was an ordinary Tuesday morning, just like any other Tuesday morning. There was much for Eleanor to do. There was the cleaning to do, and the beds to be made, and the meals to be prepared so that she could keep home nice for her men. Andy went off to school, Gary off for a short cruise in the park, Steve went off to his job, and Donald went off to scrape and save, pimp and push. God assigns my friend Elaine to impersonate a next-door neighbor who upsets Eleanor.

(Ronald exits. Enter Eleanor with a vacuum cleaner. Eleanor tries to turn the vacuum on, but it won't work. She starts to cry.)

ELEANOR: *(On her knees.)* Oh, please, God, please let my vacuum cleaner work. Please. And I promise I won't complain about my sons. Just please let my household appliances work. I don't care about the electric toothbrush, but I need the vacuum cleaner and the washing machine and the *(She sobs.)* refrigerator. Oh, please God! Please! Let my car start again and I promise I'll pick up hitchhikers even if they beat me with chains because I know that some of them are your angels sent in disguise to test me, I know this, my husband Steve tells me it's so, and he's much more religious than I am. I'm just an unworthy woman. Oh, God, help me.

(Enter Elaine May Alcott, dressed as a housewife. She drags a little girl behind her. The little girl is apparently entirely unconscious. The little girl is best played by a doll.)

ELAINE: *(Furious.)* Don't you ever answer your door bell, Mrs. Mann? Do you always ignore your neighbors?

ELEANOR: Oh, Mrs. Ackerman, I'm sorry. I didn't hear the bell. Can I get you coffee or…What's the matter with your daughter?

ELAINE: Well might you ask, Mrs. Mann. I found her in the bathroom this morning, passed out next to the john, and I found this hypodermic stuck in her little arm. *(She whips the hypodermic out of her purse.)* See this, Mrs. Mann?

ELEANOR: Oh, Mrs. Ackerman, how horrible!

ELAINE: Horrible, she says. You hear that, God? The dope pusher's mother is horrified.

(Elaine jabs Eleanor's arm with the hypodermic.)

ELEANOR: *(Screams.)* Oh, my God, you've punctured me.

ELAINE: *(Mimicking.)* Oh, my God, you've punctured me. Damn right I've punctured you. What about my daughter? Do you know how much weekly allowance we have to give Caroline to feed her habit? Fifty dollars a week. You hear that, Mrs. Mann? We have to pay my hop head daughter fifty dollars a week, all of which goes to your hateful, sick son.

ELEANOR: Oh, Mrs. Ackerman.

ELAINE: Your family is the bane of Maplewood, Mrs. Mann. My husband has been attacked in the garage by your pansy son twice now, and just last week we found your little son's penis in our driveway. My little Bobby was going to use it for fish bait until I took it away from him. Do you think I like to live in this atmosphere of sickness, Mrs. Mann? Do you think I want to live near your horrible family?

ELEANOR: Oh, Mrs. Ackerman, I know how you must feel. But do you think we might possibly have my son's penis back?

ELAINE: Certainly not! I put it right down the garbage disposal. I don't want your family's private parts hanging around my kitchen.

(Elaine jabs Eleanor with the hypodermic again.)

ELEANOR: Mrs. Ackerman, please. I'm bleeding.

ELAINE: Bleeding, she says. You hear that, God? My little daughter Caroline is o.d.ing and Mrs. Mann is complaining about a few punctures. *(Screaming.)* What about my daughter? I want some reparation. Reparation, Mrs. Mann!

ELEANOR: Oh, Mrs. Ackerman, what can I say?

ELAINE: Give me your color TV! I want your color television.

ELEANOR: Oh no, please. Donald would beat me. He watches TV all the time.

ELAINE: I don't care what he does. I just know that I'm taking your television set or I'm calling the police.

ELEANOR: Please, please, Mrs. Ackerman.

(Elaine picks up the television set.)

ELAINE: *(Shouting.)* KEEP YOUR HORRIBLE FAMILY AWAY FROM ME, DO YOU HEAR? Do you hear? *(She exits with television, leaving little Caroline behind.)*

ELEANOR: There, there, Caroline, it's all right.

(Enter Ronald. Action freezes, then actors exit.)

RONALD: The Nature and Purpose of the Universe. Chapter 3. It was an ordinary Tuesday morning, but oh God, thought Eleanor, what has happened over the years? All my hopes dashed, she thought, all my illusions crushed. I remember how happy I was in high school, playing the lead in a Chekhov play. What one was it, I wonder? And while Eleanor thought these despairing thoughts, she did the wash and baked a cake. And while Eleanor prayed to God, God was busy communicating a message to Steven about the New Pope. God's instrument on earth is again my friend Elaine May Alcott, whom God this time assigns to masquerade as Sister Annie De Maupassant, the radical nun of Bernardsville.

(Ronald exits. Enter Elaine dressed as a nun. Since Elaine has little time to change costumes, her costumes should be minimal. In this case, a nun's veil. Elaine sits at a desk, blesses a cigarette, then smokes it. Enter Steve.)

ELAINE: How do you do, Mr. Mann. I am Sister Annie De Maupassant, the radical nun of Bernardsville.

STEVE: I have heard much of your reputation, Sister.

ELAINE: And I of yours, Mr. Mann. I am told that you are one of the most thoughtful and brilliant of Catholic laymen within a radius of five dioceses. The Jesuits speak well of you.

STEVE: I am humbled by your thinking well of me.

ELAINE: But enough of this small talk. We are here on more important matters. Something is awry in Rome. The Pope is not the proper Pope. He is a fraud. He is not the Deity's choice.

STEVE: Sister Annie De Maupassant, what can this mean? You mean Pope Paul is not a proper Pope?

ELAINE: Pope Paul is a false Pope. He speaks with the Papal wee wee.

STEVE: As bad as that?

ELAINE: I fear so.

STEVE: What must be done?

ELAINE: In a few weeks Pope Paul is coming to New Jersey to bless the air in Weehawken. God has communicated to me that we must spirit him away, reveal him as a fraud, and instate the true Pope in his proper place. Only then will the Church be able to gain its rightful and dominant place in the world.

STEVE: Sister Annie De Maupassant, you may certainly depend on me.

ELAINE: God bless the laity! Thank you, Mr. Mann, I knew I could. My agents will get in touch with you soon. Simply continue your life as you normally would, stay close to the sacraments, and make ready for the Holy Spirit.

STEVE: Sister Annie De Maupassant, I have one question. Has God perhaps revealed to you who the true Pope is?

ELAINE: Yes, Mr. Mann, He has.

STEVE: Who is it to be?

(Elaine stands on her desk.)

ELAINE: Mr. Mann, it is I, Sister Annie De Maupassant, who is the true and only Pope. *(She throws a handful of glitter into the air and stamps her foot in triumph. Then she opens her mouth and lets out a high, continuous shrieking sound, while her tongue flies in and out of her mouth. She places her hand on her throat, in surprise, as if she has no control over the noises she is making. The noises stop, and she speaks.)* Bon jour, Jean. Comment ca va? Auf wiedersehn. Oh my God, I'm speaking in tongues. *(She shrieks again, her tongue going in and out, it's a gibberish sound half-sung, half-screamed. Then she speaks again.)* Moo goo gai pan. *(Swedish.)* Yo. Inga Swenson gunnar cheese. *(Shrieks again. Has Steve help her exit. Then while she is exiting:)* Flores, flores para los muertos.

(She and Steve exit. Ronald enters and addresses the audience again.)

RONALD: The Nature and Purpose of the Universe. Chapter 4. The sun hit its zenith shortly after noon that day, just as Gary and his new friend scuttled behind a bush in the park. It was a Tuesday like any other Tuesday, except that Eleanor got a call from Andy's junior high school principal. It seems that Andy had upset his athletic teacher. God assigns Elaine to play the role of the Principal's secretary, and the athletic coach plays himself.

(Ronald exits. Enter Elaine, Coach Griffin, and Andy. Elaine sits at a desk, ripping up papers and/or shooting rubber bands into the air. Andy's shirt is off, and Coach Griffin is whipping him on the floor. Enter Eleanor, carrying a full laundry basket.)

ELEANOR: Oh, dear, oh, dear. What is the matter?

ELAINE: I'm sorry to interrupt your busy day, Mrs. Mann, but we have a little problem here. *(Offers her hand, gracious.)* I'm Miss Mansfield, Mr. Watson's secretary. Mr. Watson is on sabbatical this semester, and in his absence I have complete power. *(Looking around room, cheerfully awed.)* I don't know what to do with it all, really.

ANDY: *(Being whipped.)* Mommy!

ELAINE: *(Charming.)* Oh, I'm sorry. Coach Griffin, please don't inflict any more corporal punishment on Master Mann right now. *(To Eleanor.)* Discipline is a delicate thing. Mrs. Mann, I'm going to be frank. We've all been worried about Andrew in school lately.

COACH: I won't have no boy without a male organ in my gym class.

ELEANOR: That seems to me prejudiced.

COACH: If he doesn't have an organ, he should be on the girls' side. I'm not having no girl in my gym class.

ELAINE: *(Smiles.)* You see our problem.

ELEANOR: Well, I guess there's nothing I can say. Can Andrew be exempted from gym?

COACH: Certainly not.

ELAINE: We have our rules.

ELEANOR: Well I guess he'll have to have gym with the girls then.

COACH: Damn right.

ELAINE: *(Pleased.)* I'm glad that's settled.

COACH: And he can't wear an athletic supporter either.

ELEANOR: I'm sure he wouldn't want to, Coach Griffin. Mr. Griffin, I only hope that someday you are mangled by a McReilly's reaper, and then I hope you shall have more sympathy for people without organs.

ELAINE: Please, let us remain ladies and gentlemen.

ELEANOR: Might I go now?

ELAINE: I'm afraid we have another complaint to deal with, from the Mother's Cake Committee of the PTA. I have here a letter from Mrs. Samuel Fredericks which I must read to you. *(Reciting.)* Dear Miss Mansfield, I am shaken...

ELEANOR: Where is the letter?

ELAINE: *(Smiles.)* I've committed it to memory. Dear Miss Mansfield, I am shaken and upset. At our otherwise successful Mother's Cake Sale at the children's playground the other day, our festivities were disturbed by the actions of a certain young man who my daughter says was Andrew Mann. This young boy had the temerity to approach our Mother's Cake Counter where he proceeded to undo his pants and to expose himself to the baking mothers present. We were all appalled. There was nothing there. New Paragraph. Now, Miss Mansfield, I am as much in favor of charity and kindness as the next mother, but enough is enough! I have been sick to my stomach all day, and expect to be so for much of tomorrow. Surely there must be a fit punishment for this crime, Miss Mansfield, for as our crowded prisons attest, crime is encouraged by leniency. I leave this matter in your capable hands. Sincerely, Mrs. Samuel Fredericks, 31 Club Drive, Maplewood. *(Pause.)* Have you anything to say, Andrew?

ANDY: *(Softly.)* I hate school.

ELAINE: All children think they hate school. No, my task is to do the right thing, to perpetrate the correct punishment. So I've decided that to symbolize the ungentlemanly nature of Andrew's behavior he will be required to wear girls' clothing for one month, at which time I will reconsider his case.

ELEANOR: *(Concerned.)* Do you think that that will help him realize the wrongness of his action?

ELAINE: I don't know. But if he doesn't expose himself again, I shall feel we have succeeded. *(Lowering her voice.)* Exhibitionism of a sexual nature must be checked early, Mrs. Mann. Repression is a gift from God, and we must honor it as such.

ELEANOR: I worry that such punishment might be harmful.

ELAINE: Well, time will tell. Oh, and, by the way, Mrs. Mann, I'm afraid that Mrs. Fredericks requested that you return your PTA membership card and that your car be denied use of the school parking lot. Since parents are frequently partly to blame for the failings of their children, I think that this is only just. Thank you for coming, Mrs. Mann. I've enjoyed meeting you.

ELEANOR: Miss Mansfield, I can only apologize from the depth of my heart to you, and to you, Coach Griffin, for the pain and anguish my son Andrew has given you. And I only hope that never again will I be made to feel as embarrassed and humiliated by a member of my family, and I beg you all to forgive me. *(She exits with her wash.)*

ANDY: Mommy!

(Coach whips him again, Elaine rips papers, perhaps all in rhythm. Enter Ronald. Action freezes, actors exit.)

RONALD: The Nature and Purpose of the Universe. Chapter 5. It was an ordinary Tuesday afternoon, just like any other Tuesday afternoon, and Donald was doing so well that he had no more rooms to send his girls to, so he brought Crystal home. God assigns my friend Elaine to play Crystal.

(Exits. Enter Eleanor, still with the wash. Enter Donald and Elaine, who is dressed as a prostitute.)

DONALD: Now look, Mom, there's no more room in the city so Crystal's gonna meet her trick here, and she's gonna use your room.

ELEANOR: Oh, Donald, please.

DONALD: Look, can it, bitch. *(He pushes her slightly.)* I'm going to watch some...WHERE'S THE TV?

ELEANOR: Oh Donald!

ELAINE: Jesus.

DONALD: Where is the friggin' television?

ELEANOR: Donald, your language.

(He pushes her to the ground.)

DONALD: *(Hissing.)* Where is it?

ELEANOR: Mrs. Ackerman took it in reparation.

DONALD: Who is Mrs. Ackerman?

ELEANOR: She lives down the street. You sell her little daughter drugs.

DONALD: Your story better be true. I'll be back. *(Exits.)*

ELAINE: *(Cheap dame voice.)* Your son's very violent.

ELEANOR: It was that year we lived in Union that did it. Donald used to be such a quiet boy, but the other children were so rough in Union. He had to learn how to defend himself. They used to fight with Coke bottles and power saws.

ELAINE: *(Getting on the ground next to her.)* You know, if you didn't have such dish pan features, you could almost be attractive, honey.

ELEANOR: Oh, dear God.

(Elaine inches closer.)

ELAINE: Have you ever made it with another woman?

ELEANOR: Life Magazine was right! You *are* all lesbians!

ELAINE: Hey, come on, relax.

ELEANOR: Get away from me! Steve! Donald! Where are you?

(Elaine tackles Eleanor. Eleanor screams. Enter Coach Griffin. Elaine is on top of Eleanor.)

COACH: Hey what's going on? Which one of you is Crystal?

ELAINE: *(Points to Eleanor.)* She is.

ELEANOR: No, I'm not.

ELAINE: See ya later, Crystal.

(Coach Griffin picks up Eleanor, carries her out as she screams. Enter Ronald.)

RONALD: Hello, Elaine. How are you?

ELAINE: All right. Excuse me. I've got to go change. *(Exits.)*

RONALD: The Nature and Purpose of the Universe. Chapter 6. It no longer seemed an ordinary Tuesday to Eleanor. Coach Griffin's hot sweating body came down upon her with the force of a thousand violins. The sun was like a hot pomegranate. Coach Griffin did degrading things to Eleanor, some of them very athletic. At the end of three hours, he kicked her very hard with his boot.

(Exits. Enter Eleanor, worn, and Coach Griffin.)

COACH: That was lousy. That was among the worst I've ever had. Boy, you're lousy. You can tell Donald if he thinks I'm paying you for that, he's crazy. I should be paid for putting up with you, you aging slob. *(He spits on her, kicks her, exits.)*

ELEANOR: Oh, God, please let this day come to a close. Please!

(She sinks to the floor, weeping. Enter Ronald. Ronald should be very sincere in the next scene.)

RONALD: Excuse me. Your door was open. I'm the Fuller Brush Man.

ELEANOR: Please, please, leave me alone. I can't stand anymore.

RONALD: *(Takes her face in his hands.)* Eleanor, let me look at you.

ELEANOR: You know my name.

RONALD: Eleanor, I can see suffering in your eyes. Let me kiss them. *(He kisses her eyes lightly.)* You're a fine, noble woman Eleanor. God doesn't mean for you to suffer.

ELEANOR: He doesn't?

RONALD: No. He wants you to accept His will and be happy. *(His hand lightly caresses the top of her head.)*

ELEANOR: I do accept His will. *(Rather suddenly.)* Oh, please, please take me away from here. Far, far away.

RONALD: Yes, Eleanor. I will take you away. I will come for you next week.

ELEANOR: Oh, please. I must leave here.

RONALD: Eleanor, do not give up hope. I will take you away. Next week. *(He kisses her forehead, exits.)*

ELEANOR: Oh, thank you, God. Please let me be happy. I'll promise never to complain again.

(Enter Gary and a female impersonator.)

GARY: Hello, Eleanor. I'm home.

ELEANOR: Oh, Gary. Gary. I'm so happy. You've brought home a young girl for me to meet. You don't know how happy this makes me. What's your name, dear?

FRIEND: Ralph.

ELEANOR: Oh, Gary. Gary, Gary.

GARY: Can it, Eleanor. Ralph and I are going to be up in your bedroom, so don't bother us.

ELEANOR: Please don't use my room. Gary, please!

GARY: Shut up!

RALPH: *(Politely.)* It was nice to meet you, Mrs. Mann.

(Exit Gary and Ralph. Enter Donald.)

DONALD: There you are, you slut! I'll have you know Mrs. Ackerman's never heard of you or our television set, and I told her it figured cause you're a filthy liar anyway.

ELEANOR: Oh, Donald, please don't hit me. I'll ask your father to buy us all a new television.

DONALD: You'll pay for this, Mom. *(Kicks her a little.)* I'm kind of tired. Where's Crystal?

ELEANOR: I don't know. She must have left.

DONALD: Did she give you the money?

ELEANOR: No. There wasn't any money.

DONALD: What do you mean there wasn't any money? *(He hurls her to the ground.)*

ELEANOR: Don't hit me, Donald! That man thought I was Crystal and he raped me!

DONALD: Well, give me the money!

ELEANOR: He didn't give me any. He made me do awful things.

DONALD: PAY ME!

ELEANOR: Have mercy! Donald!

DONALD: Pay me, you slut!

(Enter Andy, dressed in a pink dress. He jumps rope.)

ELEANOR: Donald, please! Andy, help me. Run for help!

(Andy keeps jumping rope.)

DONALD: You pay me the money. Crystal gets thirty dollars, so cough up thirty.

ELEANOR: Donald, the bank is closed.

DONALD: I want it now. *(Donald is perched over his mother, more or less straddling her. He slaps her face lightly but continually.)*

ELEANOR: Stop! Help me! Help! Help!

DONALD: *(Slapping.)* You slut! Trollop! Tramp!

(Steve enters.)

STEVE: I'm home, Eleanor. Is dinner ready?

(Slapping stops.)

ELEANOR: *(Still under Donald.)* What, dear? I couldn't hear you.

STEVE: I said is dinner ready yet? Have you done your duty as a wife and cooked me and my sons dinner?

ELEANOR: Oh, Steve, I'm sorry. I haven't had time...

STEVE: What do you mean, you haven't had time? Great God almighty!

(Steve pushes Donald away and gets on top of Eleanor, slapping her.)

ELEANOR: But Steve I was raped!

STEVE: What kind of wife are you? You give my children a bad example, you don't make supper, you don't make beds, you're incompetent, you're a failure as a woman.

ELEANOR: Oh, God, help me.

(Enter Ronald—though "outside" of the set.)

RONALD: Do not fear, Eleanor, I will save you in a week.

ELEANOR: Oh, God.

(A couple of lines before now, Elaine has entered, and she stands by Ronald's side. When Eleanor says "Oh God," Elaine picks up the phrase and sings it, thereby giving the entire company the starting note for the song they are about to sing.)

ELAINE: *(Sings.)*

 Oh God.

(Ronald and Elaine now sing the hymn "O God, our Help in Ages Past;" the whole company joins in, not so much in response to Ronald

and Elaine singing, but as if they were all overcome with an urge to sing a hymn at this time. Eleanor joins in the hymn also, on the last three lines, though still in much despair.)

RONALD AND ELAINE *(And eventually everyone else, sing:)*

O God, our help in ages past,
Our hope for years to come,
Our shelter from the stormy blast,
And our eternal home.
O God, our light against the dark,
We bow down to thy might,
Please help us understand thy bark,
Is far worse than thy bite.
(An elaborate, pretty ending:) Alleluia!

RONALD: The Nature and Purpose of the Universe. End of part I.
(All exit except Ronald.)

RONALD: The Nature and Purpose of the Universe. Chapter 7. It was Tuesday of the following week. It was an ordinary Tuesday, much like any other Tuesday. Truth was still beauty, and trudy booth... and yet still Eleanor woke with some hope; for today was the day that the Fuller Brush Man was supposed to save her.
(Enter actors: Steve, Andy, and Donald are eating breakfast. Andy has a bow in his hair. Enter Eleanor, followed by Gary and Ralph.)

GARY: God damn it, Eleanor. Where is Ralph's bra?

ELEANOR: Gary, I said I just don't know.

DONALD: *(Throws a spoon.)* You're making too much noise.

GARY: Ralph says you've been trying on all his clothes.

ELEANOR: But, Gary, I have my own clothes.

RALPH: Oh. She doesn't like my clothes, she says.

GARY: Why do you insult my guests?

ELEANOR: I don't mean to, dear. Please believe me. I think Ralph's clothes are fine.

GARY: Well, where's his bra?

ELEANOR: I don't know, maybe Andy took it.

DONALD: Shut up!

GARY: *(To Andy.)* Did you take Ralph's bra? Did you?

ANDY: I put it back!

GARY: You little bastard!

RALPH: *(Grabbing the bow from Andy's hair.)* And that's my bow!

ANDY: It is not. Miss Mansfield gave it to me.

RALPH: He's taking my clothes!

GARY: *(To Andy.)* I'll kill you!

ELEANOR: *(Pulling Gary back.)* Don't hit him, he hasn't any genitals!

DONALD: SHUT UP! *(He kicks over the table.)* Why is there never any quiet in this house? Woman, it's your fault. You don't know how to run a house. Now pick up this table and clean up this mess.

(He stalks out. After a stunned silence, Andy starts to leave.)

RALPH: *(To Gary.)* Let's get him!

(Andy screams, runs out.)

ANDY: I don't have your stupid bra.

(Exits. Gary and Ralph run out after him.)

ELEANOR: Gary! Wait! Don't touch his bandage!

STEVE: Eleanor, will you stay out of the boys' fights for God's sake? No wonder Andy's wearing dresses, you take on so. And pick up the table. Really, you are the worst wife and mother I've ever seen. You deserve an amateur hysterectomy.

ELEANOR: *(Truly horrified.)* Oh, Steven. Can't you please be nice to me?

STEVE: Don't snivel, Eleanor. *(Phone rings.)* Hello? Why, hello, Sister Annie De Maupassant. I'm delighted to hear from you. Yes, I'm quite ready. Today's the day then. Alright. I'll be by for you shortly. Will we have any additional help? Oh, fine. I like a good Jesuit on a job. See you later, Sister Annie De Maupassant. Glory be to God. *(Hangs up.)*

ELEANOR: Is this some more Catholic Action work, Steve?

STEVE: Mind your business, woman. And clean this house. We're having ecclesiastic guests tonight, and I don't want them to know that I'm married to a pig.

ELEANOR: Oh, Steve, please be kind to me.

STEVE: Kneel down.

(She kneels.)

STEVE: Leniency is not kindness, Eleanor. Overlooking faults is not a kindness. It is a sin.

(He kicks her, exits. Eleanor picks up the table, sets things straight. She brings the vacuum cleaner over toward table, tries to turn it on, it won't function. She starts to cry.)

ELEANOR: Why doesn't the vacuum cleaner work? Oh, God. Oh, please God, let the Fuller Brush Man come tonight. Please. I know You don't mean for me to be this unhappy. *(Phone rings.)* Hello?

(Ronald stands D., not holding a phone. Eleanor does not see him. The following scene is played mostly sincerely.)

RONALD: *(Facing out.)* Hello, Eleanor. This is the Fuller Brush Man speaking.

ELEANOR: Oh, God, is it really you? Oh, help me. You will take me away tonight, won't you?

RONALD: Yes, Eleanor. I will. Are you sure you want to leave your family and home?

ELEANOR: Oh, please. I can't stand anymore. I'm bruised all over, but it is my heart that is truly wounded.

RONALD: Eleanor, Eleanor. I will come for you tonight at midnight. Have your bags packed.

ELEANOR: Oh I will! I will! But...please don't fail me. Hello? Hello? *(She hangs up. Eleanor exits.)*

RONALD: The Nature and Purpose of the Universe. Chapter 8. No one breathes much in Weehawken, New Jersey. The air drips with a veritable venereal disease of industrial waste. The atmosphere is slowly turning to sludge. It is very romantic. Pope Paul the Sixth was due to arrive in Weehawken that ordinary Tuesday morning, to bless the air. Meanwhile, Sister Annie De Maupassant and her Jesuit friend, Fr. Anthony Hemmer, meet with Steve to discuss their plans. God has assigned Elaine once more to the role of Sister Annie De Maupassant. Fr. Hemmer plays himself.

(Enter Elaine, dressed as a nun.)

RONALD: Hello, Elaine. How are you finding the role of the radical nun of Bernardsville?

ELAINE: All right. I was surprised to see you getting in on things with that Fuller Brush Man routine.

RONALD: God works in strange and mysterious ways, Elaine.

(Ronald exits. Enter Steve and Fr. Anthony Hemmer.)

ELAINE: Ah, there you are. Hurry. The Pretender is about to enter. Fr. Anthony, I presume you've met Mr. Mann, the brilliant Catholic layman Fr. Obediah told you about.

FR. ANT.: Yes I did. You certainly are a brilliant Catholic layman, sir.

STEVE: Why thank you, Father. I try.

ELAINE: Mr. Mann has some fascinating thoughts on the connection between the guitar folk Mass and the Albigensian heresy, but we have no time to discuss them now. I see the Papal Pretender fast approaching.

FR. ANT.: We seem to be in luck. We seem to be the only ones here.

ELAINE: I'm not surprised. The Lord is thy shepherd. Ssssh.

(Enter Pope Paul, dressed in a gold outfit with gold slippers and a diamond tiara and droop earrings. He is accompanied by several monks [the other actors in monk robes, with cowls over their heads, covering their faces]; the monks enter in procession, singing in a Gregorian chant fashion:)

MONKS: *(Singing.)*

Amo, amas, amat

Amamus, amatis, amant.

(Over and over as needed. The Pope follows behind them. When he nears D., he smiles graciously at the audience and then sings in a piercing, too high ecclesiastic voice; he has a small scrap of paper that he checks for the words.)

POPE: Agricula,

Agriculae,

Agriculae,

Agriculam,

Agricula, Ah-men.

Agriculae,

Agricularum,

Agriculis,

Agriculas,

Agriculis, Ah-men.

Sum es est,

Sumus, estis, sunt.

(One of the monks leads the Pope away from the audience, and to the place where he is to speak.)

POPE: My brothers and sisters in Christ, we are gathered here in Weehawken in the face of this smog, which is a symbol of evil in the world, to stand up once again for all that is just and right and proper for salvation. God created man, and the word was made flesh, as it was in the beginning and in the middle and I feel faint. Help me. I feel faint. I am going to faint. Someone help me. I am faint. Where is the Curia? I shall faint.

(Two monks clutch the Pope on either side.)

MONK: Take deep breaths, Your Holiness.

(The Pope breathes in deeply, giving out terrible gasps at the bad air. Elaine and Steve creep up behind the two monks and strangle them to

death. The Pope is oblivious to this and shortly passes out due to all his deep breaths. Steve and Fr. Anthony pick the Pope up.)

ELAINE: *(Crosses herself.)* All that I do I do for God! Forward march for the New Church!

(Enter Ronald. Action freezes, then actors exit.)

RONALD: The Nature and Purpose of the Universe. Chapter 9. It was an ordinary day no longer. Eleanor looked at herself in the mirror and felt an inner joy. At least it was joy compared to what she usually felt. For tonight would be her redemption, her escape. For a few moments, she harbored the fear that something would go wrong, that the Fuller Brush Man would not come, that her life would continue as a hell. Her packing is interrupted as God sends Elaine to impersonate the Census Lady.

(Enter Eleanor with a suitcase. Enter Elaine.)

ELEANOR: Oh! You startled me.

ELAINE: CENSUS!

ELEANOR: What?

ELAINE: I am the census lady come to get you.

ELEANOR: What do you mean?

ELAINE: How many children do you have?

ELEANOR: Three.

ELAINE: Are you married?

ELEANOR: Yes.

ELAINE: Don't get uppity with me. This is a with-it world. You can never tell who's married nowadays. *(Shouts.)* WHAT DOES YOUR HUSBAND DO?

ELEANOR: Please don't shout.

ELAINE: I'm sorry. *(Shouts.)* WHAT DOES YOUR HUSBAND DO?

ELEANOR: He's a salesman.

ELAINE: I see. A salesman. Attention must be paid, my ass!

ELEANOR: What do you mean?

ELAINE: Does he have sex with you?

ELEANOR: Is this necessary for the census?

ELAINE: The census itself is not necessary, so your question is irrelevant. Do you have sex with your husband?

ELEANOR: I don't think that...

ELAINE: Answer the question.

ELEANOR: Yes, when he demands his rights by marriage.

ELAINE: What do you do?

ELEANOR: I don't see how this affects...

ELAINE: Do you have oral sex? Do you have anal sex? Do either of you use chains?

ELEANOR: I will not answer any of these...

ELAINE: Have you ever had nasal intercourse?

ELEANOR: I...don't think I know what it is.

ELAINE: Look at these. *(She takes some photos from her purse.)*

ELEANOR: *(Pushing photos away.)* I don't want to see any more.

ELAINE: Well, have you?

ELEANOR: Certainly not.

ELAINE: Does your husband do anything to your nose at all?

ELEANOR: No.

ELAINE: What do yours sons do?

ELEANOR: My two oldest are presently unemployed, waiting to return to college, and my youngest is in the eighth grade.

ELAINE: Oh, is that so?

ELEANOR: Yes.

ELAINE: Really?

ELEANOR: Yes.

ELAINE: It is not!

ELEANOR: Yes, it is!

ELAINE: It is not. *(Shouting.)* You phony liar. Your oldest son pushes dope and is a pimp. I have here a signed affidavit from three hundred badly used women. *(She takes out the paper.)* And your second son is a homosexual. I have Super 8 film of him. *(She takes out a roll of film.)* And your youngest son lost his penis in a reaping accident and I have here a signed statement attesting to that fact from the entire eighth grade girls' gym class. So don't try to fool me with your pathetic lies. Admit that you lead a lousy life. Do you know on a national scale of one to 800, you rank 92; and on a local scale you are 33, and on an international scale 106, and on an all-white scale 23, and on an all-black scale 640, and on a pink scale 16, and that your capability ranking places you in the lowest percentile in the entire universe? It's a sad life I see before me, Mrs. Mann. You haven't any friends. None. Do you realize that you never call anybody up and that nobody ever calls you up? And that you're universally snubbed and pitied at PTA cocktail parties? And that your husband married you only because he had to, and your housekeeping is among the most slovenly on the eastern seaboard, and your physical appeal is in the lower quadrangle of the pentanglical scale—and that's not very high, Mrs. Mann—and that your children rank as among the foremost failed children in the nation and are well below the national level in areas of achievement, maturity, and ethical thinking. WHY DO YOU CONTINUE LIVING, MRS. MANN? WHY DON'T YOU DO YOURSELF A FAVOR?

ELEANOR: Please leave now.

ELAINE: One more thing, Mrs. Mann. Even though you and your family are going to have to leave tonight before the Fuller Brush Man is scheduled to arrive, he isn't going to come for you anyway. But you'll never know for sure, cause you'll be gone. So long, Mrs. Mann! Enjoy Iceland!

ELEANOR: Wait! How do you know about the Fuller Brush Man? Who are you? He will come! I know it. God has promised that he will come.

ELAINE: So long, you slob! *(Elaine exits.)*

ELEANOR: The Fuller Brush Man will come. I know it. He will come!
(Enter Ronald. Freeze. Exit Eleanor.)

RONALD: The Nature and Purpose of the Universe. Chapter 10. This particular Tuesday Andy sat in the last row in health class and watched the other boys play with themselves. Andy realized that he would never be able to masturbate. Egged on by the other boys, Andy tried rubbing his sensitive skin, but the stitches popped and he started to bleed. The school nurse gave him a sanitary napkin and took his temperature rectally, in order to humiliate him. Life is going to be difficult for Andy. And all throughout the city of Weehawken, a great search was begun for His Holiness, Pope Paul, and for the assailants of His Holiness' two body guards.
(Exit Ronald. Enter Steve and Fr. Anthony, carrying the limp body of Pope Paul. Elaine, as Sister Annie, follows, carrying a pistol, and shooting behind her.)

ELAINE: *(Firing.)* Take that, you anti-Christ copper!
(Enter Eleanor.)

ELEANOR: Steve, what's the matter?

ELAINE: Everybody duck down!
(Everybody drops to the floor except Eleanor.)

ELEANOR: Steve, who are these people?

ELAINE: I'm the new Pope, and that's the old Pope, and this is Fr. Anthony. *(She fires her gun.)* Pow pow.

ELEANOR: Who is the Pope?

STEVE: Shut up, Eleanor, and make some coffee.
  (Enter Andy, bleeding.)
ANDY: Mommy, Mommy, I've been shot!
ELEANOR: Oh, my God! Steve! Call an ambulance.
ELAINE: What is it? The dirty anti-Christ copper get you, little boy? Huh?
ANDY: I think it came from the house. I got shot in the stomach.
ELEANOR: Oh, Steve! I'll call the hospital.
STEVE: Don't you dare go to that phone!
ELEANOR: But, Steve, we don't know how seriously Andy's been hurt.
STEVE: Look, Eleanor, Sister and I are on a dangerous mission together. If you go to that phone, I'll be forced to kill you.
ELEANOR: Steven. Steven, what's happening?
STEVE: Shut up.
ELAINE: *(Firing.)* Pow pow pow. Pow. Hey, I seem to have run out.
FR. ANT.: Are you sure?
ELAINE: I think so. *(She aims her gun at the Pope. The gun goes off, the Pope's body jumps.)* Pow. Oh, my God.
FR. ANT.: You've shot the Pope!
ELAINE: The Pretender Pope, you fool. Well, it was meant to happen. Give me his tiara. *(She puts tiara on her head. Shooting out window.)* Pow pow pow.
ELEANOR: Steven, I think Andy's passed out.
STEVE: Would you shut up? Where's the coffee?
ELAINE: Well, now that the old Pope's dead, we won't have to take him with us tonight.
FR. ANT.: Just as well.
ELEANOR: Who are you? Where are you going?
ELAINE: *(To Steve.)* You didn't tell her.
STEVE: She can't be trusted.
ELAINE: She can be trusted under gunpoint. Look here, Mrs. Mann. At exactly midnight tonight the Mystical Body of Christ Kaffe-Klatch Club of Bernardsville is lowering a helicopter into your backyard, and you and your family will have the honor of accompanying me, Sister Annie De Maupassant, the radical nun of Bernardsville and the once and future Pope, as I leave for my exile in Iceland.
ELEANOR: Iceland. Why Iceland?
STEVE: Eleanor, don't ask the Pope questions.
ELAINE: Go ahead. Ask me. I just won't answer.

ELEANOR: She's not the one I'm asking. I'm asking you.

ELAINE: "She" is the cat's mother. I am the Pope.

ELEANOR: Steven, as your wife, I ask you why we have to go to Iceland.

STEVE: You're not my wife. You're a piece of dirt. Now make the coffee.

ELEANOR: I won't go to Iceland!

(Fr. Anthony looks at her kindly.)

FR. ANT.: It would be better for you, Mrs. Mann, if you did go. If you stay here, your husband will go to jail for killing one of the Pope's guards.

STEVE: The hell I will. I'll say my wife did it.

ELAINE: This talk is boring. Tell the tiresome woman to go make coffee before I shoot another one of her children.

STEVE: Eleanor, make coffee before the Pope shoots another one of our children. Then pack our bags and tell Donald and Gary to get ready. We've got to sit tight until midnight.

(Exit Eleanor, dragging Andy behind her. Enter Ronald. Actors freeze but do not exit.)

RONALD: The Nature and Purpose of the Universe. Chapter 11. That Tuesday night Eleanor's mind was a shambles of thoughts. She worried that Andy would die, she worried that the police outside the house would kill them all or that maybe the Sister Pope inside the house would kill them all. But most of all she worried that she would not be able to get away at midnight with the Fuller Brush Man. And the strange prophecy of the Census Lady about going to Iceland came back to haunt her with an uncomfortable persistence. *(Exit Ronald. Enter Donald, Gary. End freeze, action resumes.)*

GARY: *(Seeing the Pope.)* Oh my God. *(Bends down.)* Look at those earrings.

DONALD: God damn. I'll have to start all over again in Iceland. I have my clientele all settled out here in Maplewood and everything. I'm a familiar face. No one wants to have to start up all over again. Especially in Iceland.

STEVE: Donald, we've got to keep the family together at all costs. Isn't that so, Your Holiness?

ELAINE: The family is the essential unit of man. When the family crumbles, society crumbles. When society crumbles, man crumbles. But God never crumbles. *(Starts to shriek in her "speaking in tongues" manner.)*

FR. ANT.: Your Holiness, calm yourself. We have a long helicopter flight in front of us.

(Enter Eleanor, weeping into dish towel.)

ELEANOR: Andy's dead.

ELAINE: Let me see if I can raise him up.

ELEANOR: *(Very angry.)* You stay away from him.

STEVE: Eleanor, don't talk to the Pope that way.

ELEANOR: *(Crying.)* Andy was the only one of my sons who was even remotely kind and gentle.

DONALD: Shut up. Every mother wants an emasculated son. You got your wish, so shut up.

FR. ANT.: Perhaps His Holiness should speak on death.

ELAINE: Yes. Yes. I should. *(She stands on a table.)* Death comes to us all, my brothers and sisters in Christ. It comes to the richest of us and to the poorest of us. Our days on this earth are rounded by a little sleep. On the one hand, pre-birth. On the other hand, post-death. It's six of one, half a dozen of another. The world about us is but a valley of tears, full of sorrows for the just and blessings for the unjust. But yet even in the appalling spectacle of death we can see God's face looking down on us. We can see His Great Plan. Like some great spider, God weaves an immense web in which to trap us all and then in a fit of righteous rage, He eats us. The Eucharist at last finds its just and fitting revenge. But we must not despair that we do not understand God. Rather must we rejoice in our confusion, for in our ignorance is reflected God's wisdom, in our ugliness His beauty, in our imperfections His perfections. For we are the little people of the earth, and His is the power and the glory, and never the twain shall meet. Hubb-ba, hubba-ba, hubb-ba.

STEVE: Thank you, Your Holiness. *(Elaine steps off table.)*

FR. ANT.: Hark. I hear the helicopter now.

STEVE: Are the bags packed, Eleanor?

ELEANOR: Yes.

ELAINE: All right. Get ready to board. Fr. Anthony, I've decided that you must stay behind in the living room and cover us as we fly away.

FR. ANT.: But, Your Holiness, I shall be arrested.

ELAINE: Casuistry is not my forte, Fr. Anthony. If you die I shall proclaim you a martyr and wear a red gown. Alright, I'm ready to board.

(They start to exit.)

STEVE: Eleanor, why aren't you moving?

ELEANOR: Steven, I'm not going. I've packed my bags but not to go to Iceland. At midnight I shall be carried away by a kind man who has seen my pain and who in his pity and love has vowed to take me away from this hell.

STEVE: Eleanor, get into the helicopter.

ELEANOR: Steven, no! I will not go!

STEVE: You are my legal wife. I will need you in Iceland to cook and to sew and to clean and to scrub and to get on your back and fulfill your wifely duty.

ELEANOR: Steven, I will not go. I am going to be rescued! I know it!

(Ronald, D., not visible to the actors, not in the room.)

RONALD: Eleanor, I'm on my way. Don't fear. I'll save you.

ELEANOR: I hear him now! He's coming!

STEVE: Get into the helicopter!

RONALD: Eleanor! Eleanor!

ELEANOR: I hear him. Come quickly. Save me!

ELAINE: *(Slaps her.)* You stupid woman. You hear nothing. Do you think anyone in the entire world would run off with you? You are worth nothing. This man is entirely a sick invention of your sick and pathetic mind. You are going to go to Iceland with your husband, as is your duty, and you will suffer through a long succession of tedious days and tedious nights, and you will have no rest because you are not meant to have any rest, and you will not complain because you are doing the will of God. *(Slaps her.)* You are supposed to suffer, you stupid, stupid woman!

ELEANOR: *(Hysterical.)* No!! Help me!

RONALD: Eleanor!

ELAINE: Sons, take your mother forcibly to the helicopter. Knock her unconscious if she gives you any trouble.

ELEANOR: Help me!

DONALD: Shut up, slut!

(Donald and Gary carry Eleanor offstage.)

ELAINE: What a thoroughly trivial woman.

FR. ANT.: Perhaps you should have shown more charity, Your Holiness.

ELAINE: Charity schmarity. Come on, Mr. Mann. To the helicopter. So long, lackey!

(Elaine and Steve exit. Sound of helicopter. Action freezes, Fr. Anthony and the dead Pope exit. Ronald comes forward.)

RONALD: The Nature and Purpose of the Universe. Chapter 12. That

Tuesday night the police finally got Fr. Anthony Hemmer, and he was tried for the murder of Pope Paul and of little Andy. Fr. Hemmer was sentenced to death, but then the sentence was mitigated to life imprisonment and no rest room facilities. And on that Tuesday night on the helicopter ride to Iceland, Sister Annie De Maupassant, the once and future Pope, mysteriously disappeared midflight, Elaine having more important things to do. The Mann family settled in Iceland, much the same as always except that Eleanor was in a deep depression. Steve, having lost his interest in the new Catholicism, now nurtured an infatuation with the First Lady of the Icelandic Stage, the distinguished Olga Rheinholtenbarkerburkerburr. God assigns Elaine to impersonate Olga in a last effort to finish off Eleanor.

(Ronald exits. Enter Eleanor and Steve. They sit in two chairs. Eleanor hardly moves, just stares off in complete distraction. She appears to hear very little.)

STEVE: Stop looking like a zombie, for God's sake, Eleanor. My God, you should be counting your blessings. The igloo takes care of itself, our son Gary is engaged to the son of the Prime Minister, and our son Donald has the Prime Minister's daughter pulling in $900 a week. With those sorts of connections, I expect I'll be a big shot in Icelandic politics in a few months. Are you listening, Eleanor? Eleanor? Talking to you is like talking to a mop. So, you see, you should cheer up. Your husband's gonna be quite a big shot.

(We hear the voice of an announcer.)

ANNOUNCER: Good evening, lady and gentleman. Tonight the Baked Alaska is proud to present that first lady of the Icelandic Stage, Dame Olga Rheinholtenbarkerburkerburr!

(Enter Elaine.)

ELAINE: *(Bowing graciously.)* Thank you. Thank you. I should like to do a dramatic reading for you. *(She dimples.)*

How do I love thee?

Let me count the ways.

One. Two. Three. Four, five, six…Seven. Eight.

STEVE: Hey! Don't forget nasal intercourse!

ELAINE: Oh, yes. Thank you. Nine. Ten, eleven, twelve, thirteen, fourteen, fifteen, sixteen, seventeen…and…eighteen! And now I should like to give you another reading. It is from *Macbeth* by William Shakespeare.

Tomorrow and tomorrow,
And tomorrow... *(Goes blank.)*
And tomorrow, and tomorrow, and tomorrow, and tomorrow,
and tomorrow, and tomorrow, and tomorrow...

STEVE: A song! Sing us a song! Would you look at her, Eleanor. What a
piece she is.

ELAINE: I would like to sing a little song for you that was written for me
by a little man in a little black hat with beady little eyes and greedy
little thighs. *(Sings, tune is "Tiptoe Through the Tulips".)*
Tiptoe through the tundra,
It's a wundra,
We don't catch a chill,
We tiptoe as we use our free will.
Ice-skate round the igloo,
If we dig through,
All the tundra here,
We'll find we will be happy next year.
We'll freeze our knees and our toes,
A sneeze will freeze on our nose,
And we will...
Tiptoe through the tundra,
And we'll wundra,
When the world will end,
And Jesus is our very best friend!
Dum-dee-dee-dum-dee-dee-dum, dee-dum!
(Steve applauds.)

STEVE: Olga. Come join my table.

ELAINE: *(Crossing to him.)* Oh, Mr. Mann, what a faithful fan you are.
What's the matter with your wife?

STEVE: She hasn't made the transition from New Jersey yet.

ELAINE: Oh, I see.

STEVE: Give me a kiss.

ELAINE: Oh, Mr. Mann. Do you think I should? What about your wife?

STEVE: She won't notice. *(They kiss.)* Hey, when am I going to get into
your pants?

ELAINE: Oh, Mr. Mann, the things you say! Sometimes I'm surprised out
of my little biddle empty-headed mind. But I'll tell you. you aren't
ever going to get into my pants because I love my husband. *(Louder,
directed at Eleanor.)* Yes, my sweet husband used to be a Fuller Brush

Man from New Jersey. But now he's found the love of his life in little iddle me. The Fuller Brush Man loves me.

ELEANOR: *(Stirring.)* What?

ELAINE: Oh, Mrs. Mann. I was just telling your husband how I'm married to an ex-Fuller Brush Man from New Jersey, and how happy I am. Why, here he comes now. You can meet him.
(Enter Ronald. He kisses Elaine.)

RONALD: Hello, darling. How are you? I caught your act from the back. It was magnificent as usual.

ELAINE: Thank you, dear. I'd like you to meet...

ELEANOR: It's you. *(Hysterical.)* Oh, please save me, please save me!

STEVE: *(Shakes her.)* STOP THAT. What sort of display are you making? You're embarrassing me!

ELEANOR: Save me, please. It's not too late!

STEVE: Eleanor!

ELAINE: Mr. Mann, let's leave them alone. My husband is very good at dealing with hysterical women.
(Elaine and Steve step aside. In the next section Ronald acts nonchalant and charming and not outwardly mean.)

ELEANOR: Please, let me explain why I wasn't there that night. The helicopter had come and...

RONALD: There, there, Eleanor, don't be so sentimental...

ELEANOR: But if you understood why I wasn't there...

RONALD: You weren't there?

ELEANOR: No...I...but didn't you know?

RONALD: No, silly. I never intended to go back to your house. I just wanted you to buy a brush.

ELEANOR: But you said you saw my suffering, and that you'd take me away.

RONALD: My goodness, you're a silly woman. I say that to all my customers. You're not supposed to believe me.

ELEANOR: Save me!

RONALD: Perhaps you'd like a brush now.

ELEANOR: Save me. Take me away from here!
(Steve and Elaine cross back to the two.)

RONALD: There's nothing I can do with her. She's just a silly little goose.
(Exit Ronald and Elaine.)

STEVE: Stop that. *(He throws her to the ground.)* Stop making a spectacle of yourself.

(Enter Gary, Donald, and Ralph.)

GARY: Hello there, Eleanor. On the ground again? Making a scene?

RALPH: Hello, Mrs. Mann, how are you? Gary and I share the Prime Minister's son now, isn't that nice?

DONALD: Stop whimpering, slut. The Prime Minister says he's willing to give me five dollars if he can urinate in your face, so he's coming over right after dinner.

STEVE: Get up, Eleanor. Time to make dinner.

(The four of them kick her lightly on the ground.)

STEVE: Come on, Eleanor. Get up. Get up. Get up now. *(Phone rings. Steve answers it.)* Hello? Oh. All right. Why, it's for you, Eleanor. Someone is actually on the telephone for you.

(Enter Elaine, way D. She stares out.)

ELEANOR: *(In tears.)* Hello? Hello? Hello?

ELAINE: *(Not holding a phone, very serious.)* Hello, Eleanor, this is Elaine speaking. I want you to come over to the slaughter house right away. Do you understand, Eleanor?

(The men exit automatically. Elaine crosses over to Eleanor, helps her to lie on the table. Elaine takes out a knife. Enter Ronald.)

RONALD: The Nature and Purpose of the Universe. Chapter 13. And God said to Elaine, take now thy charge Eleanor, whom thou lovest, and get thee into the land of Moriah; and offer her there for a burnt offering upon one of the mountains which I will tell thee of.

And Elaine came to the place which God had told her of; and she built an altar there, and laid the wood in order, and bound Eleanor her charge, and laid her upon the altar.

And Elaine stretched forth her hand, and took the knife to slay Eleanor. *(Elaine raises the knife very high and then lowers it quickly toward Eleanor.)*

BUT WAIT! And God said to Elaine, spare this woman's life, for I am merciful. And sing forth my glories and my praise, for I am God of Gods, the Father of His children.

ELAINE & RONALD: *(Sing together; Handel:)*
    Alleluia! Alleluia! Alleluia!

ELEANOR: Kill me! Please kill me! Kill me!

ELAINE & RONALD: Alleluia! Alleluia! Alleluia!

ELEANOR: I don't want to live. Please kill me. Kill me!

(Blackout. End.)

TO THE ACTOR
Radio Play Version

The "radio play" version allows the play to be done with fewer actors. The text is the same; only the staging would be different. The play is set in a radio studio, the actors stand in front of microphones; the violence is done by means of sound effects.

One of the dangers of doing the play this way, however, is that the conceit of Ronald and Elaine as agents of God becomes somewhat muddied (because there is a radio actress playing Elaine who's playing, say, Miss Manfield).

If you do try the play as a radio play, it is most important to keep the story of Eleanor's suffering the "reason" for the play, and not to let the radio "bits" take over the play. In line with that, the less done with who the people are who are putting on the play, the better.

When the play was done this way at the Direct Theatre, the play began with the following taped announcement:

Good morning, and welcome to WPAX Sunday Sermon, a series of weekly inspirational stories inspired by the spiritual lives of St. Jude, St. Sebastian, and St. Theresa of Avilla. The following schools will be closed tomorrow due to the death of Mother Charles Magdala, O.S.B.: Our Lady of Perpetual Sorrow School, Rockaway, N.J.; Our Lady of Tears School for Boys, Morristown, N.J.; Union Catholic Girls High School, Scotch Plains, N.J.; and Our Lady of Agonizing Suffering, Camden, N.J.

Our program will begin after a few short ejaculations: Mary, mother of God, pray for us. God, our saviour and our strength, deliver us. Mary, conceived without sin, protect us. Jesus, our hope, deliver us. And now our program.

Today we are privileged to have with us the St. Dominick Inspirational Society Plays from East Rutherford, N.J. They will be performing for you, live from our studios, a play by Christopher Durang entitled *The Nature and Purpose of the Universe*.

Tone and Violence in the Play

There is a difficult balance needed in the performance of this play: Eleanor's plight must be presented sympathetically so we care about her, and yet her suffering must be sufficiently distanced/ or theatricalized (particularly in the first two thirds of the play) so that we can find it funny.

In line with this, I have never seen Eleanor played by an actress who was the proper age to have grown sons; I'm sure it could be done, with the proper actress; but having a younger woman (20 to 30) play the role also works as a distancing device that may be helpful in presenting the play and, perhaps more importantly, also frees us from worry about the physical demands that the actress playing Eleanor must meet. Common sense and individual taste will have to dictate, but I at least offer that you may be safer casting someone young for Eleanor, and someone the audience can recognize as physically spry so they don't have to worry during the violence.

The violence against Eleanor in the play is a tricky problem; and again common sense and personal taste will have to find what works for each production and group of actors. On the one hand, the violence can't be totally fake or simply too mild, or else we'll never find the humor (particularly in the early scenes) of how *preposterously* awful Eleanor's life is. And on the other hand, if the violence is too convincing or too "specific," the play will turn too ugly. To give an example of the latter problem, there was a production in which Donald punched Eleanor in the stomach, the actress realistically acted loss of breath, and so forth, and the scene turned too ugly. It may have been all the fault of a too realistic reaction, or it may have been that a man punching a woman in the stomach may be too "specific" of an image ever to be funny in this play.

I have found that the violence that seems to work the best in productions I've seen is what I might call (vaguely, I realize) "generalized" violence. For instance, it always seems to work when Donald throws Eleanor to the ground: It's a large, sudden action, Eleanor gets to react in fear and terror, but she doesn't have to act a specific, localized pain. Things like the throwings to the ground, kicks, arm twists, hair pullings, anything that the audience knows can be easily faked and that also don't have particular "pain resonance" for us seem the safest things to try.

With the violence in particular and with the playing tone in general, the problem is somehow to balance letting the audience feel liking and sympathy for Eleanor at the same time that they find the humor in seeing her "get it." Each production has to find its own solutions, so I can offer no sweeping suggestions. But being aware of the problem may be helpful.

To Do the Play in Two Acts

If you want to place an intermission in the play, you can do so at the end of Chapter 6, with one small addition. At the end of the hymn, after Ronald says "The Nature and Purpose of the Universe. End of Part I.", Eleanor should then say: "Thank God." Then intermission.

Another place to put an intermission is at the end of Chapter 9. If you do that, you should cut Ronald's remarks about Andy at the beginning of Chapter 10, and only leave his comments about the Pope and the search for the Pope.

'dentity Crisis

AUTHOR'S NOTE

The summer after I graduated college and was waiting to go to Yale School of Drama, I stayed up in Cambridge, Massachusetts for the summer, working as a stock boy in the Physics Department. And I shared a house with seven or eight fellow students.

I was reading a book called *Madness, Sanity and The Family* by R.D. Laing and A. Esterson, which consisted of case studies of schizophrenic patients. It was Laing and Esterson's belief that the schizophrenia shown by the patients made sense—and was even a "normal" response——once you saw them in the context of their family interaction.

The stories were fascinating, and the interactions quite blatant. One patient told the doctors her parents were always whispering about her; when the doctors interviewed the girl with her parents, he told them what she said; the parents whispered to one another, and then said: "No, it's not true, we never whisper about her." Then they whispered some more.

Or then another pair of parents complained that their daughter masturbated. Then they said no, she was a good girl, she never did that. They didn't seem to find a contradiction in these two assertions, though the schizophrenic daughter did; from a lifetime of these contradictions, she felt totally confused and unable to see what was real and what wasn't.

Anyway I come from a family of extremely strong-willed people, especially women. And so reading these case studies, I found myself drawn suddenly to writing this play about an extreme and blatantly malfunctioning family where the craziness is totally evident and totally denied.

I wrote it all night long one night, and especially got the giggles writing the Peter Pan sequence.

ORIGINAL PRODUCTION

'dentity Crisis was first presented in 1971 at the Harvard Loeb Experimental Theatre, titled *Robert?* for some reason, and directed by Joanna Messina. It was after I graduated, and I don't have the rest of the names anywhere. Then I directed it in 1975 at the Yale Cabaret in New Haven, with the following cast:

Jane	Catherine Schreiber
Edith Fromage	Kate McGregor-Stewart
Robert	James Zitlow
Mr. Summers	Alan Mokler
Woman	Alma Cuervo

'dentity Crisis was then presented by the Yale Repertory Theatre, New Haven, Connecticut, on a double bill with *Guess Work* by Robert Auletta, on October 13, 1978. The direction of *'dentity Crisis* was by Frank Torok, scenery by Michael Yeargan, costumes by Marjorie Graf, lighting by Robert Jared. The cast was as follows:

Jane	Caitlin Clarke
Edith Fromage	Darcy Pulliam
Robert	Mark Linn-Baker
Mr. Summers	David K. Miller
Woman	Nancy Mayans

CHARACTERS
JANE
EDITH FROMAGE, her mother
ROBERT, her brother, father or grandfather
MR. SUMMERS, her psychologist
WOMAN

PRODUCTION NOTES

The setting of this play could be any living room with a couch, table, chair, and so forth. Because the living room has been presumably chosen and decorated by Edith, who is fairly insane, there should be some odd things about the decor.

The production at the Yale Repertory Theatre chose (partly due to its wide stage) to have a bizarrely symmetrical set: identical couches, chair and table Stage Left and Stage Right; there was a piano and piano bench Upstage Center. There were doors, identical, Left and Right.

On the wall there were five large, framed photographs: four utterly identical ones of Robert, two on either side; and one of Jane, in the Center above the piano.

Due to the extreme number of personalities that "Robert" turns out to possess, the four photos of him strike me as an excellent idea.

The symmetrical, mirrorlike image of the two couches, two chairs, and so on, strikes me as successfully odd and worked well in the Yale Rep production. It doesn't have the thematic resonance of the four photos of Robert, however; and so if your stage was not all that wide, or if you wanted to experiment with either a more realistic living room or with a differently odd one (one that mixed styles of furniture radically, for instance), you should feel free to experiment.

One prop note you might find helpful: The "tables" in the Yale Rep production were actually square cubes that opened on top, and inside were kept all of Edith and Robert's paraphernalia. This was both useful for staging purposes, and made sense thematically as well. (Edith and Robert keeping all their "toys" in a sort of toy chest.)

'DENTITY CRISIS

Scene: Living room. Jane, the daughter, in disheveled bathrobe, lies on the couch. She is extremely depressed and sits paging steadily through a Time Magazine, *not looking at it at all.*

VOICE: *(Offstage.)* Cuckoo. Cuckoo.
  (Enter Edith, carrying a bag of groceries and a dress in a dry cleaner's bag. Dress is very badly stained with blood.)
EDITH: Hello, dear, I'm back. Did you miss me? Say yes. *(Pause.)* Of course you missed me. A daughter always misses her mother. You're less depressed today, aren't you? I can tell. *(Puts bag down.)* I got your dress back. I'm afraid the stains didn't come out. You should have heard the lady at the cleaners. What did she do, slash her thighs with a razor blade? she said. I had to admit you had. Really, dear, I've never heard of anyone doing that. It was so awful when your father and I went into the bathroom together to brush our teeth and saw you perched up on the toilet, your pretty white dress over your head, slashing away at your thighs. I don't think your father had ever seen your thighs before, and I hope he never will again, at least not under those unpleasant conditions. I mean, what could have possessed you? No one in our family has ever attempted suicide before now, and no one since either. It's a sign of defeat, and no one should do it. You know what I think? Jane? Jane?
JANE: What?
EDITH: I don't think you ever attempted suicide at all. That's what I think.

JANE: How do you explain the stains then?

EDITH: I don't. *(Laughs merrily.)* I always say stains will explain themselves, and if they don't then there's nothing can be done about it. *(Edith empties the grocery bag on the table. It is filled with loose potato chips, which Edith playfully arranges as if it is some sort of food sculpture.)*

JANE: I did attempt suicide.

EDITH: No, dear, you didn't. A daughter doesn't contradict her mother.

VOICE: Cuckoo, cuckoo.

JANE: Did you hear the voice of my therapist just then?

EDITH: No, dear. *(Listens.)* Ah, now I hear it. He's saying what a fine daughter I have.

    (Enter Robert.)

ROBERT: Mother! I'm home.

EDITH: Oh, Jane, it's your brother.

    (Edith and Robert kiss passionately and long. Jane is very upset and rips up the plastic covering on her dress.)

ROBERT: Darling, darling.

EDITH: Oh, Dwayne, this is mad. We've got to stop meeting like this. Your father will find out.

JANE: I'll tell him!

EDITH: Jane, you'd never do anything like that.

ROBERT: I'm mad for you. I find you…exciting.

    (They kiss.)

EDITH: *(Looking off.)* Quick, there's the postman. Act busy.

    (Robert and Edith smash the potato chips on the table with their fists. Then they brush the crushed chips into a waste basket with a little broom.)

EDITH: There, he's gone.

ROBERT: *(Holding her.)* Oh, why must you taunt me? Let's get married.

EDITH: We have different blood types.

ROBERT: Oh, mother, I love you. *(They embrace.)*

EDITH: Oh, my God. Here comes your father.

    (Robert, with no change of costume and without exiting or re-entering, becomes the father.)

ROBERT: Edith, what are you doing?

EDITH: Oh, Arthur, I was just finishing off my morning shopping.

ROBERT: And how is our daughter?

JANE: You're not my father.

EDITH: Don't contradict your father. You love your father, Jane.

JANE: He's my brother.

EDITH: Dwayne is your brother, dear.

ROBERT: Has she been seeing that psychologist of hers?

EDITH: Well, not socially.

ROBERT: Good. *(Shouting at Jane.)* I don't ever want to hear of you dating a psychologist again.

JANE: I never have!

EDITH: Of course not, dear. You obey your father. You're a good daughter.

ROBERT: Not like some I could mention.

EDITH: No.

ROBERT: I could mention some.

EDITH: You could.

ROBERT: I could. I will.

EDITH: Now?

ROBERT: Now. Frances, Lucia, Henrietta, Charmant, Dolores, Loretta, and Peggy.

EDITH: Listen to your father, Jane.

ROBERT: No more of this slashing your thighs, young lady. I don't think that psychologist would ever go out with you again if he knew you were slashing your thighs.

JANE: I don't go out with my psychologist.

EDITH: Of course you don't. He has a wife and sixteen children. You're a good girl. You listen to your father.

JANE: *(To Robert.)* You're not my father.

EDITH: Jane, you know he's your father.

JANE: If you're my father, you must be close to fifty.

ROBERT: I am close to fifty.

JANE: Let me see your driver's license.

ROBERT: Here. *(Hands it to her.)*

JANE: *(Reads it.)* This says you're fifty. How did you get them to put that down?

EDITH: The truth is the truth no matter how you look at it, Jane.

JANE: How come you don't look fifty?

EDITH: Your father never looked his age. Most girls would be pleased that their father looked young.

ROBERT: Most girls are pleased.

EDITH: Jane's pleased you look young, aren't you, Jane? Don't you think Arthur looks young for his age, Grandad?

ROBERT: Eh? What?

EDITH: *(Shouting.)* Don't you think Arthur looks young, Grandad!

ROBERT: *(Smiling senilely.)* Yes, yes. Breakfast.

EDITH: Poor Grandad can't hear a thing.

JANE: Where's father?

EDITH: Isn't he here? That's funny. I didn't hear the door close.

JANE: Grandad, mother is having an affair with Dwayne!

ROBERT: *(Not hearing.)* What?

EDITH: He can't hear you. Besides you mustn't make up stories. I don't. Oh, listen to the doorbell.

(Bell rings. Enter Mr. Summers, the psychologist and the previous off-stage voice.)

EDITH: Why, Jane, it's your psychologist. *(To Summers.)* I recognized you from your photos. Jane has plastered her walls with your pictures. I don't know why.

SUMMERS: How do you do? You must be Jane's mother.

EDITH: Yes. I'm Edith Fromage. You probably saw my photo in the papers when you were a little boy. I invented cheese in France in the early portion of the century.

SUMMERS: In what way did you invent cheese?

EDITH: In every way. And this is my son, Dwayne Fromage.

ROBERT: How do you do, sir?

SUMMERS: How do you do? I didn't realize Jane's last name was Fromage.

EDITH: It isn't. I had Jane by another husband. A Mr. Carrot.

JANE: My name isn't Carrot.

EDITH: That's right, dear. It's *Jane* Carrot. *(Whispers.)* Jane's very over-wrought today. The stains wouldn't come out of her dress.

SUMMERS: Oh, I'm sorry.

EDITH: You think you're sorry. You should have seen the woman at the cleaners. I thought we'd have to chain her to the floor.

ROBERT: Perhaps Mr. Summers is hungry.

EDITH: Oh, forgive me. *(Offers him wastebasket of crushed chips.)*

SUMMERS: No thank you.

EDITH: Then how about some entertainment? Jane, play the piano for Mr. Summers.

JANE: I don't play the piano.

EDITH: Of course you do. I've heard you many times. You play very well.

JANE: I've never played the piano.

EDITH: Jane, Mr. Summers would enjoy your playing. Please play.

JANE: I don't know how!

EDITH: *(Angry.)* How do you know? Have you ever tried?

JANE: No.

EDITH: There. You see then. *(To Summers.)* Cello is her real instrument, but we never talk about it.

ROBERT: Please play, Jane.

(Jane walks hesitatingly to the piano, sits. Pause. Makes some noise on keyboard, obviously can't play, starts to cry.)

JANE: I don't know how to play piano!

EDITH: But you do! Why else would we have one? No one else in the house plays.

JANE: I don't remember taking lessons.

EDITH: You probably forgot due to all this strain. *(To Summers.)* You talk to her. She seems in a state. *(To Robert.)* Come on, dear. Call me if you want, Mr. Summers.

(Robert and Edith kiss, then exit.)

JANE: *(At piano.)* I don't *remember* taking piano lessons.

SUMMERS: Maybe you've repressed it. *(Sits.)* My wife gave me the message about your attempting suicide. Why did you do it, Jane?

JANE: I can't stand it. My mother says she's invented cheese and I start to think maybe she has. There's a man living in the house and I'm not sure whether he's my brother or my father or my grandfather. I can't be sure of anything anymore.

SUMMERS: You're talking quite rationally now. And your self-doubts are a sign of health. The truly crazy person never thinks he's crazy. Now explain to me what led up to your attempted suicide.

JANE: Well, a few days ago I woke up and I heard this voice saying, "It wasn't enough."

SUMMERS: Did you recognize the voice?

JANE: Not at first. But then it started to come back to me. When I was eight years old, someone brought me to a theatre with lots of other children. We had come to see a production of *Peter Pan*. And I remember something seemed wrong with the whole production, odd things kept happening. Like when the children would fly, the ropes would keep breaking and the actors would come thumping to the ground and they'd have to be carried off by the stagehands. There seemed to be an unlimited supply of understudies to take the children's places, and then *they'd* fall to the ground. And then the crocodile that chases Captain Hook seemed to be a real crocodile, it wasn't an actor, and at one point it fell off the stage, crushing several children in the front row.

SUMMERS: What happened to the children?

JANE: Several understudies came and took their places in the audience. And from scene to scene Wendy seemed to get fatter and fatter until finally by the second act she was immobile and had to be moved with a cart.

SUMMERS: Where does the voice fit in?

JANE: The voice belonged to the actress playing Peter Pan. You remember how in the second act Tinkerbell drinks some poison that Peter's about to drink, in order to save him? And then Peter turns to the audience and he says that Tinkerbell's going to die because not enough people believe in fairies, but that if everybody in the audience claps real hard to show that they *do* believe in fairies, then maybe Tinkerbell won't die. And so then all the children started to clap. We clapped very hard and very long. My palms hurt and even started to bleed I clapped so hard. Then suddenly the actress playing Peter Pan turned to the audience and she said, "That wasn't enough. You didn't clap hard enough. Tinkerbell's dead." Uh...well, and...and then everyone started to cry. The actress stalked offstage and refused to continue with the play, and they finally had to bring down the curtain. No one could see anything through all the tears, and the ushers had to come help the children up the aisles and out into the street. I don't think any of us were ever the same after that experience.

SUMMERS: How do you think this affected you?

JANE: Well it certainly turned me against theatre; but more damagingly, I think it's warped my sense of life. You know—nothing seems worth trying if Tinkerbell's just going to die.

SUMMERS: And so you wanted to die like Tinkerbell.

JANE: Yes.

SUMMERS: *(With importance.)* Jane. I have to bring my wife to the hospital briefly this afternoon, so I have to go now. But I want you to hold on, and I'll check back later today. I think you're going to be all right, but I think you need a complete rest; so when I come back we'll talk about putting you somewhere for a while.

JANE: You mean committing me.

SUMMERS: No. This would just be a rest home, a completely temporary thing. Tinkerbell just needs her batteries recharged, that's all. Now you just make your mind a blank, and I'll be back as soon as I can.

JANE: Thank you. I'll try to stay quiet 'til you return.

(Enter Edith.)

EDITH: Oh, you're leaving. Won't you have some of my cheese first?

SUMMERS: Thank you, Mrs. Fromage, but I have to go now. Please see to it that your daughter stays quiet.

EDITH: Oh, you can rely on me.

SUMMERS: *(To Jane.)* Chin up. *(Exits.)*

EDITH: Jane, dear, I've brought you some sheet music. I thought maybe if you got settled on where middle C was, it might all come back to you.

JANE: Please leave me alone.

EDITH: I don't know why you've turned against the piano.

JANE: *(Suddenly sharp.)* Well you know my one love was always the cello.

EDITH: *(Realizing Jane is being devious.)* A good daughter does not speak to her mother in that tone. I'm sure you didn't mean that. When you are ready to play the piano, let me know. Oh, there's the doorbell.

(Bell rings. Enter Robert.)

ROBERT: *(French accent.)* Ah, Madame Fromage.

EDITH: Oh, Count. How nice. I don't think you've met my daughter. Jane, dear, this is the Count de Rochelay, my new benefactor.

ROBERT: How do you do, Mademoiselle? My people and I are most anxious for your mother to make a comeback. All the time, the people of France say, whatever happened to Edith Fromage who gave us cheese? It is time she left her solitude and returned to the spotlight and invented something new. And so I come to your charming Mama and I convince her to answer the call of the people of France.

EDITH: Jane, say hello to the count.

JANE: Hello.

EDITH: *(Whispers.)* You have to forgive her. She's sulking because she's forgotten how to play the piano.

(He embraces her.)

ROBERT: Madame Fromage, I love you!

EDITH: Please! I don't want my son or husband to hear you!

ROBERT: *(Whispers.)* Madame Fromage, I love you. *(Kisses her.)*

EDITH: Not now. First I must invent something new. Have you the ingredients?

(Robert has paper bag. Edith takes out a family size loaf of Wonder

Bread and makes a stack of six slices. Then she takes a banana from the bag and rams it into the center of the stack of bread.)

ROBERT: Bravo, Madame!

EDITH: Voila! I have invented banana bread.

ROBERT: Bravo! Let us make love to celebrate!

EDITH: Please, my son or husband might hear.

ROBERT: *(Deaf.)* Eh?

EDITH: Shush, Grandad. Go down to the cellar.

ROBERT: Madame Fromage, France will thank you for this.

EDITH: And I will thank France. It is moments like these when I feel most alive.

(Robert carries Edith off.)

ROBERT: Vive Madame Fromage!

(Jane at piano hits middle C several times. Lights dim, slowly to blackout. As they do, the light of a flashlight flashes about the stage as Tinkerbell.)

EDITH'S VOICE: *(Offstage, as Peter Pan.)* Tink, are you all right, Tink? Tinkerbell?

(Light of Tinkerbell starts to blink on and off.)

JANE: Don't die! *(Jane's solitary clapping is heard in darkness. Tinkerbell's light goes off.)*

EDITH'S VOICE: *(Off, in darkness.)* That wasn't enough. She's dead. Tinkerbell's dead.

(Blackout.)

Scene: Lights up on Jane seated at piano with a paper bag over head.

VOICE: *(Offstage; Summers.)* Cuckoo, Cuckoo.

(Enter Robert.)

ROBERT: Have you seen your mother?

JANE: *(Under bag.)* To whom am I speaking?

ROBERT: Take off the bag and see.

(She takes off the bag.)

JANE: To whom am I speaking?

ROBERT: Don't act odd, Jane. Tell your father you'll be normal.

JANE: I'll be normal.

ROBERT: I'll be normal, comma, Father.

JANE: I'll be normal, comma, Father.

(Enter Edith.)

EDITH: Oh, there you are, children.

ROBERT: Mother, don't leave me for that Count. Edith, what is Dwayne talking about?

EDITH: I'm sure I don't know, Arthur. *(Whispers to Robert.)* Don't let your father know about the Count.

ROBERT: Mother, I love you. Edith, what did you just whisper to Dwayne?

EDITH: Oh, nothing, dear. Just that Grandad's hearing is getting worse. Look, I've invented banana bread, aren't you proud of me?

ROBERT: Congratulations, Edith. Gee, Mom. *(Deaf.)* What?

EDITH: *(Shouting.)* Banana bread, Grandad!

ROBERT: It's too early for bed.

JANE: I only see two people.

EDITH: I'm sure you see more than that, dear. Oh, the doorbell.
    (Doorbell. Enter a Woman.)

WOMAN: Hello, Mrs. Fromage. How's Jane?

EDITH: Much better. Jane, a visitor.

JANE: Who are you?

WOMAN: I'm your psychologist, Mr. Summers.

JANE: I don't...understand.

WOMAN: I guess it's confusing, but I didn't want to tell you earlier. I got a sex change this afternoon.

JANE: I don't believe you.

WOMAN: It's quite true. My wife can substantiate. *(Calls.)* Harriet.
    (Enter Mr. Summers.)

SUMMERS: Yes, dear.

WOMAN: Explain to Jane that I am Mr. Summers.

SUMMERS: How do you do, Jane? My husband has told me so much about you and your neuroses. You're one of my favorite cases.

JANE: I don't understand.

WOMAN: It simply seemed that the magic had one out of our marriage, and that we both needed a change.

JANE: You should have told me. You should have prepared me.

WOMAN: I didn't want to spring it on you too quickly.

EDITH: I think it's very courageous of you both.

SUMMERS: Thank you.

WOMAN: *(To Summers.)* Harriet, is that a banana in your trousers, or are you just happy to see me?

SUMMERS: It's a banana. *(Takes a banana out of his trousers, to Jane.)* They haven't fitted me with any male appendages yet, so I've been trying everything to get the hang of it. I think a banana's too large.

EDITH: Might I have the banana?

SUMMERS: Surely. *(Edith makes another thing of banana bread, quickly.)*

WOMAN: I've been wondering how my patients would react to the change.

ROBERT: Mother, I love you.

EDITH: Hush, dear, they'll hear you.

WOMAN: *(To Jane.)* Now tell me about the dream about the Peter Pan play again.

JANE: It wasn't a dream. It was a memory from my childhood.

WOMAN: Oh, I thought you told me it was a dream.

JANE: No, I didn't.

EDITH: I was listening at the door and feel sure you said it was a dream. Didn't you, dear?

JANE: It wasn't a dream, and I didn't say it was. *(To Woman.)* And I didn't tell you about it anyway. *(Pointing to Summers.)* I told him.

WOMAN: But you've never met Harriet until this very minute.

JANE: You're pulling a trick on me.

(Summers whispers to Woman.)

WOMAN: Oh, my God. Mrs. Fromage, have you any glue?

EDITH: Yes. I invented some this morning.

ROBERT: Ah, Madame Fromage, bravo for you.

EDITH: *(Handing Woman bottle.)* I call it mucilage.

WOMAN: *(Squeezing some on her breast.)* You must excuse me. My wife just noticed that one of my breasts was slipping off.

EDITH: Could I get you a melon?

WOMAN: No thank you. This should do it. Modern surgery is a wonder these days, but it can be sloppily done sometimes.

JANE: I don't think you can help me.

WOMAN: Oh dear. You see, Harriet.

SUMMERS: I see.

WOMAN: A hostile reaction to my change. Jane, dear, I'm just as capable as I was before.

JANE: I think you're crazy.

ROBERT: What? Eh?

JANE: Shut up! You're not my father.

EDITH: Of course not. He's your grandfather.

JANE: Let me see his driver's license.

EDITH: He doesn't drive. It wouldn't be wise.

SUMMERS: Oh my God! *(Scratches all over.)*

WOMAN: Harriet, what's the matter?

SUMMERS: I feel so unused to these clothes. The pants rub my legs and the shoes are too heavy and I miss my breasts.

WOMAN: Harriet. Please. We can talk about this after my session with Jane.

SUMMERS: Walter, we can't. I feel very nervous all of a sudden. May I see you in the other room for a second?

WOMAN: Very well. Mrs. Fromage, might my wife and I talk in your bedroom for a second?

EDITH: Surely. Don't step on the potato chips.

WOMAN: I'll be right back, Jane.

SUMMERS: Do excuse me. I guess I'm making the transition poorly.

(Woman and Summers exit.)

ROBERT: Madame Fromage, now that your husband and son and father have gone down to the cellar for a minute, let me ask you to become my wife. We could live in France, your true home, where the people love you for the great gift you have given them.

(Jane puts her hands over her ears.)

EDITH: What about my husband and the rest of my family?

ROBERT: Bring them all along. I have a big heart.

EDITH: That's most generous, but I must consult my daughter. Jane, did you hear the Count's offer.

(She takes Jane's hands off her ears.)

JANE: No.

EDITH: Yes you did. Do you approve?

JANE: No.

EDITH: Yes you do. Do you want to come with us to France?

JANE: No.

EDITH: Yes you do. Oh, Count, Jane's agreed to everything.

ROBERT: Darling!

EDITH: My count!

(They embrace.)

ROBERT: *(Suddenly.)* Mother, what is the meaning of this? Edith!

EDITH: Now, Dwayne, Arthur.

ROBERT: Edith, I'm shocked. *(Count.)* Don't jump to any hasty presumptions, Monsieur Fromage.

EDITH: Arthur, the Count and I were discussing my going back to the stage.

ROBERT: You've used that story before.

EDITH: Never.

ROBERT: Yes you have.

EDITH: Albert, you're belligerent.

ROBERT: Arthur.

EDITH: Arthur, you're belligerent.

ROBERT: Father, don't use that tone with my mother.

EDITH: Dwayne, don't speak crossly to your father.

ROBERT: *(Count.)* I think it is terrible any of you speak rudely to Madame Fromage. *(He coughs violently.)*

EDITH: Oh, dear, Grandad's having a coughing fit. Dwayne, run and get your grandfather some water.

ROBERT: *(Stops coughing.)* You're just trying to distract from the issue. *(Coughs.)*

EDITH: Your grandfather's choking. How can you be so cruel?

ROBERT: *(Stern.)* Listen to your mother. *(Coughs.)* Mother, we've got to get this settled first. Who do you love more—me, father, or the Count?

EDITH: Do you mean more frequently, or in greater degree?

ROBERT: Degree. *(Coughs, drops to the floor.)*

EDITH: Oh my God, he's fainted.

ROBERT: Good God, Edith, is he dead? *(Count, stooping down.)* No. He is just sleeping.

EDITH: Oh good.

ROBERT: Well, who do you love?

EDITH: Dwayne, when you ask a woman that you ask her to explain her existence. And so I will. Dwayne, I love you as a mother loves a son, as a wife loves a husband, and as a woman loves a lover. Arthur, I love you as a wife loves a son, a husband loves a lover, and a mother loves a woman. Count, I love you as a son loves a husband, as a lover loves a mother, as a wife loves a brother. It's one for all, and all for one. There, are you satisfied?

ROBERT: Mother, you're wonderful. *(Kisses her.)* Edith, I'm touched. *(Kisses her.)* Madame, you are charmant. *(Kisses her.)*
(Enter Woman and Summers. They have switched clothes: Woman wears Summers' clothes, he wears hers. That is, Summers is dressed like a woman, the Woman is dressed like a man.)

JANE: Oh God, help me.

WOMAN: Now Jane, there's no need to overreact. Harriet just felt uncomfortable.

SUMMERS: *(Looking at his flat chest.)* I don't look like I used to. Not at all. *(Places a stray banana in his bosom.)*

EDITH: I don't think I've introduced you properly. This is my husband, Arthur.

ROBERT: How do you do?

WOMAN: How do you do? I'm Mr. Summers and this is my husband Harriet.

SUMMERS: How do you do?

ROBERT: I do very well, thank you.

EDITH: And this is my son Dwayne.

SUMMERS: How do you do? I'm Mr. Summers and this is my wife Walter.

ROBERT: How do you do?

EDITH: And this is the Count de Rochelay.

ROBERT: *Comment ca va?*

WOMAN: *Très bien, merci. Je m'appele Jacqueline, et voici mon fromage, Claud.*

SUMMERS: *Bonjour, bonjour.*

EDITH: And this is my new invention, banana bread. I dedicate it to Jane, my wonderful daughter. I call the recipe "Banana Bread Jane."

ROBERT: Did you hear that, Jane?

JANE: I don't know who you are.

EDITH: Come. Let us taste of the banana bread. Jane, it's your birthday, you cut the first piece.

JANE: It isn't my birthday.

EDITH: It is. We've been wishing you happy birthday all day.

ROBERT: Happy birthday, Jane. We're going to get the piano tuned for you.

JANE: Who are you?

ROBERT: What? Eh?

SUMMERS: *Joyeux Noël,* Jane.

WOMAN: *Allez-vous à la bibliothèque?*

EDITH: Jane, cut the banana bread.

(The Woman and Summers sing the Marseillaise. Jane takes a knife and goes to cut the bread.)

EDITH: That's right, dear.

(Jane suddenly takes the knife and whacks off the top of the banana sticking out of the bread.)

WOMAN: *(Screams in agony, holds between her legs.)* That's a very inconsiderate thing for you to do. I'm going to have nightmares now.

SUMMERS: Jane, you've upset my wife.

JANE: I thought she was your husband!

EDITH: Jane, I'd like you to meet my daughter Jane.

SUMMERS: How do you do, Jane?

ROBERT: How do you do?

WOMAN: How do you do?

JANE: I don't understand. Which one is Jane?

EDITH: Don't play games with me. You know which one.

JANE: No I don't!

(Edith, Robert, Woman, and Summers keep shaking hands, introducing themselves to each other over and over. However, now instead of saying their names, they each are singing different French songs to one another. Robert and Summers sing "Frères Jacques"; Woman sings "The Marseillaise"; Edith sings "Sur le pont d' Avignon" or some other song in French. The whole thing, rather cheerful sounding, sounds like a music box gone mad. Jane runs to the side and screams.)

JANE: Help! HELP! HELP!

(Lights go out. The French singing continues in the blackout. The singing fades after a bit, and the lights come up again, with only Jane and Edith on stage. Jane is on the couch. Her hands are tied together, or else she's in a straitjacket, and tape is across her mouth. Edith sits watching her.)

VOICES: *(That of Summers and Woman alternatively.)* Cuckoo, cuckoo. Cuckoo, cuckoo.

EDITH: Oh, time for the bandage to come off. *(Takes tape off Jane's mouth.)* How are you, Jane?

(Jane smiles.)

EDITH: Jane? How are you?

JANE: Jane isn't here.

EDITH: Oh. Then who are you?

JANE: I'm Jane's mother.

EDITH: How do you do? I'm Edith Fromage. I invented cheese and banana bread.

JANE: I'm Emily Carrot. I discovered radium in carrots.

EDITH: Really? That's the last time I ever put them in a salad.

JANE: Untie me.

EDITH: Certainly, Emily. *(Does so.)* I was about to make something good to eat for my husband, son, father, and lover. They're tired of cheese and banana bread. Would you help me cook something?

JANE: Yes, Edith.

EDITH: What should we make?

JANE: Let's make a child.

EDITH: I don't know if I have a big enough bowl.

JANE: That's all right. We don't have to put the yeast in. We'll make a small child.

EDITH: Oh fine. What ingredients do we need?

JANE: Cheese and banana bread.

EDITH: I have that.

(They begin to put ingredients into a vat.)

JANE: Lots of eggs.

EDITH: Lots of eggs.

JANE: Olives for the eyes.

EDITH: Olives.

JANE: Wheat germ for the hair.

EDITH: Oh really? I didn't know that.

JANE: Oh yes. When I was in Germany, we made the most beautiful children with wheat germ hair.

EDITH: Emily, dear?

JANE: Yes?

EDITH: Welcome home.

(They embrace. Enter Woman and Summer's holding hands.)

WOMAN AND SUMMERS: *(In unison.)* At this point it seems in order to offer the psychological key to this evening's performance.

SUMMERS: Jane's repressed fear of carrots, indicated by her refusal to acknowledge her proper surname, mirrored a disorder in her libidinous regions...

WOMAN: ...which in turn made her unable to distinguish between her father and her brother and her grandfather; as long as she could not recognize to whom she was speaking...

SUMMERS: ...she would not have to react to them sexually. When Jane finally released the forces of her libido by whacking off the banana bread...

WOMAN: ...she freed her imprisoned personality...

SUMMERS: ...and enabled herself to face...

WOMAN: …her festering…
SUMMERS: …competition…
WOMAN: …with her mother.
  (Woman and Summers kiss.)
SUMMERS: The moral of the play is that through the miracle of modern psychology…
WOMAN: …man is able…
SUMMERS: …to solve his problems…
WOMAN: …and be happy.
BOTH: Thank you and good night. *(They kiss and keep kissing.)*
  (Jane and Edith continue baking. Enter Robert.)
ROBERT: Identity. I dentity, you dentity, he she or it dentities. We dentity, you dentity, they dentity. Cuckoo. Cuckoo. Cuckoo. *(As the Count.)* I dentity. *(As Dwayne.)* You dentity, *(As grandfather.)* he she or it dentities…
  (Lights fade.)

TO THE ACTOR

   I don't make this crystal clear in the play—I prefer it retain some ambiguity, to match Jane's own confusions…but I do think of Robert as actually Jane's brother; and I have always seen Robert cast as Jane's contemporary in terms of age.

   Thus the implied psychology is that Robert and his mother Edith are having an incestuous affair. Edith and Robert both admit and relish their affair, and yet minutes later will seemingly deny it to Jane, with all conviction. And Robert's switching personalities seems a genuine thing he does: I think he believes he's the father and the grandfather when he becomes them, and Edith accepts this too, and sees nothing wrong with it. Only poor Jane is thrown by their crazy games.

   Well, one can't get too heavy playing all of this…but I thought it might be helpful to specify that Robert is probably the brother.

Death Comes To Us All,
Mary Agnes

My uncle, Barry Mansfield, was an actor for a while, and then he went into stage design. Then in his forties, when I was a young teenager, he moved back to New Jersey, and ended up directing local productions of plays, including the two musicals I wrote during my high school years.

He was clevèr and smart, and for a while was a large influence on me. (I remember his calling me up when I was 13, telling me to turn on TV to see the movie *The Letter* with Bette Davis, and to watch the moody things director William Wyler did with the moon at the beginning of that film.)

One day he was quoting something, and said in a quavering voice, "Here lies Mary Agnes...", to which he replied in another, more patient voice: "Mary Agnes isn't dead, dear."

I, of course, asked him what he was talking about it. And he said that in the play *Ladies in Retirement*, there were two nutty aunts, and one of them kept going around reciting people's epitaphs: Here lies Mary Agnes...here lies so and so. And the other one, who wasn't as crazy, would say: "Mary Agnes isn't dead, dear."

So I always had this sort of phrase in my head. And during my senior year when I felt that surge of energy to write again, I wrote this play triggered by the phrase...something about death, something about crazy people.

Years later, I saw the movie *Ladies in Retirement* (with Ida Lupino, and the wonderful Elsa Lanchester as one of the crazy aunts), but I didn't hear the specific lines about saying people's epitaphs. I wonder if I heard the title wrong, or if the line was in the play version, but not the movie version; or if maybe my Uncle Barry made it up in the world of his own head and/or memory.

So I wrote this play. It was also influenced by the grand narcissism in Arthur Kopit's *Oh Dad, Poor Dad, Mama's Hung You in the Closet and I'm Feeling So Sad*, which in turn was influenced by Tennessee Williams' *Suddenly Last Summer.*

And I also thought of some distant relative my mother told me of, who used to make her grown son get in bed with her in the morning, while they both had coffee, and then would say to whomever walked in, "Isn't my son handsome?"

Alice Miller in her famous *The Drama of the Gifted Child* (which had the more accurate title *Prisoners of Childhood* before some publisher forced her to the less depressing one) defines parental narcissism as parents using their children to satisfy their own psychological and emotional needs; babies, who are very intuitive, start to pick up that they exist to please and nurture their parent; they disassociate themselves from any parts of their developing personalities that do not please or "nurture" their parents, and so have buried within them these rejected parts of their personalities; this process interferes with normal ego development, and it's passed on from generation to generation.

It's very hard to raise a child, isn't it? And this play isn't meant as seriously as the Alice Miller paragraph may imply. But that is the underlying theme of the play—parental narcissism—and I was writing about it mostly unconsciously at the time.

ORIGINAL PRODUCTION
Death Comes to Us All, Mary Agnes was first presented at the Yale School of Drama on April 22, 1975, directed by Robert Lewis. The cast was as follows:

Martin, a butler	Ben Halley, Jr.
Margaret, a maid	Denise A. Gordon
Coral Tyne	Joyce Fideor
Herbert Pomme	Jeremy Smith
Margot Pomme, his daughter	Christine Estabrook
Mrs. Jansen-Hubbell	Marcell Rosenblatt
Vivien Jansen-Hubbell Pomme	Martha Gaylord
Tod Pomme, her son	Alan Mokler
Tim Pomme, her son	Brian McEleney
A&P Delivery Boy	John L. Weil
Mary Agnes Simpson	Bever-Leigh Banfield
Grand Union Delivery Boy	Mark Boyer

Death Comes to Us All, Mary Agnes was also produced in New York City on May 13, 1988, by the Wordplay Ensemble Theatre at 339 East 28th Street, directed by Anthony Koplin. The cast was as follows:

Margaret, a maid	Abigail Gampel
Coral Tyne	Sherry Anderson
Martin, a butler	Frank Dowd
Herbert Pomme	Ron Leir
Margot Pomme, his daughter	Deborah LaCoy
Mrs. Jansen-Hubbell	Dion Murphy
Vivien Jansen-Hubbell Pomme	Lorraine Lanigan
Tod Pomme, her son	John Augustine
Tim Pomme, her son	John Jenis
A&P Delivery Boy	Anthony Koplin
Mary Agnes Simpson	Jennifer Wollerman
Grand Union Delivery Boy	Robert Bender

CHARACTERS

MARGARET, a maid
CORAL TYNE, Mr. Jansen-Hubbell's secretary
MARTIN, a butler
HERBERT POMME
MARGOT POMME, his daughter
MRS. JANSEN-HUBBELL, Margot's grandmother, very elderly
VIVIEN JANSEN-HUBBELL POMME
TOD POMME, her son
TIM POMME, her son
A&P DELIVERY BOY, an A&P delivery boy
MARY AGNES SIMPSON, Martin's niece
GRAND UNION DELIVERY BOY, a delivery boy from the Grand Union

DEATH COMES TO US ALL, MARY AGNES

SCENE 1

The setting is a Victorian drawing room in East Haddam, Vermont. Couch, chairs, and so forth. An oriental rug. A telephone on a telephone stand. After a few beats, the phone rings. Enter Margaret, a maid, about 50- years-old.

MARGARET: Hello, Mr. Jansen-Hubbell's residence, East Haddam, Vermont, the scullery maid speaking. No, I'm sorry, Mr. Jansen-Hubbell cannot come to the phone. He is upstairs dying, Lord have mercy on his soul, and cannot be disturbed. Can I take a message? Yes, you could speak to Mrs. Jansen-Hubbell, if you like, but she's mad as a hatter, poor dear, and as liable to clip herself to death with scissors as not. Why don't you just give me the message? I am a trusted and beloved servant of many years distinguished service. I first came to work for Mr. Jansen-Hubbell in early May of 1942, during the war. It was a terrible war, it was, I had just come over from England on ship, it was a stormy and...
(Enter Coral Tyne, age 33 or so, elegant, mean. She is dressed in a man's suit, tie, and so forth.)
CORAL: Margaret, go back to the scullery please. I've told you to keep to the kitchen, and that Martin takes care of the living quarters.
MARGARET: *(Nasty.)* Well, I don't see that he answered the phone, did he? The way you treat Martin with such kowtowin' and praise, you'd think he was the King of England or something...

CORAL: Don't waste my time with your petty complaints. Just give me the phone and withdraw to the lower recesses of the house please.

MARGARET: You can go straight to hell, Missy. *(Exits.)*

CORAL: *(Into phone.)* Hello. This is Coral Tyne speaking, Mr. Jansen-Hubbell's secretary. May I help you? What? You make what? Speak up. Light bulbs? Why are you calling me, selling light bulbs? Because you're what? Try to enunciate please. Hand what? Oh. Handicapped. Oh, I see. Well, I'm sorry, I'm not interested. You should sell your light bulbs to someone else. Stop stuttering. Good-bye.

(Hangs up. Enter Martin, the butler, distinguished, older.)

MARTIN: Miss Tyne, perhaps you should prepare Mrs. Jansen-Hubbell. Her son-in-law and granddaughter have just arrived.

CORAL: If you mean Herbert and Margot, why don't you say Herbert and Margot? Drop the formality, for God's sake.

MARTIN: I have never understood why Mr. Jansen-Hubbell allows you to be so rude to me.

(Coral exits. Enter Herbert Pomme, age 58, all gray, smallish man, quiet, missing one arm, his jacket sleeve hanging loosely. With him is his daughter Margot, age 24, dressed drably, hair puled back, unhappy, manic.)

MARGOT: Oh, Daddy, look—the mansion's the same as it always was.

HERBERT: So few things change.

MARGOT: And there's Martin.

MARTIN: Hello, Miss Margot. Mr. Pomme.

HERBERT: Martin.

MARGOT: You look much older, Martin. How is Grandad? Is he very bad?

MARTIN: Yes. He awaits death. He refuses his morning juice. His chronic wince worsens.

MARGOT: Does Grandma know what's going on?

MARTIN: Mrs. Jansen-Hubbell has feigned madness so long that she barely has to feign it any more.

MARGOT: *(Upset.)* Grandad hasn't been keeping her in the Tower again, has he?

HERBERT: You mustn't fight it, angel.

MARGOT: Grandad has such a cruel streak in him. It must be where my mother gets her meanness from. *(To Martin.)* Oh, please send for Grandma from the Tower.

MARTIN: I've already done so, Miss Margot.

HERBERT: Has Vivien arrived yet?

MARTIN: Not yet, Mr. Pomme.

HERBERT: I don't much look forward to seeing my wife again after all these years.

MARGOT: She's your ex-wife. Just as she's my ex-mother.

(Enter Coral and Mrs. Jansen-Hubbell. Mrs. Jansen-Hubbell is 68, dressed in black, her hands are bound together at the wrists, her eyes are wild and deeply circled. As she enters she spits out butterscotch pudding all over the stage.)

MARGOT: Grandma! What's the matter?

CORAL: *(Calling offstage.)* Margaret! *(Holding a dead rat.)* I found her chewing on this when I went up there! *(To Mrs. J-H, meanly.)* I've told you you'll make yourself sick! *(Waves dead rat in Mrs. J-H's face.)*

MARGOT: Miss Tyne, please.

(Enter Margaret.)

MARGARET: What do you want? Oh, it's Miss Margot. Are your two handsome brothers here yet?

MARGOT: No, they're not! *(Hysterical.)* Oh, why does everyone always favor my brothers over me? They were always the pretty ones, the ones who were excused when they were bad, the ones who were loved! I want love!

HERBERT: Margot, please. Control yourself.

MARGOT: *(Whimpering.)* I'm sorry, Father. It must be the strain of grandfather's oncoming death.

CORAL: Margaret, Mrs. Jansen-Hubbell has spit something up on the floor. Wipe it up, will you please?

MARGARET: May your soul rot in hell and the devils cause you unspeakable torment. *(She wipes up mess.)*

CORAL: There is no hell, Margaret. *(To others.)* I shall leave you to your memories. Martin, please remove the rat.

(Martin and Coral exit. Margaret exits as soon as she's finished cleaning up.)

MARGOT: *(Bringing Mrs. Jansen-Hubbell to sofa.)* Grandma, do you remember me? It's your little Margot. Sit down, let me look at you. Do you remember me? I remember you, way back before you first feigned madness. Do you remember that summer I was fifteen, and Daddy and I came to visit right after he'd found the French orphanage my mother had put me in? And Grandad had just got the first of his secretaries. Remember? It was Miss Willis, then, I think. And I asked you why Mama had put me in an orphanage like I didn't belong to her, just so she could go to Italy with her two boys, her two sons, my twin brothers! She left me there for five years! *(Getting teary and hysterical.)* And I said to you, Grandma, will there ever be anyone in this world who will love me? Love *me* for what I am, and love me and not pity me? And you looked at me and you said, "No," and I said, "But Grandma, Why?" And you said, "Because there never was for me!" Do you remember, Grandma? There never was for me!

(She weeps hysterically, Mrs. Jansen-Hubbell wails and wails, raising her tied hands up and down in rhythm.)

HERBERT: Margot, please! These memories do us no good. Margot.

(Enter Coral with a large gong, which she strikes three times.)

CORAL: May I remind you that we have a dying man in this house. We must have quiet.

(Enter Martin.)

MARTIN: Mr. Pomme, your ex-wife has just arrived. If you wished to avoid seeing her right away, might I suggest retiring to your room?

HERBERT: Yes. I think I might take a nap. It's been a hard trip, eh, Margot?

MARGOT: Father, you've got to face her. Don't be afraid. I'll help you.

HERBERT: There's plenty of time, Margot. I need a hot bath. *(He exits quickly.)*

MARGOT: Oh, why is he so weak?

MARTIN: Human nature, my child.

MARGOT: Mind your place, Martin.

(Enter Margaret.)

MARGARET: They're coming! I saw them. The boys are here. And as handsome as the day I saw them last. More so.

CORAL: Get back to the scullery.

MARGARET: May eagles of the Lord tear out your heart and scatter it to the winds.

(Enter Vivien Jansen-Hubbell Pomme, flanked on either side by her sons Tod and Tim. Vivien is 45, attractive, dressed expensively. She can't walk very well, she has no feeling in her legs and can walk only with support from others. She is usually supported by her sons. Tod and Tim are 26, fraternal twins, look quite similar. They wear expensive suits, and generally look like an ad from Gentlemen's Quarterly.*)*

VIVIEN: I've returned! *(Pause.)* How nice. The servants have gathered to greet us.

MARGARET: You look wonderful, ma'am.

VIVIEN: Thank you, Margaret.

MARTIN: Superb, madame.

VIVIEN: Do I really?

MARTIN: You do indeed.

CORAL: Mr. Jansen-Hubbell has expected you.

VIVIEN: One always wants one's children at one's death bed.

MARGARET: The boys look wonderful too, ma'am. As handsome as their mother is beautiful.

VIVIEN: Thank you, dear. It's the Mediterranean sun, I expect. Men always look better tanned.

MARGOT: Hello, Mother.

VIVIEN: You must be a new maid of Father's?

MARGOT: I called you "Mother."

VIVIEN: Did you? Well, I can't be expected to listen to every word people say to me. Children, help me sit down.

(Tod and Tim help her to a chair, then stand by her.)

MARGOT: I'm your daughter, Mother. How do you think I look?

VIVIEN: I gave my daughter to a French orphanage many years ago. It was an act of kindness because I realized I had not the temperament to raise girls—as I did have the temperament to raise boys, my two fine boys, my twin stars. I expect the girl's still there, unless she drowned at sea or died in a car accident. As for your personal appearance, whoever you are, it is drab and depressing. Your entire demeanor is singularly unpleasant. The world is far too drab and depressing as it is; one should try to glitter to make up for it. But I've spent too much time discussing appearance with a complete stranger, and I've ignored my mad mother. How are you, Mother?

(Martin brings Mrs. Jansen-Hubbell closer to Vivien.)

VIVIEN: Do you have any lucid moments these days, or is it all mist and haze? Oh, you've dribbled something on your nice mourning frock. That shouldn't be. Miss Tyne, does Father know that mother is out of the Tower?

CORAL: Your father is dying, Mrs. Pomme.

VIVIEN: That was not the question. The question was why is my mother not up in the Tower where it doesn't matter if she dribbles over the sofa and the carpets? And I am not to be called Mrs. Pomme. I refer to myself by my maiden name of Jansen-Hubbell, a name you are quite familiar with, I am sure, Miss Tyne. After all, you've been under my father for many years now. *(Silence.)* His service, I mean.

CORAL: Your father wished you to greet your mother before I placed her back in the Tower.

VIVIEN: I think I've greeted her long enough. Haven't I, mother? You're not going to be lucid, are you? *(No response.)* There, you see. Take her away, Miss Tyne. And Martin, you might run my bath. My legs always ache at this time of day. And Margaret, you might bring the boys some tea and graham crackers, you remember how fond Tod and Tim are of graham crackers.

MARGARET: Indeed, I do, Ma'am.

(She and Martin exit.)

VIVIEN: And, Miss Tyne, would you relate to my Father my wishes for his continued health, and that I shall see him after I take my bath.

CORAL: Yes, Miss Jansen-Hubbell.

VIVIEN: *Mrs.* Jansen-Hubbell, *Miss* Tyne. I have two sons, you are aware.

CORAL: Yes, Mrs. Jansen-Hubbell.

(Exits with grandmother. Tod and Tim sit on couch together.)

VIVIEN: Well, children, I expect once the will is revealed, we'll be able to count on a good many more summers in Italy together.

MARGOT: Maybe he'll leave all his money to me.

VIVIEN: Children, do you hear an additional voice?

(Tod and Tim grin at one another, enjoying the joke.)

VIVIEN: I hope I'm not losing my grasp like my poor lamented mother.

TOD: I'm sure you're perfectly sane, Mother.

VIVIEN: Before I take my bath, we can have a nice talk about art and literature.

MARGOT: Mother, someday you will be punished.

VIVIEN: Tell me, Tod, about your new idea for a play. And Tim, why don't you sketch me. Mother listening to her sons.

(Tim sketches.)

TOD: I thought of it the other day when Tim and I were sunbathing. The play would deal with a society where women were completely outlawed, except for a few captives who were allowed to have male offspring. They'd be impregnated by artificial insemination. And so all the women would be cut off and separated from the male society, because they were the cause of evil, all except for one woman who was worshipped by the men as a goddess.

TIM: You can pose for the goddess, Mother. We could do it in oils.

TOD: And all the men worship this woman-goddess, and then in the evenings when all the men retire to their various chambers, the woman-goddess would cry herself to sleep because none of the men will touch her.

VIVIEN: What would the ending be?

TOD: I haven't one yet.

TIM: A bolt of lightning could kill everybody.

VIVIEN: It's not one of my favorite ones. I prefer the one about the wonderful Princess who has to choose between two beautiful Princes and she can't make up her mind and so she runs off with both of them and lives happily ever after.

TOD: I never wrote that.

VIVIEN: I know. I just did, and I love it.

(Enter Martin.)

MARTIN: Your bath is ready, madam.

VIVIEN: Thank you, Martin. Children, you stay here for tea. Martin will help me to my room.

(Martin helps Vivien hobble off.)

MARGOT: For a second, I thought I was included in the "children."

TIM: Isn't it time you outgrew these petty jealousies, Margot?

MARGOT: Oh, so I'm actually going to get talked to, am I?

TOD: It's only Mama who's good at games. We're much more direct.

TIM: *(To Tod.)* I'm bored already. Do you want to play pot luck?

TOD: Why not? There's the phone.

TIM: *(Dials.)* Could I have the number of the A & P please?

MARGOT: That's domestic.

TOD: Just a game we play.

(Tim dials again.)

MARGOT: It's pretty good to be 26 and still be making prank phone calls.

TOD: There's no need to wallow in maturity.

TIM: Hello. Would you send a delivery boy out to the Jansen-Hubbell residence on Crestview Street? Just assorted groceries will do. As much as you like. Thank you. Oh, and tell him to use the front door. Yes, thank you.

MARGOT: It seems a worthless joke to charge things to grandfather. He can certainly afford it, but after all he *is* dying.

TOD: So are we all, Sis.

TIM: So how's life been since we saw you last. Did you like the orphanage?

TOD: You've grown up passably pretty, I see.

MARGOT: Not as pretty as you two, I'm sure.

TOD: Beauty, Margot, is in the eye of the beholder. If most beholders don't take to you, don't blame us.

TIM: It's probably your glum and depressing demeanor.

MARGOT: Why shouldn't I be glum? I spent the early part of my childhood in some horrible institution while mother told father I was with her traveling the continent. Getting rid of me was like drowning a kitten to her.

TIM: You rather look like a drowned kitten.

TOD: Too big. Cat.

MARGOT: I've read Freud. I know what psychological damage has been done to me. People shouldn't be allowed to have children until they've passed a test in psychology. Anyone who gets below B minus should be sterilized. My mother should be the one locked up in the Tower, not Grandma...

TOD: God'll strike you dead if you talk that way.

MARGOT: God won't, but Mama sure as hell will.

TIM: Look, Margot, you're a very neurotic girl, and you have some biological claim to be our sister, and we wish we could help you...

TOD: But we can't think of a gosh-darned thing to say, so maybe you should go off and complain to your poor, silly father. If you're here, I presume he can't be far away.

MARGOT: I never dreamed such wickedness existed. *(Exits.)*

TOD: To describe the everyday procedure of breathing, eating, and sleeping as wickedness bespeaks a parochial outlook and an alarming failure to grasp reality.

TIM: Hear, hear.

(Enter margaret with tea and graham crackers.)

MARGARET: Ah, and here's tea for my two handsome boys.

TIM: Ah, and here's Margaret, and God love her too.

TOD: We've missed you, Margaret. We've had many a wet dream over you.

MARGARET: Master Tod, what can you be thinking of?

TIM: You, Margaret, and can you blame us?

TOD: Ah, the Lord bless you, Maggie.

TIM: Better be off with you now *(He pats her rear.)* lest we can control ourselves no longer.

MARGARET: Oh Master Tim! Are you flirting with me now?

TOD: Well, knowing Tim, you better not stick around to find out.

MARGARET: Oh, the Lord up in heaven, if this isn't a day. *(She exits cheerily.)*

TIM: She's more like a cow than I remembered. *(Door bell.)* Oh, is it pot luck already?

TOD: I bet it is. Blond or dark?

TIM: Blond.

TOD: All right, if it's a blond, it's yours.
(Enter Martin.)

TOD: Oh, we'll get it, Martin. We're expecting someone.

MARTIN: Very well.
(Exits. Tim goes to door, ushers in blond grocery boy about 16, carrying several packages and wearing thick glasses.)

TIM: Ah, you've come at last.

TOD: Blond, but not too terrific. But then that's pot luck.

TIM: We haven't eaten since last Tuesday. What have you brought us?

BOY: I don't know. The manager packed it.

TOD: How clever.

BOY: Will that be cash or charge?

TIM: Charge, of course.

BOY: *(Taking out slip.)* Well, I'll just fill this out.

TIM: *(Hand on boy's shoulder.)* What's the hurry? Here, sit down. *(He forces boy to sit on couch between them.)* We can talk about life.

BOY: I have to get right back.

TIM: *(Pushing him back.)* Relax.

TOD: *(To boy, accent perhaps.)* You want to buy my sister? She is a virgin.

TIM: *(Laughs.)* Hey, you know, that might even be true.

BOY: Just let me fill out the charge form…

TIM: *(Snatching off boy's glasses.)* Hey calm down.

BOY: Wait. I can hardly see without my glasses. *(Boy's eyes are not focused.)*

TIM: *(Looking right at boy.)* Young…young…young man. Perhaps you will see better without your glasses.

BOY: What?

TIM: You want to stay with us tonight? We all have a good time. Everybody needs a little friendship. *(Arm on shoulder again.)*

BOY: Let me go.

TOD: *(Dropping the playfulness.)* If not friendship, money then. Hey, boy, look at me.
(Boy tries to.)
TOD: Would you like to make some money? Do you understand me? *(Slow.)* We...will...pay...you.
BOY: I can't see your expression clearly. If this is a joke, I can't tell.
TIM: Oh throw him back in the bay. He's too small. Here are your glasses.
(Boy leaves in a hurry.)
TIM: Don't call us, we'll call you.
TOD: Obvious latent homosexual. Did you see the way he bolted from the room?
TIM: I suspect he had acne on his back. *(Goes to phone, dials.)* Could I have the number of the Grand Union please?
(Blackout.)

SCENE 2

Vivien's bedroom. No real change of set. Just spot Vivien in bathrobe, towel around her head, she's just taken her bath. She's seated, speaking into microphone.

VIVIEN: Dear Diary, I have just finished taking my bath and have hobbled to this chair. Sometimes I think that the growing weakness in my legs, this creeping paralysis, is God's judgment on me. But I won't accept that. I refuse to be judged. And I will enjoy this last part of my life, I will. I hated the first twenty years, my father was such an unpleasant man. Father is dying, by the way, and good riddance. I hope I get most of the money.

New paragraph. I had the hiccups in the car on the way up here. Tod and Tim were very helpful. We tried holding my breath, and we tried tickling me. Then we had a car accident, and they went away.

New paragraph. With great beauty comes responsibility—to look lovely, to be charming, to wear clothes well. I feel I have met this responsibility all my life, and so have my wonderful sons Tod and Tim. I bought Tod and Tim matching olive swim trunks today, and watched them swim. I wore a sweet and rather enormous caftan, $750, Nieman Marcus. Tod said I looked rather like a circus tent, but I feel he was being witty rather than nasty. Ah, how transitory is beauty. Perhaps that should be a new paragraph.

New paragraph. Ah, how transitory is beauty. Here today, gone 40 years later, perhaps, in my case, 50. Tod and Tim exercise constantly in front of mirrors. I have always loved mirrors because they tell the truth, and I am a great believer in the truth, at least in terms of my own physical beauty. I was the most beautiful young girl who ever lived. I hope you will not think this is mere hyperbole: I have made a list of the various men and women who have expressed ecstasy at my beauty over the past many years, and on request I will give the names and addresses of those people, a list that runs on for 300 pages, single-spaced, both sides. Dr. and Mrs. Francis Wallaby, Hampshire Castle, England; the Reverend Edgar Lancaster of St. Gertrude-by-the-Tarn Church of the Martyrs, Melody Brook, New Hampshire; Dr. Harold Metterly, New York City, who treated me for a social disease in 1947. The list goes on and on. Swami Rim Krishna. Wallace Bartholomew and his mother Dame Alice Bartholomew. That drunken Irishman named Bucky or Biffy or something. Many, many people.

New paragraph. Sometimes in the early mornings I feel a sadness. I know that later in the day I will go to the hairdresser, or visit my dying father, or watch Tod and Tim swim. But nowhere in my day do I experience a kind thought or a shared response or even just a simple gesture of relaxation. And I quietly mourn the fact that I have been cast to play the role I play, that I can't be someone more elevated, more hopeful, even just more human. However, I suppose one can't have everything. I am very beautiful and charming, and everyone likes me. And I should be glad I'm not a blind person or an Avon representative or just someone who works as a clerk in an insurance company and who dies at the age of 63. And so I stare out sometimes in the morning and relish my fleeting sadness, and then I begin the day.

New paragraph. I fear that God won't think I've been a good mother. I fear that his criteria of judgment will be limited, old-fashioned. I fear I will be punished. I fear I will be punished.
(Blackout.)

SCENE 3

The drawing room. Herbert sits reading, a standing lamp by his side.
Enter Margaret; she sits and begins scouring pots she has brought with
her.

HERBERT: Margaret, please. Why aren't you in the kitchen?

MARGARET: There are all those goddamned boy scouts in the kitchen.
Mr. Jansen-Hubbell refuses to see them, and they say they won't
leave until they give him some plaque or other.

HERBERT: I don't know anything about it. *(Tries to read.)*

MARGARET: I never saw the point in being a boy scout. *(She scrubs.)*

HERBERT: Margaret, please, I'm reading.
(Enter Margot.)

MARGOT: Oh, Father, there you are. I've got to talk to someone.

HERBERT: Margot, it's been a tiring day. I'm reading.

MARGARET: Oh, God, another scene. You're a very unbalanced girl. I've
never liked you, but to be fair I guess it must be hard to have to live
up to two such wonderful people as your brothers.

MARGOT: Why do you insist on thinking of them as wonderful. Those
two fags!

MARGARET: That's a nasty thing to say. You probably only accuse them
of that because you fear it in yourself. *(To Herbert.)* Isn't that so?

MARGOT: Margaret, leave the study at once.

MARGARET: I don't see that you have no boy friend. Unless you want to
count your father. *(Exits.)*

MARGOT: Go to hell.

HERBERT: Margot, please. Your mother will hear the shouting and come
down.

MARGOT: That would be fine. It's time someone told her off. Oh, Father,
stop reading. *(She turns off his light.)* I feel so upset seeing Mother
and my brothers again, after all these years. I've hated them in the
abstract for so long that it's almost disappointing not to find them
superhumanly hateful.
(He turns on the light, she turns it off.)

MARGOT: Will you stop that? Last night I had that awful dream again.

HERBERT: Margot, you work yourself up over nothing. Lots of girls
dream they're Joan of Arc.

MARGOT: *(Angry.)* I don't mean the Joan of Arc dream. This is the one
where I'm in the orphanage and I see my mother in a field with my

two brothers, canoeing. And rather than feeling angry at her for putting me in the orphanage, I just feel this terrible longing to be accepted by them, by her. And then I find that I'm dressed like a boy and that I've even grown a mustache, and I go out to them to show my mother that I'm a boy and then I notice that I'm still wearing lipstick, and I try to wipe it off but there's so much of it I can't get it off, and I keep wiping it and wiping it, and the three of them just laugh and laugh at me, and then they steer their canoe at me and it comes racing toward me to crush me, and a great big oar from the canoe hits me on top of the head, and then the oar starts to beat me repeatedly, ecstatically. And then I wake up. Trembling.

HERBERT: What do you want me to say? The oar's a phallic symbol. You should stay away from boating. Don't grow a mustache.

MARGOT: *(Takes his book, throws it across the room.)* I feel such anger and unhappiness all the time! When you rescued me from the orphanage, I thought I was finally saved and that things would be all right. But they weren't. You don't hate mother. And you don't like me. What am I to do? I've been seeing my psychiatrist for three years now, four times a week, and I don't feel any change. I feel such a prisoner to my past. And I have such a longing for normality. I see people on the street who eat in cafeterias and have families and go to parks and who aren't burdened with this terrible bitterness; and I want to be like them. So much I want to be like them.

HERBERT: No one's going to like you if you throw books, Margot.

MARGOT: That has nothing to do with it. I don't think you've been even listening…

(Enter Mary Agnes, 19, carrying pocketbook, has coat on.)

MARY AGNES: *(To Herbert.)* How do you do? You must have come about my little dog.

MARGOT: Who are you?

MARY AGNES: You must be Margot. I'm Martin's niece, Mary Agnes Simpson. *(Back to Herbert.)* There's been a terrible accident, Doctor. My little dog has been cut into pieces. The pieces are on the bed. My husband says that roving bands of little boys did it, but I don't believe it. I think my husband did it.

MARGOT: What are you talking about?

MARY AGNES: You're probably too sweet to understand. *(To Herbert.)* You see, my husband did it as a cruelty to me. I mean the sight was quite horrible. The dog's eyes were gouged out—I found one eye in my bathroom glass, Lord knows where I'll find the other one—its stomach was slit open and its innards were mixed with some of my canceled checks. It's peculiar. I didn't even cry out, I just said, My husband has done this. *(Smiles.)* We're very eccentric, you see. *(To Margot.)* Margot, dear, when Martin comes down, tell him I want to see him in his room. *(Starts to exit, turns to Herbert.)* Oh, yes. Thank you for coming. *(Starts to exit again.)*

MARGOT: Wait. Does Martin know you're here? *(Touches her arm.)*

MARY AGNES: *(Violent.)* Don't clutch at me! Don't you clutch at me. I will not be clutched at!

(She has an epileptic fit on the ground. Herbert stands on chair to get out of way.)

MARGOT: Oh my God. What's the matter? Help!

(Margaret and Martin rush in.)

MARTIN: What's she doing here?

MARGARET: If it's not one thing, it's another.

MARGOT: What shall we do?

MARTIN: Just wait. It'll pass.

(There is silence as all watch Mary Agnes thrash about on the floor. Then she subsides. Martin helps her up.)

MARTIN: Aren't you ashamed? A girl your age. We're going to have to keep a closer watch on you.

MARY AGNES: Oh, Uncle martin, Skippy is dead. He's dead. My puppy is gone.

MARTIN: He's gone to puppy heaven. We have to face these tragedies in life, Mary Agnes, and believe that even though things seem terrible, they aren't really. Why, if I believed that things were the way they seemed, I couldn't go on for more than a day. Now, do you feel better, dear?

MARY AGNES: Yes, Uncle.

MARTIN: How did you get here?

MARY AGNES: I have my Volkswagen outside.

MARTIN: Alright. Now why don't you go get in it, and go back to your husband. I bet he's worried about you. Here, Margaret will help you to the car.

MARY AGNES: He shouldn't have killed the puppy.

MARTIN: It was probably an accident. Now, go on along.

MARY AGNES: Can't I stay with you tonight?

MARTIN: No, dear. Your husband will miss you.

MARY AGNES: All right. *(Suddenly very cheerful.)* Good-bye, everybody. *(She and Margaret exit.)*

MARTIN: *(To Herbert.)* She's just newly married and is having some trouble adjusting.

HERBERT: I think you handled it very well, Martin.

MARTIN: Thank you. One learns to cope. *(He exits.)*

HERBERT: I didn't know Martin had a niece.

MARGOT: Father, I want you to go right up to her and tell her you hate her.

HERBERT: Who? His niece?

MARGOT: No. My mother. Tell her just so she knows.

HERBERT: She knows already.

MARGOT: Then why are you afraid to tell her?

HERBERT: Margot, You're spoiling my evening. I can't read, the boy scouts are here, and we're plagued with epileptics. Why can't we be civilized?

MARGOT: She's the one who's not civilized! This is the woman who's maimed me. I'm psychologically maimed.

HERBERT: You seem fine to me, dear.

MARGOT: Well, you don't see very well, do you?
    (Enter Coral, shaken.)

CORAL: Oh, there you are. I wonder if I might see you for a moment.

HERBERT: I'll leave.

CORAL: No, I want to speak to both of you. I've just spoken to Mr. Jansen-Hubbell. He was in a wretched mood after all those boy scouts, and he told me that he plans to reveal his will tomorrow and that...he intends to leave all his money to Mrs. Pomme—that is, to Vivien, or Mrs. Jansen-Hubbell, or whatever she's being called.

MARGOT: He has so much money, surely he's leaving all of us something.

CORAL: No, he says, he plans to show the injustice of the world through his will and leave it all to that awful woman. And I feel so...so awful. *(She begins to cry, deep sobs.)*

HERBERT: Excuse me. *(Exits.)*

CORAL: I've worked for your grandfather for 12 years. When he first hired me, I slept with him only because I thought he'd eventually leave me some of his money. Not all of it, just some. It was so degrading. I don't like men much anyway, and your grandfather's mouth tasted like a septic tank. But I put up with his demands and perversions. He used to pour egg yolks on me and lick them off. I was disgusted. Egg yolks. I just kept thinking through it all, some-day it will pay off, someday I'll be rich, and then my years of bit-terness will be answered. And now I find he's planning to die and he has no plans for me at all. None at all. I could have married a drug-gist back in Hightstown if it hadn't been for your grandfather. Oh, what am I going to do?

MARGOT: *(Surprised.)* Miss Tyne, you're asking for sympathy for your own greed. People are responsible for their own actions, Miss Tyne. You can't blame my grandfather that you didn't marry a druggist. Money is so unimportant, Miss Tyne. It is love and affection, that matters. Comfort yourself with that thought.

(Exits. Coral cries. Blackout.)

SCENE 4

Vivien's bedroom. Dressed in fancy negligee.

VIVIEN: *(Seated, calling offstage.)* Tod? Tim? Are you asleep already? Tod? Tim? Are you there? Oh, dear. Oh, my. Such a long night ahead of me.

(Enter Margaret with Mrs. Jansen-Hubbell, whose hands are bound per usual.)

VIVIEN: Oh, Margaret, you've brought Mother! Thank goodness!

MARGARET: Just thought you could say goodnight to your dear mother. She needs an outing.

VIVIEN: O precious Mother. Sit down. Both of you. Oh, I'm so glad you've come. Tod and Tim have already gone to bed and I've no one to talk to, and I'm so lonely.

MARGARET: Well, your mother's here to comfort you.

VIVIEN: Is she? *(Clutching her mother.)* Are you, Mother? Are you going to be lucid, Mother, and touch my hair and say, "Vivien, my daugh-ter"? *(Pause.)* Well, I thought not. Oh, Mother, do you think Tod and Tim love me enough, do you?

MARGARET: *(Answering for Mrs. J-H.)* I'm sure they do. They love their mother.

VIVIEN: *(Looking at her mother as if she had been the one to answer.)* But do they love me enough, that's what I wonder. Oh, it reminds me of my first child, Narcissus.

MARGARET: I don't remember your having another child.

VIVIEN: *(To her mother.)* Of course, you don't, Mother, you're addled.

MARGARET: No, I mean, *I* don't remember your having another child.

VIVIEN: Oh, but I did, Margaret. You can never know. My son Narcissus was the most beautiful boy I have ever seen in my life. More beautiful than Tod and Tim even, though I'd never tell them that. His father was the North Wind and the Gulf Stream, and his skin was like pure alabaster and his hair was black like ravens' feathers gone to heaven. He was my wonderful child. And every morning, I'd wake my little boy with kisses and I'd say, "Who's the most wonderful son of the most wonderful mother in the world?" And the answer would be Narcissus and Vivien. And I remember one day, he came home from nursery school and all his jealous playmates followed angrily behind him, envious of his alabaster skin and raven black hair. The children chanted at him cruelly: "Narcissus is a sissy, Narcissus is a sissy." And I went out into our little backyard and I balanced Narcissus on my shoulders and I said, "Narcissus is the most wonderful son in the world, and Vivien is the most wonderful mother." We spoke of ourselves in the third person a lot in those days. *(Pause.)* Are you listening, Mother?

MARGARET: Yes, dear, I am.

VIVIEN: But then one day, quite suddenly, Narcissus stopped responding fully—he'd beam at my compliments to him, but he wouldn't return them. And one day down in the basement doing our laundry, we played our poem game that went: "Tyger, tyger, burning bright; in the forests of the night; who's the fairest in the land?" And the answer was always Narcissus and Vivien, Vivien and Narcissus. But one day, that one day, Narcissus said, "The answer is me. Narcissus. Not Vivien. Just me." Well…it is intolerable not to have your love returned in kind, your love should reflect right off another person and engulf you in a warm, glorious glow of light and love. But Narcissus didn't love me any more. So I picked up a wrench and I hit him over the head, my child; and then I wrapped his once beautiful body in newspapers and I threw him out in the garbage. In the garbage, you understand? Because we all need love, you see. Sigmund used to say to me, "Vivien, you're a peculiar woman and I don't like you much, but at least you don't repress your drives. And you deserve love." Ah, Sigmund. He wrote such beautiful waltzes. He was wrong, of course, I do repress my drives, some of them, but

I do deserve love. And I need it. Oh, Mother, do you love me? Do
you love me really?

MARGARET: Of course I do. You're my daughter.

VIVIEN: Oh what an ingenuous response. You're my daughter—as if that
were enough to insure love. You've a sweet, uncluttered mind,
Mother. Thank you for visiting me tonight in my sorrow. *(She kisses
her mother.)* Margaret, you can take Mother to the Tower now. I
think I'll be able to sleep.

MARGARET: Yes, Mrs. Jansen-Hubbell. Sweet dreams. Come on, dearie.
(Margaret and Mrs. Jansen-Hubbell exit.)

VIVIEN: *(Reciting softly to herself.)* Dear Diary, I fear I am not loved
enough. I fear it. *(Calling.)* Tod? Tim? Are you there? Are you there?
(Listens. Blackout.)

SCENE 5

Drawing room of the mansion again. Enter Martin.

MARTIN: And the night passeth away, and the day cometh, and the sun
also riseth. And all throughout this mansion, this mansion of life,
the human imperfections of mankind reassert themselves.
(Exits. Lights up. Enter Tod, Tim, and a boy about 17.)

BOY II: I have to go now.

TOD: Here's twenty. *(Hands him money.)*

BOY II: *(Touched.)* Thanks. Gee, thanks a lot. Usually it's ten, or even five.
Would you like some green stamps?

TOD: We have so many. Thanks anyway.

BOY II: Gee, thanks. We at Grand Union are pleased to have served you.
Call again.

TOD: We'll remember.

VIVIEN: *(Offstage.)* Is that you, boys?

TIM: Yes, mother.
(Enter Vivien, on the arm of Martin.)

TOD: Mother, I'd like you to meet Jack. He's a classmate from that school
Tim and I went to for a week in Switzerland.

VIVIEN: Oh, how do you do, Jack. I've met several of your other class-
mates, I believe.

BOY II: Yes. Well, I must be going. Excuse me. *(Exits.)*

TOD: Good-bye.

VIVIEN: *(Wistfully.)* I thought I heard three of you in there last night.

MARTIN: Perhaps Madame would like her room moved.

VIVIEN: No, I like noises. As long as I know what they are.
(Scream offstage.)

VIVIEN: Like that. That's Margot discovering the dead body of her father.
(Enter Margot.)

MARGOT: Miss Tyne has hanged herself!

VIVIEN: I was wrong. It was Miss Tyne. Well, why do you think she did it? Another depth of depression case, or did she get carried away putting on her tie?

TOD: Well, this comes as a surprise.

MARTIN: Mr. Jansen-Hubbell predicted her death to me last night before retiring.

MARGOT: And he did nothing to prevent it?

MARTIN: He's a dying man. What could he do?

VIVIEN: Is there any coffee, boys?

TIM: I think I'd like to sketch you sipping coffee. I'd call it Goddess Sipping Coffee While Awaiting the Death of Her Father.

VIVIEN: I like the goddess part.

TOD: It would make a good greeting card.

MARGOT: Is no one going to do anything about the dead woman?

MARTIN: I'll telephone the authorities.

MARGOT: *(Upset.)* Wait. Give me the key to the Tower. I want to see Grandma.

MARTIN: Miss Tyne keeps it around her neck. You can get it later. *(Exits.)*

MARGOT: I fear I could have helped her last night, and didn't.
(Enter Herbert.)

MARGOT: Father! Quick! Tell her!

VIVIEN: Why, Herbert, so you are here after all. Children, you know your father. Herbert, you've met the boys.

HERBERT: They've grown.

VIVIEN: Nonsense. You've just gotten smaller.

MARGOT: Tell her you hate her!

VIVIEN: Herbert, you're remarkably silent after all these years. Have you nothing to say?

HERBERT: How was Europe.

VIVIEN: Very pleasant. The boys had a nice puberty there. And such wonderful tans. Tod, show Herbert your tan.
(Tod lifts his shirt, showing his tanned stomach.)

MARGOT: Father, please!

VIVIEN: Herbert, can you not still this voice of conscience that keeps echoing throughout the room?

HERBERT: *(Kneeling to her, fondly.)* Oh, Vivien, I hate you.
(He caresses her, his head on her breast, she holds him.)

VIVIEN: Herbert, I'm touched. I had no idea I still had power over you. Look, children, your Father's come home to roost.

MARGOT: I hate you! I hate you all! *(She runs out.)*

VIVIEN: *(Tearing at the eyes.)* Oh, Herbert, we had good times, didn't we? Scurrying about the continent, knowing dukes and earls. Do you remember how you met me? You were just 17 and you went to your first brothel. I was just 14 and it was my first brothel too. My first night. And I remember the Madame, Madame Leore, said to me, she said, "Vera"—she got my name wrong even then—"Vera, you'll turn many a trick in your day, but you'll never turn one like your first one." And so my heart was aglow and you came up to me and in your adolescent voice you said to me, "How much?" And I thought to myself that that was the most romantic thing I had ever heard. And so you and I retired to that little room with the cobwebs and the dank smell of urine and we sat on the bed. "Is this your first?" I asked, and when you said no I didn't believe you. "And is this your first?" you asked me, and when I said yes, you didn't believe me. And one of us was lying, and to this day I don't know which one it was, but I don't care because the night air was so fragrant and love was so new, and we were so young. So very, very young. And then you began very methodically to take off my clothes, which were soaked in perspiration from my busy day and from so many other bodies. And then I bit off your buttons, one by one, and your eyes grew larger at every pop. And then I took off your pants. I was very young, you understand, and I had never seen a man, not even a statue of one because they didn't have museums in those days and I wouldn't have gone even if they had. And so then your slender form got on top of my slender form and then—pump! Pump! *PUMP!* You pumped away, and I gave in to my first experience of love—Oh! Oh! Ohhhhhhh-Ohhhhhhh. *OHHHHHHHH-HHHHHHHHHH.* Uh. Uh. And then when it was all over, I got off of you, and I looked into your blue eyes—your eyes were blue then—and I said in the pale, frightened voice of a school girl,

"Herbert, it is you I love." *(Pause.)* Do you remember, Herbert? Herbert? *(Kindly.)* Children, I think your father's fallen asleep. *(She lets go of Herbert, and he falls to the ground.)*

VIVIEN: Oh. Has he had a stroke? Do you think it's a stroke? *(Enter Martin.)*

MARTIN: Your father is about to die, Madame. He wants to see you.

VIVIEN: Oh, dear! Do I look all right?

TOD: You look wonderful Mother!

TIM: Beautiful, dear.

VIVIEN: Oh. Thank you. Help me, Martin. *(Martin helps Vivien hobble off.)*

TOD: Why does Father only have one arm?

TIM: I don't know. War wound, I suppose. Tod?

TOD: *(Knowing what's coming.)* Yes.

TIM: About last night. I felt sort of funny. I mean, I'm used to having a third in with us and all, but last night I got the feeling you preferred the Grand Union to me.

TOD: Oh, for God's sake, are we going to go through this routine again? You're as bad as mother. You think you have to be worshipped all the time.

TIM: I don't want to be worshipped. I just want to know where we stand.

TOD: Oh, I hate this. Tim, you're my brother, and I like you better than anyone except myself, but that doesn't mean I don't want a little variety from time to time. For Christ's sake.

TIM: I think you're promiscuous.

TOD: Little hypocrite. Pot luck was your game anyway. You invented it.

TIM: Oh, go to hell.

TOD: Don't take it so hard. My wanting a little variety doesn't mean I prefer that grocery boy to my own brother. Now, for God's sake, let's shake hands and forget about it.

TIM: *(Grudgingly.)* All right. *(They shake hands. Enter Margaret with tea and graham crackers.)*

MARGARET: Oh, now, isn't that nice? Brothers, shaking hands. Here, I've brought some tea for my handsome boys. What's the matter with your father?

TOD: He's just tired.

TIM: It seems Grandad's about to kick off.

MARGARET: Is he now? Well, that'll be nice for him. No sense in senseless suffering, is there?

TOD: No. By definition.

MARGARET: That'll make two deaths today, what with that awful Miss Tyne bumping herself off. I never liked her, haven't for twelve years, won't start now that she's dead. I'm no hypocrite. Hope she rots in hell.

TIM: She seemed a mean sort.

MARGARET: Oh, she was. Not a kind word for anybody. Certainly not for me. And such a slanderous tongue she had, and a filthy mind to boot. Do you know what I heard her say to Martin after setting eyes on you two?

TOD: *(Taking tea; Tim likewise.)* No. What?

MARGARET: She said, those two is queer as the day they was born. And she said that being queer was one thing, and that incest was another, but to combine the two was a truly appalling perversion. And right she was, and a sick mind she had to even think of such a thing. God bless her guardian angel for seeing she hung herself. She's happier dead than alive brooding on such thoughts.

TIM: She had a sick imagination.

MARGARET: *(Coquette.)* And I said to myself, that even if you boys were acting funny together, it was only because the proper feminine companionship hadn't offered itself to you yet. I mean, after all with your mother around all the time, I mean, a body is going to get pent up. We all have energies. And I thought, seeing how much I like both of you *(She starts to undo her blouse.)* I might be able to help you over this little hump in your lives. If you follow my meaning. *(Margaret's blouse is completely open now. She wears a bra.)* When you speak of this, and knowing you two like I do you probably will, be kind. Right?

TIM: Oh my God.

TOD: Ack.

(One or both of them throw their tea on her chest. She screams piercingly.)

MARGARET: *AAAAAHH!* You bastards!

TIM: Go run 'em under the tap, love.

MARGARET: May Saint Peter piss on your grave!

(She exits screaming. Enter Margot.)

MARGOT: What's the matter? Who's hurt?

TOD: Margaret sat on a tack.

MARGOT: What's the matter with father? *(Upset.)*

TIM: I'd forgotten. Mother thinks he might have had a stroke.

MARGOT: A stroke! Did anyone call a doctor?

TOD: A minute ago you told him you hated him. You're not very consistent.

MARGOT: Oh, please, he's all I've got.

(Enter Vivien, helped by Martin.)

VIVIEN: Children, your grandfather has just died. He's left all his money to me, and he wishes all of us ill. He was a mean-spirited man all his life, and he remained so to the end.

MARGOT: Martin, call a doctor for my father.

VIVIEN: It is not necessary. Herbert's dead too. I felt his spirit leaving him right in the middle of my remembered youth.

MARGOT: *(Crying.)* He's all I have! He's all I have!

VIVIEN: He is all you *had*, Margot. Now you have nothing. You see, Margot, only the strong survive. I'm amazed that Herbert lasted as long as he did. I think your strength kept him alive for while; for although I don't like you, you do have some strength. But I guess it wasn't enough, and now he's dead.

MARGOT: What am I to do?

VIVIEN: Leave my sight forever. Attach yourself elsewhere. And remember, I placed you in an orphanage once. Don't tempt me to do it again. *(She sits.)* Come, Tim, sketch your mother in mourning. Tod, write a poem about your mother in grief.

(Martin removes Herbert's body.)

MARGOT: *(Following body.)* I hate you, father! You're weak! Grandma! Grandma! *(She exits.)*

VIVIEN: It will have been an emotionally exhausting day, I fear.

(Vivien, Tod and Tim remain on stage, quietly posing, sketching, writing. D. C. is spotlight, becomes the Tower. Cry of "Grandma!" offstage. Enter Mrs. Jansen-Hubbell, her hands still tied, several bruises on her head. Enter Margot, frenzied.)

MARGOT: Grandma! Grandma! They're both dead! And I hate them both. Oh, please, be lucid. I know you're just pretending to be crazy. *(She begins to untie Mrs. J-H's hands.)* Grandma, say something. What shall I do? I don't feel strong anymore. Say something. Do you remember when I was a little girl? You made me cookies the day you went crazy, and you said, "Margot, whenever things get you down, just have a nice glass of milk and a couple of cookies." And then right after that you went crazy, do you remember? Grandma, say something. Please say something! *(Pause.)*

MRS. J-H: *(Shrieking.)* DON'T DEPEND ON PEOPLE!

(She reaches out to Margot and strangles her to death. Then exits, wailing. Lights off "Tower"; Margot's dead body remains til end of play.)

TIM: Don't move, mother. I can't sketch you.

TOD: I think you should get rid of Margaret.

VIVIEN: Whatever you think best, dear. You know, as your grandfather died, he called me evil. And he said he was evil. But I don't think people are evil really. I think we're all misguided. I mean, everybody wants love. That was Miss Tyne's problem. She wanted money. If she'd wanted love instead, think how happy she would have been. Everyone has the right to expect love. Everyone wants love. What's that famous poem? "It's love, it's love, it's love, it's love." Of course, everyone can't have love. Take Margot. I was never meant to love her. She's a well-meaning thing, but I had my boys and my own life, and she was conceived by mistake, as a means to facilitate sleep. Your father lost his boyish charm as time went on. Oh, well, it's been a hard day, but we can relax tonight, and tomorrow we'll return to the continent. This house has too many memories.

TOD: *(Looking at Tim.)* Do you want anything from the supermarket?

VIVIEN: *(Afraid.)* I'm sure there's plenty in the kitchen.

TOD: *(To Tim.)* Do you?

TIM: *(Angry.)* What's the matter with leftovers?

TOD: Leftovers are nice and cozy and a comfort, but fresh food adds spice to any table.

VIVIEN: *(Sadly.)* Children, mother hates metaphor.

TIM: *(To Tod.)* Very well. But not Grand Union. Is that understood?

TOD: Suits me. We haven't tried the Stop 'n' Shop.

VIVIEN: Maybe East Haddam doesn't have a Stop 'n' Shop.

TIM: All right. We can phone from upstairs.

(They start to exit.)

VIVIEN: I'm sure there's plenty of food in the kitchen.

TOD: *(Smiling.)* The food in the kitchen is burned.

TIM: See you later, mother.

(They exit.)

VIVIEN: Goodnight, my twins. Rejoice in being two. For loneliness is a terrible thing. *(To herself.)* My children are so artistic. Wonderful children of a wonderful mother. *(To herself.)* I can't help feeling sorry, though, that they're not really a bit nicer. Of course, I'm not all that nice either, I suppose, by some people's standards. But I don't think one should criticize. Let he who is without sin cast the first stone, Christ said. So they tell me. Ah, Tod, Tim. So lucky to be two. I even rather wish Herbert were alive tonight. Oh well. One does the best one can. That's what I always say. And if you're lonely one moment, you forget it the next, so it couldn't be too bad, because you forget it. Yes. I think that's the way it is. *(Sings softly to herself as lights dim. End.)*

TO THE ACTOR

The set is a Victorian drawing room; if it looks as if *The Mousetrap* is about to play there, that would be the right idea. There should be a comfortable, expensive sofa; an arm chair or two; an old coffee table; probably an Oriental rug. There should be an entrance to the house; there might also be a staircase leading to upstairs. The entranceway, or right below it, should have an old telephone and telephone stand. There should be exits, R. and L., one to servants quarters, the other to other rooms in the downstairs area.

The two non-drawing room scenes (Vivien's bedroom, and the grandmother locked up in the Tower) should be differentiated mostly by lighting; a change of set would be time-consuming and laborious. Vivien's bedroom should be D. R. in a small spotlight, with a pink boudoir chair brought in as the only piece of furniture; for the second scene set in the bedroom, a milk carton (or some particularly ratty chair) should be brought in by the maid for the grandmother to sit on. And then the brief scene in the "Tower" should be performed D. L., with the same milk carton or chair and maybe one or two dead rats, in a small spotlight.

Note on the characters of Tod and Tim: In the casting and playing of these roles, it would be a good idea to avoid effeminacy or other clichés often found in the theatrical presentation of homosexuals. I prefer that they either appear as well mannered and well dressed, rather like models from *Gentlemen's Quarterly,* or else, a somewhat more bizarre choice, as very "regular guys" (sort of like casting Paul Newman and Steve McQueen in the roles, when they were in their 20s).

Titanic

I'm fond of this play which is one of several I wrote during my three years at Yale School of Drama.

It began in a class taught my first year by Howard Stein, the Dean of Playwriting. Howard (who gives me pleasure by writing the introduction to this book) gave the first year playwriting class an assignment to write a scene about a conflict: On a train, a woman wants a man to put out his cigar.

I wrote a scene where a husband and wife were on a train, but it kept also being a boat; and though they argued about smoking some, they got off on another tangent, arguing in extremely surreal ways about the paternity of their children and who had an affair with whom, and whether it was a real affair, or whether it was possibly all done with white bread and mirrors.

Howard, happily, was not a stickler for rules, and was delighted that I wrote a crackpot reaction to his assignment. And so I then went on to make the setting be a boat, indeed to let it be the *Titanic.*

In a version my first year, the *Titanic* docked at Port Authority Bus Terminal in New York City, and the mother Victoria ended up pimping for her son Teddy.

But somehow getting off the boat seemed wrong and to lose the metaphor of these characters stuck on this doomed boat; so I threw out the second half, and kept the characters on water.

My second year at Yale, I lucked out with a guest teacher, Jules Feiffer, whose work I admired a lot. He was a very encouraging teacher, and gave good specific feedback. Also, at one point in class, he said that the play *Titanic* was emotionally like a child having a prepubescent temper tantrum (he meant this as a compliment); and in a later rewrite I added the mother Victoria telling Teddy that "this prepubescent temper tantrum is to stop this instant" as a kind of nod to Feiffer's comment.

Every Wednesday the playwrights and actors had a class together called Writers Workshop, during which the actors did readings of whatever plays the writers were working on; and then Richard Gilman, Howard Stein, and all the students would give feedback.

This was my favorite class because I found it so helpful (and often entertaining) to hear the actors read the plays aloud. And if something suddenly seemed boring or off the point, you had a viscereal feeling of that, hearing it aloud; it was much less theoretical than just discussing a play around a table with other writers (though that's valuable too; it's just I learn more hearing actors read aloud).

In class *Titanic* had a couple of bumpy readings that didn't go well; and then it had a workshop production outside of school that didn't go so well; and then, about ready to decide I should let go of expecting this play to work, I had the opportunity for a rehearsed production of the play at Yale during my final year there. And that production, and a subsequent one in New York, with the same director and same actress as Victoria, went quite well.

I made several important friendships at Yale—I've already mentioned fellow writers Albert Innaurato and Wendy Wasserstein. But of friendships among the actors, there are two in particular: Kate McGregor-Stewart and Sigourney Weaver. Both seemed to respond favorably to my work, and my work to them; when they read parts, the material came alive in surprising ways. And when we presented *Titanic* in New York City in 1975, Kate played the mother Victoria, and Sigourney played the complex part of the triple-personality Lidia.

And a few years later, when *Beyond Therapy* premiered off-Broadway at the Phoenix Theatre, Sigourney played the heroine Prudence, and Kate played the warm, expansive therapist Charlotte Wallace.

Kate, with bright red hair, a dazzling smile and a real sharpness in her comic delivery, seemed to fit all the unreasonable mother roles I wrote (even though she was in her 30s). She played Edith in *'dentity Crisis*; she created the mother in a little-known play of mine, *The Vietnamization of New Jersey*; she played Lettie Lu in *The Book of Leviticus*.

Kate once told a fellow actor who was feeling lost in a play of mine that she never worried if the transitions in my plays made "sense," she just committed fully to whatever choice her character was making at that moment and assumed that I had taken care of the transitions; if the character thought or said something contradictory a few minutes later, she then committed to that.

People are often unreasonable, after all; and in my surreal comedies, my people act very inconsistently. Victoria is concerned with appearances and what's "proper," and yet as the play goes on she's clearly exempting herself from worrying about what's "proper."

Sigourney's abilities in my work were also quite wonderful; if Kate played the hard-edged roles, Sigourney usually played the sympathetic one, or sometimes the "reasonable" one.

Due to her striking and strong looks, in movies she almost always has played bold, confident women (and did a wonderful comic variation on that as the pleased-with-herself boss in *Working Girl*), but in my plays at Yale, she surprised me by playing vulnerable sorts who did very odd things but made them psychologically believable.

In my first production at Yale, *Better Dead Than Sorry*, she played sensitive, frail Jenny who sings the title song while receiving shock treatments. Sigourney made her own headpiece to wear (using a small helmet, with little wires sticking out); and her reaction to the shocks that would interrupt her song were tiny and subtle, and this odd mixture of funny and sad.

In an early one-act version of my play *The Marriage of Bette and Boo*, she played the first version of Soot, the put-upon wife who laughs every time she's insulted. I envisioned Soot's laugh to be slightly uncomfortable, but Sigourney surprised me by playing it as a genuine laugh, which made her seem all the crazier, and which saved showing the pathos in her character until later, when it took one more by surprise and was more powerful.

Anyway, I learned a lot from many of the actors at Yale; and to Kate and Sigourney, I am especially grateful.

Oh. Back to *Titanic*. Well, make of it what you will.

By the way, the New York reviews for *Titanic* were scary…initially pretty good for the off-off-Broadway version, but negative to scathing when it was moved to off-Broadway. One should never call a play *Titanic*, as this is too great a temptation for critics to say *Titanic Sinks* and *Durang Goes Down With His Ship*. Etc., etc., all of which happened.

The day after the reviews, Sigourney and I were scheduled to appear on the *Joe Franklin Show*. It was early in our careers so we weren't known; we pretended the reviews hadn't come out yet, which was fine with him, as he had a nutritionist on and he kept wanting us to talk about that. "Sigornia!" he would say, looking up from his notes whenever the camera came back to him. "Actors and nutrition! Talk about that." Sigourney, trying to be gracious, said that she and I ate liver and green beans for energy. She claims I said I ate cookies for breakfast, but I don't really remember.

Off-Broadway *Titanic* ran two weeks—the first week to pretty good laughter, the second week to almost no one after the bad reviews.

To save the production money, I doubled as assistant stage manager and also as the dead body that gets rolled onstage wrapped in gauze.

I remember my eyes backstage meeting Richard Peterson, who was playing Teddy. He was dressed in his boxer shorts, and there I was pathetically wrapped up in a sheet and tied to this push-cart; and the audience was non-existent and silent out front. It felt like a real theatrical baptism by fire. It was painful at the time, though now it makes me laugh. Ahahahaha.

And I think the play's funny. I hope you do.

(Note: There are extensive acting notes in the Dramatists Play Service acting edition of this play, and I hope people producing the play will refer to them.)

Titanic was first presented at the Yale Experimental Theatre in May 1974, directed by Peter Mark Schifter. The cast was as follows:

Victoria Tammurai	Kate McGregor-Stewart
Richard Tammurai	Kenneth Ryan
Teddy Tammurai	Joel Polis
Lidia	Christine Estabrook
The Captain	Robert Nersesian
Higgins	Richard Bey

Titanic was then presented by the Direct Theatre, 455 West 43rd Street, New York City, in February, 1976. The production was directed by Peter Mark Schifter, setting and costumes by Ernie Smith, lighting by Richard Winkler. The cast was as follows:

Victoria Tammurai	Kate McGregor-Stewart
Richard Tammurai	Stefan Hartman
Teddy Tammurai	Richard Peterson
Lidia	Sigourney Weaver
The Captain	Jeff Brooks
Higgins	Ralph Redpath

This production was subsequently moved off-Broadway to the Van Dam Theatre in New York in May 1976, presented by John Rothman. This version was presented with a curtain-raiser, *Das Lusitania Songspiel*, co-authored by and featuring Christopher Durang and Sigourney Weaver.

CHARACTERS
VITORIA TAMMURAI
RICHARD TAMMURAI
TEDDY TAMMURAI, their son
LIDIA
THE CAPTAIN
HIGGINS, the sailor

TITANIC

SCENE 1

The dining room aboard the Titanic. *Victoria and Richard Tammurai, expensively dressed, sit at table with their son Teddy, age twenty, but dressed as a little boy in short pants. The orchestra can be heard playing "Nearer My God to Thee."*

VICTORIA: Richard, listen, they're playing our song.
     (They listen. She sings a little.)
VICTORIA: *(Singing.)*
     Nearer my God to thee,
     Floating across the sea...
RICHARD: We've had many a happy time listening to that tune.
VICTORIA: The merry-go-round was playing that tune when I first conceived Teddy. Did you know that, Teddy?
TEDDY: No.
VICTORIA: Of course you didn't. You were too young. Yes, your father was quite a devil on the merry-go-round.
RICHARD: I still am.
VICTORIA: I imagine so, although you developed a bad case of vertigo the last time we rode the Wild Mouse.
RICHARD: I've never ridden the Wild Mouse.
VICTORIA: Memories fade as one gets older. Teddy, sit up. People will think you're fourteen years old.
RICHARD: A slouch is bad for shuffleboard, son. I've entered us in the ship's match tomorrow.

VICTORIA: I love shuffleboard. And badminton. And that amusement where one bangs cars together. What is that called, Teddy?

TEDDY: Auto roulette.

VICTORIA: I don't think that's right. Oh, look. The Captain is looking our way. No, I don't think he is. He's getting something out of his eye. A speck.

RICHARD: A distinguished looking man.

VICTORIA: It's the uniform that does it. Why weren't we placed at the Captain's table?

RICHARD: I don't know. I consider it a snub actually.

VICTORIA: Granted the *Titanic's* passenger list is impressive, but I think we are still among the crème de la crème. We're certainly rich enough.

RICHARD: We may be rich enough, but perhaps the Captain looked into your family background. Your family is not precisely upper class. It's rather dreadful really. A sort of lower form of plant-life out in Indiana.

VICTORIA: Richard, is this yet another insult to me? I would not have set one foot upon this boat if I had thought you were going to persist in these endless cruelties to me.

TEDDY: *(Uncomfortable. Changing subject.)* Where's Annabella?

VICTORIA: *(Looks at him blankly; then to Richard.)* Teddy has very hairy legs for a fourteen-year-old. Do you think that's right, Richard?

RICHARD: Teddy hasn't been fourteen for years.

VICTORIA: I know, but even so. You're very nice looking, Teddy. Richard, I want a divorce. As soon as the *Titanic* docks, I am going straight to my solicitor.

TEDDY: Mommy.

VICTORIA: Shush, dear. Act your age.

RICHARD: It's high time we bought you long pants, son.

VICTORIA: Richard, you're changing the subject.

RICHARD: Then I'll return to it. Victoria, as far as I am concerned you can go right back to the pig farms of Indiana. There is no point in continuing this domestic purgatory.

VICTORIA: Not purgatory, Richard. Hell.

TEDDY: Mommy, everyone is staring at us.

VICTORIA: Nonsense, dear. They're admiring me. And don't whimper. It isn't manly.

RICHARD: Teddy, don't listen to what I'm about to say to your mother.

Victoria, I have the greatest contempt for you, but perhaps we should stay together for the sake of the children.

VICTORIA: Richard, Teddy is not your son.

RICHARD: Victoria, what do you mean?

VICTORIA: Richard, when you married me you looked down on my American ways. You made fun of the pig farm. You made rude suggestions about my mother. And one night, after you had hurt me deeply in front of our dinner guests—you had ridiculed my boeuf de bordelaise—I went out to our beach and I wept. And on the beach I met a derelict who saw my pain, and he reached out to me as a human being. It was a mad moment, Richard, but although I never saw him again, it is he who is Teddy's father.

RICHARD: Victoria, what are you saying?

VICTORIA: The meaning is clear enough. Teddy's father was some beachcomber. He is not your son.

RICHARD: I have been sorely deceived.

(Teddy starts to cry.)

VICTORIA: Your son is crying.

RICHARD: I have no son. *(To Teddy.)* I hope you realize that from this moment I want nothing more to do with you.

TEDDY: Daddy! *(Cries.)*

VICTORIA: Teddy, please act your age. I've never seen a fourteen-year-old with such hairy legs.

RICHARD: Is my daughter of my seed?

VICTORIA: *(Smiling at another table.)* What?

RICHARD: I said, am I the father of my daughter?

VICTORIA: Who? Annabella? Let me think. *(Thinks for awhile. Reminisces about a sexy encounter, then shakes head no. Thinks about a few other encounters, still no. Then recalls something unpleasant, and shakes her head affirmatively.)* Yes.

RICHARD: Then I have a daughter. *(To Teddy.)* I have no son, but I have a daughter.

TEDDY: What of the twenty years you've acted as my father?

RICHARD: This knowledge cancels them out.

VICTORIA: Smile, the Captain's looking at us.

(Richard and Victoria smile.)

RICHARD: Most distinguished looking.

VICTORIA: Don't repeat yourself, Richard.

RICHARD: Victoria, I have something to tell you.

VICTORIA: What?

RICHARD: Annabella is not your daughter.

VICTORIA: What do you mean?

RICHARD: After one of your numerous cruelties to me, I turned for comfort to Harriet Lindsay. She is Annabella's mother.

VICTORIA: Nonsense. I remember the placenta quite distinctly.

RICHARD: No. It was all a trick. You only thought you gave birth. Harriet and I did it with mirrors.

VICTORIA: You mean I went through all that labor for nothing?

RICHARD: Absolutely nothing.

VICTORIA: Well, I certainly never intend to speak to Harriet or Annabella ever again. First thing in the morning I shall have her deck chair moved away from mine.

RICHARD: And I shall withdraw Teddy's and my name from the father-son shuffleboard match.

VICTORIA: You're both embarrassing at shuffleboard anyway.

TEDDY: Please don't argue.

VICTORIA: Don't be tiresome, Teddy.

RICHARD: I'm only surprised to hear that Teddy's father was a derelict you met on the beach rather than one of your mother's prize hogs.

TEDDY: Daddy!

VICTORIA: Richard, you are pushing me to my limit. I shall now make one thing clear. *(She stands.)* THERE NEVER WAS AN ANNABELLA. *(She sits back down again.)* Harriet Lindsay and I have been having an affair since that summer we bought the beach house, and she just invented a pregnancy to keep you from getting suspicious. You never even slept with her. We did it all with mirrors and slices of white bread. You made love to pieces of white bread, you stupid man, and not only that, but I made your toast out of it in the morning. HAH! I trust you'll be more careful next time I say something is just marmalade.

RICHARD: *(Stands.)* Victoria, I shall make arrangements for private accommodations. What you have just told me is monstrous, and it is I who shall sue you for a divorce. Good evening. *(Exits in rage.)*

VICTORIA: You should have thrown your glass of water at your father when he said that, Teddy. He insulted your mother.

TEDDY: *(Looks in his glass.)* There's a guppy in my glass.

VICTORIA: I don't care what's in your glass. Manners are manners. *(Rises.)* I'm going to the cabin to rest. *(Suddenly exhausted, sad.)* Somehow I wish we had never come on the *Titanic*. Finish your dinner, Teddy. Mother still loves you.

(She exits. Teddy bends a spoon glumly in half. Enter Lidia, dressed in a pink party dress with a pink bow. She stands on a table and curtsies.)

LIDIA: Ladies and gentlemen, my father says it's all right if I want to sing a little song, and so I do and I will. *(Sings to the tune of "Frères Jacques.")*

Pudding, pudding,
I'd eat pudding,
For dessert, 'til it hurt.
When it pours vanilla,
I get my umbrella,
Sit and watch, butterscotch.

I take walks right
In the pudding,
Such a treat for my feet,
Then I lose my footing,
Fall down in the pudding,
What a mess, on my dress.

Mommy says we
Won't have pudding
Anymore 'cause I'm four,
Who'd have ever thunk it,
I'd get stuck with junket,
No more pudding, no more pudding.

(Lidia comes and sits at the table with Teddy. Pause.)

TEDDY: Are you sitting at the right table?

LIDIA: That was my favorite song in the whole world. I'm the Captain's daughter Lidia. It is my task to make the guests feel at ease. Your fly is open. *(Giggles; he goes to fix it.)*

LIDIA: No, leave it open. Better for circulation if you know what I mean. *(Pause.)* May I sit down? *(She is already seated.)*

TEDDY: *(Pause.)* Yes.

LIDIA: My father thinks I'm very promiscuous for my age. What do you think?

TEDDY: I don't know your age.

LIDIA: We were all listening to your parents arguing. Do you think your father really slept with white bread?

TEDDY: I don't know. It might be a metaphor.

LIDIA: I used to keep a hedgehog up my vagina. *(Pause.)* But my parents made me stop because I kept feeding it in public. I think that's being fussy. *(Pause.)* I got a funny disease from the hedgehog. They thought it was Dutch Elm disease, but it wasn't. After a while, I got a reputation, and then none of the boys would sleep with me. *(Pause.)* I used to bring lesbians on for a while, and they all had to get rabies shots. Am I boring you?

TEDDY: No. I'm just upset because of my parents.

LIDIA: I don't blame you. Things that wouldn't bother you normally often bother you just because it's your parents who are doing it. I once saw may parents "doing it." It was on educational television. But that's not my idea of education, do you agree? I mean, certain things should be a mystery. To me, sex is a mystery. Is it a mystery to you?

TEDDY: Yes.

LIDIA: *(Laughs.)* I bet it is! I'd love to see your father on television with all that bread. But I wonder who they'd get to sponsor it? I mean, I don't know if the bread companies would think that that was good publicity or not. Of course, I'm not an advertising expert, but I don't think that's one of the twelve ways to build a strong body that Wonder Bread had in mind. *(Laughs.)* I made a joke. Could I borrow some of your lettuce?

TEDDY: Yes.

LIDIA: Thank you. *(She puts it up her dress.)* I have a couple of hamsters in here now, and do they make a mess! *(Keeps feeding the hamsters. Fairly long pause.)* My gynecologist runs the other way when he sees me coming.

(She smiles. Teddy gulps his water, a little afraid.)

TEDDY: *(Clutching his throat.)* Does anything happen to you if you swallow a guppy?

LIDIA: Did you know that guppy mothers eat their babies?

(Smiles, puts her hand over his. Lights dim. Orchestra starts playing "Nearer My God To Thee" again. Blackout.)

SCENE 2

Captain's quarters. The Captain and Victoria.

CAPTAIN: Well, here we are, Mrs. Tammurai.

VICTORIA: What a lovely cabin, Captain. Why all this pet food?

CAPTAIN: My daughter has a fondness for animals.

VICTORIA: You know, Captain, my husband finds you most distinguished looking.

CAPTAIN: And what about you?

VICTORIA: He finds me moderately attractive.

CAPTAIN: No, I mean, how do *you* find me?

VICTORIA: I find you a deeply sensitive, considerate seafarer.

CAPTAIN: I'm touched. Do you have any tin foil with you?

VICTORIA: Why should I have any tin foil?

CAPTAIN: You're a very attractive woman.

VICTORIA: And you mean attractive women carry tin foil?

CAPTAIN: No, I meant it as a non sequitur. Tin foil is a secret passion of mine. And you are very attractive, you know.

VICTORIA: The mother of my nonexistent daughter always thought so. Oh, Harriet, where are you?

CAPTAIN: Pardon me?

VICTORIA: Nothing, I was remembering other voices, other wombs.

CAPTAIN: Wombs?

VICTORIA: *(Sings sadly.)* A womb without windows, a womb without doors.

CAPTAIN: I want to show you something. *(Ducks behind couch, comes out with a dildo strapped to his forehead.)*

VICTORIA: Are you a doctor?

CAPTAIN: I find you exciting.

VICTORIA: Is this a unicorn fetish?

CAPTAIN: Do you deliver?

VICTORIA: I feel our lives becoming quickly trivial.

CAPTAIN: *(Nuzzling her with his forehead.)* Do you deliver?

VICTORIA: If the mood is right, Captain.

CAPTAIN: How can we make the mood right?

VICTORIA: *(Sadly.)* The usual ways. Soft music. *(Music starts.)* Dim lights. *(Lights dim.)* Bread.

CAPTAIN: Did you say bed?

VICTORIA: No. Bread. *(From beneath her dress she brings forth a family-size loaf of Wonder Bread.)*

CAPTAIN: You're an unusual woman, Mrs. Tammurai.

VICTORIA: I've seen too much of the world. *(Lights dim to black; in darkness.)* Oh, you men are fools. *(Blackout.)*

SCENE 3

A cabin. Lidia pulling Teddy in.

LIDIA: Come on, Teddy. You can't stay a virgin forever.

TEDDY: It's been such a trying day.

LIDIA: Come on, relax. Take your clothes off, and I'll get the rope.

TEDDY: Rope?

LIDIA: Boy, you are a novice. *(Blackout.)*

SCENE 4

The deck. Sailor is on watch. Enter Richard.

RICHARD: Hello there, sailor. What do you see?

SAILOR: Nothing much, sir. Lot of mist and haze.

RICHARD: You look rather familiar.

SAILOR: Do I, sir? Some people say I look like Leif Erickson.

RICHARD: The Nordic chap? Yes, you look rather Nordic. Actually, the person you most reminded me of was—no, I doubt it could be the same one.

SAILOR: Who did you have in mind, sir?

RICHARD: Well, this is going to sound silly—but do you go around in drag much? You know, women's clothing?

SAILOR: I beg your pardon?

RICHARD: You're not the same one then? You're not Dicky Miller from Portsmith?

SAILOR: I've never dressed as a woman in my entire life.

RICHARD: Not even as a child? Didn't you like to go rummaging through your mummy's lingerie drawer?

SAILOR: I find this conversation offensive, sir.

RICHARD: Well, very well, I guess you're not Dicky Miller. I could never tell, of course, unless you dressed up as Queen Victoria. That was Dicky's most frequent guise. We'd all be sitting around the bar in this club I belong to, and in would waltz Dicky with three tiaras on his head and a tiny poodle stuffed in his bosom. "I am Queen Victoria," he'd say. We'd all play along, all the guys. "Sorry, Your Majesty, no women allowed in this club," we'd say. "I am not a woman," Dicky would say. "I am the Queen." Strange fellow, Dicky.

SAILOR: I'm finding it difficult to concentrate on my task, sir.

RICHARD: What? Watching the sea? I can tell you if we see any icebergs. Just you relax.

SAILOR: That friend of yours doesn't sound like a regular guy to me.

RICHARD: He was. The friendliest, nicest guy you'll ever want to meet. Give you the blouse off his back, he would. We used to take him in the back room and play along with him kind of, you know, give him a pinch in the rear, or tweak his cheek; we stopped after a while though when one of the poodles smothered to death in Dicky's bodice. It kind of put an edge on things.

SAILOR: Are you a member of parliament, sir?

RICHARD: I'm just a poor soul looking for friendship on this bitch of an earth out in the middle of this bitch of a sea.

SAILOR: I think I see an iceberg!

RICHARD: Really? Where?

SAILOR: Good God! We're heading right for it!

RICHARD: Then we're done for. Sailor, before we go down, I wonder if you'd do me one small favor...

SAILOR: No time for that! I've got to find the Captain. *(He exits.)*

RICHARD: Oh, very well. *(He follows the Sailor out; blackout.)*

SCENE 5

Lidia's cabin. Teddy bound in bed. Lidia is smoking a cigarette.

TEDDY: I had no idea it would be so awful.

LIDIA: The first is always awful.

TEDDY: Why is it necessary that the man be tied?

LIDIA: So the woman can be safe, dopey, in case you try something funny.

TEDDY: The hamsters bit me.

LIDIA: That's your own fault. You did it all wrong. Those quick pokes always send 'em into hysterics.

TEDDY: Was your first as bad?

LIDIA: Course. My first was a gang bang with twenty-two Portuguese sailors. They didn't know a word of English and it lasted for two days.

TEDDY: Did they tie you up?

LIDIA: No, they punched me.

TEDDY: I guess I prefer being tied to being punched.

LIDIA: Next time we can try it with punching if you like.

TEDDY: I bet I'm going to get an infection from the hamsters.

LIDIA: You men are always complaining. Just be glad I got rid of the hedgehog.

(Enter the Captain in his underwear with a slice of bread stuck on the dildo on his forehead.)

CAPTAIN: Lidia, did you see a woman pass through here?

LIDIA: No I didn't. What *are* you up to?

CAPTAIN: I was entertaining in my cabin, but the woman seems to have slipped away.

LIDIA: You look like you've been engendering biscuits.

CAPTAIN: Biscuits? What about biscuits?

LIDIA: You have a piece of bread on your dildo.

CAPTAIN: Watch your tongue, young lady! You're incessantly vulgar. Your mother and I shall ask for a refund from your finishing school in Hampshire.

(Enter Sailor and Richard.)

SAILOR: Begging pardon, sir, but we've sighted an iceberg.

CAPTAIN: I've told you not to bother me in my quarters, Higgins. Put your complaint in the log and I'll consider it later. *(Calling.)* Mrs. Tammurai! *(He exits.)*

SAILOR: I'm afraid we're going to sink. Why will no one listen? *(He exits.)*

RICHARD: Poor chap.

TEDDY: Daddy!

RICHARD: Teddy! What are you…I don't even know who you are.

TEDDY: You didn't tell me about the hamsters.

RICHARD: Don't bother me with your tales of petulance. *(Sees Lidia.)* Oh, my God. Is it you?

LIDIA: Certainly not. I'm the Captain's daughter, Lidia. Your son's not much of a ladies' man, I might suggest.

RICHARD: I have no son, *Harriet.*

LIDIA: Why did you call me Harriet?

RICHARD: You can't fool me. White bread or no white bread, I remember Harriet Lindsay of Wallington Park.

TEDDY: Then this is the mother of my sister Annabella?

RICHARD: Shut up, Teddy. There is no Annabella.

(Enter Victoria, pursued by the Captain.)

CAPTAIN: Mrs. Tammurai, don't tease.

RICHARD: Victoria!

VICTORIA: Good evening, Richard. I believe you should speak harshly to the Captain. He is attempting to violate my bread box.

RICHARD: Your doings are no longer a concern of mine. You can run a whole wheat brothel as far as I'm concerned.

TEDDY: I'm all tied up.

LIDIA: Hello, Victoria.

VICTORIA: Oh my God. That voice.

LIDIA: *(Sings seductively.)*
   A womb without windows,
   A womb without doors.

VICTORIA: Harriet, Harriet. You've come back.

CAPTAIN: I don't understand. Who is Harriet?

VICTORIA: She is.

CAPTAIN: But this is my daughter Lidia.

VICTORIA: Certainly I can be expected to recognize my own sister Harriet!

RICHARD: I didn't realize Harriet Lindsay was your sister!

VICTORIA: There are many things you don't realize, Richard.

CAPTAIN: But I don't understand. What is the meaning of this, Lidia?

VICTORIA: This is not Lidia. This is my sister Harriet.

TEDDY: I'm all tied up.

VICTORIA: Teddy. Why are you here?

TEDDY: I don't know.

CAPTAIN: I don't understand. Who is Harriet?

LIDIA: *(Triumphant.)* I am Harriet Lindsay, sister of Victoria Tammurai. I am Eternal Youth.

CAPTAIN: My daughter Lidia was blond. You're not blond—now that I look. Where is my daughter?

LIDIA: Your daughter Lidia is in locker #2838 in Port Authority Bus Terminal in New York and has been for three years. *(She suddenly feels pangs within her, reaches up in her skirt and pulls out two dead hamsters.)* My hamsters are dead! Too much marmalade. Here's a souvenir of your first night with your mother's sister, Teddy! *(She whirls the hamsters around her head and then throws them at Teddy.)*

VICTORIA: *(Somewhat concerned.)* Oh dear. Teddy really shouldn't be witnessing all this.

RICHARD: Victoria, I am appalled. When we reach London, I am going to *my* solicitor. I intend to take custody of the boy regardless of his parentage.

TEDDY: Daddy, untie me!

VICTORIA: No court would separate a mother and her son.

RICHARD: When the mother's moral life is at the level your is, Victoria, the court will jump at the chance.

VICTORIA: Don't speak to me of morals, Richard. I know all about your secret life in that so-called club in London. Masquerading as royalty, suffocating poodles. What court would let a child enter that sort of life?

RICHARD: You are an incestuous snail.

(Enter Sailor.)

RICHARD: Hello there, young man.

SAILOR: Captain, please sir! We're going to ram the iceberg!

CAPTAIN: Very well, Higgins. I heard you the first time. *(To Lidia.)* Don't think I'll forget this, Lidia. I shall resent you to my last living day. *(Exits.)*

VICTORIA: Come, Harriet, let's pack. You and I must prepare to shoulder the burden of being new parents to Teddy.

RICHARD: You'll hear from me, Victoria. No incestuous slattern is going to turn my boy into a degenerate.

VICTORIA: He's not your son!
  (Victoria and Lidia exit.)
SAILOR: I'm afraid we're done for. That berg's going to rip right through
  us. *(Exits.)*
RICHARD: Don't worry, Teddy. Daddy still loves you. *(Exits after the
  sailor.)*
TEDDY: It's chilly. I wish they'd have pulled blankets up over me. *(Calls
  plaintively.)* Blankets! Blankets!
  *(A loud crash. Sounds of enormous ripping, water gushing, alarms,
  sirens, and so forth. Teddy, still tied, rushes off, screaming. Various en-
  trances of shipwreck chaos: The Captain and Sailor are hysterical; Lidia
  fairly calm; Richard has trouble with his life jacket; Victoria is hysterical. The Sailor, from entrance to entrance, inexplicably is losing his uniform. The final crossover is Teddy, tied and hopping, calling "Daddy!
  Mommy!" etc. Blackout.)*

SCENE 6

*The noise stops. Teddy re-enters, unbound, and having found the
Sailor's uniform, which he begins to put on in audience view. The
Captain's voice comes over the loudspeaker.*

CAPTAIN: This is your Captain speaking. Do not panic. We have not hit
  an iceberg. What you have just heard is a sound effects record. My
  wife put it on. It is her idea of a little joke. Please return to your cab-
  ins. There is no cause for alarm.
  (Enter Sailor who sees Teddy with his clothes.)
SAILOR: I beg your pardon? Are those my clothes?
  *(Teddy rushes off. Before Sailor has a chance to pursue him, enter
  Richard who sees Sailor.)*
RICHARD: Hello there, young man. Forget something?
SAILOR: Where's the Captain?
RICHARD: He's…on the loudspeaker.
SAILOR: Forget it. *(Runs off after where Teddy went.)*
RICHARD: Do you play bridge? Ah well…
  (Enter Teddy, now completely dressed as Sailor, from other side.)

RICHARD: Hello there, Sailor.

TEDDY: I couldn't find my other clothes.

RICHARD: What other clothes? These suit you remarkably well, young man.

TEDDY: I think I have an infection.

RICHARD: Oh, piffle. You can't scare me off with that. Say, I know this is going to sound like a line, but you look awfully familiar.

TEDDY: What do you mean, I *look* familiar?

RICHARD: I suppose it's just that you're wearing the same kind of uniform the other fellow was wearing.

TEDDY: This *is* his uniform.

RICHARD: You share it? That's oddly titillating.

TEDDY: I've lost my shoes.

RICHARD: So you have. Have you ever read Nietzsche's *Genealogy of Morals?*

TEDDY: I don't remember.

RICHARD: I want you to come to my cabin and reevaluate your concepts of good and bad.

TEDDY: I don't know if I have any concepts of good and bad.

RICHARD: Well, we must in any case evaluate what you *do* have.
      (They exit. Blackout.)

SCENE 7
      The cabin. Victoria, nervous.

VICTORIA: Oh my God, my God. Harriet, where are you?
      (Knock on door. Enter Sailor.)

SAILOR: Captain requests your presence on deck, Ma'am. Oh, I'm sorry. I was looking for his wife. Have you seen her?

VICTORIA: No, I haven't. Where's Harriet?

SAILOR: Lidia?

VICTORIA: Harriet.

SAILOR: I don't know. *(Exits.)*

VICTORIA: Oh, Harriet, so many illusions shattered, so many dreams trodden in the dust.

(Enter Richard in his bathrobe from the bedroom.)

RICHARD: Oh, Victoria. I didn't know you were here. Are you about to leave?

(Enter Teddy in underwear, also from the bedroom.)

VICTORIA: Richard, where *is* Harriet?

TEDDY: Harriet has my clothes somewhere.

VICTORIA: Teddy, why are you here?

RICHARD: My God! Are you Teddy?

VICTORIA: Of course, he's Teddy. Who did you think he was?

RICHARD: I thought he was a sailor.

VICTORIA: Teddy doesn't look anything like a sailor. Where are your clothes, Teddy?

RICHARD: Give me back the money I gave you at once!

VICTORIA: What money?

RICHARD: I am hardly going to pay my own son!

VICTORIA: Pay him for what? Richard, what did you pay him for?

TEDDY: I don't feel well.

RICHARD: You should have told me who you were. Give me back the money.

TEDDY: No, I earned it.

VICTORIA: Teddy, did you solicit your father?

TEDDY: I don't have a father.

VICTORIA: That's no excuse to solicit him, Teddy. I'm surprised at you. That's *two* bad things you've done today. And you, Richard. What sort of example is this for you to give your son? Picking up male riffraff on the deck.

RICHARD: I would hardly call my son riffraff.

VICTORIA: Well, I should hope not. Really, Richard, what could you have been thinking of?

RICHARD: Victoria, mistakes happen.

VICTORIA: Well, I suppose they do.

RICHARD: I forgive you with the derelict on the beach, if you forgive me with Teddy.

VICTORIA: That's a generous offer, Richard.

(They kiss.)

VICTORIA: Now Teddy, give your father the money back.

(Enter Lidia, who watches from the back.)

TEDDY: I don't want to.

VICTORIA: Teddy, is this any way for a ten-year-old to behave?

RICHARD: He needs to see a psychologist.

VICTORIA: *(Horrified.)* Oh, Richard—no!

LIDIA: *(Very harsh.)* That's no way to speak to your parents, Teddy. *(Slaps him.)* APOLOGIZE!

TEDDY: *(Stunned.)* I don't want to.

LIDIA: APOLOGIZE! *(Slaps him again.)*

TEDDY: I'm sorry. *(Gives money to Richard.)*

VICTORIA: After all, Teddy, you really shouldn't charge your father. We can't be proud of you if you're rude, Teddy.

RICHARD: I'm sure Teddy didn't mean it. All's forgiven.

(Richard kisses Teddy; Victoria and Lidia kiss.)

LIDIA: *(Clutches her stomach.)* I caught a sea gull up on deck. It's not sitting well. *(Feathers fall from beneath her dress.)* Look. I'm molting. I am a sea gull. I am a sea gull.

(Sudden Crash. Everyone is thrown to ground.)

CAPTAIN: *(On loudspeaker.)* This is your Captain. Please do not be alarmed. Would anyone seeing a woman carrying a sound effects record please advise the Captain of this fact as soon as possible? Thank you.

LIDIA: *(Hating life.)* Oh, why won't we sink, why?

(Blackout.)

SCENE 8

The Titanic *lounge. At table: Victoria, Richard, Teddy, Lidia.*

VICTORIA: *(Distressed.)* Richard, why will the Captain never eat with us?

RICHARD: There, there, get a hold on.

(Enter the Sailor with dish of mints.)

SAILOR: The Captain sends his regrets and promises to join you for coffee momentarily. He offers you these delicious after-dinner mints. *(Offers them.)*

VICTORIA: How nice. I love mints.

(Lidia takes dish. Puts a mint up her dress. Pause.)

VICTORIA: Harriet, don't do that.

LIDIA: What? *(Puts another mint up her dress.)*

RICHARD: Harriet, please. This is a public lounge.

LIDIA: *(Pretending not to understand.)* What's the matter?

VICTORIA: Harriet, people are staring at us. They won't know what you're doing.

LIDIA: *(Loudly, to supposed onlookers.)* I'VE GOT A SEAGULL IN HERE.

VICTORIA: Harriet!

RICHARD: Victoria, let's just ignore her. *(Pause.)*

LIDIA: You wanna try, Teddy?

(Teddy feeds Lidia's seagull.)

RICHARD: Teddy, behave!

VICTORIA: Harriet, I hardly think after-dinner mints are suitable eating for sea gulls. No wonder you're molting.

LIDIA: My gynecologist says my molting disease is catching.

VICTORIA: I don't believe you *have* a gynecologist. Really, Harriet, a douche is one thing but a vaginal zoo is quite another!

RICHARD: I couldn't agree more. Next thing we know she's going to install trapeze artists.

VICTORIA: We can do without your contributions, Richard.

RICHARD: I was agreeing with you.

VICTORIA: I don't want you to agree with me.

TEDDY: I agree with mother *and* father. *(Feeds Lidia again.)*

RICHARD: Teddy, mother and I do not wish you to feed Annabella's seagull.

VICTORIA: Richard, you called Harriet Annabella.

RICHARD: Did I? I get so confused.

VICTORIA: Ah, "Confusion," that famous poem by A. E. Housman. *(Begins to recite.)*
  Ah, Confusion, with rue my heart is laden;
  For golden friends I had,
  For many a rose-lipped maiden,
  And many a lightfoot lad.
  (During above, Lidia whispers to Teddy. Then suddenly they get up, attacking the Sailor and removing his clothes. Lidia is the driving force behind this.)

VICTORIA: Children, children!

RICHARD: No, let them be, Victoria. I want to see what they come up with.

(Teddy puts on the Sailor's clothes.)

SAILOR: I shall have to report this to the Captain.

LIDIA: Teddy is a passenger on this boat, and he needs to have clothes.
  (Enter the Captain. He hulks sorrowfully.)
CAPTAIN: I'm sorry I'm late.
SAILOR: Captain, they've taken my clothes.
CAPTAIN: *(Sadly.)* Ah, Higgins. *(To all.)* I fear I've just been through a
  rather harrowing experience. We've had to execute my wife. It's nau-
  tical law. You're not allowed to incite to sinking. We hanged her
  from the mast.
VICTORIA: Oh, Captain, how difficult for you.
CAPTAIN: Well, the others did it actually. I just blew the whistle. *(Blows
  whistle.)* So you'll excuse me. We're holding the burial tomorrow at
  dawn. I'd appreciate it if you could make it. Good evening.
  (Exits. Sailor follows.)
RICHARD: How unfortunate for the man.
VICTORIA: He's taking it well, I think.
LIDIA: *(Taking last mint.)* Here goes the last one.
VICTORIA: Wait. Let's make a wish on it.
RICHARD: Victoria, one doesn't make wishes on after-dinner mints.
VICTORIA: One can if one wants to.
RICHARD: Very well, have it you own way.
VICTORIA: *(Wishing on mint.)* I wish for happiness and good fortune and
  love and faithfulness. Harriet?
LIDIA: I wish that the ship would sink.
VICTORIA: Harriet, don't say that! *(Knocks on the table three times.)*
LIDIA: We keep almost sinking. I'm tired of not sinking.
VICTORIA: Let's just close the subject.
LIDIA: What do you wish for, Teddy?
VICTORIA: I don't even want to know. Here, feed your damn seagull.
  (Feeds Lidia.) It's time for bed.
RICHARD: Ah, bed, a good suggestion. Come along, Teddy. *(Takes Teddy's
  arm.)*
TEDDY: I wish for...
VICTORIA: That's enough, Teddy. We *don't* want to hear. Harriet, when
  you feel more civil, we'll be in the cabin. Richard, take *my* arm.
TEDDY: Good night, Aunt Harriet.
  (Exit Richard, Victoria, Teddy.)
LIDIA: I still hope the boat sinks. *(Lidia takes out large hand drill, tries to
  make holes in the floor. Singing while drilling.)*

Death by drowning,
Death by water,
Father mother, son and daughter…
(Re-enter Sailor. Sailor takes drill away from her.)

SAILOR: I'm sorry, I can't allow you to do that.

LIDIA: I don't know what you're talking about.

SAILOR: It wouldn't do any good. We're several floors above the water anyway.

LIDIA: *(Seductive.)* That's a nice uniform you've got there, Sailor.

SAILOR: You've taken my uniform.

LIDIA: Don't be a stranger, sailor.

(Blackout.)

SCENE 9

The cabin. Teddy, in his sailor suit, sits on Richard's knee.

RICHARD: Come on. Sing!

TEDDY: I don't want to.

RICHARD: Please. *(Puts money in Teddy's pocket.)*

TEDDY: *(Sings.)*
On the good ship lollipop,
It's a short trip into bed you hop
And dream away, something something something
Butterneck bay…
(Richard bounces Teddy up and down.)

TEDDY: Don't do that. You'll make me seasick.

RICHARD: You know, Dorothy, you could make an effort to be a little more pleasant.

TEDDY: Don't call me Dorothy. I don't feel right. I don't have my own clothes.

RICHARD: You look very charming in these.

TEDDY: Where's mommy and Aunt Harriet?

RICHARD: They're in the bedroom.

TEDDY: Is Aunt Harriet a man?

RICHARD: Your Aunt Harriet is an enigma.

(Scream offstage. Enter Victoria, hysterical.)

VICTORIA: She did it again! Something bit me!

TEDDY: Of course, it was a seagull.

(Enter Lidia.)

VICTORIA: You said you took the seagull out.

LIDIA: I was mistaken.

RICHARD: Annabella, why do you treat your mother this way?

VICTORIA: *(Looking at her hand.)* Oh God, it might be rabid.

RICHARD: *(Looks at her hand.)* Dorothy, get your mother's hypodermic, love.

(Teddy does.)

RICHARD: He's very handsome today.

VICTORIA: It's this sea air that does it.

RICHARD: You know, Harriet, these constant booster shots for Victoria are pushing us straight to the poor house. Lie down, Victoria.

VICTORIA: Oh God, the pain! I want Harriet to do it.

LIDIA: Very well. Lie down, Victoria.

(Victoria lies down, bares her stomach.)

LIDIA: Is it nine times or six?

RICHARD: I'm not a doctor.

LIDIA: All right. Ready, on your mark, get set, go!

(Lidia jabs Victoria's stomach nine times, very fast. Awful screams.)

VICTORIA: Oh it's so sordid. Richard, take me away. Help me to the bathroom.

(Richard helps Victoria off.)

LIDIA: Hello, Teddy.

TEDDY: Aren't you my sister Annabella?

LIDIA: What if I am?

TEDDY: Then there really *is* an Annabella?

LIDIA: Yes.

TEDDY: And there isn't a Harriet?

LIDIA: I suppose not.

TEDDY: Why haven't mommy and daddy recognized you?

LIDIA: Because they're very bad parents.

TEDDY: *(A true realization.)* Yes they are. They're very bad. Do you think the boat will ever dock and we can get away from them?

LIDIA: The ship isn't going to dock. It's going to sink.

TEDDY: Soon?

LIDIA: I hope so.

TEDDY: Do you think we should tell our parents you're their daughter and not Harriet?

LIDIA: Not until I'm good and ready.

TEDDY: *(Disappointed.)* Oh.

LIDIA: Poor Teddy.

(Enter Higgins.)

SAILOR: Is the Captain here?

LIDIA: Oh, good, I have nothing in here now. Come on, Teddy.

(Exit Lidia, Teddy, Sailor. Enter the Captain.)

CAPTAIN: Hello? Anyone home?

(Enter Richard.)

CAPTAIN: Is Mrs. Tammurai at home?

RICHARD: Well, it is rather late.

(Enter Victoria, quickly, all cheered up.)

VICTORIA: That's all right, Richard. I'm feeling better. Oh, Captain. How nice of you to visit us. Won't you have tea, Captain?

CAPTAIN: If it's no bother.

VICTORIA: No bother.

(No one gets tea. All sit.)

CAPTAIN: Now that my wife is dead, I would like to propose to you.

RICHARD: Perhaps I should leave.

VICTORIA: Richard's such a gentleman. *(Kisses him.)* I have always loved men. *(Kisses the Captain.)* How did your wife die?

CAPTAIN: I had her executed.

VICTORIA: Oh yes, of course.

CAPTAIN: Nautical law.

VICTORIA: Well that happens at sea. How sad to view death. Someday I shall face my death, and I shall look back and see the overview of my life. And what shall I see? Rabies shots. Deceit. Mirrors. White bread. More white bread. Ah, Captain, you remember the bread.

CAPTAIN: Fondly, Madam.

VICTORIA: *(Takes bread from his vest pocket.)* Here's some here. *(Offers it to Richard.)* Richard?

RICHARD: No thank you.

VICTORIA: For a while I was the toast of this city. What days they were, Richard. Muffins in the winter, popovers in the fall; strawberry tarts during the Mardi Gras. But then one realizes how empty and sterile it has all been. And what do we see, when we bread awaken? We see that we have not really been alive, that a crust of bread has mattered more than we. *(To Richard.)* Oh, Richard, if only we could have made one another happy; *(Looks at Captain.)* or if all three of us could have made one another happy. If only I was not cursed with loving Harriet…Harriet…WHERE IS HARRIET?

RICHARD: WHERE IS TEDDY?

VICTORIA: OH MY GOD!

RICHARD: DOROTHY!

(Victoria and Richard exit hysterical. They bring back Lidia, Teddy, and Sailor, the last two of whom are in their underwear.)

VICTORIA: Dirty! That's dirty! *(Hits Teddy's hand.)*

RICHARD: Little girls don't play with other little girls that way, Teddy. *(Slaps him.)*

CAPTAIN: Good God, Higgins, you're not on deck. Who's on watch?

SAILOR: I can't do everything.

VICTORIA: Big boys don't sleep with their aunts, Teddy.

RICHARD: How could my son behave this way?

CAPTAIN: Higgins, report to deck at once. And put on your uniform. *(Exit Sailor.)*

VICTORIA: Harriet, Teddy is too young to be treated in a carnal manner.

LIDIA: You're right. But I see a solution.

RICHARD: You do?

VICTORIA: *(Sits; speaks with a true and deep yearning.)* I have always *longed* for a solution.

LIDIA: The Captain can marry us all. Ship captains can do that, can't they?

CAPTAIN: But only on board ship.

(All look deeply disappointed; then Lidia with irritation snaps them out of it.)

LIDIA: Well, then that's perfect!

VICTORIA: Oh Harriet, what a wonderful idea.

TEDDY: Do I have to, Daddy?

RICHARD: Shush, Dorothy. Act your age.

CAPTAIN: I do have to bury my wife at dawn.

LIDIA: What better time. A burial, that's death; and a marriage, that's life.

VICTORIA: At dawn.

TEDDY: Who's steering the ship now?

CAPTAIN: I could check.

VICTORIA: Don't bother. First, let's have that tea.

(They sit and wait. Fog horn. Blackout.)

SCENE 10

*Deck of ship at dawn. Ship whistle. Rooster crows. Wedding march.
Enter the Captain. He is followed by the Sailor who is still in his underwear and is wheeling in a wrapped dead body on a hand cart. Enter
Richard, Teddy, Lidia, Victoria all wearing bridal veils. They stand in
front of Captain.*

CAPTAIN: Dearly beloved and dearly bereaved, we are gathered here to
bury my wife and we are gathered here today in the face of God to
join these men and these women in the holy sacrament of marriage,
which is an honorable estate. Bring my wife closer, Higgins, I shall
use her for inspiration.
(Sailor brings body closer.)
Some people might consider this ceremony sick. Who among you
think it is sick?
(Lidia and Teddy raise their hands. After a while, so does the Sailor.)
Well, I think that is wrong. Because you see, there is no right or
wrong. And thus my thinking your rejection is wrong because nothing is wrong. And nothing is right. We have passed from the rigid
law of the Old Testament—how many of you have read the Old
Testament?
(Richard and Sailor raise hands.)
—to the more humane law of love in the New Testament—how
many of you believe in love?
(Victoria raises her hand.)
—onward finally to the new nonexistent law of today, to the deep-
think of nothingness. If God is alive, he is a crackpot. If he's dead,
he's causing a terrible stink. How many of you know of the death
stench of Father Zossima in Dostoevsky?
(Sailor raises his hand.)
You're doing very well today, Higgins. Who can tell about these
things? Can you? Can I? I used to go to the movies with my wife,
and we wouldn't understand a *single* thing we saw on the screen.
(Pause.) Let me put it this way. Right or wrong, up or down, dead
or alive, I have no opinion on it either way because—who am I to
say? I'm nobody. Do what you want then because I have no advice
to give you. In the name of the Father, of the Son, and of the Holy
Spirit. Amen.

ALL: Amen.

CAPTAIN: Do you, Harriet, take this woman as your...*(Can't think of a word, moves on.)*...to amuse and enjoy, to frighten and destroy, 'til whatever time you cease being interested?

LIDIA: Yes.

CAPTAIN: And vice versa?

VICTORIA: Yes, thank you.

CAPTAIN: I pronounce you...married. And do you, Richard, take... *(Pause.)*

RICHARD: Dorothy, your Reverend.

CAPTAIN: Take Dorothy, to love and correct, to bend and erect, 'til things do you in?

RICHARD: I do.

CAPTAIN: And vice versa?

TEDDY: I do.

CAPTAIN: I pronounce you...man 'n' wife. You may kiss your son.

RICHARD: I have no son.

CAPTAIN: I can sympathize, having no wife or daughter. Though once I did...*(Gets teary.)*

SAILOR: Get a hold on, sir.

CAPTAIN: Before you all embark on your honeymoons below decks, I think I should tell you that Higgins here has graciously offered to marry my wife. However, I have not accepted his offer. It's touching when an enlisted man tries to warm an old man's heart, but we cannot lose our grip on reality. So as planned, I have ordered a full military burial for my wife and ask only to see her face one more time before we hurl her over. Higgins.

(Sailor brings body closer. Captain peeks under sheet.)

CAPTAIN: This isn't my wife! My wife wasn't Chinese!

RICHARD: Perhaps it's the effects of hanging.

CAPTAIN: Nonsense. My wife never wore a lotus blossom in her entire life. She'd sooner be found dead. Higgins, cancel the funeral. Oh, and take this thing with you. Toss it over first chance you get.

SAILOR: Yes, sir. *(Sailor exits with body.)*

CAPTAIN: Well, this has soured my day.

RICHARD: Now, now. Don't let it. Why don't you join us for dinner? We'll make it a fivesome.

CAPTAIN: Very well. I accept your invitation.

RICHARD: Good. Let's just get out of these wet things, and meet in the dining room.

(All start to exit. Richard catches Victoria.)

RICHARD: You see, Victoria, we're ending up at the Captain's table after all. Why, Victoria, you're crying.

VICTORIA: It's happiness. Or maybe the absence of it. Leave me by myself for a moment.

(All exit but Victoria.)

VICTORIA: Weddings make me cry. I guess I must be a sentimental goose. Harriet had a goose once, but I don't want to go into that. Isn't love a strange thing? I find it very humiliating. I love the movies, especially Jennifer Jones. *The Portrait of Jennie,* and the lighthouse and the hurricane. Teddy loves me. When all else fails, the love of a son for his mother is a sturdy thing. That was a *wonderful* movie. She was Eurasian in that one. Who was Eurasian? What am I talking about? *(Thinks for a while, but can't get a bead on what she was talking about; laughs.)* Sometimes when I don't make connections between statements, I worry. And sometimes I'm like the Captain, and I don't care.

(Blackout.)

SCENE 11

The Titanic *dining room. The Captain, Richard, Victoria.*

CAPTAIN: Where are your spouses?

VICTORIA: They're changing still, I guess. Richard, this is the second honeymoon we've had together, isn't it? I've always been fond of Richard.

RICHARD: Oh, here comes Higgins. Nice looking, don't you think, Victoria?

VICTORIA: Richard. You're worse than Dicky Miller.

RICHARD: I've never worn a tiara in my life.

CAPTAIN: What is it, Higgins?

SAILOR: Sir, there's a heavy fog out, and there's been a general warning about...

CAPTAIN: Higgins, I've told you to put these comments in the log. Stop worrying about the weather, son.

SAILOR: But...

CAPTAIN: Yes, I know. *Icebergs. (Cocks his head at Richard and Victoria, makes a little joke.)* But my wife's dead, that's taken care of *one* iceberg.

(Laughs lightly; Richard and Victoria don't really like the joke.)

CAPTAIN: By the way, have you found her body yet?

SAILOR: There are several waiting for your identification, sir.

CAPTAIN: I'm sure she's one of them. Good night, Higgins.

SAILOR: But sir...

CAPTAIN: That will be all.

(Sailor exits.)

VICTORIA: He seems a charming young man.

CAPTAIN: Bit of a stickler for the rules.

VICTORIA: Oh here come Harriet and Teddy.

(Enter Lidia and Teddy, dressed in mourning. They look attractive, very grown-up and somehow dangerous. Lidia's "mourning" in particular is disturbing—shiny black material, low-cut, sexy, but sort of perverse. She might be on her way to a Black Mass.)

VICTORIA: Oh.

TEDDY: Don't stand up.

LIDIA: Good evening.

VICTORIA: Oh, Harriet. You look like you're...in mourning.

LIDIA: Yes?

VICTORIA: But this is a celebration.

LIDIA: Well one should always be prepared for everything.

VICTORIA: Richard, she's acting hostile.

CAPTAIN: Here, here, let's keep our tempers. How about a jolly song, Lidia? I mean, Harriet.

VICTORIA: Yes, something festive.

RICHARD: Why are you wearing black, Teddy?

TEDDY: I'm in mourning for my life. *(Grins.)*

LIDIA: Song time. Come on, Teddy.

VICTORIA: Oh, good, this will be a celebration then.

(Teddy and Lidia get in place to sing. Enter the Sailor.)

SAILOR: Captain, an iceberg's been...

CAPTAIN: Hush, Higgins. They're singing.

TEDDY & LIDIA: *(Singing, alternating lines; to "Twinkle, Twinkle.")*

Hedgehog, hedgehog,
Burning bright,
In the forests of the night,
Hedgehog, hedgehog,
Can't you see?
You were always meant for me.
Who knows what I'm waiting for,
When I sit I feel quite sore,
Hedgehog, hedgehog, come with me,
Away, away to Innisfree.

LIDIA: In this next part of the song, Teddy plays the hedgehog.
(Teddy gets on his hands and knees. Lidia insinuatingly begins to lift her skirt. Teddy begins to crawl toward her as Lidia sings. The song is turning obscene.)

LIDIA: *(Lidia sings.)*
Teddy, Teddy,
You're alright,
In the forests of the night...

VICTORIA: *(Interrupting.)* Stop it! It's horrible.

SAILOR: Captain, I've sighted one. It's...

CAPTAIN: *(In a foul humor from the song too.)* Go away, Higgins!
(Sailor exits.)

VICTORIA: *(To Lidia.)* That wasn't a particularly winning song. Did you think it would be winning?

LIDIA: You didn't like it?

RICHARD: Now, now. Harriet always knew the off songs, we used to say.

VICTORIA: Well I'm sure you thought I'd like it. It was a nice gesture, Harriet. *(Having convinced herself.)* I loved it. Oh, I'm all aglow with happiness tonight.

LIDIA: Why, because I'm legally bound to you?

VICTORIA: Harriet, the wedding was your idea. *(Angry.)* And I wish you hadn't worn mourning.

RICHARD: Let's not bicker on our honeymoons. Let's start over. Harriet, you look ravishing.

TEDDY: What about me?

RICHARD: You're a nice looking boy, Teddy.

VICTORIA: I didn't know you had long pants, did you, Harriet?

LIDIA: Why don't you call me Annabella?

VICTORIA: What?

CAPTAIN: *(Embarrassed.)* I wonder if the orchestra would play something else.

RICHARD: What orchestra?

CAPTAIN: I don't know. I'll go check. *(Exits.)*

RICHARD: Harriet, I don't know why you're acting this way, but have the decency to control your tongue in front of the Captain.

TEDDY: You shouldn't talk about tongue at the table.

RICHARD: Teddy, are you trying to give us difficulty?

VICTORIA: Don't be harsh with Teddy, Richard, he's confused. Have you spoken to him about that bad word beginning with "m" yet? He's that age.

RICHARD: What bad word beginning with "m"?

VICTORIA: I'm embarrassed to say it.

RICHARD: What? Menstruation?

VICTORIA: No, silly, that's girls. Masturbation.

TEDDY: Oh, that bad word beginning with "m." I thought you meant "mother."

VICTORIA: *(Stunned.)* That's very unkind. *(Cries.)*

RICHARD: Look what you've done to your mother.

VICTORIA: Give me your leg, Teddy.

TEDDY: You shouldn't talk about leg at the table.

VICTORIA: This prepubescent temper tantrum is to stop this instant. GIVE ME YOUR LEG. *(She grabs his leg.)* You are obviously too young for long pants. *(Shrieking, Victoria tears off the bottom part of Teddy's pants legs, making his long pants now short pants. This is a sudden and insane motion, and is quite ferocious. Upon completion of her task, Victoria returns to a calm if strained manner.)* Harriet, you're very silent. As an adult, you should give Richard and me your support.

LIDIA: Why did you call me Harriet?

VICTORIA: What?

(Enter the Captain, with a dildo strapped to his nose.)

CAPTAIN: Guess who I am!

LIDIA: I thought you had caught on by now. Teddy caught on. I AM YOUR DAUGHTER ANNABELLA.

VICTORIA: What do you mean? There is no Annabella. It was a trick you and I played on Richard.

CAPTAIN: Guess who I am.

VICTORIA: *Hush,* we haven't time.

(Captain is abashed, sulks.)

LIDIA: I've tricked you, mother. You never had an affair with your sister Harriet. You had an affair with me. You don't even have a sister. You're an only child.

VICTORIA: I was a *lonely* child.

LIDIA: Teddy and I have been mistreated.

VICTORIA: This is all petty complaining, meant to distract from the main issue.

LIDIA: We're the main issue, we're the only issue.

VICTORIA: *(Slaps her.)* Don't you ever play with words that way again.

(Teddy slaps Victoria.)

VICTORIA: Teddy!

(Richard slaps Teddy.)

VICTORIA: Thank you, Richard.

(Lidia slaps Richard. Victoria slaps Lidia. Teddy slaps Victoria and Richard. They all slap one another, grow furious, throw food, and so forth)

RICHARD: *(Stopping it.)* Teddy, you're to go to bed at once, without supper.

CAPTAIN: Guess who I am!

RICHARD: Look, nobody cares.

CAPTAIN: I'm supposed to be Cyrano de Bergerac.

(Enter the Sailor.)

SAILOR: Captain! The iceberg!

CAPTAIN: Not now, Higgins.

SAILOR: Captain, we're done for.

(Sound of ship scraping the iceberg, water gushing in, sirens, and so on.)

VICTORIA: Richard, we're sinking.

RICHARD: Wait, maybe it's that record again.

CAPTAIN: Let's listen and see if the Captain says anything on the loudspeaker.

(They all listen. Nothing but the noises of sinking.)

CAPTAIN: Oh my God. *(Takes off dildo.)*

RICHARD: Victoria, this is the end.

VICTORIA: Richard, where did we go wrong?

RICHARD: Do you think we could try again?

(Orchestra plays "Nearer My God to Thee.")

VICTORIA: Richard, let's try.

(They sing "Nearer My God to Thee." Captain joins them. Lidia and

Teddy keep interrupting them. Sailor keeps trying to get the Captain away from the singing. Captain gets annoyed.)

VICTORIA, RICHARD, CAPTAIN: *(Singing.)*

Nearer my God to Thee,

Nearer to thee…

SAILOR: Captain, please, the lifeboats, sir…

CAPTAIN: Keep your pants on, for God's sake! *(Goes back to singing.)*

VICTORIA, RICHARD, CAPTAIN:

E'en though it be a cross,

That raiseth me,

LIDIA: *(Shouting over the singing.)* Teddy and I have an announcement!

RICHARD: We've heard quite enough from you, thank you.

VICTORIA: Teddy and you have both become spiteful.

VICTORIA, RICHARD, CAPTAIN:

Still all my song shall be,

Nearer my God to Thee,

Nearer my God to Thee,

Nearer to…

LIDIA: *(Shouting over the above singing.)* This isn't Teddy. There is no Teddy. This is my hedgehog. GO GET 'EM, HEDGEHOG!

(Victoria, Richard, and the Captain continue singing Teddy takes out a gun and shoots Victoria and Richard. The Captain does not notice.)

RICHARD: *(Dying.)* Victoria.

VICTORIA: *(Dying.)* Richard.

(Blackout. In blackout, the sounds of sinking continue until suddenly we hear the sound of a needle being knocked off a record and then silence.)

VOICE OF CAPTAIN: This is your Captain speaking. Everything is all right again.

SCENE 12

Same as before. The dead bodies of Victoria and Richard have been propped up in chairs, side by side for the coming funeral. Teddy and Lidia are apart by themselves.

LIDIA: We keep almost sinking.

TEDDY: I wonder where I got the gun.

LIDIA: Do you think the Captain noticed who shot them?

TEDDY: No. Do you?

LIDIA: No.

> *(Enter the Captain and Sailor. Captain wears a black arm band. Sailor perhaps has flowers for the two corpses. Captain speaks a eulogy.)*

CAPTAIN: We are gathered here to mourn the passing of Richard and Victoria Tammurai, passengers on the S.S. *Titanic* and fellow sea-farers on the voyage of Life. They were fine, worthy people, good manners, good stock, good breeding, generally the sort of people one would want to be passengers on one's boat. I remember the first time I met Mr. and Mrs. Tammurai. It was... *(Can't remember, becomes disturbed.)* Higgins...

> *(He and Sailor whisper for a bit; Sailor can't seem to help him.)*

TEDDY: *(During Captain's whispering.)* I feel better having killed them, don't you?

LIDIA: I miss my hedgehog. Listen! I think I hear something. Like the ship scraping an iceberg...

> *(They listen.)*

CAPTAIN: *(Having remembered; starting again.)* I first met Mr. and...

LIDIA: SSSSSHH! *(She and Teddy listen; Captain is insulted.)*

TEDDY: I don't hear anything.

LIDIA: Oh why won't we sink, why? *(To Captain.)* You can go on.

CAPTAIN: You've made me forget again. *(Sour humor.)* Higgins, the funeral's over. Throw them overboard.

SAILOR: Yes, sir.

LIDIA: Sssssh. *(Teddy and she listen.)* No.

SAILOR: *(Trying to budge them.)* I can't move them alone, sir. *(Looks at Captain and Teddy.)*

TEDDY: I don't want to touch them.

CAPTAIN: Well, I can't lift them, Higgins.

LIDIA: Sssssss. Listen. No.

SAILOR: But what shall I do?

CAPTAIN: *(Irritated.)* Well, we'll just have to let them sit here and decompose until they're lighter and you can lift them.

SAILOR: Yes sir.

CAPTAIN: This has been a most dissatisfactory...

LIDIA: Sssssh! *(Listens.)*

CAPTAIN: I do not wish to be shushed again, young lady.

LIDIA: I'm listening for the bottom to rip.

CAPTAIN: In my day young ladies occupied themselves in more constructive social activities. Higgins, bring me the log.

SAILOR: Yes sir. *(Gives it to him.)*

CAPTAIN: *(With great authority, glaring at Lidia.)* I am now going to enter a complaint against you in the log. What longitude and latitude are we, Higgins?

SAILOR: I don't know, sir.

CAPTAIN: No matter. *(Makes them up.)* Longitude 35, latitude 87. I hereby register a complaint against a certain young woman...
(Continues writing, moving his lips to himself. Sailor stands at attention.)

TEDDY: I'm going to wake up now. *(Closes his eyes, opens them again, hoping to have awakened out of a dream; he hasn't though; patiently he tries again; then again, this time pinching himself; he can't wake up; keeps trying.)*

LIDIA: Listen...
(She listens hopefully. Lidia keeps listening; Teddy keeps trying to wake up; Captain keeps writing in his log and moving his lips; Sailor stands at attention. Lights fade to black. End.)

The Actor's Nightmare

AUTHOR'S NOTE

I assume that most people who are in theatre, or even have just dabbled in it, have had these "actors' nightmares"—you dream that you have to go onstage, but for some reason you've never attended rehearsal and you don't know a single line.

After writing this play, I've learned that in psychological literature this dream is called "the good student's dream," and the prototype is the high school or college student, in life usually quite conscientious, who dreams that he has to take a test, but that he is totally unprepared: He has forgotten to study, or has lost his book, or he can't read the questions, and so on.

My personal variations have included dreaming I was playing Edmund in *Long Day's Journey Into Night*, and thinking to myself, well, I know the story, I just don't know the lines, maybe I can fake it. Or once dreaming I was acting at Yale Repertory Theatre, but that they had re-designed the backstage area so that I kept getting lost in hallways and couldn't find my way onto the stage. Or once dreaming I was in a musical that I knew nothing about—never rehearsed, never read it—and finding myself onstage needing to sing along with an orchestra, guessing at what the melody was, and ad-libbing lyrics, including some that rhymed. They didn't make sense, but they rhymed.

Recently I had the best actor's nightmare, for me at least. I have acted the role in *The Actor's Nightmare* twice (covering for my friend Jeff Brooks when he went on vacation from the Off-Broadway version); and in the dream I am about to go on in my own play as George Spelvin, but I haven't done it in over ten years, I haven't rehearsed it, and even though I'm the author, I'm not sure if I still know the lines. So I keep wandering about backstage looking for copies of the script—with minutes until I go on—but the stage manager for some reason doesn't have any copies of the play. I keep looking at the stage manager's book—which normally has the play being done—but it just has words and words on it, not my play, and when I read the words, they make no sense, my brain can't compute the meanings of what's on the page.

So it's from a lifetime of dreams like this that I wrote this play. And from hearing and enjoying the theatrical war stories of some friends who were understudies and had to go on with very short notice.

I also wrote the play specifically as a companion piece to *Sister Mary Ignatius*. For that purpose, I made sure the main character was male, that there was a meaty but very different, somewhat glamorous part for the actress who would play Sister Mary; and I also added some positive thoughts about religion, as spoken by the man reminiscing about his days at a monastery school.

ORIGINAL PRODUCTION

The Actor's Nightmare was first presented by Playwrights Horizons in New York City on a double bill with *Sister Mary Ignatius Explains It All For You* on October 14, 1981. The production was directed by Jerry Zaks; set design by Karen Schulz; costume design by William Ivey Long; lighting design by Paul Gallo; sound design by Aural Fixation; production stage manager was Esther Cohen. The cast was as follows:

George Spelvin. . . . . Jeff Brooks
Meg . . . . Polly Draper
Sarah Siddons . . . . Elizabeth Franz
Ellen Terry . . . . Mary Catherine Wright
Henry Irving . . . . Timothy Landfield

CHARACTERS
GEORGE SPELVIN, an accountant, 20s–30s
MEG, a stage manager, 25–30
SARAH SIDDONS, a grand actress
ELLEN TERRY, another actress, not as grand
HENRY IRVING, a grand actor

(Note: There is also the part of the Executioner, but I prefer that that part not be listed in the program. It is normally double-cast with HenryIrving, but you could have a separate actor do it if you preferred.)

During the subsequent run of *The Actor's Nightmare*, the following actors also joined the production: as George, Christopher Durang, Brian Keeler, John Short; as Meg, Carolyn Mignini, Brenda Currin, Madi Weland; as Sarah, Nancy Marchand, Mary Louise Wilson, Kathleen Chalfant, Lynn Redgrave, Patricia Gage; as Ellen, Deborah Rush, Alice Playten, Cynthia Darlow, Winnic Holzman, Angee Cockcroft; as Henry, Jeffrey Hayenga, Mark Herrier, Kevin O'Rourke. The understudies during the run included Claudette Sutherland, Merle Louise, Helen-Jean Arthur (all three for Sarah) and Mark Arnott, Tracey Ellis, Debra Dean, James Eckhouse, and Ian Blackman.

The final performance off-Broadway was January 29, 1984.

THE ACTOR'S NIGHTMARE

Scene: Basically an empty stage, maybe with a few set pieces on it or around it. George Spelvin, a young man, wanders in. He looks baffled and uncertain where he is. Enter Meg, the stage manager. In jeans and sweatshirt, perhaps, pleasant, efficient.

GEORGE: Oh, I'm sorry. I don't know how I got in here.

MEG: Oh, thank goodness you're here. I've been calling you.

GEORGE: Pardon?

MEG: An awful thing has happened. Eddie's been in a car accident, and you'll have to go on for him.

GEORGE: Good heavens, how awful. Who's Eddie?

MEG: Eddie.

(He looks blank.)

MEG: Edwin. You have to go on for him.

GEORGE: On for him.

MEG: Well, he can't go on. He's been in a car accident.

GEORGE: Yes I understood that part. But what do you mean "go on for him"?

MEG: You play the part. Now I know you haven't had a chance to rehearse it exactly, but presumably you know your lines, and you've certainly seen it enough.

GEORGE: I don't understand. Do I know you?

MEG: George, we really don't have time for this kind of joshing. Half-hour. *(Exits.)*

GEORGE: My name isn't George, it's…well, I don't know what it is, but it isn't George.

(Enter Sarah Siddons, a glamorous actress, perhaps in a sweeping cape.)
SARAH: My God, did you hear about Eddie?

GEORGE: Yes I did.

SARAH: It's just too, too awful. Now good luck tonight, George darling, we're all counting on you. Of course, you're a little too young for the part, and you are shorter than Edwin so we'll cut all the lines about bumping your head on the ceiling. And don't forget when I cough three times, that's your cue to unzip the back of my dress and then I'll slap you. We changed it from last night. *(She starts to exit.)*

GEORGE: Wait, please. What play are we doing exactly?

SARAH: *(Stares at him.)* What?

GEORGE: What is the play, please?

SARAH: Coward.

GEORGE: Pardon?

SARAH: Coward. *(Looks at him as if he's crazy.)* It's the Coward. Noel Coward. *(Suddenly relaxing.)* George, don't do that. For a second, I thought you were serious. Break a leg, darling. *(Exits.)*

GEORGE: *(To himself.)* Coward. I wonder if it's *Private Lives.* At least I've seen that one. I don't remember rehearsing it exactly. And am I an actor? I thought I was an accountant. And why does everyone call me George?

(Enter Dame Ellen Terry, younger than Sarah, a bit less grand.)
ELLEN: Hello, Stanley. I heard about Edwin. Good luck tonight. We're counting on you.

GEORGE: Wait. What play are we doing?

ELLEN: Very funny, Stanley.

GEORGE: No really. I've forgotten.

ELLEN: *Checkmate.*

GEORGE: *Checkmate?*

ELLEN: By Samuel Beckett. You know, in the garbage cans. You always play these jokes, Stanley, just don't do it onstage. Well, good luck tonight. I mean, break a leg. Did you hear? Edwin broke *both* legs. *(Exits.)*

GEORGE: I've never heard of *Checkmate.*
(Re-enter Meg.)
MEG: George, get into costume. We have fifteen minutes. *(Exits.)*
(Enter Henry Irving, age 28–33, also somewhat grand.)
HENRY: Good God, I'm late. Hi, Eddie. Oh you're not Eddie. Who are you?

GEORGE: You've never seen me before?

HENRY: Who the devil are you?

GEORGE: I don't really know. George, I think. Maybe Stanley, but probably George. I think I'm an accountant.

HENRY: Look, no one's allowed backstage before a performance. So you'll have to leave, or I'll be forced to report you to the stage manager.

GEORGE: Oh she knows I'm here already.

HENRY: Oh. Well, if Meg knows you're here it must be all right I suppose. It's not my affair. I'm late enough already. *(Exits.)*

MEG: *(offstage.)* Ten minutes, everybody. The call is ten minutes.

GEORGE: I better just go home. *(Takes off his pants.)* Oh dear, I didn't mean to do that.

(Enter Meg.)

MEG: George, stop that. Go into the dressing room to change. Really, you keep this up and we'll bring you up on charges.

GEORGE: But where is the dressing room?

MEG: George, you're not amusing. It's that way. And give me those. *(Takes his pants.)* I'll go soak them for you.

GEORGE: Please don't soak them.

MEG: Don't tell me my job. Now go get changed. The call is five minutes. *(Pushes him off to dressing room; crosses back the other way, calling out:)* Five minutes, everyone. Five minutes. Places.

(A curtain closes on the stage. Darkness. Lights come up on the curtain. A voice is heard.)

VOICE: Ladies and gentlemen, may I have your attention please? At this evening's performance, the role of Elyot, normally played by Edwin Booth, will be played by George Spelvin.

(Sound of audience moans.)

VOICE: The role of Amanda, normally played by Sarah Bernhardt, will be played by Sarah Siddons. The role of Kitty the bar maid will be played by Mrs. Patrick Campbell. Dr. Crippin will play himself. The management wishes to remind the audience that the taking of photographs is strictly forbidden by law, and is dangerous as it may disorient the actor. Thank you.

(The curtain opens. There is very little set, but probably a small set piece to indicate the railing of a terrace balcony. Some other set piece [a chair, a table, a cocktail bar] might be used to indicate wealth, elegance, French Riviera.

Sarah Siddons is present when the curtain opens. She is in a glam-

orous evening gown, and is holding a cocktail glass and standing behind the terrace railing, staring out above the audience's head. There is the recorded sound of applause.

After a moment George arrives onstage, fairly pushed on. He is dressed as Hamlet—black leotard and large gold medallion around his neck. As soon as he enters, several flash photos are taken, which disorient him greatly. When he can, he looks out and sees the audience and is very taken aback. We hear music.)

SARAH: Extraordinary how potent cheap music is.

GEORGE: What?

SARAH: Extraordinary how potent cheap music is.

GEORGE: Yes, that's true. Am I supposed to be Hamlet?

SARAH: *(Alarmed; then going on:)* Whose yacht do you think that is?

GEORGE: Where?

SARAH: The duke of Westminster, I expect. It always is.

GEORGE: Ah, well, perhaps. To be or not to be. I don't know any more of it.

(She looks irritated at him; then she coughs three times. He remembers and unzips her dress; she slaps him.)

SARAH: Elyot, please. We are on our honeymoons.

GEORGE: Are we?

SARAH: Yes. *(Irritated, being over-explicit.)* Me with Victor, and you with Sibyl.

GEORGE: Ah.

SARAH: Tell me about Sibyl.

GEORGE: I've never met her.

SARAH: Ah, Elyot, you're so amusing. You're married to Sibyl. Tell me about her.

GEORGE: Nothing much to tell really. She's sort of nondescript, I'd say.

SARAH: I bet you were going to say that she's just like Lady Bundle, and that she has several chins, and one blue eye and one brown eye, and a third eye in the center of her forehead. Weren't you?

GEORGE: Yes. I think so.

SARAH: Victor's like that too. *(Long pause.)* I bet you were just about to tell me that you traveled around the world.

GEORGE: Yes I was. I traveled around the world.

SARAH: How was it?

GEORGE: The world?

SARAH: Yes.

GEORGE: Oh, very nice.

SARAH: I always feared the Taj Mahal would look like a biscuit box. Did it?

GEORGE: Not really.

SARAH: *(She's going to give him the cue again.)* I always feared the Taj Mahal would look like a biscuit box. Did it?

GEORGE: I guess it did.

SARAH: *(Again.)* I always feared the Taj Mahal would look like a biscuit box. Did it?

GEORGE: Hard to say. What brand biscuit box?

SARAH: I always feared the Taj Mahal would look like a biscuit box. Did it? *(Pause.)* Did it? Did it?

GEORGE: I wonder whose yacht that is out there.

SARAH: Did it? Did it? Did it? Did it?

(Enter Meg. She's put on an apron and maid's hat and carries a duster, but is otherwise still in her stage manager's garb.)

MEG: My, this balcony looks dusty. I think I'll just clean it up a little. *(Dusts and goes to George and whispers in his ear; exits.)*

GEORGE: Not only did the Taj Mahal look like a biscuit box, but women should be struck regularly like gongs. *(Applause.)*

SARAH: Extraordinary how potent cheap music is.

GEORGE: Yes. Quite extraordinary.

SARAH: How was China?

GEORGE: China?

SARAH: You traveled around the world. How was China?

GEORGE: I liked it, but I felt homesick.

SARAH: *(Again this is happening; gives him cue again.)* How was China?

GEORGE: Lots of rice. The women bind their feet.

SARAH: How was China?

GEORGE: I hated it. I missed...Sibyl.

SARAH: How was China?

GEORGE: I...miss the maid. Oh, maid!

SARAH: *How was China?*

GEORGE: Just wait a moment please. Oh, maid!

(Enter Meg.)

GEORGE: Ah, there you are. I think you missed a spot here. *(She crosses, dusts, and whispers in his ear; exits.)*

SARAH: How was China?

GEORGE: *(With authority.)* Very large, China.

SARAH: And Japan?

GEORGE: *(Doesn't know, but makes a guess.)* Very...small, Japan.

SARAH: And Ireland?

GEORGE: Very...green.

SARAH: And Iceland?

GEORGE: Very white.

SARAH: And Italy?

GEORGE: Very...Neapolitan.

SARAH: And Copenhagen?

GEORGE: Very...cosmopolitan.

SARAH: And Florida?

GEORGE: Very...condominium.

SARAH: And Perth Amboy?

GEORGE: Very...mobile home, I don't know.

SARAH: And Sibyl?

GEORGE: What?

SARAH: Do you love Sibyl?

GEORGE: Who's Sibyl?

SARAH: Your new wife, who you married after you and I got our divorce.

GEORGE: Oh were we married? Oh yes, I forgot that part.

SARAH: Elyot, you're so amusing. You make me laugh all the time. *(Laughs.)* So, do you love Sibyl?

GEORGE: Probably. I married her.

(Pause. She coughs three times, he unzips her dress, she slaps him.)

SARAH: Oh, Elyot, darling, I'm sorry. We were mad to have left each other. Kiss me.

(They kiss. Enter Dame Ellen Terry as Sibyl, in an evening gown.)

ELLEN: Oh, how ghastly.

SARAH: Oh dear. And this must be Sibyl.

ELLEN: Oh how ghastly. What shall we do?

SARAH: We must all speak in very low voices and attempt to be civilized.

ELLEN: Is this Amanda? Oh, Elyot, I think she's simply obnoxious.

SARAH: How very rude.

ELLEN: Oh, Elyot, how can you treat me like this?

GEORGE: Hello, Sibyl.

ELLEN: Well, since you ask, I'm very upset. I was inside writing a letter to your mother and wanted to know how to spell apothecary.

SARAH: A-P-O-T-H-E-C-A-R-Y.

ELLEN: *(Icy.)* Thank you.

(Writes it down; Sarah looks over her shoulder.)

SARAH: Don't scribble, Sibyl.

ELLEN: Did my eyes deceive me, or were you kissing my husband a moment ago?

SARAH: We must all speak in very low voices and attempt to be civilized.

ELLEN: I was speaking in a low voice.

SARAH: Yes, but I could still hear you.

ELLEN: Oh. Sorry. *(Speaks too low to be heard.)*

SARAH: *(Speaks inaudibly also.)*

ELLEN: *(Speaks inaudibly.)*

SARAH: *(Speaks inaudibly.)*

ELLEN: *(Speaks inaudibly.)*

SARAH: I can't hear a bloody word she's saying. The woman's a nincompoop. Say something, Elyot.

GEORGE: I couldn't hear her either.

ELLEN: Elyot, you have to choose between us immediately—do you love this creature, or do you love me?

GEORGE: I wonder where the maid is.

ELLEN AND SARAH: *(Together, furious.)* Forget about the maid, Elyot! *(They look embarrassed.)*

ELLEN: *(Trying to cover.)* You could never have a lasting relationship with a maid. Choose between the two of us.

GEORGE: I choose...oh God, I don't know my lines. I don't know how I got here. I wish I *weren't* here. I wish I had joined the monastery like I almost did right after high school. I almost joined, but then I didn't.

SARAH: *(Trying to cover.)* Oh, Elyot, your malaria is acting up again and you're ranting. Come, come, who do you choose, me or that baggage over there.

ELLEN: You're the baggage, not I. Yes, Elyot, who do you choose?

GEORGE: I choose...*(To Sarah.)* I'm sorry, what is your name?

SARAH: Amanda.

GEORGE: I choose Amanda. I think that's what he does in the play.

ELLEN: Very well. I can accept defeat gracefully. I don't think I'll send this letter to your mother. She has a loud voice and an overbearing manner and I don't like her taste in tea china. I hope, Elyot, that when you find me hanging from the hotel lobby chandelier with my eyes all bulged out and my tongue hanging out, that you'll be very, very sorry. Good-bye. *(Exits.)*

SARAH: What a dreadful sport she is.

GEORGE: *(Doing his best to say something his character might.)* Poor Sibyl. She's going to hang herself.

SARAH: Some women should be hung regularly like tapestries. Oh who cares? Whose yacht do you think that is?

GEORGE: *(Remembering.)* The Duke of Westminster, I exp...

SARAH: *(Furious.)* How dare you mention that time in Mozambique? *(Slaps him.)* Oh, darling, I'm sorry. *(Moving her cigarette grandly.)* I love you madly!

GEORGE: *(Gasps.)* I've inhaled your cigarette ash.

(He coughs three times. Sarah looks confused, then unzips the front of his Hamlet doublet. He looks confused, then slaps her. She slaps him back with a vengeance. They both look confused.)

SARAH: There, we're not angry anymore, are we? Oh, Elyot, wait for me here and I'll pack my things and we'll run away together before Victor gets back. Oh, darling, isn't it extraordinary how potent cheap music can be?

(She exits; recorded applause on her exit. George sort of follows a bit, but then turns back to face the audience. Flash photos are taken again; George blinks and is disoriented. Lights change, the sound of trumpets is heard, and Henry Irving, dressed in Shakespearean garb, enters and bows grandly to George.)

HENRY: Hail to your Lordship!

GEORGE: Oh hello. Are you Victor?

HENRY: The same, my Lord, and your poor servant ever.

GEORGE: This doesn't sound like Noel Coward.

HENRY: A truant disposition, good my Lord.

GEORGE: You're not Victor, are you?

HENRY: My Lord, I came to see your father's funeral.

GEORGE: Oh yes? And how was it?

HENRY: Indeed, my Lord, it followed hard upon.

GEORGE: Hard upon? Yes, I see.

(Enter Meg.)

GEORGE: Oh, good, the maid.

(She whispers to him.)

GEORGE: Thrift, thrift, Horatio. The funeral baked meats did coldly furnish forth the marriage tables. What does that mean?

(Meg exits.)

GEORGE: Ah, she's gone already.

HENRY: My Lord, I think I saw him yesternight.

GEORGE: Did you? Who?

HENRY: My Lord, the king your father.

GEORGE: The king my father?

HENRY: Season your admiration for a while with an attent ear till I may deliver upon the witness of these gentlemen this marvel to you.

GEORGE: I see. I'm Hamlet now, right?

HENRY: *Sssh! (Rattling this off in a very Shakespearean way:)*
    Two nights together had these gentlemen,
    Marcellus and Bernardo, on their watch
    In the dead waste and middle of the night
    Been thus encountered. A figure like your father,
    Arméd at point exactly, cap-a-pe,
    Appears before them and with solemn march
    Goes slow and stately by them. Thrice he walked
    By their oppressed and fear-surprised eyes
    Within his truncheon's length, whilst they, distilled
    Almost to jelly with the act of fear,
    Stand dumb and speak not to him. This to me
    In dreadful secrecy impart they did,
    And I with them the third night kept the watch,
    Where, as they had delivered, both in time,
    Form of the thing, each word made true and good,
    The apparition comes. I knew your father.
    These hands are not more like.

GEORGE: Oh, my turn? Most strange and wondrous tale you tell, Horatio. It doth turn my ear into a very...*(At a loss.)* merry...bare bodkin.

HENRY: As I do live, my honored lord, tis true,
    and we did think it writ down in our duty
    To let you know of it.

GEORGE: Well, thank you very much. *(Pause.)*

HENRY: Oh yes, my Lord. He wore his beaver up.

GEORGE: His beaver up. He wore his beaver up. And does he usually wear it down?

HENRY: A countenance more in sorrow than in anger.

GEORGE: Well I am sorry to hear that. My father was a king of much renown. A favorite amongst all in London town. *(Pause.)* And in Denmark.

HENRY: I war'nt it will.

GEORGE: I war'nt it will also.

HENRY: Our duty to your honor. *(Exits.)*

GEORGE: Where are you going? Don't go.

(Smiles out at audience. Enter Sarah dressed as Queen Gertrude.)

GEORGE: Oh, Amanda, good to see you. Whose yacht do you think that is?

SARAH: O Hamlet, speak no more.

Thou turn'st mine eyes into my very soul,

And there I see such black and grainéd spots

As will not leave their tinct.

GEORGE: I haven't seen Victor. Someone was here who I thought might have been him, but it wasn't.

SARAH: Oh speak to me no more.

These words like daggers enter in mine ears.

No more, sweet Hamlet.

GEORGE: Very well. What do you want to talk about?

SARAH: No more! *(Exits.)*

GEORGE: Oh don't go. *(Pause; smiles uncomfortably at the audience.)* Maybe someone else will come out in a minute. *(Pause.)* Of course sometimes people have soliloquies in Shakespeare. Let's just wait a moment more and maybe someone will come.

(The lights suddenly change to a dim blue background and one bright white spot center stage. George is not standing in the spot.)

Oh dear. *(He moves somewhat awkwardly into the spot, decides to do his best to live up to the requirements of the moment.)* To be or not to be, that is the question. *(Doesn't know any more.)* Oh maid! *(No response; remembers that actors call for "line.")* Line. Line! Ohhhh. Oh, what a rogue and peasant slave am I. Whether tis nobler in the mind's eye to kill oneself, or not killing oneself, to sleep a great deal. We are such stuff as dreams are made on; and our lives are rounded by a little sleep.

(The lights change. The spot goes out, and another one comes up stage right. George moves into it.)

Uh, thrift, thrift, Horatio. Neither a borrower nor a lender be. But to thine own self be true. There is a special providence in the fall of a sparrow. Extraordinary how potent cheap music can be. Out, out, damn spot! I come to wive it wealthily in Padua; if wealthily, then happily in Padua. *(Sings.)* Brush up your Shakespeare; start quoting him now; Da da...

(Lights change again. That spot goes off; another one comes on, center stage, though closer to audience. George moves into that.)

I wonder whose yacht that is. How was China? Very large, China. How was Japan? Very small, Japan. I pledge allegiance to the flag of the United States of America and to the republic for which it stands, one nation, under God, indivisible with liberty and justice for all. Line! Line! Oh my God. *(Gets idea.)* O my God, I am heartily sorry for having offended thee, and I detest all my sins because I dread the loss of heaven and the pains of hell. But most of all because they offend thee, my God, who art all good and deserving of all my love. And I resolve to confess my sins, to do penance, and to amend my life, Amen.

(Friendly.) That's the act of contrition that Catholic school children say in confession in order to be forgiven their sins. Catholic adults say it too, I imagine. I don't know any Catholic adults. Line!

(Explaining.) When you call for a line, the stage manager normally gives you your next line, to refresh your memory. Line! The quality of mercy is not strained. It droppeth as the gentle rain upon the place below, when we have shuffled off this mortal coil. Alas, poor Yorick. I knew him well. Get thee to a nunnery. Line.

Nunnery. As a child, I was taught by nuns, and then in high school I was taught by Benedictine priests. I really rather liked the nuns, they were sort of warm, though they were fairly crazy too. Line. I liked the priests also. The school was on the grounds of the monastery, and my junior and senior years I spent a few weekends joining in the daily routine of the monastery—prayers, then breakfast, then prayers, then lunch, then prayers, then dinner, then prayers, then sleep. I found the predictability quite attractive. And the food was good. I was going to join the monastery after high school, but they said I was too young and should wait. And then I just stopped believing in all those things, so I never did join the monastery. I became an accountant. I've studied logarithms, and cosine and tangent...

(Irritated.) LINE!

(Apologetic.) I'm sorry. This is supposed to be *Hamlet* or *Private Lives* or something, and I keep rattling on like a maniac. I really do apologize. I just don't recall attending a single rehearsal. I can't imagine what I was doing. And also you came expecting to see Edwin Booth and you get me. I really am very embarrassed. Sorry. *Line!*

I have always depended on the kindness of strangers. *Stella!* It is a far, far better thing I do than I have ever done before. It's a far, far better place I go to than I have ever been before. *(Sings the alphabet song.)* a, b, c, d, e, f, g, h, i, j, k, l, m, n, o, p, q, r, s, t . . .

(As he starts to sing, enter Ellen Terry, dragging two large garbage cans. She puts them side by side, gets in one.)

GEORGE: Oh, good. Are you Ophelia? Get thee to a nunnery.

(She points to the other garbage can, indicating he should get in it.)

GEORGE: Get in? Okay. *(He does.)* This must be one of those modern *Hamlets.*

(Lights change abruptly to stark "Beckett lighting.")

ELLEN: Nothing to be done. Pause. Pause. Wrinkle nose. *(Wrinkles nose.)* Nothing to be done.

GEORGE: I guess you're not Ophelia.

ELLEN: We'll just wait. Pause. Either he'll come, pause pause pause, or he won't.

GEORGE: That's a reasonable attitude. Are we, on a guess, waiting for Godot?

ELLEN: No, Willie. He came already and was an awful bore. Yesterday he came. Garlic on his breath, telling a lot of unpleasant jokes about Jews and Polacks and stewardesses. He was just dreadful, pause, rolls her eyes upward. *(She rolls her eyes.)*

GEORGE: Well, I am sorry to hear that. Pause. So who are we waiting for?

ELLEN: We're waiting for Lefty.

GEORGE: Ah. And is he a political organizer or something, I seem to recall?

ELLEN: Yes, dear, he is a political organizer. He's always coming around saying get involved, get off your behinds and organize, fight the system, do this, do that, uh, he's exhausting, he's worse than Jane Fonda. And he has garlic breath just like Godot, I don't know which of them is worse, and I hope neither of them ever comes here again. Blinks left eye, blinks right eye, closes eyes, opens them. *(Does this.)*

GEORGE: So we're really not waiting for anyone, are we?

ELLEN: No, dear, we're not. It's just another happy day, pause, smile, pause, picks nit from head. *(Picks nit from head.)*

GEORGE: Do you smell something?

ELLEN: That's not your line. Willie doesn't have that many lines. *(Louder.)* Oh, Willie, how talkative you are this morning!

GEORGE: There seems to be some sort of muck at the bottom of this garbage can.

ELLEN: Mustn't complain, Willie. There's muck at the bottom of everyone's garbage can. Count your blessings, Willie. I do. *(Counts to herself, eyes closed.)* One. Two. Three. Are you counting, Willie?

GEORGE: I guess so.

ELLEN: I'm up to three. Three is my eyesight. *(Opens her eyes.)* Oh my God, I've gone blind. I can't see, Willie. Oh my God. Oh what a terrible day. Oh dear. Oh my. *(Suddenly very cheerful again.)* Oh well. Not so bad really. I only used my eyes occasionally. When I wanted to see something. But no more!

GEORGE: I really don't know this play at all.

ELLEN: Count your blessings, Willie. Let me hear you count them.

GEORGE: Alright. One. Two. Three. That's my eyesight. Four. That's my hearing. Five, that's my...Master Charge. Six, that's...

ELLEN: Did you say God, Willie?

GEORGE: No.

ELLEN: Why did you leave the monastery, Willie? Was it the same reason I left the opera?

GEORGE: I have no idea.

ELLEN: I left the opera because I couldn't sing. They were mad to have hired me. Certifiable. And they were certified shortly afterward, the entire staff. They reside now at the Rigoletto Home for the Mentally Incapacitated. In Turin. Pause. Tries to touch her nose with her tongue. *(Does this.)*

VOICE: Ladies and gentlemen, may I have your attention please?

ELLEN: Oh, Willie, listen. A voice. Perhaps there is a God.

VOICE: At this evening's performance, the role of Sir Thomas More, the man for all seasons, normally played by Edwin Booth, will be played by George Spelvin. The role of Lady Alice, normally played by Sarah Bernhardt, will be played by Sarah Siddons. The role of Lady Margaret, normally played by Eleanora Duse, will be read by the stage manager. And at this evening's performance the executioner will play himself.

GEORGE: What did he say?

ELLEN: The executioner will play himself.

GEORGE: What does he mean, the executioner will play himself?

(Lights change to Man for All Seasons *general lighting. Enter Sarah as Lady Alice [Sir Thomas More's wife], and Meg with a few costumed*

touches but otherwise in her stage manger's garb and carrying a script as Lady Margaret [Sir Thomas More's daughter]. Note: Though Meg starts by referring to her script, quite quickly it becomes clear that she knows the lines and does her best to play Sir Thomas' daughter with appropriate passion and seriousness.)

MEG: Oh father, why have they locked you up in this dreadful dungeon, it's more than I can bear.

SARAH: I've brought you a custard, Thomas.

MEG: Mother's brought you a custard, father.

GEORGE: Yes, thank you.

MEG: Oh father, if you don't give in to King Henry, they're going to cut your head off.

SARAH: Aren't you going to eat the custard I brought you, Thomas?

GEORGE: I'm not hungry, thank you.

(Sudden alarming crash of cymbals, or something similarly startling musically occurs. The Executioner appears upstage. He is dressed as the traditional headsman—the black mask, bare chest and arms, the large ax. The more legitimately alarming he looks the better. He can be played by the same actor who plays Henry Irving if his build and demeanor are appropriate. If not, it is possible to have a different actor play this role.)

GEORGE: Oh my God, I've got to get out of here.

MEG: He's over here. And he'll never give in to the King.

GEORGE: No, no, I might. Quick, is this all about Anne Boleyn and everything?

MEG: Yes, and you won't give in because you believe in the Catholic Church and the infallibility of the Pope and the everlasting life of the soul.

GEORGE: I don't necessarily believe in any of that. *(To Executioner.)* Oh, sir, there's been an error. I think it's fine if the King marries Anne Boleyn. I just want to wake up.

MEG: Oh don't deny God, father, just to spare our feelings. Mother and I are willing to have you dead if it's a question of principle.

SARAH: The first batch of custard didn't come out all that well, Thomas. This is the second batch. But it has a piece of hair in it, I think.

GEORGE: Oh shut up about your custard, would you? I don't think the Pope is infallible at all. I think he's a normal man with normal capabilities who wears gold slippers. I thought about joining the monastery when I was younger, but I didn't do it.

ELLEN: *(Waking up from a brief doze.)* Oh I was having such a pleasant dream, Willie. Go ahead, let him cut your head off, it'll be a nice change of pace.

(The Executioner, who has been motionless, now moves. In a sudden gesture, he reveals the cutting block that waits for George's head. Note: In the Playwrights Horizons production, our set designer constructed a square furniture piece that doubled as a settee and/or small cocktail table during the Private Lives *section. However, when the Executioner kicked the top of it, the piece fell open, revealing itself to contain a bloodied cutting block.)*

GEORGE: That blade looks very real to me. I want to wake up now. Or change plays. I wonder whose yacht that is out there.

(Sarah offers him the custard again.)

GEORGE: *No, thank you!* A horse, a horse! My kingdom for a horse!

EXECUTIONER: Sir Thomas More, you have been found guilty of the charge of High Treason. The sentence of the court is that you be taken to the Tower of London, thence to the place of execution, and there your head shall be stricken from your body, and may God have mercy on your soul.

(Meg helps George out of the garbage can.)

GEORGE: All this talk about God. All right, I'm sorry I didn't go to the monastery, maybe I should have, and I'm sorry I giggled during Mass in third grade, but I see no reason to be killed for it.

ELLEN: Nothing to be done. That's what I find so wonderful.

(Meg puts George's head on the block.)

GEORGE: No!

EXECUTIONER: Do I understand you right? You wish to reverse your previous stand on King Henry's marriage to Anne and to deny the Bishop of Rome?

GEORGE: Yes, yes, God, yes. I could care less. Let him marry eight wives.

EXECUTIONER: That's a terrible legacy of cowardice for Sir Thomas More to leave behind.

GEORGE: I don't care.

EXECUTIONER: I'm going to ignore what you've said and cut your head off anyway, and then we'll all pretend you went to your death nobly. The Church needs its saints, and school children have got to have heroes to look up to, don't you all agree?

ELLEN: I agree. I know I need someone to look up to. Pause smile picks her nose. *(Does this.)*

GEORGE: Yes, yes, I can feel myself waking up now. The covers have fallen off the bed, and I'm cold, and I'm going to wake up so that I can reach down and pull them up again.

EXFCUTIONER: Sir Thomas, prepare to meet your death.

GEORGE: Be quiet. I am about to wake up.

EXECUTIONER: Sir Thomas, prepare to meet your death.

GEORGE: I'm awake!

(Looks around him. Sarah offers him custard again.)

GEORGE: No, I'm not.

SARAH: He doesn't know his lines.

EXECUTIONER: Sir Thomas, prepare to meet your death.

GEORGE: Line! Line!

MEG: You turn to the executioner and say, "Friend, be not afraid of your office. You send me to God."

GEORGE: I don't like that line. Give me another.

MEG: That's the line in the script, George. Say it.

GEORGE: I don't want to.

MEG: Say it.

ELLEN: Say it, Willie. It'll mean a lot to me and to generations of school children to come.

SARAH: O Hamlet, speak the speech, I pray you, trippingly on the tongue.

EXECUTIONER: Say it!

GEORGE: Friend, be not afraid of your office. You send me... Extraordinary how potent cheap music is.

MEG: That's not the line.

GEORGE: Women should be struck regularly like gongs.

MEG: George, say the line right.

GEORGE: They say you can never dream your own death, so I expect I'll wake up just as soon as he starts to bring the blade down. So perhaps I should get it over with.

MEG: Say the proper line, George.

(George kneels down.)

GEORGE: Friend, be not afraid of your office.

(Executioner raises his ax.)

ELLEN: Good-bye, Willie.

SARAH: Good-bye, Hamlet.

MEG: Good-bye, George.

EXECUTIONER: Good-bye, Sir Thomas.

GEORGE: You send me to God. *(Executioner raises the ax to bring it down. Blackout. Sound of the ax coming down.)*

EXECUTIONER: *(In darkness.)* Behold the head of Sir Thomas More.

ELLEN: *(In darkness.)* Oh I wish I weren't blind and could see that, Willie. Oh well, no matter. It's still been another happy day. Pause, smile, wrinkles nose, pause, picks nit from head, pause, pause, wiggles ears, all in darkness, utterly useless, no one can see her. She stares ahead. Count two. End of play.

(Music plays. Maybe canned applause. Lights come up for curtain calls. The four take their bows [if Henry Irving does not play the executioner, he comes out for his bow as well]. Sarah and Ellen have fairly elaborate bows, perhaps receiving flowers from the executioner. They gesture for George to take his bow, but he seems to be dead. They look disorientated and then bow again, and lights out. End.)

TO THE ACTOR

Normally this play is a lot of fun to do; and it seems to be my most popular play in high schools.

Auditioning actors to play George Spelvin, I was surprised to see that it was kind of a hard part in some ways...or maybe I should put it another way: It didn't seem to be open to too many interpretations.

George says he's an accountant, and I think we should accept that. Some people get hung up by the thought that the play is George's "dream", and that it clearly shows he has more than average knowledge of theatre (Noel Coward, Beckett, Shakespeare), and so that maybe he really is an actor, but he's just dreaming he's an accountant.

Yes, yes, yes...that's all possible, but it seems way too complicated. The play works better if George is a true innocent who has wandered into this situation and who knows almost nothing of what's going on around him. (Indeed if he were actually an actor, he would probably make a better stab at the Noel Coward style than he does.)

So let George be an accountant...and I'm the author of the play, not George.

Another trap is to get stuck in playing George's fear. I have found that professional actors sometimes like to bring their own feelings about stage fright into the play, but it doesn't really fit with the comedy. During the ad-lib monologue in particular, if George starts going to too much angst, it becomes boring for us to watch.

Rather I think the part of George gives the actor a real opportunity for audience rapport and lightness. Once George gets over his initial shock at this crazy dream-like situation, he becomes involved with a "game"—he is trying to guess what might be the right thing to say next.

Along those lines, when he makes a good guess, I think it's perfectly acceptable that he smiles and nods at the audience, as if to say to them, "I'm actually doing okay now, aren't I?" Or when the Shakespeare starts and he hears a line like "He wore his beaver up," his total bafflement on how possibly to guess what this line means is also worthy of a look to the audience.

I have found if an actor focuses instead on George being fearful, that that makes the actor afraid to "bond" with the audience. And that's where a lot of the comedy and the fun lie.

Also, Jerry Zaks, who directed this play and *Sister Mary* (and several others of my plays), is always telling actors the wonderful advice that they should make "positive" choices. So if George is stuck in this fairly no-win situation, rather than choosing "fear" or a depressed "I can't win" attitude, there's a lot more energy and comedy in choosing the positive: Maybe I'll guess the next line right; well, even if it was wrong, it was a good try, wasn't it? And in the context of this dream play, George can kind of get into the "game" aspect of it all...the game is to guess the possibly right next line; and his attitude is also "game," he's willing to try all this.

If George has been sufficiently willing throughout the play (even through the Beckett, about which he has no idea: he's seen sophisticated comedy and Shakespeare, it seems, but not this absurdist tragedy), then when the executioner comes on, an actual fear can then be appropriate to play...something feels more threatening to George in this section. If he hasn't been playing strong fear up until then, it's a better switch.

Ellen's lines in the Beckett have normally gone well, but it's important that all her "pause, pause, wrinkle nose" sorts of lines are done with commitment as if they are appropriate lines. (The idea is that she is saying her stage directions aloud...though it's not meant to be that she's making a mistake, it's meant to be that that's how this play is done in this dream.)

Well, that's all.

Sister Mary Ignatius
Explains It All for You

I am happy to be ending this volume with this play. I think it and *The Marriage of Bette and Boo* are my two best plays so far.

Sister Mary Ignatius was an enormous step up in my career, both financially and critically.

I followed the critical debacle of *Titanic* with regional successes of a full-length play called *A History of The American Film.* This got such good reviews around the country and had such good word of mouth that I thought we had a really strong chance of succeeding on Broadway.

The year the play was scheduled to come in I was "hot" with movie offers and TV offers, all of which I turned down as not quite right. (Sometimes they were inappropriate offers—like being asked to write *Elvis-mania* for Broadway; other times they were viable offers that I chose not to pursue as too "conventional" or mainstream; I'm not sure if that's fear of success, or marching to my own drummer; not sure.)

Anyway, *A History of The American Film* got a good though flawed production; the reviews were not horrible, but they were just lackluster enough that we didn't sell tickets. And so it closed after two weeks' preview and two weeks' run.

And suddenly I wasn't "hot" at all. And I wasn't sure what writing I could do that would earn me money.

At the same time, my mother became quite ill. She had had breast cancer in 1972; she had been all right for a while, but then in 1976, they discovered she had bone cancer in her hip. This cancer was moving at an ambiguous pace—her doctors told me she had between one year to two years to ten years. But by 1978 the cancer was clearly getting worse. Her ability to walk was going; very poignantly, just about the last time she was able to walk was at the opening of *A History of The American Film* on Broadway. By the very next week, she couldn't walk at all.

Sudden death is a terrible way to go; and prolonged death is a terrible way to go. One way you don't have a chance to say good-bye. The other way, you have to watch the person inch bit by bit toward death; you have to watch the person try to deal with fear of the unknown and sorrow about not wanting to go; and you want, of course, to offer emotional comfort, but what comfort can you offer?

In 1978, I was twenty-nine and I had no religious beliefs. I had rejected the complex theology of my Catholic upbringing during my college depression. I just didn't believe there was a God up there, paying attention to what went on on earth in the way that the priests and nuns had taught us He did.

I didn't believe He sat up in heaven listening to antiwar protesters praying to stop the killing in Vietnam, to stop the dropping of napalm on people. Remember napalm? The burning gas from Dow Chemical designed to stick to the skin? I didn't believe God had anything to do with allowing or not allowing napalm; or the atom bomb; or the Holocaust; or an earthquake. But if He had nothing to do with any of human suffering, then I didn't know the point of praying; or the point of any of it.

But this isn't something you want to say to someone who's dying. "Yes, I think it's a great big empty void you're going to. So long!"

But what could I say to my mother? Or to anyone dying?

My mother's sisters would often say they were praying for my mother, and that I should pray. And I would think...and then what? God will say, "Yes, I will lessen her suffering today." Or He'll say, "No, I think I'll let it intensify today. How about I make her bones so brittle she breaks a leg just moving in bed? I think I'll do that today."

I know I'm describing a child's view of God really—and yet I think most (or many) adults who believe in God ascribe to this view of God.

And in my later years, Catholic school boy that I am at heart, I find myself becoming more open to more mystical interpretations of God.

But the highly anthropomorphic God I was raised on—the Father Figure in heaven, loving but with a bad temper, who watched over everybody and everything; who created original sin when Adam and Eve sinned, and then the only way He could expiate this sin was to offer up the sacrifice of His own son through gruesome torture—this view of God just didn't work for me.

But being around my mother and around her understandable panic, how I wished it did. How, at the time, I wished I could repeat soothingly, after death there's heaven, and you see all the people who've gone before you, and there's eternal life.

So my mother's impending death made me think a lot about religion, and what I grew up believing.

Looking back, I realized that the Catholicism of my childhood had an answer for absolutely everything—it was extremely thorough. I had this impulse to write a play in which a nun came out and explained *everything*—the nature and purpose of the universe, if you will, but as told through the prism of Catholic dogma.

When I stopped believing in God—for my very typical, young man–existentialist reasons—I stopped thinking about the rules of Catholicism that I had accepted as fact when I was a child.

But suddenly writing this play, I found myself re-steeped in the specifics of what I had been taught.

The church of the 1950s (and before) didn't teach a generalized sense that there was serious sin (like murder, say) and less serious sin (like telling a minor lie).

It was very specific, and very dogmatic. It didn't say, Christ said such and such, and we *interpret* that to mean x, y , or z. Instead, it said, Christ said this, and we as His representatives on earth are infallible because Christ said we were, and so everything we say is *fact*, not interpretation.

Well, I believed them when I was seven (and up until I was twenty). They were teaching me the facts of existence, not any interpretation.

And these "facts" were complicated, and built on top of one another.

The Church at that time offered an intricately woven set of specifics, on many topics and with many rules. On sin: There was something called mortal sin, which sent you to hell for eternity. And there was something called venial sin, which sent you to a place called purgatory to undergo some mild punishment for an unspecified time (though it seemed it might be long) until your sin was "worked off" and you were ready to be accepted into heaven. Purgatory was sort of like a jail sentence with an eventual parole into heaven; hell was like capital punishment, except dragged on for an eternity of hideous torture.

And then there were long lists of which sins were mortal, and which were venial. Murder was mortal. But also eating meat on Fridays was mortal. (Because Christ died on a Friday, the church felt we should fast and avoid meat on Fridays out of respect. This custom somehow got blown up into this "rule" with the threat of eternal punishment behind it. Kind of unreasonable, whoever thought it up. Doesn't sound too much like Christ. "Blessed are the peacemakers, but be sure to send to hell anyone who doesn't show me enough respect on Fridays." But at age seven I accepted what they said. And my family seemed to accept it even though they were in their fortiess.)

Anyway, I'm starting to rehash some of the material that is in the play. So I'm going to stop doing that.

But writing this play was a prime example of the old adage, "Write about what you know." My conclusions about the Catholic dogma of the 1950s are debatable and open to challenge; but you can't challenge, I hope, that I have the background and personal experience (of twelve years of Catholic schooling and religious instruction) to write this play.

By the way, this play was an enormous critical hit for me, and was the turning point when I started to be able to make a living as a writer.

It also, a year or so into its run in New York, started to cause controversy around the country, where some conservative Catholic groups claimed the play was "anti-Catholic" and wanted it shut down. I've written a bit about this aspect of the play's effect at the end of this book. These protests, which occurred especially between 1983 and 1986, are important and worrisome in terms of how we in this country are having serious and recurring problems tolerating difference of opinion.

But more on that later.

I wrote the first part of the play during my mother's final year. I wrote the second half of the play about six months after she died.

I didn't write the play "because" my mother died. But there's no question that thoughts about religion and dogma were triggered in me because of my mother's painful struggle with cancer.

And I wasn't angry when I wrote the play…though when I read it now, I can see that it seems angry sometimes.

My mother was an emotionally honest person. She wasn't wise in her handling of an alcoholic husband or in dealing with her disappointment that a blood incompatibility with my father precluded their having children after me. But I felt a real sense of security in my mother's willingness to tell me what she thought and felt. The bad side of this was I became her "confidante" at an early age; but that aside, it's pleasurable to be around honesty.

I feel I've followed my mother's example and have been emotionally honest in my writing about my Catholic upbringing. It's not all inclusive, it doesn't take in all the positive teachers I had (I really liked and learned from the Benedictine monks who taught me in high school, for instance)…but this play is not a *documentary* on all the varieties of people in the Catholic Church. Rather it is about the specific rules and dogma that the Church has been teaching for much of the 20th century; I question much of this dogma in my play, and I ask you to question it too.

Once again, looking back, it's my amazement that these rules were taught to me ages seven to thirteen as FACT that so startles me—that's what a lot of my upset and surprise comes out of; and that's what also fuels the satire in this play.

ORIGINAL PRODUCTION

Sister Mary Ignatius Explains It All for You was first presented by the Ensemble Studio Theatre, in New York City, on a bill with one-act plays by David Mamet, Marsha Norman, and Tennessee Williams, on December 14, 1979. Artistic director, Curt Dempster. The production was directed by Jerry Zaks; set design by Brian Martin; light design by Mary Louise Moreto; costume design by Madeline Cohen. The cast was as follows:

Sister Mary Ignatius . . . . Elizabeth Franz
Thomas . . . . Mark Stefan
Gary Sullavan . . . . Gregory Grove
Diane Symonds . . . . Ann McDonough
Philomena Rostovich . . . . Prudence Wright Holmes
Aloysius Busiccio . . . . .Don Marino

Sister Mary Ignatius Explains It All for You was then presented at Playwrights Horizons in New York City, on a double bill with *The Actor's Nightmare,* on October 14, 1981. Andre Bishop, artistic director; Paul Daniels, managing director. The production was designed by Jerry Zaks; set design by Karen Schulz; costume design by William Ivey Long; lighting design by Paul Gallo; sound design by Aural Fixation; production stage manager was Esther Cohen. The cast was as follows:

Sister Mary Ignatius . . . . Elizabeth Franz
Thomas . . . . Mark Stefan
Gary Sullavan . . . . Timothy Landfield
Diane Symonds . . . . Polly Draper
Philomena Rostovich . . . . Mary Catherine Wright
Aloysius Benheim . . . . Jeff Brooks

This production subsequently moved with the same cast to off-Broadway at the Westside Arts Theatre, where it played until January 29, 1984. During the subsequent run of *Actor's* and *Sister,* the following actors also joined the production:

As Sister Mary and Sarah Siddons: Nancy Marchand, Mary Louise Wilson, Kathleen Chalfant, Lynn Redgrave, Patricia Gage.

As Thomas: Guy-Paris Thompson, Evan Sandman, Damon Dukakis, Vaughan Sandman, Timmy Geissler.

As Gary and Henry Irving: Jeffrey Hayenga, Mark Herrier, Kevin O'Rourke.

As Diane and Meg: Carolyn Mignini, Brenda Currin, Madi Weland.

As Philomena and Ellen Terry: Deborah Rush, Alice Playten, Cynthia Darlow, Winnie Holzman, Angee Cockcroft.

As Aloysius and George Spelvin: Christopher Durang, Brian Keeler, John Short.

Understudies during the run included Claudette Sutherland, Merle Louise, Helen-Jean Arthur (all three for Sister Mary); and Mark Arnott, Tracey Ellis, Debra Dean, James Eckhouse, and Ian Blackman.

CHARACTERS
SISTER MARY IGNATIUS
THOMAS, her 7-year-old student
GARY SULLAVAN
DIANE SYMONDS
PHILOMENA ROSTOVICH
ALOYSUIS BENHEIM

SISTER MARY IGNATIUS
EXPLAINS IT ALL FOR YOU

Enter Sister Mary Ignatius, dressed in an old-fashioned nun's habit. Sister is of indeterminate age, though probably anywhere from 45 to a vigorous 65.

The stage is fairly simple. There should be a lectern, a potted palm, a chair to the side for Sister to sit on.

There is also an easel, or some sort of stand, on which are several drawings made on cardboard; the only one we can presently see is either blank or is a simple cross.

Sister crosses to the lectern and looks out at the audience until she has their attention. She then smiles, perhaps wearily, perhaps in a welcoming manner. Sister is charismatic and likes to address the audience. She makes the sign of the cross.

SISTER: *(Crossing herself.)* In the name of the Father, and of the Son, and of the Holy Ghost, Amen. *(Sister moves to the easel, and removes the cover drawing, revealing beneath it the first drawing for her lecture. It is a neat if childlike drawing of the planet earth, the sun and moon. She picks up a pointer and points to the picture.)*

First there is the earth. Near the earth is the sun, and also nearby is the moon. *(Sister smiles at the audience, and checks to make sure they have followed what she has said. She then removes the drawing, revealing the second drawing for her lecture.*

This picture is split in three: On top it shows the gates of heaven amid some clouds; in the middle it shows some sort of murky area of paths, or some other image that might suggest waiting, wandering; and on the bottom is a third area, showing people burning up in flames with little devils with little pitchforks, poking them.)

Outside the universe, where we go after death, is heaven, hell and purgatory.

(Points to the picture of heaven.)

Heaven is where we live in eternal bliss with our Lord Jesus Christ. *(Bows her head reverently; then points to the bottom part of the picture.)*

Hell is where we are eternally deprived of the presence of our Lord Jesus Christ... *(Bows her head again.)* ...and are thus miserable. This is the greatest agony of hell, but there are also unspeakable physical torments, which we shall nonetheless speak of later.

(Points to the central area of the picture.)

Purgatory is the middle area where we go after death to suffer if we have not been perfect in our lives and are thus not ready for heaven, or if we have not received the sacraments and made a good confession to a priest right before our death. Purgatory, depending on our sins, can go on for a very, very long time and is fairly unpleasant. Though we do not yet know whether there is any physical torment in purgatory, we do know that there is much psychological torment because we are being delayed from being in the presence of our Lord Jesus Christ. *(Bows her head again.)*

For those non-Catholics present, I bow my head to show respect for our Savior when I say His name. Our Lord Jesus Christ. *(Bows her head.)*

Our Lord Jesus Christ. *(Bows her head.)*

Our Lord Jesus Christ. *(Bows her head.)*

You can expect to be in purgatory for anywhere from 300 years to 700 billion years. This may sound like forever, but don't forget in terms of eternity 700 billion years does come to an end. All things come to an end except our Lord Jesus Christ.

(Bows her head; takes the pointer, and recaps what she has just explained to the audience.)

Heaven, hell, purgatory.

(Smiles; she now reveals the third prepared drawing, which, like that of purgatory, is of a murky area, perhaps with a prisonlike fence, and which has unhappy babylike creatures floating about in it.)

There is also limbo, which is where unbaptized babies were sent for eternity *before* the Ecumenical Council and Pope John XXIII. The unbaptized babies sent to limbo never leave limbo and so never get to heaven. *Now* unbaptized babies are sent straight to purgatory where, presumably, someone baptizes them and then they are sent on to heaven. The unbaptized babies who died before the Ecumenical Council, however, remain in limbo. Limbo is not all that unpleasant, it's just that it isn't heaven, and you never leave there.

(Puts the pointer down, finishes with the drawings for now; looks out to the audience with focus.)

I want to be very clear about the Immaculate Conception. It does not mean that the Blessed Mother gave birth to Christ without the prior unpleasantness of physical intimacy. That is true, but is not called the Immaculate Conception; that is called the Virgin Birth. The Immaculate Conception means that the Blessed Mother was herself born without original sin. Everyone makes this error, it makes me lose my patience.

That Mary's conception was immaculate is an infallible statement.

A lot of fault-finding non-Catholics run around saying that Catholics believe the Pope is infallible whenever he speaks. This is untrue. The Pope is infallible on only certain occasions, when he speaks "ex cathedra," which is Latin for "out of the cathedral."

When he speaks ex cathedra, we must accept what he says at that moment as dogma, or risk hell fire; or, now that things are becoming more liberal, many, many years in purgatory.

I would now like a glass of water. Thomas.

(Enter Thomas, a sweet-faced, obedient boy of age seven. He is dressed in a parochial school boy's uniform of gray dress pants, white shirt and navy blue tie, navy blue blazer. He hands Sister a glass of water. Sister proudly introduces Thomas.)

SISTER: This is Thomas, he is seven years old and in the second grade of Our Lady of Perpetual Sorrow School. Seven is the age of reason, so now that Thomas has turned seven he is capable of choosing to commit sin or not to commit sin, and God will hold him accountable for whatever he does. Isn't that so, Thomas?

THOMAS: Yes, Sister.

SISTER: Before we turn seven, God tends to pay no attention to the bad things we do because He knows we can know no better. Once we turn seven, He feels we are capable of knowing. Thomas, who made you?

THOMAS: *(Reciting his answers.)* God made me.

SISTER: Why did God make you?

THOMAS: God made me to show forth His goodness and share with us His happiness.

SISTER: What is the sixth commandment?

THOMAS: The sixth commandment is thou shalt not commit adultery.

SISTER: What is forbidden by the sixth commandment?

THOMAS: The sixth commandment forbids all impurities in thought, word or deed, whether alone or with others.

SISTER: That's correct, Thomas.

(Sister gives Thomas a cookie from her pocket, which he gratefully eats. Sister sips her water, and then addresses the audience again.)

SISTER: Thomas has a lovely soprano voice which the Church used to preserve by creating castrati. Thomas unfortunately will lose his soprano voice in a few years and will receive facial hair and psychological difficulties in its place. To me, it is not a worthwhile exchange. You may go now, Thomas.

(Sister gives Thomas back her glass of water, and he starts to leave. Sister abruptly calls out to him:)

SISTER: What is the fourth commandment?

(Thomas stops, turns out front, and recites the proper answer:)

THOMAS: The fourth commandment is honor thy mother and thy father.

SISTER: Very good.

(Sister offers him another cookie, which Thomas takes from her and then goes offstage, happy. Sister beams at him and at the audience. Thomas is clearly her favorite, prized student of the moment.

After smiling, she looks after him for a moment, then back to the audience.)

SISTER: Sometimes in the mornings I look at all the children lining up in front of school, and I'm overwhelmed with a sense of sadness and exhaustion thinking of all the pain and suffering and personal unhappiness they're going to face in their lives. *(Looks sad; eats a cookie.)*

But can their suffering compare with Christ's on the cross? Let us think of Christ on the cross for a moment. Try to feel the nails ripping through His hands and feet. Some experts say that the nails actually went through his wrists, which was better for keeping Him up on the cross, though of course most of the statues have the nails going right through His palms. Imagine those nails being driven through: pound, pound, pound, rip, rip, rip. Think of the crown of thorns eating into His skull, and the sense of infection He must have felt in His brain and near His eyes. Imagine blood from His brain spurting forth through His eyes, imagine His vision squinting through a veil of red liquid. Imagine these things, and then just *dare* to feel sorry for the children lining up outside of school.

We dare not; His suffering was greater than ours. He died for our sins! Yours and mine. We put Him up there, you did. *(Points accusingly at a member of the audience, chosen at random.)*

All you people sitting out there. He loved us so much that He came all the way down to earth just so He could be nailed painfully to a cross and hang there for three hours.

Who else has loved us as much as that?

(Looks at the audience to make sure they have understood the importance of her last remark; then:)

I come from a large family. My father was big and ugly, my mother had a nasty disposition and didn't like me; and there were twenty-six of us. It took three hours just to wash the dishes, but Christ hung on that cross for three hours and *He* never complained. We lived in a small, ugly house, and I shared a room with all of my sisters. My father would bring home drunken bums off the street, and let them stay in the same room as himself and my mother. "Whatever you do to the least of these, you do also to Me," Christ said. Sometimes these bums would make my mother hysterical, and we'd have to throw water on her. Thomas, could I have some more water please? And some chocolates?

(Thomas comes back with a full glass of water, and with a nice red box of chocolates.)

SISTER: *(To Thomas.)* Who made you?

THOMAS: God made me.

SISTER: What is the ninth commandment?

THOMAS: The ninth commandment is thou shalt not covet thy neighbor's wife.

SISTER: What is forbidden by the ninth commandment?

THOMAS: The ninth commandment forbids all indecency in thought, word and deed, whether alone or with thy neighbor's wife.

(Sister smiles at the audience, extremely pleased by Thomas' knowledge

and good example. He is a student to be proud of. Sister sips the water and looks at the chocolates Thomas is holding, and chooses one.)

SISTER: Thank you. Go away again.

(Thomas obediently exits.)

SISTER: Bring the little children unto me, Our Lord said. I don't remember in reference to what. *(Goes to the lectern and picks up a stack of 3 x 5 cards.)* I have your questions here on some little file cards.

(Sister smiles at the audience, and looks at the first card, which she reads aloud:) "If God is all powerful, why does He allow evil in the world?" *(Looks at the card a moment; then goes on to the next card with no reaction.)*

"Tell us some more about your family." *(Smiles; is happy to have been asked this.)*

We said grace before every meal. My mother was a terrible cook. She used to boil chopped meat. She hated little children, but they couldn't use birth control. Let me explain this one more time.

Birth control is wrong because God, whatever you may think about the wisdom involved, created sex for the purpose of procreation, not recreation. Everything in this world has a purpose. We eat food to feed our bodies. We don't eat and then make ourselves throw up immediately afterward, do we? So it should be with sex. Either it is done for its proper purpose, or it is just so much throwing up, morally speaking. Next question.

(Reads.) "Do nuns go to the bathroom?" *(Answers:)* Yes.

(Reads.) "Was Jesus effeminate?" *(Answers:)* Yes.

(Reads.) "I have a brain tumor and am afraid of dying. What should I do?" *(Faintly annoyed.)* Now I thought I had explained what happens after death to you already. There is heaven, hell and purgatory. What is the problem?

O ye of little faith, Christ said to someone.

All right. As any seven-year-old knows, there are two kinds of sin: mortal sin and venial sin. Venial sin is the less serious kind, like if you tell a small lie to your parents, or when you take the Lord's name in vain when you break your thumb with a hammer, or when you kick a barking dog. If you die with any venial sins on your conscience, no matter how many of them there are, you can eventually work it all out in purgatory.

However—mortal sin, on the other hand, is the most serious kind of sin you can do: murder, sex outside of marriage, hijacking a plane, masturbation. And if you die with any of these sins on your soul, even just one, you will go straight to hell and burn for all of eternity.

Now to rid yourself of mortal sin, you must go make a good confession and vow never to do it again. If, as many of you know, you are on your way to confession to confess a mortal sin and you are struck by a car or bus before you get there, God may forgive you without confession if before you die you manage to say a good act of contrition. If you die instantaneously and are unable to say a good act of contrition, you will go straight to hell.

Thomas, come read this partial list of those who are going to burn in hell.

(Thomas enters and crosses to Sister, who holds up a sheet of paper that was on the lectern. Sister hands him the paper, and Thomas reads it aloud.)

THOMAS: *(Reading.)* Christine Keeler, Roman Polanski, Zsa Zsa Gabor, the editors of *After Dark* magazine, Linda Lovelace, Gergina Spelvin, Big John Holmes, Brooke Shields, David Bowie, Mick Jagger, Patty Hearst, Betty Comden, Adolph Green.

SISTER: This is just a partial list. It is added to constantly. Thomas, how can we best keep from going to hell?

THOMAS: *(Recites.)* By not committing a mortal sin, by keeping close to the sacraments, especially going to confession and receiving communion, and by obeying our parents.

(Sister gives him a cookie.)

SISTER: Good boy. Do you love our Lord, Thomas?

THOMAS: Yes, Sister.

SISTER: How much?

THOMAS: *(Holds out his arms wide.)* This much.

SISTER: Well, that's very nice, but Christ loves us an infinite amount. How do we know that, Thomas?

THOMAS: Because you tell us.

SISTER: That's right. And by His actions. He died on the cross for us to make up for our sins. Wasn't that nice of Him?

THOMAS: Very nice.

SISTER: And shouldn't we be grateful?

THOMAS: Yes, we should.

SISTER: That's right, we should. *(Starts to give him a cookie, but suddenly pulls it back.)* How do you spell "cookie"?

THOMAS: C-o-o-k-i-e. Cookie.

SISTER: Very good. *(Gives him the cookie.)* Mary has had an argument with her parents and has shot and killed them. Is that a venial sin or a mortal sin?

THOMAS: That is a mortal sin.

SISTER: If she dies with this mortal sin on her soul, will she go to heaven or to hell?

THOMAS: *(Firmly.)* She will go to hell.

SISTER: Very good.

> *(Thomas reaches for a cookie, though Sister hadn't offered one. She smiles at the audience, and gets a cookie from her pocket; but before giving it to him asks him this:)*

SISTER: How do you spell "ecumenical"?

THOMAS: *(Sounds it out.)* Eck— "e-c-k." You— "u." Men— "m-e-n." Ical— "i-c-k-l-e." Ecumenical.

SISTER: Very good. *(Gives him the cookie.)* What's two plus two?

THOMAS: Four.

SISTER: What's one and one and one and one and one and one and one and one and one?

THOMAS: Nine.

SISTER: Very good. *(Gives him another cookie.)* Because she is afraid to show her parents her bad report card, Susan goes to the top of a tall building and jumps off. Is this a venial sin or a mortal sin?

THOMAS: Mortal sin.

SISTER: And where will she go?

THOMAS: Hell.

SISTER: Sit on my lap.

> *(Sister sits on the chair, and Thomas sits on her lap. She hugs him fondly.)*

SISTER: Would you like to keep your pretty soprano voice forever?

THOMAS: Yes, Sister.

SISTER: Well, we'll see what we can do about it. *(Sings; bounces him on her knees.)*

Cookies in the morning,
Cookies in the evening,
Cookies in the summertime,
Be my little cookie,
And love me all the time.

> *(Stops bouncing him.)* God, I've done so much talking, I've got to

rest. *(Hands Thomas her stack of file cards.)* Here, you take care of some of these questions, Thomas, and I'll sleep a little. All right? *(To audience.)* I'll just be a minute. *(Closes her eyes, takes a tiny cat nap.)*

THOMAS: *(Reading a card.)* "How do we know there is a God?"

(Recites the answer.) We know that there is a God because the Church tells us so. And also because everything has a primary cause. Dinner is put on the table because the primary cause, our mother, has put it in the oven and cooked it. *(Reads next card.)*

"If God is all powerful, why does He allow evil?" *(Pauses; skips to the next card.)*

"What does God look like?" *(Answers.)* God looks like an old man, a young man, and a small white dove.

(Sister, refreshed, opens her eyes.)

SISTER: I'll take the next one.

(Reads.) "Are you ever sorry you became a nun?"

(Looks at the audience; answers with great simplicity.) I am never sorry I became a nun.

(Reads the next card.) "It used to be a mortal sin to eat meat on Fridays, and now it isn't. Does that mean that people who ate meat on Fridays back when it was a sin are in hell? Or what?"

(Answers.) People who ate meat on Fridays back when it was a mortal sin are indeed in hell if they did not confess the sin before they died. If they confessed it, they are not in hell, unless they did not confess some other mortal sin they committed. People who would eat meat on Fridays back in the 50s tended to be the sort who would commit other mortal sins, so on a guess, I bet many of them *are* in hell for other sins, if they did confess the eating of meat.

(Reads.) "What exactly went on in Sodom?"

(Irritated.) Who asked me this question?

(Looks suspiciously at certain members of the audience, especially if they are two men sitting together; then skips ahead to the next question:)

"I am an Aries. Is it a sin to follow your horoscope?"

(Answers.) It is a sin to follow your horoscope because only God knows the future and He won't tell us. Also, we can tell horoscopes are false because according to astrology, Christ would have been a Capricorn, and Capricorn people are cold, ambitious and attracted to Scorpio and Virgo, and we know that Christ was warm, loving, and not attracted to anybody. Give me a cookie, Thomas.

(He gives her one of his; Sister looks thoughtful.)

SISTER: I'm going to talk about Sodom a bit. Thomas, please leave the stage.

(Thomas obediently gets up off Sister's lap and exits. Sister crosses back to center stage and addresses this problem that concerns her.)

SISTER: To answer your question, Sodom is where they committed acts of homosexuality and bestiality in the Old Testament, and God, infuriated by this, destroyed them all in one fell swoop. Modern day Sodoms are New York City, San Francisco, Amsterdam, Los Angeles... well, basically anywhere where the population is over 50,000. The only reason that God has not destroyed these modern day Sodoms is that Catholic nuns and priests live in these cities, and God does not wish to destroy them. He does, however, give these people body lice and hepatitis.

It's so hard to know why God allows wickedness to flourish. I guess it's because God wants man to choose goodness freely of his own free will; sometimes one wonders if free will is worth all the trouble if there's going to be so much evil and unhappiness, but God knows best, presumably. If it were up to me, I might be tempted to wipe out cities and civilizations, but, luckily for New York and Amsterdam, I'm not God.

(Reads next card.) "Why is St. Christopher no longer a saint, and did anyone listen to the prayers I prayed to him before they decided he didn't exist?"

(Answers; smiles warmly; she likes this saint.) The name Christopher means "Christ bearer" and we used to believe that he carried the Christ child across a river on his shoulders. Then sometime around Pope John XXIII, the Catholic Church decided that this was just a story and didn't really happen. I am not convinced that when we get to heaven we may not find that St. Christopher does indeed exist and that he dislikes Pope John XXIII; however, if he does not exist, then the prayers you prayed to him would have been picked up by St. Jude.

St. Jude is the patron saint of hopeless causes. When you have a particular problem that has little hope of being solved, you pray to St. Jude. When you lose or misplace something, you pray to St. Anthony. *(Reads.)* "Tell us some more about your family." *(Smiles again, pleased.)*

I had twenty-six brothers and sister. From my family five became priests, seven became nuns, three became brothers, and the rest were institutionalized. My mother was also institutionalized shortly after she started thinking my father was Satan.

(Telling a sweet story:) Some days when we were little, we'd come home and not be able to find our mother and we'd pray to St. Anthony to help us find her. Then when we'd find her with her head in the oven... *(Sister's voice cracks with sudden sadness.)* ...we'd pray to St. Jude to make her sane again. *(Goes to next question.)*

"Are all our prayers answered?"

(Sudden joyful energy:) Yes, they are! What people who ask that question often don't realize is that sometimes the answer to our prayers is "no."

"Dear God, please make my mother not be crazy." God's answer: No. "Dear God, please let me recover from cancer." God's answer: No. "Dear God, please take away this toothache." God's answer: All right, but you're going to be run over by a car.

(Full of faith and joy:) But every bad thing that happens to us, God has a special reason for. God is the good shepherd, we are His flock. And if God is grouchy or busy with more important matters, His beloved mother Mary is always there to intercede for us. I shall now sing the Hail Mary in Latin.

(Sister motions to the lighting booth, and the lights change to a pre-arranged special spotlight for her—atmospheric, close on her face, with lots of blue light surrounding her. The rest of the stage becomes fairly dim.

Sister sings with great reverence and faith. The "Ave Maria" can be either the Schubert version, or the Bach-Gounod version.

Depending on the actress, she may sing well or poorly, but the attitude is one of sharing a gift with the audience, and basking in her love for the Blessed Mother.)

SISTER: *(Sings.)*

Ave Maria,

Gratia plena,

Maria, gratia plena,

Maria, gratia plena, ... *(and so on).*

(As Sister sings, enter four people, ages 28–30. The four people are: a woman dressed as the Blessed Mother; a man dressed as St. Joseph; and a large camel [made up of two people, a woman playing the front, a man playing the back].

Because of the dim lights, we don't see this foursome too clearly at first.

Sister, in the midst of her singing, senses that someone has entered, looks over and sees this religious apparition and screams.)

ST. JOSEPH: We're sorry we're late.

SISTER: Oh dear God. *(Kneels.)*

ST. JOSEPH: Sister, what are you doing?

SISTER: You look so real.

ST. JOSEPH: Sister, I'm Gary Sullavan, and... *(Points to the person playing the Blesses Mother.)* ...this is Diane Symonds. We were in your fifth grade class in 1959, and you asked us to come today. Don't you remember?

SISTER: 1959?

GARY: Don't you remember asking us?

SISTER: Not very distinctly. *(Calls out to the lighting booth.)* Could I have some lights please?

(Stage lights come back bright as they were before Sister's "Ave Maria."

In the brighter lights, it is clear that the four people are in very homemade costumes such as one might see in a Biblical pageant.

Gary, playing St. Joseph, is dressed in a colored bathrobe, with a multicolored towel tied around his head, and carrying a staff.

Diane, playing the Blessed Mother, has a blue veil pinned to her head, a white sweater with pearl or rhinestone buttons, and a long white or blue dress.

The camel is played by Philomena and Aloysius, whom we don't see yet. It is made out of some brown material: The front legs belong to Philomena, and the back legs belong to Aloysius.

The head of the camel is actually a hand puppet at the end of Philomena's arm [the arm is the camel's neck]; and the humps are actually the heads of Philomena and Aloysius, covered with material in a baglike fashion. [They can see out of little eye slits that we maybe can't see.]

The face of the camel has large eyes and a sweet, somewhat goofy expression.

Sister, seeing in better light, looks at Gary, no longer frightened, but still a bit confused.)

SISTER: What did I want you to do?

GARY: You wanted us to put on a pageant.

SISTER: That camel looks false to me.

PHILOMENA: *(From the front of the camel.)* Hello, Sister.

SISTER: I thought so.

PHILOMENA: It's Philomena, Sister. Philomena Rostovich.

ALOYSIUS: *(From the back of the camel.)* And Aloysius Benheim.

SISTER: I don't really recognize any of you. Of course, you're not wearing your school uniforms.

DIANE: 1959.

SISTER: What?

DIANE: You taught us in 1959.

SISTER: *(Excited.)* I recognize you. Mary Jean Mahoney.

DIANE: I'm not Mary Jean Mahoney. I'm Diane Symonds.

SISTER: *(To the audience.)* This is all so confusing.

GARY: Don't you want to see the pageant?

SISTER: What pageant is it?

GARY: We used to perform it at Christmas in your class; every class did. You said it was written in 1948 by Mary Jean Mahoney, who was your best student, you said.

DIANE: You said she was very elevated, and that when she was in the 7th grade, she didn't have her first period, she had a stigmata.

SISTER: Oh yes. *(To audience.)* They discovered it in gym class. Mary Jean Mahoney. She entered a cloistered order of nuns upon her graduation from 12th grade. Sometimes late at night I can hear her praying. Mary Jean Mahoney. Yes! Let's see her pageant again.

(Upon that okay from Sister, the four students get in position to perform the pageant, including moving the easel and lectern if they need to.)

SISTER: *(To audience.)* She was such a bright student. I remember asking them to come now. I think. I wanted to tell you about Mary Jean Mahoney, and the perfect faith of a child. Yes, the pageant, please. Thomas, come watch with me.

(Sister sits in her chair on the side of the stage to watch the pageant. Thomas comes and joins her, and sits on her lap.

Gary blows a little flourish on a kazoo and begins the pageant. He, Diane, and the camel stand in a clump together.)

GARY: *(Announcing.)* The pageant of the birth and death of Our Beloved Saviour Jesus Christ, by Mary Jean Mahoney as told to Mrs. Robert J. Mahoney. The setting: a desert near Bethlehem. St. Joseph and the Virgin Mary and their trusty camel must flee from the wicked King Herod.

(Sister looks out at the audience, smiling. She always found Mary Jean's pageant charming, and she's hoping that they enjoy it as well.)

DIANE: *(Sings; to the tune of "We Gather Together To Ask the Lord's Blessings.")*
Hello, my name's Mary,
And his name is Joseph,
We're parents of Jesus,
Who's not been born yet.

We're fleeing from Herod,
And nobody knows if,
We'll make it to the town,
But we'll try, you can bet.

And I'm still a virgin,
And he's not the father,
The father descended
From heaven above,

And this is our camel,
(Camel nods to the audience.)
He's really not much bother,
We're off to Bethlehem,
Because God is love.

GARY: Here's an Inn, Mary. But there doesn't look like there's any room.

DIANE: Well, ask them, Joseph.

GARY: *(Knocks on imaginary door.)* Excuse me. You don't have room at your Inn, do you? *(Listens.)* I thought not… What? You would? Oh, Mary, this kind Innkeeper says that even though he has no room at the Inn, we can sleep in the stable.

DIANE: Do I look like a barn animal?

GARY: Mary, we really haven't any choice.

DIANE: Yes we do. *(Looks out front, sort of like Thomas does when answering questions.)* Sister says we have choice over everything, because God gave us free will to decide between good and evil. *(To Gary.)* And so I *choose* to stay in the stable.
(Sister looks out at the audience, amused by her mention in Mary Jean's pageant.)

GARY: Well, here it is.

DIANE: Pew.

GARY: I don't think there are any sheets.

DIANE: I don't need sheets, I'm so tired, I could sleep anywhere.

GARY: Well, that's good. Good night, Mary.

DIANE: But I do need pillows.

GARY: Mary, what can I do? We don't have any pillows.

DIANE: I can't sleep without pillows.

GARY: Let's pray to God then. If you just pray, He answers your prayers.

DIANE: Sometimes He says no, Joseph.

GARY: I know, but let's try.

    (They both kneel.)

GARY: Dear God, we beseech thee, hear our prayer.

DIANE: Pillows! Pillows! Pillows!

GARY: And behold, God answered their prayers.

CAMEL: *(Philomena.)* We have an idea, Mary and Joseph. We have two humps, and you can use them as pillows.

DIANE: Thank you, God. Come on, Joseph. Let's go to sleep.

    (The camel sits, and Gary and Diane lean against the two humps and go to sleep. The camel sings a lullaby:)

CAMEL: *(Philomena and Aloysius; singing.)*

Rockabye, and good night,

May God keep you and watch you,

Rockabye, and good night, *(and so on.)*

(Gary and Diane fall asleep. Aloysius makes baby crying noises, and then abruptly tosses a baby over his hump and onto the floor.)

DIANE: *(Seeing the doll, picking it up.)* Look, Joseph, He's born. Jesus is born.

    (All four stand and sing triumphantly.)

GARY, DIANE AND CAMEL: *(Singing.)*

Joy to the world, the Saviour's come,

Let earth receive her king,

La la la la la la-la-la,

La la la la la la-la-la,

(Softer.)

Let heaven and nature sing,

Let heaven and nature sing,

(Louder, triumphant.)

Let heaven, and heaven, and nature sing!

(Diane holds up the doll for Gary to speak to. The doll is a happy look-ing commercial doll with straight blond hair and blue eyes. It looks very American and not in anyway Christlike.)

GARY: *(To doll.)* Can you say Poppa, Jesus? Can you say Momma?

DIANE: He's not that kind of child, Joseph. He was born without original sin, like me. *(To the audience, sternly.)* This is called my Immaculate Conception, which is not to be confused with my Virgin Birth. Everyone makes this error, it makes me lose my patience.

(Sister shares a look with the audience, a little amused, a little chagrined. She knows the pageant is poking fun at her here, but she's big enough to accept a few jokes about some of her foibles.)

DIANE: *(Back to Gary.)* We must learn from Him, Joseph.

GARY: *(To audience.)* And so Jesus instructed His parents, and the priests in the Temple. And He performed many miracles.

DIANE: He turned water into wine.

GARY: He made cripples walk.

DIANE: He walked on the water.

GARY: And then came the time for His crucifixion. And His mother said to Him:

DIANE: *(To doll.)* But why, Jesus, why? Why must you be crucified? And what do you mean by "I must die so that others may know eternal life"?

GARY: And Jesus explained that because Adam and Eve, especially Eve, sinned, that mankind was cursed until Jesus could redeem us by dying on the cross.

DIANE: *(To doll.)* But that sounds silly. Why can't God just forgive us?

GARY: But Jesus laughed at her and said: "Yours is not to reason why, yours is but to do and die." And then He said, "But seriously, mother, it is not up to God to justify His ways to man; rather man must have total and complete faith in God's wisdom, he must accept and not question, just like an innocent babe accepts and doesn't question his parents." And then Mary said:

DIANE: *(To doll.)* I understand. Or rather, I understand that I am not supposed to understand. Come, let us go to Golgotha and watch you be crucified.

GARY: And Mary and the apostles and the faithful camel, whose name was Misty, followed Jesus to the rock of Golgotha and watched Him be nailed to a cross.

(Gary takes a previously hidden small wooden cross and places it on the ground.

He places the doll on the cross, and then takes a hammer from beneath his robe and pounds the floor next to the doll energetically.

Then he stands the doll upright, now attached to the cross.

The cheery, happy expression of the blond-haired doll looks eerie and incongruous hanging on the cross.

[Note: Gary can get the cross from either offstage, or from Aloysius, who can keep it under the camel costume. The doll can be attached using either Velcro, or using little elastic bands that attach to the doll's hands.]

Sister stares at this part of the pageant with a very disturbed expression.

In her recollection, when the children showed the doll being crucified, it always felt innocent and reverent, though childishly simple.

But with adults doing it now, and with the choice of this particular doll, it seems disturbing and inappropriate.

But she can't really decide if it's wrong or not. But she's made uncomfortable and faintly disapproving; and her facial expression shows this.)

GARY: And then He hung there for three hours in terrible agony.

DIANE: Imagine the agony. Try to feel the nails ripping through His hands and feet. Pound, pound, pound, rip, rip, rip. Washing the dishes for three hours is nothing compared to hanging on a cross.

GARY: And then He died.

(Sister bows her head in reverence, trying to keep in the spirit of the original pageant.

Gary moves the doll and the cross out of audience view. He then turns to Diane.)

GARY: He's dead now, Mary.

DIANE: *(Sad, lost.)* Oh.

GARY: Let's go for a long walk.

(They mime walking for a second.)

DIANE: Oh, Joseph, I feel so alone.

GARY: So do I, Mary.

DIANE: *(Sad, confused, truly wondering.)* Do you think He was just a nut? Do you think maybe the Holy Ghost isn't His father at all, that I made it all up? Maybe I'm not a virgin... Maybe... *(Holds her head in existential confusion.)*

GARY: *(To audience.)* But then Misty said:

CAMEL: *(Philomena.)* Do not despair, Mary and Joseph. Of course, He is God. He'll rise again in three days.

DIANE: Oh, if only I could believe you. But why should I listen to a dumb animal?

(The Camel gives Diane-Mary an annoyed head turn.)

CAMEL: *(Philomena.)* O ye of little faith.

DIANE: *(Sad.)* Oh, Joseph, I'm losing my mind.

GARY: *(To audience.)* And so Mary and Joseph and the camel hid for three days and three nights.

(Gary, Diane and the Camel run around in circles for a second, as they "run" and "hide.")

GARY: And on Sunday morning, they got up...

(They all stretch their arms, and yawn.)

GARY: ...and went to the Tomb where Christ was buried. And when they got there, standing by the Tomb was an angel. And the angel spoke.

ALOYSIUS: *(As voice of angel; he is still the back of the camel, however.)* Mary and Joseph! Your son has risen from the dead, just like your dumb animal Misty told you He would.

DIANE: Thank you, Misty, you were right! *(Kisses Misty's head.)*

GARY: And then Mary and Joseph, realizing their lack of faith, made a good Act of Contrition. And then Jesus came out from behind the tree where He was hiding, they spent forty days on earth enjoying themselves...

(Diane, Gary and the Camel sort of dance around happily in place.)

GARY: ...and setting the groundwork for the Catholic Church, and then Jesus, Mary, Joseph and Misty ascended into heaven and lived happily ever after.

(Diane and Gary, holding the happy doll between them, stand in front of the Camel. All four sing the final jubilant phrase of the "Angels We Have Heard On High" Christmas carol, as Diane and Gary mime ascension by waving their arms in a flying motion.)

DIANE, GARY, CAMEL: *(Singing.)* Glor-or-or-or-or-ia! In Excelsis Deo!

(All four bow. Sister applauds enthusiastically.

After their bow, the four students get out of their costumes and put them and their props offstage while Sister talks to them and to the audience.

Out of their costumes, we have a clearer sense who they are. Diane is attractive, plainspoken, a little serious, calm surface but with something going on underneath. She wears slacks or jeans, with a simple blouse, a nice blazer.

Gary is appealing looking, wears chinos, a nice shirt, maybe a loosened tie or even a vest—not corporate, sort of aging preppylike.

Philomena is sweet but nervous, shy. She wears a simple dress; she seems less together than Diane.

Aloysius is a little squarer than Gary; maybe dress pants, shirt, tie.)

SISTER: Oh, thank you, children. That was lovely. Thank you. *(To audience.)* The old stories really are the best, aren't they? Mary Jean Mahoney. What a good child. And what a nice reunion we're having. *(To the four students.)* What year did you say you were in my class again?

GARY: 1959.

SISTER: 1959. Oh, those were happy years. Eisenhower, Pope Pius still alive, then the first Catholic president. And so now you're all grown up. Let's do some of the old questions, shall we? *(To Aloysius.)* Who made you?

ALOYSIUS: God made me.

SISTER: Quite correct. *(To Philomena.)* What is the seventh commandment?

PHILOMENA: The seventh commandment is thou shalt not steal.

SISTER: Very good. What is contrition? *(To Diane.)* You.

DIANE: Uh… being sorry for sin?

SISTER: *(Cheerfully chastising.)* That's not how we answer questions here, young lady. Thomas?

(Thomas stands and answers with authority.)

THOMAS: Contrition is sincere sorrow for having offended God, and hatred for the sins we have committed, with a firm purpose of sinning no more.

DIANE: Oh yes. Right.

SISTER: *(Still kindly.)* For someone who's just played the Virgin, you don't know your catechism responses very well. What grade are you in?

DIANE: I'm not in a grade. I'm in life.

SISTER: Oh yes. Right. Well, cookies, anyone? Thomas, go bring our nice guests some cookies.

(Thomas exits.)

SISTER: It's so nice to see you all again. You must all be married by now, I imagine. I hope you all have large families like we encouraged?

PHILOMENA: I have a little girl, age three.

SISTER: That's nice.

ALOYSIUS: I have two boys.

SISTER: I like boys. *(To Gary.)* And you?

GARY: I'm not married.

SISTER: Well, a nice-looking boy like you, it won't be long before some pretty girl snatches you up. *(To Diane.)* And you?

DIANE: I don't have any children. But I've had two abortions.

(Enter Thomas with a plate of cookies.)

SISTER: No cookies, Thomas. Take them away.

(Thomas exits immediately. Sister is appalled at what Diane has said.)

SISTER: *(To Diane.)* You are in a state of mortal sin, young woman. What is the fifth commandment?

DIANE: Thou shalt not kill.

SISTER: You are a murderer.

DIANE: *(Unemotional.)* The first one was when I was raped when I was eighteen.

SISTER: Well I am sorry to hear that. But only God has power over life and death. God might have had very special plans for your baby. Are you sure I taught you?

DIANE: Yes, you taught me.

SISTER: Did I give you good grades?

DIANE: Yes. Very good.

SISTER: Have you told these sins in confession?

DIANE: What sins?

SISTER: You know very well what I mean.

DIANE: I don't go to confession.

SISTER: Well, it looks pretty clear to me, we'll just add you to the list of people going to hell. *(Calls offstage.)* Thomas, we'll put her name right after Comden and Green.

(Thomas appears when called; nods his head obediently.)

THOMAS: All right. *(Exits.)*

SISTER: *(Moves away from Diane.)* Somebody change the subject, I don't want to hear anymore about this.

GARY: *(Trying to oblige.)* Ummmmmmm… it certainly is strange being able to chew the communion wafer now, isn't it?

SISTER: What?

GARY: Well, you used to tell us that because the communion wafer was really the body of Christ, if we chewed it, it might bleed.

SISTER: I was speaking metaphorically.

GARY: Oh.

(Sister looks over at Diane.)

SISTER: Well, I still feel shaken by that girl over there. *(Wanting to change the atmosphere.)* Let's talk about something positive. *(To Philomena.)* You, with the little girl. Tell me about yourself.

PHILOMENA: Well my little girl is three, and her name is Wendy.

SISTER: There is no Saint Wendy.

PHILOMENA: Her middle name is Mary.

SISTER: Wendy Mary. Too many Y's. I'd change it. What does your husband do?

PHILOMENA: I don't have a husband.

(Long pause.)

SISTER: Did he die?

PHILOMENA: I don't think so. I didn't know him for very long.

SISTER: Do you sign your letters "Mrs." or "Miss"?

PHILOMENA: I don't write letters.

SISTER: Did this person you lost track of *marry* you before he left?

PHILOMENA: *(Sad.)* No.

SISTER: Children, you are making me very sad. *(To Philomena.)* Did you get good grades in my class?

PHILOMENA: No, Sister. You said I was stupid.

SISTER: Are you a prostitute?

PHILOMENA: Sister! Certainly not. I just get lonely.

SISTER: *(To Philomena and the audience both.)* The Mother Superior of my own convent may get lonely, but does she have illegitimate children?

ALOYSIUS: There was that nun who stuffed her baby behind her dresser last year.

(Sister stares at him.)

ALOYSIUS: It was in the news.

SISTER: No one was addressing you, Aloysius. Philomena, my point is that loneliness does not excuse sin.

PHILOMENA: But there are worse sins. And I believe Jesus forgives me. After all, he didn't want them to stone the woman taken in adultery.

SISTER: That was merely a *political* gesture. In private Christ stoned many women taken in adultery.

DIANE: That's not in the Bible.

SISTER: *(Suddenly very angry.)* Not everything has to be in the Bible! *(To audience, trying to recoup.)* There's oral tradition in the Church. One priest tells another priest something, it gets passed down through the years.

PHILOMENA: *(Unhappy.)* But don't you believe Jesus forgives people who sin?

SISTER: Yes, of course, He forgives sin, but he's *tricky.* You have to be *truly* sorry, and you have to *truly* resolve not to sin again, or else He'll send you straight to hell just like the thief He was crucified next to.

PHILOMENA: I think Jesus forgives me.

SISTER: Well I think you're going to hell. *(To Aloysius.)* And what about you? Is there anything the matter with you?

ALOYSIUS: Nothing. I'm fine.

SISTER: But are you living properly?

ALOYSIUS: Yes.

SISTER: And you're married?

ALOYSIUS: Yes.

SISTER: And you don't use birth control?

ALOYSIUS: No.

SISTER: But you only have two children. Why is that? You're not spilling your seed like Onan, are you? That's a sin, you know.

ALOYSIUS: No. It's just chance that we haven't had more.

SISTER: And you go to Mass once a week, and communion at least once a year, and confession at least once a year? Right?

ALOYSIUS: Yes.

SISTER: Well, I'm very pleased then.

ALOYSIUS: *(Somehow feels he has to be honest.)* I am an alcoholic. And recently I've started to hit my wife. And I keep thinking about suicide.

SISTER: *(Thinks for a moment.)* Within bounds, all those things are venial sins. *(To audience.)* At least one of my students turned out well. *(To Aloysius.)* Of course, I don't know how hard you're hitting your wife; but with prayer and God's grace...

ALOYSIUS: My wife is very unhappy.

SISTER: Yes, but eventually there's death. And then everlasting happiness in heaven. *(With real feeling.)* Some days I long for heaven. *(To Gary.)* And you? Have you turned out all right?

GARY: I'm okay.

SISTER: And you don't use birth control?

GARY: *(Trying to stay off the hook.)* Definitely not.

SISTER: That's good. *(Looks at him.)* What do you mean, "Definitely not"?

GARY: I... don't use it.

SISTER: And you're not married. Have you not found the right girl?

GARY: In a manner of speaking.

SISTER: *(Grim; choosing not to pursue it.)* Okay. *(Walks away, but can't leave it, comes back to him.)* You do that thing that makes Jesus puke, don't you?

GARY: Pardon?

SISTER: Drop the polite boy manner, buster. When your mother looks at you, she turns into a pillar of salt, right?

GARY: What?

SISTER: Sodom and Gomorrah, stupid. You sleep with men, don't you?

GARY: Well... yes.

SISTER: Jesus, Mary and Joseph! We have a regular cross section in here.

GARY: I got seduced when I was in the seminary.

(Sister looks horrified.)

GARY: I mean, I'd been denying it up to then.

SISTER: We don't want to hear about it.

GARY: And then when I left the seminary, I was very upset, and then I went to New York and I slept with five hundred different people.

SISTER: Jesus is going to throw up.

GARY: But then I decided I was trashing my life, and so I only had sex with guys I had an emotional relationship with.

SISTER: That must have cut it down to about three hundred.

GARY: And now I'm living with this one guy who I'd gone to grade school with and only ran into again two years ago, and we're faithful with one another and stuff. He was in your class too. Jeff Hannigan.

SISTER: He was a bad boy. Some of them should be left on the side of a hill to die, and he was one.

GARY: You remember him?

SISTER: Not really. His type.

GARY: Anyway, when I met him again, he was still a practicing Catholic, and so now I am again too.

SISTER: I'd practice a little harder if I were you.

GARY: So I don't think I'm so bad.

SISTER: *(Makes a "vomit" sound.)* Bleeeeeeeeeeeeggghhhhh. You make me want to "bleeeegghhh." *(To all four students, angry.)* Didn't any of you listen to me when I was teaching you? What were you all doing??? *(Mad; trying to explain the whole thing to them again:)* There is the universe, created by God. Eve ate the apple, man got original sin. Jesus said to St. Peter, "Upon this rock," rock meaning Peter, "I build my Church," by which He meant that Peter was the first Pope and that he and subsequent Popes would be infallible on matters of doctrine and morals. So your way is very clear: You have this infallible Church that tells you what is right and wrong, you follow its teaching, and then you get to heaven.

Didn't you all hear me say that? Did you all have wax in your ears? Did I speak in a foreign tongue? Or what???

And you've all sinned against sex... *(To Aloysius.)* ...not you, you're just depressed, you probably need vitamins... *(To the other three.)* But the rest of you! Why this obsession with sex? The Church has been very clear setting up the guidelines for you. *(To Diane and Philomena.)* For you two girls, why can't you marry one Catholic man and have as many babies as chance and the good Lord allows you to? Simple, easy-to-follow directions. *(To Gary.)* And for you, you can *force* yourself to marry and procreate with some nice Catholic girl—try it, it's not so hard. Or you can be celibate for the rest of your life. Again, simple directions. *(Suddenly in a fury.)* THOSE ARE YOUR OPTIONS!!! No others. They are your direct paths to heaven and salvation, to everlasting happiness. Why aren't you following these paths? Are you insane????

DIANE: *(Strong and clear.)* You're insane.

(Sister looks at Diane for a half a second.)

SISTER: You know, you're my least favorite person here today. I mean, the little effeminate one over there... *(Points to Gary, who is not effeminate, by the way.)* ...makes me want to "bleeeeggghh." But I can tell he once was nice, and he might get better with shock treatments and aversion therapy. But I can tell shock treatments wouldn't help you. You're fresh as paint, and you're nasty. I can see it in your face.

DIANE: You shouldn't be teaching children. You should be locked up in a convent somewhere where you can't hurt anybody.

SISTER: Me hurt someone. You're the one who runs around killing babies at the drop of a hat.

DIANE: It's a medical procedure. And even the Church admits it can't pinpoint *when* life begins in the womb. Why should you decide that the minute the sperm touches the ovum...

SISTER: Don't talk filth to me, I don't want to hear it. *(Pauses; suddenly very suspicious.)* Why did you all come here today? I don't remember asking you.

GARY: It was Diane's idea.

SISTER: What? What was?

PHILOMENA: We wanted to embarrass you.

ALOYSIUS: None of us ever liked you.

SISTER: What do you mean? My students always loved me. I was the favorite.

ALOYSIUS: No. We thought you were a bully.

SISTER: I was the *favorite.*

ALOYSIUS: You never let me go to the bathroom when I needed to.

SISTER: All you had to do was raise your hand.

ALOYSIUS: *(Argumentative.)* There were sixty children, and I sat in the back of the room; and I did raise my hand, but you never acknowledged me. Every afternoon my bladder became very full, and I always ended up wetting my pants.

SISTER: Big deal.

ALOYSIUS: I spoke to you about recognizing me sooner, and about my problem, but all you said then was "big deal."

SISTER: I remember you. You used to make a puddle in the last row every day.

ALOYSIUS: I have bladder problems to this day.

SISTER: What a baby. You flunked. I was giving you a lesson in life, and you flunked. It was up to you to solve the problem: Don't drink your little carton of milk at lunch; bring a little container with you and urinate behind your desk; or simply hold it in and offer the discomfort up to Christ. He suffered three hours of agony on the cross, surely a full bladder pales by comparison. I talk about the universe and original sin and heaven and hell, and you complain to me about bathroom privileges. You're a ridiculous crybaby. *(Cuffs him on the head.)*

PHILOMENA: You used to hit me too.

SISTER: You probably said stupid things.

PHILOMENA: I did. I told you I was stupid. That was no reason to hit me.

SISTER: It seems a very good reason to hit you. *(Looks out to the audience; wants to keep them on her side.)* Knock some sense into you.

PHILOMENA: You used to take the point of your pencil and poke it up and down on my head when I didn't do my homework.

SISTER: You should have done your homework. *(Smiles at the audience, as if to say "You have to be tough with these students.")*

PHILOMENA: And when I didn't know how to do long division, you slammed my head against the blackboard.

SISTER: Did I ever break a bone?

PHILOMENA: No.

SISTER: There you see! *(To Gary.)* And what about you?

GARY: You didn't do anything to me in particular. I just found you scary.

SISTER: Well I am scary. *(Gives conspiratorial look to the audience; she's scary, and it's a good thing to be.)*

GARY: But my lover Jeff doesn't like you cause you made him wet his pants too.

SISTER: All this obsession with the bladder. *(To Diane.)* And you, the nasty one, why did you want to embarrass me?

DIANE: *(Said simply.)* Because I believed you. I believed how you said the world worked, and that God loved us; and the story of the Good Shepherd and the lost sheep; and I don't think you should lie to people.

SISTER: But that's how things are. I didn't lie.

DIANE: *(Without too much emotion; presenting facts, so she can be understood.)* When I was sixteen, my mother got breast cancer, which spread. I prayed to God to let her suffering be small, but her suffering seemed to me quite extreme. She was in bad pain for half a year; and then terrible pain for much of a full year. The ulcerations on her body were horrifying to her, and to me. Her last few weeks she slipped into a semiconscious state, which allowed her, unfortunately, to wake up for a few minutes at a time and to have a full awareness of her pain and her fear of death. She was able to recognize me, and she would try to cry, but she was unable to; and to speak, but she was unable to. I think she wanted me to get her new doctors; she never really accepted that her disease was going to kill her, and she thought in her panic that her doctors must be incompetent and that new ones could magically cure her. Then, thank goodness, she went into a full coma.

A nurse who I knew to be Catholic assured me that everything would be done to keep her alive—a dubious comfort. Happily, the doctor was not Catholic, or if he was, not doctrinaire, and they didn't use extraordinary means to keep her alive; and she finally died after several more weeks in her coma. *(Somewhat to Sister, somewhat to the audience.)* Now there are, I'm sure, far worse deaths—terrible burnings, tortures, plagues, pestilence, famine; Christ on the cross even, as Sister likes to say.

But I thought my mother's death was bad enough, and I got confused as to why I had been praying, and to whom. I mean, if prayer was really this button you pressed—admit you need the Lord, then He stops your suffering—then why didn't it always work? Or ever work? And when it worked, so-called, and our prayers were supposedly answered, wasn't it as likely to be chance as God? *(To Sister directly.)* God always answers our prayers, you said, He just sometimes says no. But why would he say no to stopping my mother's suffering.

(Diane's voice becomes vulnerable here, and Sister takes her hand in sympathy.)

I wasn't even asking that she live, just that He end her suffering. And it can't be that He was letting her suffer because she'd been bad, because she hadn't been bad and besides suffering doesn't seem to work that way, considering the suffering of children who've obviously done nothing wrong.

(Takes her hand away from Sister; having momentarily accepted Sister's sympathy, she now rejects it.)

So why was He letting her suffer? Spite? Was the Lord God actually malicious? That seemed possible, but far-fetched. Maybe He had no control over it, maybe He wasn't omnipotent as you taught us He was. Maybe He created the world sort of by accident by belching one morning or getting the hiccups, and maybe He had no idea how the whole thing worked. In which case, He wouldn't be malicious, just *useless.*

(Sister starts to give up on trying to reach Diane here; she sees she's too far gone in her disbelief.)

Or, of course, more likely than that, He didn't exist at all, the universe was hiccuped or belched into existence all on its own, and my mother's suffering just *existed,* like rain or wind or humidity.

(Back directly to Sister again.) I became angry at myself, and by extension at you, for ever having expected anything beyond randomness from the world. And while I was thinking these things, the day that my mother died, I was raped.

(To audience.) Now I know that's really too much, one really loses all sympathy for me because I sound like I'm making it up or something. But bad things sometimes happen all at once, and this particular day on my return from the hospital, I was raped by some maniac who broke into the house. He had a knife and cut me up some.

Anyway, I don't really want to go on about the experience, but I got very depressed for about five years. Somehow the utter randomness of things—my mother's suffering, my attack by a lunatic who was either born a lunatic or made one by cruel parents or perhaps by an imbalance of hormones or whatever, etc., etc.—*this randomness seemed intolerable.*

(*To Sister.*) I found I grew to hate you, Sister, for making me once expect everything to be ordered and to make sense. My psychiatrist said he thought my hatred of you was obsessive, that I was just looking for someone to blame. Then he seduced me, and he was the father of my second abortion.

SISTER: (*To audience.*) I think she *is* making all this up.

DIANE: (*To audience.*) He said I seduced him. And maybe that's so. But he could be lying just to make himself feel better. (*To Sister.*) And, of course, your idea that I should have had this baby, either baby, is preposterous. Have you any idea what a terrible mother I'd be? I'm a nervous wreck.

SISTER: God would have given you the strength.

DIANE: (*To audience.*) I suppose it is childish to look for blame, part of the randomness of things is that there is no one to blame. (*To Sister.*) But basically I think everything is your fault, Sister.

SISTER: You have obviously never read the Book of Job.

DIANE: I have read it. And I think it's a nasty story.

SISTER: (*To audience and Diane both.*) God explains in that story why He lets us suffer, and a very lovely explanation it is too. He likes to test us, so that when we choose to love Him, no matter what He does to us, that proves how great and deep our love for Him is.

DIANE: That sounds like *The Story of O.*

SISTER: Well, there's obviously no talking to you. You don't want help or knowledge or enlightenment, so there's nothing left for you but an unhappy life, sickness, death, and hell.

DIANE: Last evening I killed my psychiatrist, and now I'm going to kill you.

(*Diane takes out a gun from a pocket in her blazer. Gary, Philomena, and Aloysius all look frightened and surprised; this had not been part of the plan.*)

GARY: (*Taken aback.*) Oh dear. I thought we were just going to embarrass her.

SISTER: (*Stalling for time.*) And you have, very much so. So no need to kill me at all. Good-bye, Diane, Gary, Aloysius…

DIANE: (*Pointing the gun at Sister.*) You're insane. You shouldn't be allowed to teach children. I see that there's that little boy here today. You're going to make him crazy.

SISTER: *(Calls.)* Thomas, stay offstage with the cookies, dear.

DIANE: I want you to admit that everything's your fault, and then I'm going to kill you.

PHILOMENA: Maybe we should all wait outside.

SISTER: Stay here. Diane, look at me. *(With great sincerity.)* I was wrong. I admit it. I thought everything made sense, but I didn't understand things properly. There's nothing I can say to make it up to you but... *(Sees something awful behind Diane's head.)* LOOK OUT!

(Diane turns to look behind her; Sister whips out her own gun and shoots Diane dead. Then like a circus artist completing a stunt, she throws her hands into the air:)

SISTER: Ta-da! *(Energetic, to the audience.)* For those non-Catholics present, murder is allowable in self-defense, one doesn't even have to tell it in confession. *(Calls out.)* Thomas, bring me some water.

GARY: We didn't know she was bringing a gun.

(Thomas brings in a glass of water to Sister.)

SISTER: I remember her from class now. *(Sips her water; looks at the dead body.)* She had no sense of humor.

ALOYSIUS: I have to go to the bathroom.

SISTER: *(Aims the gun at him.)* Stay where you are.

(Aloysius puts up his hands.)

SISTER: Raise your hand if you want to go to the bathroom, Aloysius, and wait until I have acknowledged you.

(She ignores him now, though keeps gun aimed at him most of the time; Aloysius raises up one hand and holds it up.)

SISTER: Thomas, bring me a cookie.

(Thomas gives her a cookie from his pocket.)

SISTER: *(To audience:)* Most of my students turned out beautifully, these are the few exceptions. But we never give up on those who've turned out badly, do we, Thomas? What is the story of the Good Shepherd and the Lost Sheep?

THOMAS: The Good Shepherd was so concerned about his Lost Sheep that He left his flock to go find the Lost Sheep, and then He found it.

SISTER: That's right. And while he was gone, a great big wolf came and killed his entire flock. No, just kidding. I'm feeling lightheaded from all this excitement. No, by the story of the Lost Sheep, Christ tells us that when a sinner strays, we mustn't give up on the sinner.

(Sister indicates for Thomas to exit, which he does.)

SISTER: So I don't totally despair for these people standing here. *(To*

Gary.) Gary, I hope that you will leave your friend Jeff, don't even tell him where you're going, just disappear. And then I hope you will live your life as a celibate. Like me. Celibate rhymes with celebrate. Our Lord loves celibate people. *(To Philomena.)* And you, Philomena, I hope you will get married to some nice Catholic man, or if you stay unmarried, then you too will become a celibate. Rhymes with celebrate!

ALOYSIUS: Sister, I have my hand up.

SISTER: Keep it up. And you, Aloysius, I hope you'll remember not to kill yourself, which is a mortal sin. For if we live by God's laws even though we are having a miserable life, remember heaven and eternal happiness are our reward.

GARY: Should we help you with the body, Sister?

SISTER: *(Disoriented for a moment, then:)* The janitor will help me later, thank you. *(To Gary and Philomena.)* You two may go now, so I can finish my lecture.

GARY: Why don't you let him go to the bathroom?

SISTER: *(Bothered by something.)* Gary?

GARY: Yes, Sister?

SISTER: You still believe what you do with Jeff is wrong, don't you? I mean, you still confess it in confession, don't you?

GARY: Well, I don't really think it's wrong, but I'm not sure, so I do still tell it in confession.

SISTER: When did you last go to confession?

GARY: This morning actually. I was going to be playing Saint Joseph and all.

SISTER: And you haven't sinned since then, have you?

GARY: No, Sister.

(Sister shoots Gary dead. Then throws her arms in the air for joy.)

SISTER: *(Triumphant.)* I have sent him to heaven! *(Points gun at Philomena.)* Okay, you with the little girl. Go home before I decide your little girl would be better off in a Catholic orphanage.

(Philomena rushes off in terror.)

SISTER: *(To audience:)* I'm not really within the letter of the law shooting Gary like this. But really if he did make a good confession, I have sent him straight to heaven and eternal, blissful happiness. And I'm afraid otherwise he would have ended up in hell. I think Christ will allow me this little dispensation from the letter of the law, but I'll go to confession later today, just to be sure.

ALOYSIUS: Sister, I have to go to the bathroom.

SISTER: Wait until I recognize you, Aloysius.

ALOYSIUS: *(Takes down hand.)* I'm going to leave now.

SISTER: *(Re-aims gun, angry.)* I've used this twice today, don't tempt me to use it again!

(Aloysius re-puts his one hand up in the air, afraid.)

SISTER: *(Calls.)* Thomas!

(Thomas enters.)

SISTER: Who made you?

THOMAS: God made me.

SISTER: Why did God make you?

THOMAS: God made me to show forth His goodness and share with us His happiness.

ALOYSIUS: If you don't let me go to the bathroom, I'm going to wet my pants.

SISTER: We all have free will, Aloysius. Thomas, explain about the primary cause again.

THOMAS: Everything has a primary cause. Dinner is put on the table because the primary cause...

SISTER: Thomas, I'm going to nap some, I'm exhausted.

(Puts her gun in Thomas' hands.)

SISTER: You keep that dangerous man over there covered, and if he moves, shoot him. And also, recite some nice catechism questions for us all while I rest. All right, dear?

THOMAS: Yes, Sister.

(Sister sits in her chair, exhausted by all the emotional excitement and activity.)

SISTER: Sit on my lap.

(Thomas sits on Sister's lap. He keeps the gun aimed at Aloysius, who stays with his hand up in the air. Sister takes comfort from Thomas' presence and his words. She smiles at the audience a bit, and holds him close while he recites:)

THOMAS: "What must we do to gain the happiness of heaven?"

To gain the happiness of heaven, we must know, love and serve God in this world.

(Lights start to dim.)

"From whom do we learn to know, love and serve God?"

We learn to know, love and serve God from Jesus Christ.

"What are some of the perfections of God?"

Some of the perfections of God are: God is eternal, all-good, all-knowing, all-present, and almighty.
(The lights have dimmed to black on the three figures: Aloysius with his hand up; Thomas aiming the gun and reciting his questions, Sister seated with Thomas on her lap. End.)

TO THE ACTOR

It's a mistake to have an actress play (or, worse, seem to be) mean...we see Sister kill two people at the end of the play, we shouldn't expect her to do so five minutes after we first see her. (There are places, of course, where Sister *should* be strident and bullying; but it should be underneath and revealed only sometimes.) Also, the strength and power of figures like Sister Mary (or, say, Jean Brodie) is in their charm; we believe them because they take us in. If Sister were obviously a horror, we'd know not to believe her.

In line with this, the relationship between Sister and Thomas should have warmth and even love. It's true that she presents him as one might present a dog doing tricks; and yet he does the tricks well, and she rewards him with not only cookies but warmth, approval, bounces on the knee, and so on. All this fondness and attention could easily make Thomas adore Sister.

The actress playing Sister should avoid commenting on her role. (All the actors should avoid commenting.) The humor works best when presented straight. That is, it's fine that we as an audience think it outrageous that Sister contemplates Thomas' castration to save his pretty voice; the actress should not indicate her own awareness of this outrageousness (that kind of comic-wink acting that is effective sometimes in a skit, rarely in a play). Sister thinks nothing is wrong with her contemplation, and it's only her feelings we should see.

I urge the actress to play that Sister really *does* want the best for her students, it's just that she feels she has the infallible truth on most matters and so is understandably confused and angered when here students turn out not to have followed her teachings. Thus, she should be *really* furious during what director Jerry Zaks and I call her "Bleegggggghhh!" speech (p.402); we often used this speech to audition understudies and replacements and found that it was important to see if the actress was willing to commit to the enormity of Sister's anger there; without Sister's out and out exploding at this point, the shape of the play goes off, and the seriousness of Diane's speech and the later killings will seem unprepared for and stylistically out of the blue.

Sister, like Mrs. Sorken, speaks densely, with many words. It's important to move through to the end of these speeches, to always remember the content of the "whole sentence," and not get bogged down staying too long on the by-ways of her thoughts.

In line with this, when Sister explains all the rules, much of the humor is in how matter-of-factly she says them. I don't mean for the whole part to be done in monotone or without affect; but I have seen the play become laborious if the actress chooses to color and emphasize every single adjective Sister has. For instance, "There are also unspeakable physical torments, which we shall nonetheless speak of later." most likely works best without coloring the words "unspeakable physical torments"; that way, the content of what she says is funny. (Common sense and acting intuition need to be added to following my notes; there are other places in the text where it would no longer be appropriate to only be matter-of-fact.)

Much of what I say in the notes to *Mrs. Sorken* in how to handle lengthy speeches and sentences also applies here.

Miscellaneous thought: "Celibate" does not rhyme with "celebrate," nor in my mind does Sister think it does. I prefer that she pronounce both words properly and then just says they rhyme because she wants them to; it sort of extends her power to say blatantly false things when she feels like it, to make a point (as when she says Christ stoned many women taken in adultery).

About Diane's speech: It is obviously meant seriously and has a high emotional content, but the actress should be careful how much emotion she lets through and when. In some auditions when actresses have chosen to rant and rave and weep, the speech has seemed ungodly. Diane's speech is very verbal, and very methodically point-by-point; hysteria is an illogical approach to the speech; if she were that hysterical, she couldn't be as verbal as she is, she'd just weep and weep.

It's useful to remember that what Diane is describing happened several years ago, and so some of the immediacy has faded; also, and importantly, Diana tries to *distance* herself from the pain she feels by being analytic. The tone of much of the speech, whatever underlying sadness comes through, should be factual: This happened to me, and then I thought that, but that wasn't true, so then I thought this and this, and so forth.

There are places where a more raw emotion can break through, but then I think it important that she gather herself back together and back to her "distancing" mode, until she finally shows her anger at Sister. (Her out-of-proportion anger by the way; when she says "Basically I think everything's your fault, Sister", the audience usually laughs; Sister is culpable of a lot, but every single thing that happened to Diane, it is inappropriate to blame on her. People offended by the play often assume I agree with every single thing Diane says; I only agree with a lot of it.)

Afterword

Sister Mary Ignatius Explains It All For You, after its critical success in New York, ran into censorship problems around the country starting in 1983.

Some Catholics felt offended by the play, and tried to shut it down in various cities. They asserted that the play was "anti-Catholic" and "bigoted" and ridiculed their beliefs.

"Anti-Catholic and bigoted." I was really startled and unprepared for these accusations. I was raised Catholic and went to Catholic schools for twelve years; though "lapsed," I still felt an identity as a Catholic.

In my high school years, 1963–67, I was very connected to my Catholic faith. This was the period of Pope John XXIII, who initiated the Second Vatican Council; this was a liberalizing movement in the church that wanted to "open the windows," to bring religion closer to the people. Along those lines, the Mass in Latin was changed to the Mass in the vernacular. Vatican II also wanted to stress the core of Christ's message over what had become rigid rules (just as Christ Himself disapproved of the Pharisees for valuing the letter of the law over the spirit.)

In high school, influenced by some of the younger priests at my school, I became very much a committed "liberal" Catholic. I questioned whether warfare could ever be moral; Christ after all said, Turn the other cheek, do not resist the evildoer. I started to wonder whether Ghandi and Martin Luther King, both proponents of nonviolence, were the true followers of Christ.

Like many people in the church, I began to question the Church's rules on sexuality. Any kind of sex outside of marriage was taught to be a mortal sin. But I started to believe that a couple who lived together in a loving relationship and who were engaged in their Christian calling to help people were more moral, in the spirit of the law, than was a couple who lived together, married but in mutual dislike, and who had no real interest or commitment to following Christ's commandment of love.

Caring about the poor and the needy was also highly important in this more liberal theology, based on countless things Christ said in the gospels—but which didn't show up much in the more rule-oriented teaching of the Church.

So in my own development, I went from the religion of rote when I was a child (following rules rather literal mindedly) to what seemed like a richer, more compassionate religion focusing on the more radical, love-affirming things that seem to be the main part of Christ's message.

And then, as I have indicated in other places, in college I lost my faith. This was for various reasons, having to do with personal sadness and depression, despair about people's ability to get on with one another, and a sudden lack of belief that God watched over us as I had been taught and wanted to believe.

Indeed, I remember the day I realized this had happened. At Harvard I regularly attended an experimental Mass at a Jesuit house. It was a small gathering, mostly of priests, nuns, and Divinity School students; and in place of the priest giving a homily, each person was free to share his or her thoughts, Quaker–meeting–style.

And this particular day, with Vietnam much on everyone's mind, this one young nun said that even though everyday the news showed more killing and suffering, and even though our leaders did not seem to be responding to the protests to stop the war, still she felt hope. And I thought to myself, I don't.

I just didn't feel hope anymore. So I stopped going to church, and I never recaptured that feeling of hope I used to have when I believed in a Divine Being overseeing all. (Though as I've said elsewhere, I have come to believe in a more mystical view of a Divine Intelligence that isn't as literal-minded as what I initially was stuck on.)

But during my "liberal" Catholic phase, I definitely considered myself a Catholic. And I felt alignment, as did many Catholic people in those days, with the sense of renewal and reform that had been started by the Second Ecumenical Council. I very much valued Pope John XXIII, and thought he was leading the church back to the original message of Christ in the gospel.

I wrote Sister Mary Ignatius 12 years after the day I felt hopeless at that mass.

I wrote it, looking back. And I wrote it from the same theological place I was in back when I was still a believing Catholic: I felt that the church I had grown up with had gotten stuck in rules, and that some of the rules were illogical, and some had misled people and caused them psychological pain.

I did not believe my views to be "anti-Catholic." These were the same views I held even as a practicing Catholic.

As to what I expected audience response to be, I guess I was naive. I thought most people would agree with me—the nitpicking rules of the pre-Vatican II church seemed false to me and not in alignment with Christ's teachings of love. And I've made it clear in the play how much Sister Mary Ignatius dislikes and disagrees with Pope John XXIII and the Vatican Council. She likes the old rules.

And I assumed that the people who didn't like the play or its point of view would simply dismiss it, avoid it, tell their friends not to go.

I did not expect that some of them would try to shut it down, or would say my play should not be performed in any theatre with tax funding. (Almost all theatre in America has some federal or state arts funding.)

So starting in 1982, protests against the play began. I'd like to give you a bit of their history because I think it's unusual, and because the arguments triggered by my play are still with us, and seem on the brink of destroying the National Endowment for the Arts.

CHRONOLOGY OF PROTESTS

Sister Mary Ignatius opened in the fall of 1981 at Playwrights Horizons Theatre in New York, was much acclaimed, and moved to an off-Broadway venue. It ran a bit over two years. In 1982, a successful production was done in Los Angeles and it ran a year.

In the fall of 1982 a small theatre in St. Louis, the Theatre Project, announced their intention to present *Sister Mary Ignatius* in January of 1983, in their rented space at the Mayfair Hotel.

The St. Louis chapter of the Catholic League for Religious and Civil Rights had heard of the play from New York City. They read the script, and then asked the Theatre Project to change their choice of the play, claiming *Sister Mary* was bigoted against Catholics. The Theatre Project refused.

The Catholic League approached the Mayfair Hotel, asking the management to cancel its arrangement with the Theatre Project.

The Catholic League then brought the play to the attention of the St. Louis Archbishop, John May, who wrote an editorial in a Catholic newsletter condemning the play as "a vile diatribe against all things Catholic." He urged St. Louis Catholics not to attend.

A few days later, the Mayfair Hotel withdrew from its tentative agreement with the Theatre Project, citing "technical difficulties."

Two local universities now offered their spaces to the Theatre Project; the privately funded Washington University and the publicly funded University of Missouri.

Senator Edwin L. Dirck, the democratic chairman of the Senate Appropriations Committee in the Missouri state senate, threw his support to the Catholic League in opposing the play.

He called in Arnold B. Grobman, the Chancellor of the University of Missouri, to ask him to defend his choice of allowing this "anti-Catholic" play to be done on property that was publicly funded.

Mr. Grobman responded he had allowed the Theatre Project to use space at the University in the past, and that "I don't tell them what plays to perform any more than I tell teachers what to teach or students what to read." He added that he didn't find the play anti-Catholic, but rather a satire on parochial education.

Senator Dirck told the newspapers that the Chancellor had "offended every member of the committee" and threatened budgetary reprisals.

The Theatre Project had a small grant from the Missouri State Arts Council—about three percent of its budget—and Senator Dirck also called in Talbot McCarthy, the chairperson of the Missouri Arts Council, to defend her action in having given a grant to a theatre doing "an anti-Catholic play."

Dirck warned McCarthy that the art council's funding was in jeopardy unless she took action against the Theatre Project; he wanted her to withdraw the grant.

McCarthy declined. She was quoted in the papers as being sorry she offended the Senate Committee, but said the Council made its grant decisions based on the past performance of theatre applicants, and that "our role is not to censor every work by the 500 groups we support."

By now this controversy was front-page news in St. Louis almost daily. The two major newspapers traded editorials back and forth, one in favor of the play's right to be performed, the other against. The play still hadn't opened.

National press followed: the *Charles Kuralt CBS News Sunday Morning, Entertainment Tonight, the Phil Donohue Show*. This publicity increased attendance at the box offices in New York and Los Angeles.

The play opened in St. Louis (to mediocre reviews actually) and sold out for its entire run. According to *Variety*, it was the first production in the Theatre Project's history to have made a profit.

The controversy didn't die down, and both newspapers continued to run editorials about the play. There were many emotional letters to the editors, pro and con.

In spring of 1983, Senator Dirck followed through on his threat to Talbot McCarthy. He put forth an appropriations bill cutting funds to the Arts Council by $60,000. He was quoted as saying that it would be better to give the funds to something more wholesome, like county fairs. This led to the rather amusing headline "Senate To Cut $60,000—Pigs More Wholesome Than Theatre." (And so they are.)

A rider was added to this bill, specifying that the Theatre Project in particular was never to be given a state arts grant again because it had presented the play.

In a close vote, the Missouri senate defeated the proposed arts council budget cut; but it overwhelmingly approved (22-8) the ban on future grants to the Theatre Project.

The American Civil Liberties Union was prepared to initiate a lawsuit if the ban stood. However, in subcommittee conference, the ban was killed and was not a part of the final bill.

In its place a letter of warning was written, warning the Arts Council to be more careful in the future to avoid funding any works that might cause offense.

And so concluded the St. Louis part of the *Sister Mary* story.

At the time, I considered the St. Louis events a fluke. But over the next several years, *Sister Mary Ignatius* caused controversy wherever it appeared, usually triggered by protests from the Catholic League for Religious and Civil Rights.

The next major incident occurred in the fall of 1983 in Boston. Elizabeth Franz was about to recreate her portrayal of Sister Mary at the Charles Playhouse.

The Catholic League tried to convince the management of the theatre to cancel the play. They also threatened to boycott another play at the same theatre, *Shear Madness*.

They approached the Mayor of Boston, Raymond L. Flynn. A couple of days before the play started previews, the Mayor released a statement "repudiating" the play and calling it "blatantly and painfully anti-Catholic."

The New England chapter of the Anti-Defamation League of the B'nai B'rith joined forces with the Catholic League, and released a statement to the press calling the play "offensive, demeaning, and misrepresentative of the Catholic faith and of those who believe and practice it."

The protests intensified during the preview period, with large picket lines and daily statements in the press and on television.

They defused some when it turned out to be totally commercial—there were no ties to tax funding and this precluded the tax money argument.

They defused further when the reviews came out. The reviews were extremely favorable, and, more importantly for the protests, many of the reviewers, including Catholic ones, expressed their opinion that the play was not anti-Catholic; it was antiauthoritarian.

A small picket line remained for most of the run, but the daily barrage on television and in the newspapers stopped, and the play was quite successful in Boston.

The Catholic League is a national organization, however, and trying to keep *Sister Mary Ignatius* from being performed had become one of the League's chief activities. Opposition to the play was listed on their flyers as one of the things they did. After Boston, other protests came fast and furious.

In Detriot a production of the play was canceled due to an organized letter-writing campaign. The producers just didn't want the hassle.

In Glen Ellyn, Illinios, a small college scheduled four performances of a student production and was unprepared for the sudden avalanche of animosity. The drama department received petitions with 2,000 signatures each from two parishes, urging the cancellation of the "bigotry." Intimations of lawsuits were made concerning the misuse of public funds.

The college, scheduled to host a well-known playwright later in the year, felt it could not retreat on the principle of free speech, and they did not cancel. A student threatened to disrupt each performance, though he did not follow through, and the four performances came and went. At their next meeting, the Board of Directors of the college were greeted by picketers holding large blow-up photos of each of the directors with the word "Bigot" scrawled across the face. The protest was photographed and published in the newspapers. The head of the drama department was told unofficially to avoid such controversy in the future.

A protest against a production of *Sister Mary Ignatius* in Erie, Pennsylvania. was heating up when the press revealed that the director was a Polish emigre who had come to America looking for "artistic freedom." So they backed down on that one.

An announced production of *Sister Mary* was canceled in Ponca City, Oklahoma, after a campaign that included: anonymous phone calls warning prominent citizens that the proposed play might "destroy" the community, a letter writing campaign to the theatre, attempts made to revoke the theatre's lease, ads in the newspaper advising "Catholics and all concerned Christians" to attend the theatre's next board meeting.

A local priest met with the theatre and expressed his concern over the perceived anti-Catholic conspiracy of the theatre due to the proposed *Sister Mary Ignatius* and the previous *Man of La Mancha,* which he felt was also anti-Catholic, citing its reference to the Spanish Inquisition. The theatre canceled the production.

In Coral Gables, Florida, a small production of the play was met with condemnation by both the local bishop and the city council. The theatre, undaunted, put on the play and it sold out. However, they received three death threats which included a picture of a car exploding and the words "Death to Infidels" as well as phone calls to the theatre's secretary warning her not to open letters addressed to the management as they might contain bombs.

Other protests continued. Sometimes the play would be canceled; sometimes it would sell out. There were always angry, unresolved emotions surrounding it.

I wanted to write this closing note to the volume because I think the protests that happened against Sister Mary Ignatius are important. The issue is what to do about speech we don't like or agree with. Do we suppress it? Or do we let it be, and counter it with other speech? My own belief is that suppression of speech is always dangerous. If you suppress my play today, I or others may try to suppress what you write tomorrow. This suppressing of speech is dangerous whether it comes from the right or the left. So don't do it. Speak up, protest, picket, write your own play or essay. But don't try to shut others up.

The Catholic League went on to sponsor protests against the movie *The Last Temptation of Christ.* In New Jersey there was a bomb threat against a theatre showing *Priest,* and the theatre owner canceled any further showings of the film. In St. Louis, a proposed college production of Larry Kramer's gay rights-AIDS play, *The Normal Heart,* so enraged someone in that community that they burned the student director's house to the ground. In Cobb County, Georgia, a production of Terrence McNally's play *Lips Together, Teeth Apart,* which received funding from a county arts commission, offended a local couple who complained to the city council. Then the city council disbanded the entire arts funding system.

I'd like to end with a story about the *Sister Mary* protests that I learned only recently.

At a Dramatists Guild function, I met Kitty Carlisle Hart, the actress wife of the late Moss Hart. Kitty Hart was the chairperson of the New York State Arts Council for many years, including the year that *Sister Mary Ignatius* played in New York City. After the St. Louis and Boston protest occurred, I learned that there had been a behind-the-scenes protest about *Sister Mary* in New York that preceded both of those events. I now had the opportunity to ask Ms. Hart about it personally.

Once again it was the Catholic League for Religious and Civil Rights, and they wanted the Arts Council to repudiate and/or penalize Playwrights Horizons, which received a grant from the Arts Council, for having presented *Sister Mary Ignatius.* Ms. Hart said it wasn't the Arts Council's mandate to judge specific plays but rather to award monies to theatres doing good work in general.

Unsatisfied with her response, the League then appealed to the state legislature in Albany. Kitty Hart was summoned to Albany to explain the Arts Council's position. She told me that the atmosphere was tense until one of the senators admitted to having had a very tough nun in grammar school who reminded him of Sister Mary; and then another senator said, "I remember having a nun a bit like Sister Mary." And then a Jewish woman senator, older, raised her arm and showed the numbers on her wrist which came from the death camps, and she said, "And I remember when they burned the books." Everyone was speechless, and the issue was closed.

For that meeting anyway.

Christopher Durang
August 1995

Smith and Kraus *Books For Actors*

YOUNG ACTORS SERIES

CONTEMPORARY PLAYWRIGHTS SERIES

GREAT TRANSLATION FOR ACTORS SERIES

CAREER DEVELOPMENT SERIES

If you require pre-publication information about upcoming Smith and Kraus books, you may receive our semi-annual catalogue, free of charge, by sending your name and address to *Smith and Kraus Catalogue, P.O. Box 127, One Main Street, Lyme, NH 03768. Or call us at (800) 895-4331, fax (603) 795-4427.*